BLACK FARCE AND CUE BALL WIZARDS

BLACK FARCE AND CUE BALL WIZARDS

THE INSIDE STORY OF THE SNOOKER WORLD

CLIVE EVERTON

MAINSTREAM
PUBLISHING

EDINBURGH AND LONDON

First published in Great Britain in 2007 by
MAINSTREAM PUBLISHING COMPANY
(EDINBURGH) LTD
7 Albany Street
Edinburgh EH1 3UG

ISBN 9781845961992

A catalogue record for this book is available
from the British Library

Typeset in Billboard and Palatino

Printed in Great Britain by
William Clowes Ltd, Beccles, Suffolk

CONTENTS

PROLOGUE

JUST PAST MIDNIGHT ON THE 1985 MAY BANK HOLIDAY, 18.5 MILLION BBC2 viewers saw Dennis Taylor pot the last black of the deciding 35th frame to beat Steve Davis in their epic Embassy World Championship final.

To anyone who remembered snooker sinking so low in public esteem that it could boast no more than half a dozen professionals, with the championship itself dormant for seven years because no one thought it worth promoting, it was amazing that the game had become a prime television attraction and that its leading exponents could become millionaires through prize money generated principally by sponsorship and television fees.

For 50 years, snooker had been a widely played folk sport whose grass roots following had always been underestimated. Now, it was right up there in sport's major league and success would beget success.

That, at least, was the theory. Instead, snooker frittered away its potentialities through incompetence, mismanagement and worse. Through my magazine, *Snooker Scene*, and elsewhere, I charted the careers of the leading players and, with horrified fascination, the sport's eternal internecine strife as it missed one chance after another to consolidate its future.

My emotional commitment to the game dated back to boyhood and one rainy London afternoon when my father and I settled into the plush fauteuils of Leicester Square Hall, which was then the 220-seat home of the professional game. From the first click of the balls, I was entranced and even now, in the imperishable action replay of my memory, I see Sidney Smith completing the first century break I ever saw.

Back home, I had a friend who had a quarter-size table we used to play on. I pestered my parents for one of my own. A few months later, by special dispensation, my father took me into his club. A full-size table looked like a 40-acre field. I played when and where I could. There was a disreputable billiard hall in an alley in the Shambles area of Worcester, where I was at school. I saw a newspaper article and entered the 1951 British Under 16 Billiards Championship.

As I had been playing on a full-size table for only three months, I was not surprised to lose in the first round, but the experience of playing in the womb-like amphitheatre of Burroughes and Watts, Soho Square, the Mecca of the amateur game, which was just as plush and even more intimate than Leicester Square Hall, sank the hook of the game deeper into me.

BBC Television, casting about desperately for Saturday afternoon sporting action, covered the final the following year with Sidney Smith, the commentator, seated in the back row. I found it disconcerting at times to hear him predict more than once a shot different to my own choice, but I won easily and Alec Bedser, the Surrey and England cricketer, presented me with the trophy. Far from making me any kind of hero at school – King's, Worcester – this success made me more of an outsider and nurtured, in turn, my anti-establishment instincts. My headmaster, F.R. Kittermaster, an Old Rugbeian from the Thomas Arnold tradition, wrote in *Sport and Society* that only sports with an element of physical danger, like rugby, cricket or hockey, were 'character building'. He was fond of insisting: 'You came here to be made into gentlemen.' Proficiency at billiards, the classic sign of a misspent youth, did not fit into his definition.

In practical ways, my father was always very helpful but like many parents of his generation – because this had been done to him – he was incapable of praising me to my face.

'You didn't have much to beat, did you?' he said in the immediate aftermath of me winning the 1952 British Under 16 Billiards. 'Well, what does it mean? What can you do? Who'd give you a job? I wouldn't,' he was to say genially of my BA Hons on degree day at Cardiff University. When I won the Welsh Billiards Championship at the age of 22, he said: 'Yes, but you can't make a living out of it, can you?' He was right about that at the time, as the professional game had sunk to an all-time low.

Save for wanting to get married, I would have stayed in Cardiff, but a friend of Valerie's father fixed me up with a teaching job at a college of further education in Halesowen on the outskirts of Birmingham. I taught English and liberal studies – though I never found out what they were – and at the time it was the only job which would guarantee me £750 a year. I was neither unselfish enough to want to devote my career to teaching nor callous enough to do it so lazily that my students would not pass their exams, but journalism was what I'd always wanted to do. In my innocence, I thought it would be better than working.

The problem was a point of entry. I was willing to start small and I could not have started smaller. I used to practise sometimes with Rex Williams who, frustrated by lack of competitive opportunities and mindful of the need to keep in the public eye, negotiated two columns, one with the *Wolverhampton Express and Star*, the other with its sporting pink. Each paid two guineas, which we split down the middle. Around this time, I also sold printing and stationery part-time for his father's Blackheath Printing Works.

In the summers, tennis was my game. From when I won the under 15 singles on Malvern's centre court under its grassy bank of spectators, I was just as keen on it as I was on billiards and snooker in the winters. The summer holidays I spent going from one junior tournament to another were irretrievably happy times with enough success for hope and enjoyment to carry me forward.

My decent serve and backhand, my slowness on the turn and my suspect forehand, particularly out wide, added up to a game unfitted for glorious achievement but sufficient to keep me in the

Worcestershire team for 13 years. At County Week, the inter-county grass court championships, we travailed between groups three and five as we explored each July a succession of politely run-down English seaside resorts, Felixstowe, Cromer, Frinton, Scarborough, Budleigh Salterton, Southsea and Minehead amongst them. I was in a winning pair against Mike Sangster two weeks after he reached the Wimbledon semi-finals; I was in a losing pair to Bedfordshire's non-playing captain, called up in desperation and borrowed gear to play his first match in five years.

In the days before Open tennis, before prize money and before sponsorship, there were a lot of tournaments. This was partly because the players did not have to be paid, except with a few unofficial pounds, meal vouchers and indulgent private hospitality. Hordes of Australians and South Africans would appear each spring to bum their way around the circuit. David Talbot, who was tennis and hockey correspondent of the *Birmingham Post* and whom I'd known since I was a junior, mentioned one day that he was off to Rome and Paris for the next few weeks for the Italian and French championships. I asked who, in that case, would be covering the tournaments at two other of the world's great capitals, Sutton Coldfield and Wolverhampton. David said they had no one as yet. I asked him if I could do it. He fixed it for me with the sports editor – 200 words plus results each day.

Getting the hang of small-time freelancing, I scratched round for a few other bits and pieces and turned in my teaching job after a year. What it amounted to was that I loved sport and wanted to spend my life in it. There was no living to be had in snooker in its depressed state and even less in billiards, which was always my better game, and at tennis I was just solid county standard. I had a fair working knowledge of most sports, I could write and it looked as if it would be enjoyable.

The *Birmingham Post* appointed a new editor, David Hopkinson, who had made his reputation by revealing that certain Sheffield policemen had been apt to use rhino whips as tools of interrogation. He wanted to beef up the *Post*'s news features and thought that David Talbot was too good to waste on hockey, then an important sport with the *Post*'s predominantly business middle class readership. Hockey was a sport I had never played and about which I knew next to nothing, but this was no bar to the *Post*, at David's suggestion, offering or me accepting the position of hockey correspondent. England v. West Germany was the first match I covered and within weeks I was pontificating with the best of them. I got to know the hockey writers from the nationals and when there was a game in the Midlands which was worth covering but not match of the day for them to attend in person, I started to work for the *Daily Telegraph*, *The Times* and *The Guardian*. Before long, it was not uncommon for me to churn out six or seven reports on the same match for a variety of locals and nationals.

There were two long established agencies, Cater's and Moxley's, who virtually monopolised the football and cricket coverage from Birmingham because, in those pre-mobile days, they controlled the press-box phones at the main grounds, which they would hire out only to newspapers not competing freelances. But everything else that moved – hockey, tennis, badminton, squash, quite a bit of athletics – kept me productive. I could not earn £100 a year out of snooker at this stage.

It did not take me long to become professionally well regarded but fees were so poor that quantity was the only route to a livelihood. Woodrow (later Lord) Wyatt set up a group of local weeklies that included the *Birmingham Planet*. To convey the impression of a cast of dozens in the writing department, different bylines were appended to my three weekly columns: squash by Angus Devitt, badminton by Harold Stringer and hockey by Rory McFarlane. They paid £2 each. 'It's only fag money,' my father would cry when I told him. 'You can't make a living like this.'

My first bylined piece for a national was in *The Observer*. A World Amateur Snooker Championship, first mooted in 1952 but deferred 'until some improvement in the Billiards Association and Control Council's [BA&CC] finances takes place', would never have been staged if this had remained the sole criterion, but the chief Indian bigwig of the day, M.M. Begg, donated a trophy and concluded arrangements for a tournament in Calcutta. England's representative was a Birmingham fireman, Gary Owen, with whom I sometimes practised at the Central fire station. My profile of him was published as 'Clearing top tables' and he duly won the title.

The BA&CC was an organisation in genteel decay. It always had been. This was exemplified by its magazine, *Billiards and Snooker*, formerly *The Billiard Player*, which was edited by an ancient retainer, Richard Holt. Certain that I could produce something more interesting, I offered my services. December 1966 was my first issue.

The BA&CC had allowed the British Junior Championship to lapse and showed no signs of reviving it, so I did it myself through the magazine, obtaining sponsorship from Accles and Pollock, who were trying to promote a new tubular steel cue. 'There's no doubt about it. They'll be great for poking the fire with,' was Fred Davis's unpromising reaction to this technological innovation. Their theory, unfounded as it was to prove, was that young players would be readier to accept an alternative to the traditional ash and maple cues. The finals were played at their own sports club in Oldbury, near Birmingham. Watching Dennis Taylor practise, I put him among the favourites only to discover that he had lost in the Lancashire qualifying area. He was there for the billiards and won it. He obviously enjoyed it because he never played billiards again.

Editing *Billiards and Snooker* was not a full-time job, but it took me to London a couple of days a week. The administration of the BA&CC offices at 15 Exeter Street, just off the Strand, was in the hands of two ladies of mature years, Betty and Renee. There was also an elderly fellow – Tom, I think his name was – whom I never actually caught working. His duties were indiscernible to the naked eye except that upon receipt of a phone call from Harold Phillips, the chairman, he would descend to the betting shop beneath to place his bets.

Brought up to have at least a vestigial respect for established authority, it shocked me to witness how run-down, unambitious and ineffective the BA&CC was. Snooker's underlying problem clearly was – as it was to remain – an inept governing body. Greatly daring, it updated its name from the Billiards Association and Control Council to the Billiards and Snooker Control Council (B&SCC) but had no idea how to harness the mass strength represented by its participants into a powerful, logically structured governing body which could develop the game.

Originally, much on the lines of the Marylebone Cricket Club, the B&SCC was a self-perpetuating oligarchy of bungling amateurs, well meaning in the main, with one or two dominant figures who utilised their involvement to satisfy their urge to exercise power. An attempt at democracy went well wide of the mark. Deciding that the number of county representatives on the control council should be based on the number of clubs affiliated at five shillings – yes, 25p – per club produced a situation in which Lancashire and Yorkshire could outvote not only the rest of England but also the rest of the world, overseas and national associations being limited to one representative each with all meetings held in England.

'What's wrong wi' that?' was the response when this anomaly was pointed out.

The B&SCC's precarious solvency depended on facility fees from television of the order of £100 a broadcast. Chairman Phillips, a clerk at the Admiralty whose patrician bearing was more that of a First Lord, had responded to an overture from the fledgling ITV, who wanted to stage a tournament in which four professionals would play four amateurs over the best of five frames. When all four professionals – Fred Davis, John Pulman, Kingsley Kennerley and Rex Williams – lost in the first round, it was clear that lack of competition had in only a few years blunted the edge of the professionals' games.

The professionals were summarily dropped and amateur matches continued on ITV for a few years until the *Sunday Times* revealed that the B&SCC, in dire financial straits and needing television fees, modest as they were, to ensure its survival, had put pressure on players to prearrange certain matches so that the fifth frame would be the decider.

One lunchtime, I was in a Fleet Street pub with two tennis journalists, Jimmy Jones and Bill Edwards, and the newly appointed sports features editor of the *Sunday Times*, John Lovesey. Chatting of this and that, I described what was going on, which was common knowledge in the snooker world. Lovesey was appalled and thus I became involved in an investigative story for the first time. I was appointed snooker correspondent of the *Sunday Times* – for the little that was initially worth – and remained so until a bust-up in 1997.

There was no betting element involved in the match fixing, but it was disgraceful that a governing body was colluding in such a deception of the viewing public. There was a furore and snooker disappeared from ITV's screens. Phillips, who was attracting criticism for the spending of meagre resources on wining and dining, was ousted from the chairmanship by Jack Karnehm, a billiards player who was loud in his condemnation of both this and the fixed matches on television. As chairman, though, Karnehm soon became hooked on the taste of power, petty as this was, and was disappointed that I would neither collude in his lust for personal publicity nor agree with his opinions.

The editorship of *Billiards and Snooker* took me past the point at which I could cope on my own. I rented an office in Edgbaston, one of Birmingham's leafier districts, set up as Everton's News Agency and engaged Mike Brettell, who had been sports editor at the *Birmingham Planet* until it folded. Mike departed after a year or so to become a district freelance in Dudley and I soldiered on with a couple of not very satisfactory replacements, a nucleus of casuals and a good-natured, sport-loving secretary, Ann Jefferson.

My workload was nothing if not various. I covered some football for *The Times* and some rugby for the *Sunday Telegraph*, chiefly from Leicester, Moseley and Coventry, which were the leading Midlands sides of the day. At Leicester, I sometimes sat next to John Morris, who became secretary of the British Boxing Board of

Control. I covered Wimbledon for *The Times of India* – 1,000 words on the Indian interest to be on the cable by five o'clock, as long as there was any Indian interest. Otherwise, I just covered the main matches, which included Ann Jones's capture of the 1969 women's title. I ghosted her subsequent book, *A Game to Love*.

Out of the blue, in January 1968, another project landed in my lap. I had walked into the Lansdowne Club in London to research a profile of Jonah Barrington, the world no. 1 squash player, for the *Birmingham Post* and walked out as his manager. Sharing an instinctive suspicion of officialdom and a frustration that our chosen sports, squash and snooker, were showing few signs of being properly developed, we discovered an instant kinship.

Beyond his playing ambitions, Jonah was taking it upon himself to transform a minority middle class sport into one of mass participation in Britain and to extend its frontiers internationally. In those days, squash professionals coached, re-strung rackets and played in one or two tournaments a year for derisory prize money. The great Hashim Khan's racket contract was £50 a year plus free rackets. Jonah wanted to be the first travelling tournament professional and to do so he had both to help set up tournaments and gather a troupe around him. My accountant, Tony Hughes, and I set up Squash Rackets Promotions, whose first venture was to bring over from Australia for a 15-match series Geoff Hunt, who had just beaten Jonah for the world amateur title.

To show how clever we were, we had 15 sell-outs and broke even, an outcome which could be attributed to some venues being able to accommodate no more than 50 uncomfortably confined spectators, all this being prior to the advent of glass-walled courts. Jonah, who was underwriting this project, was slaughtered 13–2 but beat Geoff in an epic British Open final, which was then the sport's premier event.

I left contract negotiations to Tony. Meetings echoed to his cry of 'But what are you going to give him for his name?' as he concluded the deals with Dunlop, Banbury Squash Courts and others, which might not seem very special now but certainly were then. I wrote a couple of books with Jonah, the alternately biographical/autobiographical *Book of Jonah* and an instructional volume elucidating such arcane techniques as 'the gobbling stride'.

Jonah was friendly with the managing director of Pakistan International Airlines and conceived the idea of a travelling circus, much on the lines that Jack Kramer had pioneered in tennis. It was no problem to obtain the players – two of whom hated each other – and the details were left to me and PIA's London public relations manager.

'Mr Clive, can you tell me what is happening, please? I am in the darkness,' he began one of our meetings. So were we all much of the time, but amazingly it all happened somehow – Tokyo, Manila, Bangkok, Pakistan, Australia and home to a ten-venue British finale.

Needing a sponsor for the British leg of Jonah's Flying Circus, I went to see Peter West, a BBC sports commentator, and Patrick Nally, a bright young marketing man, who were setting up West Nally, a consultancy specialising in the new but rapidly expanding world of sports sponsorship. They confided that they were pitching for the Gallaher account – Park Drive and Benson and Hedges being among its brands – and quickly agreed to make squash part of their pitch.

What other ideas did I have? Off the cuff, I suggested hockey's county championship – I was still hockey correspondent of the *Birmingham Post* – and snooker. West Nally won the account and all three projects I had suggested were given the green light. The fruition of my snooker idea, the Park Drive 2000, placed the four best available professionals into a league spread over eighteen clubs in which they played each other three times. Peter, with his BBC contacts, arranged for the top two to contest a final of which the highlights would be shown on BBC's *Grandstand*, the channel's Saturday afternoon sports flagship. In a 1970 context, this was big news for snooker. I put pictures of the four players on the front cover of *Billiards and Snooker*.

Karnehm hit the ceiling, incensed that I was 'giving professionals publicity' when they were at loggerheads with the B&SCC, the owners of the magazine. My response was that, like it or not, this tournament had come to pass and it was absurd for the magazine to pretend it had not. Karnehm persuaded the Control Council to sack me. The professionals declared their autonomy soon afterwards as the World Professional Billiards and Snooker Association.

I instantly decided to set up a rival magazine, *World Snooker*, whose first issue, three weeks later, also acted as the programme on sale at the 18 Park Drive venues. At that sort of notice, we could not sell the back cover to an advertiser but with the one marketing masterstroke of my career I left it blank save for the word 'Autographs'. This proved a vital stimulus to sales. We printed 3,000 and sold out.

Fifteen months later, the B&SCC came crawling back. The circulation of their magazine had sunk so low that they could not afford to keep it going. They did not want to be seen to be failing to meet their obligations to pre-paid subscribers. They gave me £1,000 to take it off their hands and the publication united under my owner/editorship as *Snooker Scene*. Its first issue, April 1972 (12p), led with Alex Higgins becoming world champion at his first attempt.

About this time, Jonah and I agreed to part professionally. He was guaranteed a basic income from contracts; I felt, having so many other commitments, that the time required for organising his non-contractual activities was disproportionate to the return from any fair percentage of the fees. Managing Jonah struck me rather as national service struck some of my contemporaries: glad to have done it but relieved not to have to do it anymore.

Sportsmen are accustomed to planning their days exclusively around themselves: 'Show me a champion and I will show you a selfish man,' Jonah would say unrepentantly. He was usually late unless it was important to him to be on time and could be irritating in small ways, although I invariably warmed to his basic goodness of heart. Here was a man with unblinking self-knowledge who had demonstrated what it took to rise from casual mediocrity to no. 1 in his sport. He wanted not just to be better, not just to be the best, but to be outstandingly the best and was prepared, as few genuinely are, to pay the price.

Jonah was an agent of change, the harbinger of a new order in squash, and this alone was enough to put a lot of backs up. Most sporting establishments are resistant to change, largely because the people who comprise them fear that they will lose position, power, influence, the comfort of familiarity even. A succession of snooker establishments reacted in this way and I was to be at war with them for more than 30 years.

Even without Jonah, I had plenty on my plate. Cherishing the delusion that business success would be automatic if I worked hard enough, I made mistakes, one of the most costly of which was to float *Hockey Scene* which in less than two years lost every penny that *Snooker Scene* had ever made. My agency's staff grew to six and we were doing a sizeable gross. Unfortunately, we were not ending with much of a net. It was hopeless with journalists who were not up to it and those who were up to it soon realised that there were jobs out there paying much more than an agency like mine could afford.

The classic example of this was Jim Rosenthal, who became a highly accomplished ITV Sport front man. Having kept goal for Oxfordshire, Jim knew quite a bit about hockey, but it was not a sport which attracted him and he did not much care for virtually editing *Hockey Scene*. He wrote a syndicated cricket column which we set up with the England opener, John Edrich, and on alternate Saturdays would cover Walsall's matches for Radio Birmingham, for whom I had a Sunday morning programme called *Scoreboard*. It was obvious how capable Jim was and Radio Birmingham promptly offered him a job as a junior producer at £2,950 a year, a sum not beyond the dreams of avarice but considerably more than he was getting from me. A couple of years after that, he was recruited by BBC Radio in London, graduated to presenting the Saturday afternoon sports show and thence to ITV. Another bright young man, Richard Eaton, who covered squash, badminton, table tennis and tennis for the agency, set up on his own and spread his wings to cover the international circuit of these sports. I decided simply to re-vamp the business, getting rid of virtually everything except snooker, which was just starting to make headway.

While I was trying to make my way in journalism and broadcasting, I was still investing as much emotional energy and practice time as I could into my own game for my experience was, as it has remained, that there is no commentary, no incisive editorial, nothing in my professional life which could reproduce the visceral satisfactions of competition. I won six Welsh amateur billiards titles, lost in five English Championship finals and reached the World Amateur Championship semi-final in Auckland in 1975. I travelled to Melbourne in 1977 with high hopes, having just had an epidural injection for a niggle in my lower back. It felt fine until, on my second day in Melbourne, it seized up. I could hardly move; physiotherapy, osteopathy and another epidural made very little difference. I spent most of my time lying on my bed gazing at the ceiling. Dosed up to the eyeballs on painkillers, I played with an improvised half-upright stance and somehow reached the semi-finals again, but my heart was heavy. Instinctively, I sensed that my back problem was very serious. In fact, I was never the same again. By spending a fortune on physiotherapy, I gained intermittent relief, but it was never more than a few weeks before my back gave way again. To protect it, I stood more and more square on, but this affected my eye–arm alignment and I started hitting across the ball. My standard deteriorated rapidly and I was frequently sunk in gloom.

I did enjoy one bizarre success. In the late '70s, a Canadian Open used to be staged at the Canadian National Exhibition Centre in Toronto. Once, it could not be accommodated in the main building and was instead played in the middle tent of three in the grounds, with a circus on one side and a non-stop steel band on the other. The highlights of the circus included a man being shot from a cannon every hour and an elephant dancing. The snooker MC nevertheless took his responsibilities seriously: 'I must ask you to be very quiet because the least distraction can upset the players,' he solemnly told the audience prior to each session. On another occasion, Terry Griffiths was introduced as 'from Wales, England'.

Even in the main building, it was very hot and noisy, with snooker players battling against the relentless thrum of the air-conditioning plant and myriad lights from other attractions. Every hour, there was a fashion show with electric organ accompaniment; the Mounties had a show which entailed frequent use of police sirens. Anything less like the Crucible would be difficult to imagine, but most of the top players competed because the tournament circuit was not yet very extensive and the standard was astonishingly high in the circumstances. Snooker was the main attraction, but there was also a billiards event, which I won in 1980. In a field of variable quality, I beat Long John Baldry's pianist in the first round and Steve Davis in the final.

Eventually, there was no alternative to surgery, a fusion at the base of my spine. It transpired that my bottom disc had worn away to just a few flakes. This was at a time when the professional game was opening up. Amazing to relate, there was even some prize money coming into billiards. I knew that even my best snooker would not win titles, but it was certainly good enough to win sufficient matches to obtain a respectable ranking and, above all, enjoy competing. Naively, I thought that once an operation had taken the pain away I would be able to regain my old standard. I turned professional on what proved to be this unfounded assumption. There was no pain but neither was there the natural twist in my back which would have enabled me to regain my original alignment. On top of this, the balance of my eyesight changed to make me preponderantly right-eyed.

With nothing else to do, I might just possibly have sorted these problems out, but snooker was taking off in a big way and so was my television and radio career. It was no situation for a part-time player. There were a few isolated moments when I seemed to be getting somewhere – I beat a young John Parrott and the 1977 UK champion, Patsy Fagan, and was ranked 48th – but they did not last long. My game never felt right and to cap it all I was to have problems with my knees as well, having two cartilage operations on my right and two on my left.

I battled on long after I had lost all confidence in my snooker before retiring in 1991. I persisted with billiards, which was lower profile with fewer quality players and not so demanding in terms of practice. I reached three world quarter-finals, two in India, to which I made five trips, falling ill with stomach problems each time. I did struggle up to ninth in the world rankings but always had a sense of a wonderful future behind me.

The bedrocks of my working life out on the circuit became four interlocking freelance contracts with BBC TV, BBC Radio, *The Guardian* and the *Sunday Times*. For example, the way this worked at the Crucible was to commentate on two of the day's three sessions and supply radio with reports of 40–50 seconds every hour on the half-hour when I was available. Somewhere amongst the television and radio commitments, usually including pieces at close of play for morning output, I wrote two stories for *The Guardian*, one for first edition with a 7.30 deadline, the rewrite at close of play. On Saturdays, I performed similarly for the *Sunday Times* until I moved to the *Independent on Sunday*.

Janice Hale, who joined the agency in 1971, put her heart and soul into *Snooker Scene* and virtually ran it administratively, as well as developing into a very able journalist and broadcaster. Sometimes when she was out on the road on her own, she was given a rough time by establishment figures who wanted to get at me through her. On the other hand, she could drink most of them under the table, with which process she frequently extracted much useful information. I could see something going seriously amiss with her for about a year before she cracked into a full-scale nervous breakdown in 1993. She retired into private life and married shortly afterwards.

Subsequently, no one could have wished for better or more

loyal supporters than Phil Yates and David Hendon. Apart from all our freelance, television, radio and newspaper work, there was *Snooker Scene* to produce every month. I had started this as a simple journal of record of what was happening on the table, but it became a crusading vehicle for getting the game openly, honestly and efficiently run, an objective which at best bobbed about on a distant horizon and at worst dropped out of sight. Taking *Wisden* and *Private Eye* as our models, we sometimes made our point through hard reporting, sometimes through satire. At times, our crusading made me part of the story, a position in which few journalists feel comfortable, but we had some fun as we battled and each successive WPBSA establishment came to loathe us heartily. I was working for a living, a good one, but I was also living for my work.

1

JOE DAVIS SETS THE BALL ROLLING

IF YOU WANTED TO PAINT HIGH CEILINGS IN MICHELANGELO'S DAY, it paid to know the Pope; if you wanted to be a professional snooker player just after the 1939–45 war, you needed Joe Davis's papal seal of approval.

The governing body, the Billiards Association and Control Council, was like most British sporting governing bodies of the day: patrician, patronising and lazy. It declared a player ineligible for amateur competition if he so much as served a cup of tea in a billiard hall. In this way, Fred Davis, Joe's younger brother by 13 years, automatically became a professional on his 16th birthday.

But as far as the tournament scene went, Joe had it all sewn up. If anyone wanted to compete professionally, there was only one way: Joe's way. He had been responsible for the game's emergence as a public entertainment; he had developed, virtually in a vacuum, many of the breakbuilding techniques which came to be taken for granted; he was, said Fred, a very good player before anyone else knew how to play the game.

Joe was chairman of the Professional Billiard Players Association (PBPA); he was a one-third shareholder of Leicester Square Hall; if there were any endorsement contracts, he had them; and in the early years of television it was with him that negotiations were conducted.

For this was a business, a cartel almost, of which Joe was

effectively the godfather and from which newcomers could be excluded on his say-so as somehow not the right type. Through his force of personality, he controlled the game.

It had been Joe and his friend, Bill Camkin, a Birmingham billiard table maker, who had originated the World Snooker Championship in the 1926–27 season. As with billiards, the senior game, there were no third party prizes to play for, no sponsorship. Players sank or swam through gate money. Matches usually lasted a week, three days minimum.

'It is doubtful whether snooker as a spectacular game is sufficiently popular to warrant the successful promotion of such a competition,' the BA&CC secretary, A. Stanley Thorn, had sniffed in 1924 when a snooker championship had first been mooted, but Camkin could see from his halls in Birmingham, and Davis from his family's around Chesterfield, how popular the shorter, sharper, more gambling-orientated snooker was becoming at the expense of billiards.

For the first championship, the nine entrants paid a five guinea entry fee and advanced a five guinea sidestake. Half the entry fees were to be divided 60/40 between winner and runner-up with the other half going to the BA&CC. After expenses, the profit from each match, if any, was to be shared between the two players.

Under these terms, Davis pocketed £6 10s for beating Tom Dennis 20–11 in the first final. The BA&CC, pleading shortage of funds, used the players' half of the entry fees to buy a trophy, the one that is still competed for annually in front of millions of television viewers. *The Billiard Player*, the official magazine of the day, awarded the occasion a mere four paragraphs. There was no master plan to develop snooker. 'We were all scraping and scrattin' to get a living,' Davis was to tell me 40 years later.

Davis promoted snooker as best he could, but it was uphill work. With the 1931 championship attracting only two entries, the title match was played in the back room of Dennis's pub in Nottingham. Gate receipts being certain to be affected by as one-sided a contest as he could have made it, Davis was content to do enough to win 25–21. By 1937, though, snooker had advanced sufficiently – and billiards declined – for Thurston's, the forerunner of Leicester Square Hall, to switch its main attraction, the *Daily Mail* Gold Cup, to snooker.

For the first time, Joe had a serious rival, the Australian Horace Lindrum, nephew of Walter Lindrum, the only billiards player Joe was compelled to admit was in a different class to everyone else. From 27–24 down in their 1937 world final, Davis won 31–27. Lindrum's freshness and inspiration would soon start to burn out as the burden of the family name and reputation began to weigh heavily upon him, not least because his overbearing mother never let him forget it. He remained a class player, but at the point where winning or losing became the issue he tended to fade.

Fred, Joe's younger sibling, began to emerge as his main rival, running him to 17–14 in their 1939 world semi-final and 37–35 in the 1940 final, at which point Fred went away to war and Joe toured the country for war charities, mostly playing in clubs and public venues but also working up a trick shots act which he presented at the London Palladium and in various variety halls.

The first post-war championship was a triumph for Joe, particularly financially. Full-house crowds of 1,200 for the final twice a day filled the Royal Horticultural Hall, London, for a fortnight. Each player took away the unheard-of sum of £1,500 for his trouble. There was radio commentary – no simple task with the position of so many balls to describe – from Joyce Gardner, a doyenne of the women's game. 'Ooh, you are a good player, Joe,' she trilled as he completed one of his six century breaks.

Joe's victory over Lindrum, 78–67, fulfilled his ambition to hold the title for 20 years and retire undefeated. His motives were an excessive fear of losing, particularly to Fred, and a conviction that it was in his own commercial interests. Instead of rising above the bad old practices of the early billiards greats, Joe perpetuated them. The idea was to win the championship, not enter the following year and, finally, take the lion's share of the gate for matches with whoever did win it. As every tournament except the championship was handicapped, Joe could also protect his reputation by giving starts. If he won, this emphasised how good he was. If he lost, even conceding only 7, then, of course, he was, after all, giving a start. Four defeats by Fred were his only losses on level terms in his entire career.

Such an attitude seems barely conceivable now, but it had been common since the days of John Roberts junior, who in the late nineteenth century grandly offered the BA&CC a venue, a table and a trophy for their championship – but declined to play in it. Everyone knew he was the best player and that his personality was stronger than the game's administration. Joe had absorbed all those lessons, but his retirement from championship play was soon to devalue the championship itself. In less than ten years, professional snooker was to decline from the peak of the 1946 final almost to the point of extinction.

Joe continued to play so well that it remained clear for almost another 20 years that he was still, apart from sporadic threats from Fred, the best player. To rule as the king in exile was an ideal situation for him.

His assumption that Fred would immediately succeed him as champion proved misplaced. The 1947 championship was played in various venues in the early part of the year so that the final between Fred and Walter Donaldson could be the opening attraction for Leicester Square Hall in the autumn. Fred expected to win and saw no reason to practise through the summer. Donaldson, a Scot who had done nothing in his pre-war career to suggest he would be a threat, had been too hard for Lindrum in the semi-finals and prepared himself single-mindedly for his great opportunity, locking himself away to practise each day in a friend's loft. He won easily, 82–63.

This was the first of the eight consecutive finals they contested, Donaldson winning only once more, in 1950. Most of the season, though, was occupied by handicap events sponsored by newspapers, the *Empire News* and the *Sporting Record* (both now defunct), and the *News of the World*. These were round robin events of three or even six day matches. In fact, Fred Davis held so strongly to the view that a mere three days did not provide an adequate test that he declined to play in the *News of the World* tournament in the 1949–50 season.

Prominent in the cast with the two Davises and Donaldson was Sidney Smith, who had lost to Joe in the 1938 and 1939 world finals. He had become the first player to compile a total clearance – all 15 reds with colours, plus the colours in sequence – on 11 December 1936 but, as this happened to be the date of Edward VIII's abdication speech, Smith's feat, to his mortification, did not register on the day's news agenda.

This merely confirmed Smith's long held view that the fates were against him and that their malign influence could be mitigated only by unflagging endeavour and parsimony. His staple income came from the club exhibition circuit: Labour clubs, Conservative clubs, workingmen's clubs, social clubs, church institutes; any of the 15,000 clubs of all sorts in Britain that had a billiard table.

He would start with billiards, not leaving off until he had made a 200 break, and proceed to a few frames of snooker – 'frimes', as he called them in his strangulated accent – and trick shots. Many tours were on behalf of charities, such as Missions for Seamen, where his fee would be determined by a percentage of the take. To this end, he was an inspired auctioneer of miscellaneous gifts to the cause.

Repeat bookings seldom far from his mind, he never forgot the name of a club secretary, was invariably receptive to any offer of a bed for the night and when none was forthcoming thought nothing of waiting half the night on a station in midwinter to catch the first morning train home or to his next port of call. He wrote a column for the *Sporting Record* and coached at every opportunity, even between sessions of his matches at Leicester Square Hall, in which he was a one-third shareholder with Joe Davis and a table maker, Bob Jelks. When he was sitting out during his matches there, he habitually counted the number of spectators, not only because he was a shareholder but also because as a front-rank player he was on 20 per cent of the gate, below Fred on 25 per cent and Joe on 30 per cent, but above the stragglers at 15 per cent. On many a day, his calculations would not have taken him long.

Snooker's television success story could not have been predicted from the BBC's first outside broadcast from Leicester Square Hall on 8 October 1950. The facility fee was £75 and the entire budget, including £50 for sound-and-vision lines and £5 for contingencies, was £160.

Michael Henderson, the pioneer producer in this field, was keen in that black and white era that 'there shall be numbers on all balls except white and black – six numbers on each ball'. The Composition Billiard Ball Supply Company obliged, although that first transmission proved they were too small to be readable except in intense close-up.

The format was for Joe Davis and Walter Donaldson to finish the frame in progress – everything was done live in those days – and for a competition then to take place in which each in turn would try to make a break. Another professional, Albert Brown, was cast in the humble role of scattering the pack from behind with a break-off shot for each in turn.

To this day, I can remember Smith, the commentator, saying sorrowfully: 'No, Joe's shaking his head,' as the break-off shot left the cue ball touching one red and with no glimmer of a chance of potting any other.

Henderson shied away from the very form of lighting which makes snooker attractive today, when the well-lit shots of the non-striker in his chair are often emotionally very informative. He did not see it that way. 'We gave pictures of what a snooker hall really looked like,' ran his producer's internal report. 'If the audience were to be lit, we might as well do it in the studio.' Of course, years later, this is exactly what *Pot Black* did.

Human error caused one element of that initial broadcast to go awry. Henderson asked for 'a microphone [to be] hidden in the overhead lighting to pick up the balls and the remarks of the players'. A sound engineer found that this 'picked up some hum from the lighting fitting' and unilaterally decided to place it out of harm's way.

'The microphone was actually placed at one end of the room on top of the scoreboard,' reported Henderson. There, it did not pick up any hum, but it did not pick up the click of the balls either, still less any remarks.

Still and all, it went down well. F. Hirst, a viewer from Manchester, wrote in to report that 'reception in this area was very clear' and Henderson, as was the BBC's meticulously courteous way in those days, sent thank you letters to everyone – even Albert Brown.

The next broadcast on 17 October 1950 featured authentic matchplay, an arbitrary slice of the three-day match in the *News of the World* tournament between Joe Davis and Alec Brown. Retirement was rare in the professional game then; players in decline simply received more start. The extent to which Brown was no longer considered a threat was reflected in being given 30 start. This inspired him to practise like a demon and he duly slaughtered everyone. Most of the transmission consisted of Joe unsuccessfully playing for an improbable number of snookers.

The producer, Alan Chilvers, summed up: 'The match did not provide very good television material as Alec Brown was five frames ahead and increasing his lead, with the result that it was very difficult to work up any enthusiasm for the play itself.'

Once the viewing public had briefly marvelled at professional techniques for their own sake, it soon dawned on television producers that professional matches of such epic length, at least best of 37 running up to best of 145 for the world final, could not be relied upon for dramatic climaxes. A couple of frames out of so many was meaningless, so snooker tended to be covered on a Buggins' turn basis as a duty to a minor sport. Drafting in Raymond Glendenning, the doyen of football and racing commentary, only made matters worse.

'Why was Glendenning chosen?' demanded a memo from the director of television, George Barnes. 'He did it amateurishly and made mistakes which no viewer who knows the game would condone.'

Ted Lowe, appointed Leicester Square Hall's manager for its post-war re-opening, whose duties embraced everything from selling the tickets to introducing the players and cleaning the toilets, took to sitting with Glendenning to guide him along and one day found the microphone thrust upon him when the master wordsman was stricken with laryngitis. There was no commentary box and he was seated only four rows from the players. So it was that 'Whispering Ted' developed the characteristic style that was to serve him till retirement in 1996.

In all, there were 17 telecasts from Leicester Square Hall. From snooker's point of view, the basic idea seemed to be merely to get snooker on the air somehow or other. The professional establishment never seriously considered budging from their standard fare of three day matches, so the chance of anything dramatic happening, particularly as all transmissions had to be live, was slight. In the absence of planning, the BBC simply came along on a date convenient to them and covered whichever match happened to be in progress. Their penultimate transmission was from John Barrie v. John Pulman, who were vying for bottom place in the *News of the World* tournament on 3 December 1954.

The Leicester Square Hall era ended on 29 January 1955, an occasion presented by one of the BBC's most highly regarded broadcasters, Wynford Vaughan-Thomas, who was reminded by internal memo that he would need a dinner jacket and would be expected to 'evoke a tear or two at the end'.

John Clark, 78, who had been in charge of the scoreboard for the very first match at Thurston's in 1901, was invited to perform this function for the last. 'Truly a great honour,' his wife wrote a few weeks later, 'but is it not worthy of a small fee?' Apparently, it was not.

The advent of such a major new source of entertainment as television and the imposition of a new entertainment tax were making snooker a very tough market in which to make a living.

The closure of Leicester Square Hall had been prompted by the expiry of the lease from the Automobile Association and the low likelihood of snooker generating the income to cope with the proposed increase. Like Burroughes and Watts, it was a delightful venue, redolent with atmosphere and history but belonging to a period in which professional snooker was a cosy little world in which everyone knew everyone and regular patrons and front row ticket holders were easily recognisable.

The *News of the World*, to whom Joe Davis contributed a column for more than 20 years, invested only £1,500 in their annual tournament, in return for which their name was illuminated in neon on a prime West End site for the duration of the 28 three day matches which the event comprised. This was one of the sponsorship bargains of the century.

The players were extremely grateful for any prize money – £500 for the winner – to supplement their often meagre earnings from the gate. In addition, Joe had a unique bonus scheme: his father-in-law, 'Bonky' Triggs, would write out a cheque for £114, £110 or whatever it was every time Joe made a century there.

On 22 January 1955, just before it ceased its 54 year career as the shop window of the game, Joe made the first officially recognised 147 in an exhibition there against an adversary of long ago, Willie Smith, who had won his two world billiards titles in 1920 and 1924. E.J. 'Murt' O'Donoghue, a New Zealander who both hustled in and owned billiard halls in Australia, had made a 147 – witnessed and signed for by 135 spectators – in Griffith, New South Wales, in 1934, but Davis's maximum met the criteria for official recognition: that it be made on a table with championship-size pockets in a public venue with a certificated referee officiating.

Even Davis's 147 was not recognised at once because the professionals had by then cut themselves adrift of the bumbling BA&CC. The professionals invented the 'play again' rule whereby the non-offender had the option of requiring his opponent to play from the position left after committing a foul. For this reason, although it had been irrelevant to this particular frame, the BA&CC

pettily refused official recognition but relented in April 1957 and adopted the rule itself in 1958.

Earlier, the pros had fallen out with the BA&CC over money so violently that they decided in 1952 to organise their own world championship. All the leading players (except Joe) entered the PBPA's World Matchplay Championship, which was regarded by the public as the genuine article. The BA&CC stubbornly organised its own for which there were only two entries: the cussed New Zealand veteran Clark McConachy and Horace Lindrum, who was so far past his best that Joe and Fred had both been handicapped to give him 23 start in the *Sporting Record* tournament two years earlier.

Lindrum had taken this as an affront to his dignity and refused to play. The potential humiliation of losing in receipt of such a large start was too dreadful to contemplate. His mother, though, could think only of having his name on the illustrious trophy and this duly came to pass when he beat McConachy, who was essentially a billiards player, 94–49, in a fortnight's match at the Houldsworth Hall, Manchester. Lindrum was considered a renegade. In Australia, he described himself as the 'undefeated champion' but he never played in England again and only shortly before his death in 1974 was his personal breach with Joe bridged.

The 'real' world championship continued much as before through a series of week's matches spread throughout the season with the final in early April at Blackpool Tower Circus. Initially, these were so popular that this capacious venue could be filled two sessions a day for a fortnight, even with one player already holding a match-winning lead in the best of 145 and dead frames being solemnly played out. In 1950 and '51, it was decided that the market would bear only the best of 97 and thereafter only the best of 73.

BBC TV visited one of these finals, installing Ted Lowe, without the aid of a monitor, 'so far up in the gods that the only way I could even tell who was at the table was by Walter's bald head. As for what they were doing . . .' Another year, two lion cubs were born in the animal quarters during the final. One was named Fred, the other Walter.

Donaldson, disillusioned with dwindling returns and the slog of it all, retired to his Buckinghamshire farm and converted his billiard room into a cowshed. Born in Coatbridge, he had originally come south to manage billiard halls for the Davis family in Chesterfield. A dour, uncompromising Scot with a dour, uncompromising game, he was not eagerly sought after for exhibition engagements. Even when he was world champion, he drove only a modest Ford Popular.

Alec Brown also drifted out of the game, as did his unrelated namesake, Albert, a former Birmingham bus driver who, in his fast-bowling youth, had taken five wickets for Warwickshire against the Indian tourists in 1935. Barrie Smith, who on the basis of 'That's enough Smiths' – the professional ranks already boasting Willie and Sidney – played professionally as John Barrie, also drifted away. Prone to absent-mindedness and later depression, he once broke off at Leicester Square Hall with the yellow. Kingsley Kennerley, who had failed to fulfil the exceptional promise of an amateur career, which had included English titles at both billiards and snooker, continued to coach and plough a decreasingly productive furrow on the club exhibition circuit.

Sidney Smith eventually succumbed to the pressures of incessant striving, scrimping and saving. In the latter days of Leicester Square Hall, his cue action became so eccentric that even Joe, not noted for his sympathetic nature, offered to try to sort him out. Smith, deeply frustrated by being in the shadow of Joe for so long, rebuffed him. Having scraped together just enough to retire, he severed all contact with the game.

A Canadian, George Chenier, and a South African, Peter Mans (father of the 1978 world runner-up, Perrie) both showed useful form in the 1949–50 season but neither was attracted by the financial potential of a second visit. Jack Rea, an engaging Irishman who had been working as a marker in the billiard room of the East India Club, was one year given his chance in section B of the *News of the World* tournament, the winner of which qualified for the main event, and went on to win the £500 first prize with the aid of what proved to be excessively generous handicapping. As the professional scene fell apart, it was fortunate for him that he had the personality to turn club exhibitions into a form of cabaret, his gift for repartee and an impressive range of trick shots helping evenings go with a swing.

Rex Williams, who had turned professional in 1951 at the age of 17 as the youngest ever English amateur champion, was confidently expected, not least by himself, to become world champion and possibly would have done in different circumstances. In the short term, though, the gulf between professional and amateur standards at the time was illustrated by his 39–22 defeat by the ageing Alec Brown on his 1952 championship debut.

Amidst the exodus of has-beens and never-wasers and the continuing presence of not-quites like Rea and Williams, the chief championship rival to Fred Davis emerged as John Pulman to whom Joe was still giving 14 start in the *News of the World* tournament. Their two Blackpool finals were closely contested with Pulman, 31–29 ahead going into the last day, having a great chance to win in 1956. Pulman loved wine, women and, at times, song, but in retrospect believed it had done him no good to spend two hours in bed with the daughter of a snooker dignitary just prior to the resumption of play. Fred won that session 5–1 and the match 38–35.

Pulman won the title in Jersey the following year, but it was an empty triumph. The promoter was unable to convince Fred that it was financially worthwhile playing. There were only four entries. Pulman beat Rea for a title he was to hold unchallenged until 1964. So low had professional snooker sunk in the esteem of a public bored by endless permutations of the same few players – with Joe, the best, not even competing – that for seven years no promoter would gamble on staging the game's premier event.

A much truncated version of the *News of the World* tournament was staged for a couple of years at Burroughes and Watts, Soho Square, but this 180-seat match hall was given over almost for an entire season to the English Amateur Championships and other events under the auspices of the B&SCC. Staging one match every afternoon and another every evening, six days a week, the London and also the Home Counties qualifying rounds would occupy several months prior to the competitions proper, which would also feature the survivors of other area eliminators.

Burroughes Hall was steeped in history. It was there in 1907 that Tom Reece, playing a match with Joe Chapman of 500,000 up, swiftly obtained 'anchor cannon' position with the three balls grouped around a corner pocket. With the object-white on one of its jaws and the red on the other, Reece maintained a cannon sequence which took him to his target with an unfinished run of 499,135.

This took six weeks of afternoon and evening sessions. Reece, who did not much care for Chapman, favoured him with such remarks as, 'How do you find the table?' and 'What sort of chalk do you use?', as he forged relentlessly on. Gentry arriving from lunch or dinner found the atmosphere congenial to a pleasant doze. Chapman, recognising the inevitable, departed long before the end.

The anchor cannon and subsequently the pendulum cannon, in which the two balls were actually trapped in the jaws, were banned, much to the disgust of Reece, a cannon artist and billiards purist who was to greet the rise of snooker with unconcealed derision. 'A game to be played in clogs and corduroys, a splendid game for navvies in their lunch hour,' he sneered.

Not just Burroughes and Watts but their competitors, Thurston's, operated their match halls on the sites of their showrooms for tables and equipment. A Hitlerite bomb demolished Thurston's – although Leicester Square Hall re-opened on that site in 1947 – but Burroughes continued unchanged. I never played there without a sense of awe, and most other players felt similarly. It had a plush, uniquely intimate ambience and a sleekly smooth-running table with strict pockets. Nevertheless, Burroughes and Watts, like much of post-war Britain, was living in a time warp. It epitomised all the traditional, gentlemanly, complacent, inefficient qualities that exposed the fiction that Britain was the centre of the universe and that the world owed it a living.

The reality of this hit home in 1967 when Burroughes and Watts was bought by the Hurst Park Syndicate, whose chief figures were Jarvis Astaire, a property magnate with boxing interests, Sam Burns, a bookmaker and boxing manager, and Terry Downes, whose boxing career included a world middleweight championship. Property was their game and it was abundantly obvious that a prime site in Soho Square could be utilised much more remuneratively. Hurst Park then sold the equipment and repair side of its purchase to a northern firm, E.J. Riley, for £55,000, not a huge sum even in 1967. Bruce Donkin, who spent a lifetime in snooker as a referee, MC and, predominantly, in trade areas, was then appointed by Riley to supervise the takeover.

On first opening the safe at Soho Square, Donkin found in one of its drawers six First World War hand grenades and in the other twelve glass phials of mustard gas, these to be used, it seemed, in the event of enemy invasion. The bomb disposal unit was summoned from Horsham to deal with them.

Familiarising himself with the shape of the table-making works at Bow, Donkin found some discrepancy between the rooms he knew about and the total area of the premises. Pinning this discrepancy down, he discovered one bricked-up room to be full of best Brazilian timber. Someone had over-ordered and decided that this was the best way of covering up his mistake. There was also a stack of brown paper parcels. The brown paper disintegrated to the touch. Within were pocket nets tied in sixes. These disintegrated, too. His curiosity was then drawn to a stack of manila folders on the office manager's desk. The folders had clearly been there for variable lengths of time; the bottom two had been there so long that they had sweated into the desk and become part of it. The free-standing ashtrays in the match hall, some two foot six high and rounded at the bottom so that they could not overturn, attracted his attention. He asked for one to be emptied and discovered that this was very difficult, as they had never been emptied before. Smokers had simply continued to jam one cigarette butt after another into them, forming a compacted mass both in the bottom and up the stem. Some items had been there since 1914.

He found that there were several law firms paying half a crown (12½p) per week to store tables. Some of them had been doing this for so long that it was no longer possible to trace the owners. In the north, many Riley employees had slate paths – obviously broken-up table beds – to their terraced houses. One Manchester branch was discovered to be operating from a room so small that a cushion could not be placed on the bench for re-rubbering without putting half of it out of the window. If it was raining, something else had to be done until the weather changed.

Inadvertently, Riley also acquired a chalk factory, F.N. Locke of Merton, where liquid chalk used to be poured from jugs into small square moulds and then placed in the oven. Four weeks after the takeover, someone from Locke's rang up to ask the whereabouts of their wages. This was the first Donkin knew that Locke's was supposed to have been part of the deal. Unintentionally, all mention of them had been omitted from the contract.

Back in 1967, the closure of Burroughes Hall was lamented as the end of an era. So it was, but it was symptomatic of the new start which was needed and without which snooker could never have been reinvented as a public entertainment.

2

FROM BUST TO THE CREST OF A BOOM

LATE IN HIS CAREER, JUST AS TELEVISION AND SPONSORSHIP were beginning to transform the players' earning power, John Pulman was waiting to be introduced by an MC who, extolling his experience, delivered himself of the opinion that he 'wasn't world champion all those years for nothing'.

'Next to nothing,' muttered Pulman feelingly, just loud enough for a few to hear, summarising his financial return from his 12-year tenure.

The son of an Exeter billiard hall owner, he was educated at the local grammar school and worked briefly as a clerk for the Inland Revenue, an irony in view of his subsequent proud boast that for the last 50 years of his life he did not pay a penny in income tax.

English amateur champion as an unknown in 1946, when incredibly his highest break of the competition was 25, he lived at the home, with billiard room attached, of his wealthy patron, Bill Lampard, a Bristol confectioner, who launched him into the professional game. This arrangement ceased only when Pulman was discovered in bed with Mrs Lampard.

Leaving aside that he would probably never have become champion anyway if Fred Davis, let alone Joe, had entered in 1957, few world champions can ever have been so poorly remunerated. Only summer seasons at Butlins and endless club exhibitions kept him going.

'You need a map from the AA to play on this,' he would exclaim of one poor table after another. 'All these cushions are doing is stopping the balls from falling on the floor,' was another regular quip.

One club was so riled by his remarks that it filed an official complaint, stating: 'There couldn't have been anything wrong with the table because all our players beat him.'

Having driven through atrocious weather, he arrived at one club, wearing his tuxedo and carrying his cue case, to be met with the question: 'Are you the snooker player?'

This was too much for him. 'No, I'm the fucking chimney sweep.'

Amusing though its highlights and lowlights may have been in retrospect, this sort of routine, with many long days to kill and many a beast of a table to be tamed, did his game no good. Convivial to a fault, he habitually drank long and late, even after snooker's tournament scene revived.

The handful of professionals who survived were all in the same boat. A woman who ran a club in Coventry engaged Fred Davis for an exhibition, omitting to mention that she was writing from her home address and not that of her club.

'When I eventually located her home, the only address I had, the whole road was in darkness. I was just about ready to give up. There wasn't a soul about except someone passing, who directed me to a club at the end of the road. It wasn't the right one, but someone gave me correct directions. After an hour or so hunting around Coventry, I wasn't at my most cheery, but suddenly we were there. "Lovely to see you," the lady beamed. "We were wondering what happened to you."'

For five years, Davis and Rex Williams toured on behalf of Watneys, the brewers, whose representatives made the arrangements. They arrived at one club to discover it had no table.

'Where's the table?' they asked.

'We thought you'd bring it with you,' came the artless reply.

Joe Davis maintained his BBC contacts and he and A.N. Other

(usually Fred) were sometimes engaged for *Grandstand*, more often than not in the depths of winter when outdoor events ran maximum risk of cancellation. In that pre-videotape era, everything was shown live and snooker was fitted in between other items, usually horse races. It was stressed to the players that the frame they were about to play was not to exceed the ten, twelve or however many minutes they were to fill.

The hiatus in the professional game was especially unfortunate for Williams, who in the next 40 years or so was to play many roles in snooker's 'Dance to the Music of Time', some of them simultaneously. Outstanding in his teens at both snooker and billiards, he seemed assured of a glittering future but just when he needed all the top level play and experience he could get, the professional game was falling apart. Convinced that his time would come, he continued to practise diligently on the table his father, Bill, had installed at the printing works in Blackheath, Staffordshire. His autocratic style of ownership gave Williams himself an obvious role model.

A retired chemist, Bertram Smith, whom no one ever called anything but Mr Smith, fielded out daily for the sheer pleasure of helping. In those laboratory conditions, Williams rarely failed to play to a very high standard but, out in the professional game, which another role model, Joe, was running with an imperious hand, progress had not been quite as swift as expected, even before professional snooker came to a virtual standstill. So insular had the professional game become that it was argued that there was little enough work for the handful of professionals that remained without spreading it more thinly by encouraging newcomers.

Yet even in its darker days, snooker remained popular at club and amateur championship level, with three million players in the British Isles alone and a competitive structure founded on local leagues and national associations, which in most cases dated back to the 1930s. But snooker was the last of the folk sports, very seldom mentioned and then only briefly in the national press.

The World Professional Championship was eventually resurrected on a challenge basis by Williams in 1964. No one thought any the worse of him because he was doing this primarily for his own benefit. He was the youngest and most enthusiastic of the handful of pros who remained and if he had not shown some initiative, no one else would. By the simple expedient of taking the B&SCC chairman, Harold Phillips, out to lunch, the governing body's blessing was obtained. John Pulman, who had held the title unopposed for seven years, defended it successfully against Fred Davis at Burroughes and Watts, Soho Square.

'I had deteriorated,' said Davis of his long absence from competition. 'So had he, but not as much.'

Pulman saw off six more challenges, including two from Williams, one of which was a 47-match series across South Africa. At one rural venue, no spectators showed up. Instead of playing, the players spun a coin.

An indulgent view was also taken of Williams and Davis playing a 51-match series, taking a fee from each club, for what they advertised as the World Open Matchplay Championship. It could hardly have been less open as no other entries were invited, but the rationale was that Davis had won a 'World Open' in Sydney in 1960 to which the B&SCC, on a 'why not?' basis, had awarded official sanction, although entry was by invitation and Davis the only top player in it.

The cynical were not unduly surprised when the outcome of the series depended on the very last match. 'I had a devil of a job to let him win,' said Davis, who had led 25–22. There was no betting element, but the theory was that Williams should have a title to his name to make him more promotable. As, it seemed, he could not beat Pulman for the 'real' world title, this was the solution.

Davis and Williams embarked on a nationwide club tour under the sponsorship of Watneys, who also sponsored a British Amateur Pairs Championship. The B&SCC, blissfully ignoring the underlying purpose of the sponsorship, arranged some of the later matches in temperance halls.

Tobacco sponsorship was just getting off the ground and John Player hired Pulman as world champion to tour clubs promoting their No. 6 brand. Seeing snooker's grass roots as fertile ground for sales, they also sponsored a new British team championship – Victoria and Albert Museum v. Activated Sludge Company was one first round pairing that came out of the hat – and, at Pulman's urging, his 1968 world title defence against Eddie Charlton. Impressed by the number of full houses this drew during the week to the Co-op Hall, Bolton, John Player extended its support to enable the 1968–69 championship to revert to a knockout format.

Through a combination of random circumstances, there were three new professionals of high quality: Gary Owen had won two world amateur titles, and John Spencer and Ray Reardon had met in the 1964 English Amateur Championship final at the Central Hall, Birmingham, an impressive venue by night – which was when it had been inspected by officials. The first afternoon session revealed it to be less suitable by day, as the huge uncurtained windows admitted a blaze of spring sun that blinded any player attempting pots to one of the middle pockets.

Reardon won and was invited to tour South Africa, where he made such a striking impression that he was offered a return tour as a professional. After ten years pounding the beat for the City of Stoke Constabulary, supplementing his wages by doing local club exhibitions at £2–3 a time, he took the plunge. Despite the financial uncertainty of a change of direction, it was more alluring than continuing as he was.

Spencer, who worked as a cost clerk and bookmaker's assistant, won the English amateur title in 1966 after losing the 1965 final to Pat Houlihan, a product of snooker's racier tradition, a London hustler who was once roused from his bed by an aide of the Krays to play Tommy Smithson, subsequently the victim of what the more excitable newspapers tend to describe as a 'gangland slaying'. There was no malice or violence in Houlihan, but he moved in the same circles as petty criminals.

He went to prison for breaking and entering, thus making himself unavailable for the 1966 World Amateur Championship in Karachi for which Spencer was selected instead. Runner-up to Owen there, Spencer fell out with the B&SCC on his return over expenses and the way the game was being run. He was prepared to retire – indeed, he had retired for ten years after making a 115 break at the age of fifteen at the Radcliffe Sunday School Institute – but was offered a few engagements by both the National Spastics Society and Pontin's holiday camps and decided to continue as a professional.

Owen, who turned on the strength of a £250 contract with Riley, the company wanting a fresh name to put on a range of cues, Spencer and Reardon all therefore competed in the 1968–69 championship for which there were eight entries. Pulman's 11 year reign as champion was ended by Spencer, who beat him 25–18 at Wryton Stadium, Bolton, a venue more commonly used for all-in wrestling. Pulman remarked that he had seen more attractive public conveniences.

Spencer, who had raised the £100 entry fee only through a loan from his bank manager, went on to beat Owen 37–24 at the Victoria Halls, London, for the £1,780 first prize, which was then a fortune in snooker terms.

Coincidentally, BBC2, the only channel on which colour was then available, was at this time looking for low budget programmes to which colour was intrinsic so that sales of colour TV sets could be stimulated. Ted Lowe, who had maintained his contacts with BBC producers from the days when he used to commentate on Joe Davis v. A.N. Other on Saturday afternoons, was able to say in all honesty that snooker had been enlivened by its recent influx of new professionals. Philip Lewis, a BBC producer, coined the title *Pot Black* and the first programme under that name went out on 23 July 1969.

The BBC's hopes for *Pot Black* were not immoderately high but almost at once it went to second place in the BBC2 ratings and established that the potential popularity of snooker, properly presented, was much greater than had been imagined. Programmes were recorded in the BBC's Birmingham studios and although results could not be taken all that seriously, the matches being of only one frame, the exposure the game received and the reaction to it was far-reaching in its influence.

The 1970 world championship, again sponsored by John Player, this time with nine entries, was won by Reardon, although he held the title less than seven months for in November that year the event was staged again at various venues in Australia with nine competitors from six countries, the most internationally representative field yet. A double elimination system produced as semi-finalists Reardon, Spencer and two Australians, Charlton and Warren Simpson. Behind the scenes, the semi-final draw had been changed, perhaps to ensure an Australian finalist. Charlton had lost only once to Simpson since 1964 but was involved in a minor car accident on his way to the match, lost the first three frames and never fully recovered. Spencer, at the peak of his form, demolished Reardon in the other semi-final and treated Simpson similarly to regain the title, making three centuries in four frames.

All the while, tension was building up between the B&SCC and the professionals. Williams had resurrected the Professional Billiard Players Association (PBPA), the professionals' trade union, who were initially quite content, despite historical warnings to the contrary, to play along with the B&SCC, even agreeing that 5 per cent of their world championship prize money and the entire gate for the final should go to this rickety governing body. When the chairman, Karnehm, unilaterally altered the terms agreed between Davis and Reardon and the Stoke promoter for their 1968–69 quarter-final, trust and confidence began to ebb away rapidly. The professionals remained prepared to pay the B&SCC for any services rendered but became resistant to any arrangements which smacked of a tax on earnings.

The issue which precipitated the final breach between the B&SCC and the PBPA was the World Professional Billiards Championship, which had remained dormant from 1951, when the New Zealander

Clark McConachy beat John Barrie in the title match at Leicester Square Hall, to 1968, when Williams challenged.

By then, the 73-year-old McConachy was suffering from Parkinson's disease, which made his cue arm tremble so violently that he eventually played with a 30 oz cue, nearly double the usual weight, to try to stabilise it. Even so, Williams struggled to beat him by a mere 265 points in their week's title match in Auckland.

Williams said he would defend the title if guaranteed £250 for a week's match. Leslie Driffield, a pompous, self-important Yorkshireman who had won the English amateur title eight times and the world amateur twice, was also a B&SCC council member and not even a professional when a council meeting, in which he himself took a full part, nominated him as Williams's challenger.

Williams was given five months to defend his title, a time limit that might more fairly have been imposed on Driffield to offer him terms. At the end of this period, the B&SCC nevertheless stripped Williams of the title. Williams, though a much classier player, might not have beaten Driffield and was perhaps not dying to play him, but the B&SCC put itself in the wrong and fostered suspicions that there was a hidden agenda for Driffield to play Karnehm for the professional title.

On 12 December 1970, the PBPA renamed itself the World Professional Billiards and Snooker Association and declared its autonomy as the professional governing body. Shortly afterwards, Williams defended his title under the WPBSA auspices against Bernard Bennett, who had never made a 200 break in competition, in a travesty of a match at Bennett's club in Southampton. The winning margin, 9,250–4,058, almost mirrored the margin by which Driffield beat Karnehm at Middlesbrough for the B&SCC version of the title: 9,029–4,342.

Initially, the WPBSA was run on the proverbial shoestring from the West Bromwich home of Mike Green, a snooker enthusiast who had a soft drinks business. Williams, who wanted the professional game to flourish and, within limits, expand so that he could fulfil his own dreams of glory and fame, was its chairman. None of the other players showed much interest in anything except playing – even getting them to attend committee meetings could be hard work. Once, a quorum was achieved only by keeping Pulman hanging on a phone in a public call box in Devizes.

Save for one brief intermission, Williams was to remain chairman until he was ousted in 1987 on a vote of no confidence from fellow committee members. Having valuably set up the association, he increasingly yielded to the temptation to treat it as a personal fiefdom as his arrogant, imperious streak came into play.

After ten years in the wilderness, he was to be voted in again in 1997 by which time, it was soon clear, these traits had worsened. They were to bring the game almost to its knees.

3

THE SHOT THAT SHAPED SNOOKER'S DESTINY

FROM FIRST QUALIFYING ROUND TO FINAL, IT TOOK ALEX HIGGINS only three weeks short of a year to win the world title: three days for early matches, five or six for later rounds still being the norm, each separately promoted in a different venue. This, after all, was how it had been done since 1926–27. There was no sponsor. Players were dependent on a share of the gate except that the finalists were to split half the entry fees 60/40. This produced the generally quoted figure of £480, which Higgins pocketed for winning at his first attempt.

Higgins was snooker's first anti-hero; he sought neither acceptance nor respectability. He loved and lived snooker and wanted to live the rest of his life at full throttle. He carried the seeds of his own destruction.

There had seldom been much money to spare in his family. When Alex was young, his father had been left with a learning disorder after being hit by a lorry, an accident for which he received no compensation. Nor did his father ever learn to read or write. His mother and three sisters bathed him in well-nigh unconditional love. He did as he liked, though once, with fire raging downstairs, he realised only just in time that his mother's frantic urging was not simply a ruse to get him out of bed. Respect for authority was never a strong suit; one childhood incident added rage and contempt. His mother had equipped him with a pristine football kit, but he was five minutes late getting to the pitch and the teacher in charge made him return to the dressing-room.

He served his snooker apprenticeship in The Jampot, a billiard hall off the Donegall Road in Belfast, where older men would unforgivingly take his money if they could. He lived on fizzy drinks and chocolate bars. At 15, having responded to an advert in the *Belfast Telegraph*, he was apprenticed to Eddie Reavey, the racehorse trainer, at Wantage. He tasted alcohol for the first but far from the last time on the ferry to Liverpool – half a bitter. He shovelled large quantities of manure and quickly realised that the romance of racing was better viewed as a punter than a participant. He worked in a paper mill, hustled in the London area and returned home to win the Northern Ireland Amateur Championship at the age of 18. Playing for Belfast YMCA, he won the Player's No. 6 British Team Championship almost single-handedly, playing so brilliantly that a couple of local enthusiasts fixed a few exhibitions for him. He then set sail for Blackburn, carrying only his cue and a small suitcase.

'I'm a snooker player. I play for money. Who'll play me?' was his attitude, though, contrary to reports, he denied ever uttering these words directly.

Soon, there was news of dashing centuries, high living, bust-ups and punch-ups. His first managers, John McLoughlin and Dennis Broderick, used the Post Office club, his practice base, at lunchtimes. 'He has only three vices,' said McLoughlin, 'drinking, gambling and women. Every pound he earns seems to make the bookies richer.'

He began to play challenge matches with John Spencer, initially receiving 14 start. They were invariably packed out. He was soon such an attraction that he was put into the third Park Drive series. He acquired a huge army of supporters, snooker's Stretford End, to whom he remained their man whatever he did.

In the week before Christmas 1971, Higgins beat Rex Williams 31–30 in a world semi-final at Bolton which changed the lives of both. Williams had worked and practised for the title all his life; it was his heart's desire. Higgins had the mood upon him and the sense that the force was with him, winning frames from losing positions and casting them away from winning positions with equal abandon. There was Williams, meticulous in his application and calculation; there was Higgins, impulsive, inspirational, hustling round the table, assessing his shot instantaneously and letting fly with the minimum of preparation.

In the 61st and deciding frame came a seminal moment, not just for the combatants but for snooker's history. Williams, 14 ahead, attempted the blue from its spot to a middle pocket. A slight degree of difficulty was imposed by the cue ball lying on the cushion less than an inch from the middle-pocket jaw, but the blue had only to be dropped in to leave automatic position for the five remaining reds, all of which lay in inviting positions with pink and black available. Had Williams potted the blue, he could hardly have failed to win.

The blue hit the jaw and stayed out. Higgins made 32 from the position left and Williams did not score again. This blue was to haunt Williams for the rest of his life. At the interface between long cherished ambition and achievable reality, his frailty of temperament had betrayed him. Higgins had no such self-doubts, but the snooker world could later ponder how differently snooker might have developed if Higgins had not won the 1972 title and Williams had.

It was certainly possible that Williams could have beaten a debilitated Spencer in the final. Between his quarter-final win over Fred Davis and his semi-final against Eddie Charlton, Spencer went to Canada. At the peak of his form, he made sixty breaks over 80 in the ninety-eight frames he won in two matches against Cliff Thorburn in Calgary and Edmonton. On his return, he was so tired he slept by night and, whenever he could, lay on the sofa by day. His arduous 37–32 semi-final victory over Charlton drained most of his remaining reserves; his 4–3 win over Higgins in the third Park Drive 2000 final the night before the world final drained him dry.

Higgins played with a sense of destiny and sublime confidence. Spencer could not pot a long ball to save his life but hung on till the Thursday evening, the eighth session of twelve, when Higgins went through him 6–0 to lead 27–21. Early on the Saturday evening, Higgins arrived at the finish line, 37–32.

A miners' strike and consequent power failure contributed not only to the capacity attendances but also to a bizarre second evening when, with conventional lighting and heating out of action on that cold February night, the players agreed to continue under the dull, inadequate illumination produced by a mobile generator.

Most of the crowd was accommodated on tiered seating based on stacked beer crates; a few hung precariously from any coign of vantage. Snooker was unaccustomed to the paying public being so keen to see a match. Beer supplies held up but toilet facilities proved sadly inadequate as the Ladies was ruthlessly appropriated by hordes of gents.

Apart from the light thrown over the 12 x 6, directed by the shade above it to finish at the cushion rails, the room was in such darkness that I took notes without being able to see what I was writing. Seated at the end of a row, I also wrote largely indecipherable 'runners' (reports which had to be phoned before close of play), which I passed to Janice Hale, later snooker correspondent of *The Observer*, who was a few months into her role as secretarial dogsbody at my agency. Janice then made for the only available phone, situated by the club entrance, which boasted no light, and phoned through the story as best she could.

At close of play, there were other reports to write and phone. BBC Northern Ireland asked for voice reports, as did Radio Blackburn, now Radio Lancashire. The same piece sufficed for both outlets save that he was Belfast's Alex Higgins for Northern Ireland and Oswaldtwistle's Alex Higgins for Radio Blackburn. Higgins was, in fact, successively resident, unofficially, at 9, 11, 13, 15 and 17 Ebony Street, moving along as each house was demolished.

There was also a media breakthrough with the *Daily Telegraph* for which I had covered hockey, tennis and whatever else came up.

Their redoubtable sports editor, Kingsley Wright, had responded discouragingly to my offer to provide snooker coverage a few years previously. 'The only possibility of coverage would be a world championship, preferably in London.' Now, he was commissioning four paragraphs plus frame scores with a re-write after the evening session. And I did know not to allow any paragraph to exceed 35 words.

The 1973 world championship was sponsored by Park Drive and organised by West Nally, whose success with the Park Drive 2000 prompted them, with the WPBSA's approval, to condense an event straggling out over an entire season, with no continuity of interest and scant media attention, into a fortnight with play, Wimbledon-style, in eight different arenas within a huge venue, City Exhibition Halls, Manchester. With an £8,000 prize fund and television coverage on *Grandstand* on two Saturdays, the players thought they had arrived in heaven without the prior inconvenience of dying.

Higgins was at the centre of the publicity build-up. A Thames TV documentary, *Hurricane Higgins*, which was no public relations exercise, and news page coverage of his involvement in miscellaneous off-table incidents increased his appeal at the box office. Contemptuous of social airs and graces, snooker's first authentic anti-hero attracted massive support from those socially placed to care little for traditional or established values. He was their champion – the People's Champion, as he was to call himself – against the rest of the world. Even those who did not approve of all his antics were attracted by his skill, dash and nerve.

But his title defence was an anticlimax. His 16–14 win over the veteran Fred Davis – a quarter-final which, uniquely even for Manchester, included a stoppage for rain while a section of the roof was repaired – was too close for comfort. His semi-final defeat, 23–9, by the relentlessly steady Eddie Charlton was a long drawn out execution. Reardon, down 19–12, beat Spencer 23–22 in the other semi-final and after losing the opening session 7–0 beat Charlton 38–32 in the final.

Snooker looked as if it might take off but internal feuds and cliques held it back. West and Nally set up Snooker Promotions and also Mister Billiards, an equipment company. Briefly, they attempted to manage the unmanageable Higgins. They brought in Norwich Union to sponsor a tournament at the Piccadilly Hotel, London, thus bringing ITV back into snooker for the first time since the fixed matches fiasco with the B&SCC. With Park Drive as sponsors providing increased prize money, they staged the 1974 world championship at Belle Vue, Manchester, which was won by Reardon.

Immediately afterwards, they presented to the WPBSA ambitious plans for an international circuit. Rex Williams and his coterie somehow managed to see this as a threat and to interpret what they had achieved for the game as an occasion not for gratitude but envy, jealousy and distrust. They could not seem to bear the thought that someone might make money out of snooker even if they were helping the players to make money. West and Nally gave up on the WPBSA and decided to be involved in snooker only through servicing tournaments for sponsors. Park Drive departed but on behalf of another Gallaher brand, Benson and Hedges, they set up the Masters in 1975.

The leading players – for it was they who comprised the WPBSA committee – remained suspicious of outsiders and more comfortable within their own cosier little world. *Pot Black*, for all its excellent viewing figures, fitted into this because everybody knew good old Ted Lowe, who not only commentated but also had a major say in which players were invited.

The series was recorded annually between Christmas and New Year in the otherwise deserted BBC Pebble Mill complex. Three days' attendance was required for a fee of £300; matches were of only one frame's duration; there was no practice table. The studio lighting for the match table was blinding to wearers of spectacles. John Pulman confessed to the hope that he was left nothing easy to go at in case he should look foolish through failing.

Higgins, less malleable than most, threatened not to turn up for a second day of filming. This was par for the course for this awkward Irishman if matters did not go his way. The producers simply took his refusal at face value and dropped him from subsequent series.

When it was suggested to the table makers, Thurston's, that using its table for the series had a commercial value worthy of payment – rather than the charge of an installation fee – its managing director of the day, Bob Mitchell, thought carefully and proposed to limit his charge to £90 less £1 for every time Thurston's name was mentioned. They thought big in those days. For one early *Pot Black* series, I was asked to choose the shot of the week. I was paid £15 for the series (i.e. £1 a week).

Eddie Charlton was also one of snooker's own, not an outsider who might conceivably have the temerity to make money out of the game, and was awarded the rights to promote the 1975 world championship in Australia. Some sports might have found it odd that a world championship should be promoted by one of its leading contenders but professional snooker, ever since the days of Joe Davis, was used to the idea of a player or clique of players having control of either promotion or administration, or both.

Charlton's sporting versatility had been exemplified in his youth through soccer, rowing, speed roller skating, boxing, cricket and others. He had been one of the carriers of the Olympic torch for the 1956 Olympic Games in Melbourne. Snooker had always been his best game, although he was still a miner when he turned professional at the age of 33 in 1963. He acquired a backer, Jack Chown, and challenged for John Pulman's world title in 1968 when snooker was still so deep in depression that even the championship was still being resolved on an intermittent challenge basis.

He ran Pulman close, 39–34, in a week's match at the Co-op Hall, Bolton, reached the 1972 semi-finals and the 1973 final. He was clearly the best Australian player and reinforced his dominance by his chairmanship of the Australian Professional Association, his promotions company, his connections in the billiard trade and the television and sponsorship contracts of which these interests deemed him a vital part. It was difficult to move hand, foot or finger in Australian snooker without his approval. He practised hard, worked the exhibition circuit diligently and burned with desire to win a world title.

Unfortunately, his solid, no frills, no risks game was not quite good enough for this. He resembled his fellow Australian, Ron Clarke, a phenomenal even pace runner who set several world records only to fail in the Olympic Games because there was always someone who drew inspiration on the day or possessed a killer finishing kick. Charlton was in the same category: there was always someone with more flair or a higher peak performance who could overcome him on the occasions that mattered most.

When the draw for the 1975 championship was made – contrary to WPBSA criteria – the cognoscenti were not slow to point out that the seedings placed Reardon at no. 1 and, outrageously, Spencer at no. 8, with Higgins, the only other world champion of the early '70s, also in the opposite half to the promoter, Charlton.

The matches were played all over Australia in varying conditions. Dennis Taylor, making his first significant showing in the championship, reached the semi-finals but had to endure a choppy flight in a light aircraft from Sydney to Brisbane on the morning of his match against Charlton and never recovered from a poor start.

In the best of 61 frames final in the Nunawading basketball stadium in Melbourne, the crowds were ready to salute an Australian victory when Charlton, leading Reardon 29–25, needed only the brown, not a difficult pot for a player of his calibre, to lead by five with only six to play, a position from which he would surely have secured the title. As it was, Reardon won that frame and went on to win 31–30, a psychological setback from which Charlton never recovered.

Time and again, and not just in snooker, a player's psyche becomes scarred by having failed to clinch a winning position through his own inadequacy. When this happens on an occasion of supreme personal significance, the wound goes especially deep. These moments of trauma become lodged in the mind and impede a player's efforts if he again manages to reach the brink of an important victory – maybe even the fulfilment of his heart's desire.

Such failures shake a player's sense of certainty. Charlton's had been shaken by losing the 1970 semi-final to Simpson and the 1973 final to Reardon, 38–32, after winning the opening session 7–0. His 1975 catastrophe was much worse. He remained a gritty and formidable competitor but tended to lose the important close ones: 20–18 to Higgins and 19–17 to Griffiths in the 1976 and 1979 semi-finals respectively. He never won a world title or a major tournament in Britain.

4

ENTER THE BBC AND THE CRUCIBLE

PRIOR TO THE '70s, SPORTS SPONSORSHIP HAD BEEN A HAPHAZARD business, more likely to be engaged in through a chairman's whim than as a marketing tool. The tobacco companies were first to realise its possibilities, in part out of necessity as direct tobacco advertising was banned from British television screens. Tobacco concerns could therefore maintain a television presence for their brands only through sponsorship and valuable name penetration could also be obtained through press reporting of such events.

There appeared to be a natural relationship between snooker and smoking. Snooker did not demand high levels of fitness; its players commonly smoked. There was a great deal of smoking in clubs and snooker halls; therefore it was not only events which would attract spectators and, ideally, television viewers, but also those with extensive grass roots participation which were of interest to tobacco sponsors.

John Player and Park Drive had come and gone. Benson and Hedges, rather than support a world championship that could subsequently be awarded to another sponsor, not only founded but also promoted the Benson and Hedges Masters in 1975 and continued to do so until 2003. In 1976, out of the blue, Embassy came into snooker through sponsoring the world championship.

While it was clear that substantial sponsorships were available for sports which could command significant television exposure, it did not immediately seem that snooker would fit into this category. *Pot Black*, studio recorded and therefore not open to sponsorship, provided a pleasant half-hour for 15 weeks each year and there had been some coverage on *Grandstand* of the 1973 and 1974 world championships. ITV had taken an interest for its *World of Sport* Saturday afternoon show with two Norwich Union Opens in 1973 and 1974. If a promoter or sponsor's agent came up with an event, the leading players were, with rare exceptions, only too happy to play in it. The WPBSA did not at this stage seek any role in sanctioning tournaments or regulating the game. Its committee members were all players and they simply wanted to play. There was no calendar, no structure. Everything was ad hoc.

Embassy's unlikely snooker midwife was Maurice Hayes, the secretary/treasurer of the Chester League, who worked his way up the amateur hierarchy without much difficulty to become vice-chairman of the Billiards and Snooker Control Council. This perennially cash-strapped and ineffectual amateur governing body was still, five years after the professionals' unilateral declaration of independence, claiming to be the professional governing body as well.

Eager for limelight, Hayes had become a referee although his performance in the English Amateur Championship final drew the observation that not since the days of Al Jolson had white gloves been employed to more flamboyant effect. He got to know several professionals who, at this stage of snooker's development, still depended heavily on exhibition bookings. He knew all the clubs and began to book players into them on a commission basis. Armed with the calling cards of both Q Promotions, through which he seemed to manage players from Alex Higgins downwards, and the vice-chairmanship of the apparent governing body, he approached Imperial Tobacco's special events department. Shortly afterwards, to the amazement of the snooker world, Embassy announced the sponsorship of the world championship, which was destined to endure for 30 years.

Not without teething troubles, though. As long as he kept his one-man band, Q Promotions, small and controllable, Hayes was able to cope, but his Embassy coup fired him with grandiose visions. Inevitably, desire outran performance.

He had the bright idea of concurrently playing the top half of the draw at Middlesbrough Town Hall and the bottom half at Wythenshawe Forum, a logistical nightmare. The journalistic difficulties of covering such a bifurcated event were compounded by a simple omission on the part of Hayes: no phones. At Wythenshawe, the world's media, some five of us, queued with the public for the one·public phone that the venue boasted. Middlesbrough's first day dawned to the horrified recognition that the town hall's huge windows had no curtains. Funeral directors throughout Teesside thrived on an unexpected source of revenue as they strove to meet the urgent demand for black crêpe.

Several funny things happened at the Forum as Embassy's small special events staff attempted to make up for Hayes's shortcomings. An applicant for press accreditation announced himself in a broad Manchester accent as representing the North Atlantic Press Agency. And where, he was asked, was its head office? 'St Helens,' he replied guilelessly. His application was rejected.

When Charlton made a break of 137, he enquired whether this was a championship record. When the pockets were quickly found to be of varying sizes, it was obvious that it could not be. The now defunct Raper and Sons, whose tables had been installed, were unhelpful in their response to criticism. Thus, at dead of night, an Embassy man was despatched to raise from his bed Cliff Curtis, chief fitter for a rival firm, Riley, to make the best of a bad job.

As was to happen so often, snooker was rescued by the dramatic quality of the matches, particularly a trio of wins for Higgins: 15–14 over Cliff Thorburn, 15–14 over John Spencer and 20–18 in the semi-finals over Eddie Charlton. One entranced spectator amongst the sell-out crowds was Nick Hunter, the BBC producer who had been entrusted with the coverage of the final, which was to be shown on *Grandstand*.

In a more junior role, Hunter had worked on snooker elements of black and white *Grandstand*s of long ago but appreciated that week that there was only the most superficial resemblance between a brief knockabout for an immaterial result and the championship version of the game, with pride, money and status at stake, as it was in other professional sports. As he watched, Hunter became convinced that the public, like him, would be prepared to watch these dramatic conflicts, particularly if they were more professionally presented.

Meanwhile, he had immediate problems with the final, which was staged at Wythenshawe. A table was freshly erected, as was a primitive lighting rig. Reardon, who had driven down from Middlesbrough that morning, discovered after only a few shots that he could not see properly. Trailing 4–2 at the first interval, he headed for the tournament office and insisted that the lighting be adjusted.

Reardon led 8–5 after two sessions, but it became clear the next afternoon that it was impossible to pot a ball along the left-hand-side cushion because it would invariably pull away from it; on the other side, it was virtually impossible to miss because the ball clung to the cushion as if magnetised. It was also obvious that there was something wrong with the angle of rebound from the cushions.

With Higgins leading 10–9 after three sessions, Reardon again vented his feelings in the tournament office. Behind closed doors, the table was worked upon. My reports of all this prompted Gordon Raper, head of the firm whose table it was, to have a solicitor's letter sent to *The Guardian* on the grounds that its reputation had been damaged. This raised the intriguing possibility that if a cricket correspondent described a wicket as under-prepared, over-responsive to spin or in any other way imperfect, a libel writ from the groundsman might follow. *The Guardian* fended Raper off with ease.

There was yet another problem: the referee, Bill Timms, known to irreverent hacks as Bill Pomp. Bill's eyesight and/or knowledge of the free-ball rule was not up to snuff and after the fifth of the eight sessions comprising the final, Reardon, at the time 19–13 ahead, made his now familiar journey to the tournament office.

'Either he goes or I do,' was the tenor of his message. To the unconcealed lack of surprise of all insiders, it was announced that Timms was ill and would be replaced by John Williams, later to become a familiar television face.

Reardon extended his lead to 24–15 by close of play as Higgins, wild and demoralised, conceded several frames with reds still on the table. BBC TV was now filming for *Grandstand*, but Hunter was growing concerned that there might be very little left to film. Higgins versus Thorburn, Spencer and Charlton had been dramatic; this was scarcely worth watching. Next day, Reardon took three of the first four frames to win with a session and a half to spare.

'As far as we were concerned, it was an interesting and rewarding involvement,' said Embassy's Peter Dyke in a masterpiece of polite understatement. 'Given the right opportunity, we would be very pleased to continue our association with snooker and we shall be giving this careful consideration in the near future.'

A continuing role for Hayes was not envisaged: 'At all times, we have been more than willing to do a financial reconciliation with Maurice Hayes and, in fact, we had a most friendly meeting in Bristol. For reasons unknown to us, he steadfastly refused to reveal what monies Q Promotions had received from outside sources [e.g. gate money, exhibitors' fees] through their involvement with the world championship.'

Q Promotions crashed. For months, complaints had been flooding in from clubs that had installed special seating and even a table for exhibitions for which they had sold tickets only to be let down by the non-appearance of a player, booked through Hayes, whom Hayes had neglected to inform. Bizarrely, Higgins showed up for one engagement which Hayes had failed to finalise with the club. Hayes was a man apt to confuse saying he was going to do something or even intending to do it with actually having done it. Even in the run-in to the world championship, there had been a fiasco after the BBC, eager to stimulate prior interest, had accepted Hayes's suggestion that the draw should be made live on its *Nationwide* programme.

The plan was to have Higgins in Lime Grove, Spencer in Manchester and Dennis Taylor in Birmingham, where they would each perform a trick shot and comment on the draw. Higgins arrived in Lime Grove ten minutes before the deadline but Spencer knew nothing about it. Taylor was playing in Portsmouth and his substitute, Graham Miles, became stuck in a traffic jam in Newbury. *Nationwide*, left with a hole in its programme at short notice, was furious. Hayes chanced upon Glenda Jackson, the actress and later MP and transport minister, in the hospitality lounge and persuaded her, off camera and unheralded, to draw the names from an ashtray.

Although Hayes did not have any players under contract, he gave a contrary impression because, through Q Promotions, he solicited engagements for them. Yorkshire TV, who were recording a pro-celebrity series featuring performers as various as Frankie Vaughan, Arthur Mullard and Fred Trueman, paid the players' fees to his company, a destination from which they were never re-routed. Hayes appointed himself to referee the event. He insisted on having the world championship programme rights on a profit or loss basis. It carried a full page picture of Hayes and smaller pictures of the players, but the printer was left unpaid, a fate also suffered by the Chester hotel that hosted another Hayes brainchild, a snooker Oscars dinner.

All agreed that Hayes had not begun his operations with any fraudulent intent. Nor was hope of profit even his chief motive. He craved the limelight and simply and deeply wished to be regarded as a mover and shaker. Once he overreached himself and became haplessly overcommitted to a wholly unrealistic workload, mistakes were inevitable.

When the *Sunday Times* commissioned Keith Botsford and me to write a cautionary tale – 'The man who could have been king' – we ran him to earth in a single-room office above a dentist's surgery in Birkenhead. Interviewing him was like sticking one's head inside a giant marshmallow for any answer to a question was invariably preceded by several minutes of irrelevant circumstantial detail, his mind making great imaginative leaps over chasms of inconvenient facts. It was obvious that if snooker wanted to be taken seriously, it could not afford to have a man playing ducks and drakes with television companies, major sponsors and the reputations of the players. Hayes left the country and was last spotted driving a taxi in Canada.

Pessimists feared that Embassy would pull out of snooker forthwith. They stayed because there was the prospect of more television coverage and better promotion.

Mike Watterson, an English amateur international from Chesterfield who was friendly with several leading players, had been thinking about promoting the championship. When his wife returned from an evening at the Crucible Theatre, Sheffield, she informed him that she had found the ideal venue. The WPBSA needed a promoter, as did Embassy, and when Hunter said that he would push for much more extensive television coverage, there was the makings of a deal. Embassy guaranteed a £17,000 prize fund; the semi-finals and final were covered in some depth; Watterson promoted the championship with an efficiency and flair it had never previously experienced.

From the very first morning, the Crucible seemed a natural home for the championship. Seating only 980, its auditorium was banked steeply enough to give a perfect view to all. There were some gripping matches. Higgins went out 13–12 on the final black to Doug Mountjoy, and John Pulman, making his last major effort, reached the semi-finals.

Spencer beat Reardon in the quarter-finals and went on to beat Thorburn 25–21 to win the title for the third time. Thorburn admitted that he was psychologically not quite ready to win, but his cause was not assisted by countless phone calls from Canadian well-wishers, oblivious to the time difference, in the middle of the night.

More than 20,000 paid for admission. It was clear that an important foundation had been laid for the future of the championship. Hunter persuaded his superiors to cover the following year's championship from first ball to last, as it has been ever since.

This created an opening for me at the BBC. With simultaneous action on two tables, it was obviously impossible for Ted Lowe to cope on his own. A few years into *Pot Black*'s run, the BBC had signed Ted exclusively thus ending the long-standing practice whereby not only BBC but ITV turned to him automatically whenever snooker was on the agenda. This allowed me to accumulate some experience with various ITV outlets.

My first television engagement was for HTV (Wales), which staged a Welsh amateur tournament in its Cardiff studio. Hugh Johns, HTV's resident number one for all sports, supplied the commentary; I summarised. Football was Hugh's speciality. The pinnacle of his career was doing the ITV commentary for the 1966 World Cup final; somewhere near the opposite end was his remark, as time was running down on some undistinguished lower division encounter: 'The referee's looking at his whistle. He's going to blow his watch.'

Thames TV's initial replacement for Ted, though not by a process of logic I understood, was Shaw Taylor, direct from *Police 5*, but it was then put about that auditions would be held. Mine was in the middle of an office at Thames TV. I was told I would be hearing from them and so I did. They felt I could do the job, but they would like to have another listen to 'the timbre' of my voice. This alarmed me. I could change my clothes, my haircut or my religion, but my voice I was stuck with. So many forebodings of rejection intruded that I saw nothing peculiar in being asked to go the following week to Stoke Poges golf club where a further test would decide my suitability.

There were two men from Thames and a 'sponsor's representative'. We were joined by the Oldest Member, straight out of P.G. Wodehouse. We had a few pre-lunch drinks, or at least they did. About 1.30, we sat down to a several course lunch. Wine flowed copiously. Brandy and liqueurs followed. I abstained, fearing the timbre of my voice might be altered for the worse. Details of the test remained hazy.

At about 4.30, we adjourned to the billiard room. A tape recorder and microphone were produced. I was to commentate on a frame between Fred Davis, impersonated here by the Oldest Member, and Ray Reardon, who obviously could not attend in person but who would be embodied for the occasion by the sponsor's representative.

The frame was never completed. The highest break was 1 and there were few of those. I would outline Reardon's claim to greatness in imaginary close-up and try to change gear to describe how he had failed to pot a ball lying over a pocket. I would stress Davis's incomparable experience and then attempt to explain a grotesque shot selection, grotesquely executed.

In ten minutes, it was over and I drove back to Birmingham. Next day, the phone call. My timbre had passed muster. I had the job: England v. the Rest of the World, a 15-week recorded series at the Holiday Inn, Swiss Cottage.

I fulfilled several more engagements for various ITV companies, including the Holsten International from the Fulcrum, Slough, in 1979 when Thames, wishing neither to engage two crews nor pay overtime for one, decided on the fatal economy of not covering all frames.

On top of this, viewers could easily have formed the impression that the tournament was taking place in a mortuary. As the promoter had neglected to satisfy the local authority with gangway arrangements in case of fire, not a single spectator came within range of the cameras though ghostly applause could be sporadically heard from an unseen balcony.

By the time Spencer and Thorburn, held up in traffic, arrived late for their quarter-final, most of the spectators had dispersed in the belief that there would be no further play until that evening. The promoter decided that their first three frames should be played forthwith in front of the few people who were still hanging about and without the television crew, who had been awarded a meal break.

Spencer then compiled the first 147 ever seen, albeit not by many, in tournament play. We television folk were informed of this as we emerged from the nearby McDonald's. This gave us a problem with the highlights programme. The shameful temptation not to mention that the 147 had ever happened was quickly resisted on the grounds that the news would be in the next morning's papers. We settled for a reconstruction of the last three shots. Nor could we inject any drama into the outcome of the match as the promoter had introduced a six frames aggregate score format. After the first three frames, Spencer held the not insubstantial lead of 374–1. Finally, it transpired that the middle pockets were massively oversized, so the 147 could not be officially recognised anyway.

I offered my services to the BBC for the 1978 world championship but, hearing nothing, assumed that my ITV background had ruled me out. I drove up to Sheffield in no particular hurry on the first day to report the championship for *The Guardian*, landing in the pressroom shortly before start of play.

Nick Hunter, now the BBC's executive producer, greeted me. 'Would you like to do some commentary for us this week?'

'Sure, when?' I replied. I thought he might offer half a session on a dull morning.

He consulted his watch. 'In about 20 minutes?'

So, the BBC had kept their word. I had auditioned in 1963 – in case Ted was ill – and was told that I had done well and would be hearing from them. Obviously, they had needed to chew it over but, 15 years later, there I was and there I have remained.

I made my BBC TV debut on Willie Thorne v. Eddie Charlton. Willie, who then sported a full head of hair, was subsequently to be famed for his gleaming pate – 'a very polished player', as I once murmured – while Eddie had much less hair in 1978 than he was to have, and retain, a few years later. The first sign of follicle resurgence on Eddie's noble head was a configuration of what appeared to be stapling holes. This gave way in time to a coiffure so luxuriant and so defiant of the natural laws of growth that we had seen nothing like it since the days of Liberace.

Never mind what was on Eddie's head. What was within it was a never-give-up resolve. Willie, ever the Nearly Man, missed a black which would have made him a 13–9 winner and Eddie not only won 13–12 but also effected a similar escape in the next round, beating Thorburn from four down with five to play.

These were two matches which underlined that snooker is about much more than technique. There is a shot as in itself it intrinsically is; and there is the same shot, loaded with significance, perhaps the winning shot or the one which offers the key to a winning position. On the face of it, what is happening on the table is determining the outcome; in reality, what is happening in the mind often determines what is happening on the table when winning or losing becomes the immediate issue.

The shifting psychological balance between players, which I try to convey in commentary, is one of snooker's deepest sources of fascination. The important question is not how well a player can play, but how well he can play when pressure of one sort or another is exerted upon him.

If a player accumulates a history of losing significant matches from winning positions, it tends to scar his psyche so that the scab is picked off if a similar situation arises. My name for the inability to clinch winning positions is Clincher's disease and in their time Thorburn, Charlton and Thorne all suffered from it. Charlton and Thorburn tended to counteract this, albeit not fully, by being exceptionally gritty fighters from behind.

Had Charlton not lost to Reardon from six up with nine to play in their 1975 world final, he might have had a better chance of beating him in their 1978 semi-final, in which he led 12–9 after three of the five sessions. Reardon, who had 'felt wonderful and couldn't hit a ball', gave himself a late night and many double gins. Next morning, he 'felt tired and listless and played marvellous' in taking all seven frames that session en route to victory at 18–14.

In many ways, the star of the 1978 championship was Fred

Davis, whose run to the semi-finals was aptly commemorated by a BBC musical item set to 'When I'm 64' by The Beatles. It is inconceivable that a sexagenarian could ever again reach such an advanced stage of the championship. The standard of play in 1978 was not what it was to become by 1988, still less 1998, but it was nevertheless an indication of Fred's quality, having passed his peak, that he should have done so well.

Indeed, he was a strong favourite to beat the South African left-hander Perrie Mans to reach the final but crucially missed a straight pink from its spot, which would have put him only one behind at 15–16, and eventually lost 18–16. The drama of this match was not confined to the arena. Despite winning eight world titles, Fred had never quite escaped the shadow of Joe, his elder brother, who had retired from the world championship – but nothing else – just as Fred was coming into his prime.

This was a classic sibling rivalry. Joe had to rule the roost and mostly the easy-going Fred was prepared to let him, but when it came to competition Joe brought out Fred's best. Only Fred ever beat Joe on level terms but, whatever he did, he was always the younger brother.

If Joe could not win himself, he invariably rooted for Fred and was doing so in the auditorium with such intensity in that 1978 semi-final, swinging this way and that in his seat as he tried to will the balls into the pockets, that he almost fell into the gangway when Fred missed the vital pink.

After that frame, the last before the mid-session interval, Joe was taken ill backstage. He was driven back to his London home next day but collapsed on the pavement. He survived a six-and-a-half-hour operation but died from a chest infection a few weeks later while he was convalescing in the country.

The Joe Davis era thus neatly overlapped the authentic dawn of snooker's television age, for this was the first championship that the BBC covered from first ball to last so that the public could participate in the accumulating tension not only of each match but also round by round, sharing the hopes and fears of their favourites as their deepest reserves of emotion, concentration and will had to be cashed in.

Hardcore snooker men enthused that this was the first time snooker had ever been shown properly, for it takes time for tension, the most important ingredient of a match, to build up. It is usually a while before the wills and styles of two players start to interact. Viewers could appreciate the skill of the man at the table and share the suffering of the man in the non-striker's chair. Nick Hunter's conviction that the BBC should provide a portrait of the championship rather than a few glimpses of the final was triumphantly vindicated.

Near midnight on the first Monday of the championship, there was a BBC2 audience of almost five million. This rose to a peak of seven million. In the first round, Patsy Fagan won two black ball games and the decider on the pink to beat Alex Higgins from two down with three to play. Day after day, one match or another kept the television audience riveted as the nation went red-eyed to work.

'Backstage at the Crucible,' wrote *The Guardian*'s then television correspondent, Peter Fiddick, 'there is a sense that the result scarcely matters, that something new is happening. The top players are very conscious of their new audience and its implications. For them, the game is at last being shown properly, at length, with all its tactics, and the fact that it can prove even more popular that way opens a whole new future.'

5

THE DAYS OF INNOCENCE

EVEN THOSE OF US WHO HAD WANTED SNOOKER TO BE MORE THAN the low profile folk sport it had been for as long as we could remember could scarcely adjust to its abrupt lift-off into a major television attraction, and BBC could hardly believe its luck. It was almost as if a brand new sport had been delivered gift-wrapped with an intriguing cast of characters. BBC wanted more snooker, and ITV, not wishing to be left out of the action, wanted some as well. A circuit materialised in response to this demand.

At the table, the dramatis personae were colourful and varied: there was Reardon, who had just beaten Mans 25–18 to win the 1978 world title, his sixth and, as it proved, his last; there was Spencer, who had won three championships and was already in decline. It was not long before Reardon was as well. There was Higgins, easily snooker's greatest box-office and television attraction, a prodigious talent always half in love with self-destruction. World champion in 1972, he was to regain the title in 1982.

There were veteran world champions, such as John Pulman and Fred Davis, who were clearly in the twilight of their careers. From the same era but already having missed the boat in terms of ever becoming world champion, there was Rex Williams. Eddie Charlton had also missed this boat several times and was to miss it one last time in 1979. The supporting cast included players like Graham Miles, who sighted so far on his left eye that his cue was almost resting under his ear. Inevitably, he was said to be playing by ear. Patsy Fagan, the inaugural UK champion, was to have his career destroyed by a psychological block. When he attempted to use the rest, he was unable to strike the cue ball.

Three Canadians – Cliff Thorburn, Kirk Stevens and Bill Werbeniuk – added colour to the scene. Thorburn had spent most of his adult years criss-crossing North America, as had Bill Werbeniuk, whose father, Adam 'Shorty' Werbeniuk, had been able to spare enough time from his vocation as an armed robber to become Canadian champion. To play for third party prizes on a legit circuit instead of their own money in ever more dubious halls in the bad part of town was a delightful novelty. David Taylor (aka 'The Silver Fox') was there, as was Dennis Taylor, who despite reaching the 1975 and 1977 world semi-finals did not quite appear to have the extra gear to become champion. He proved everybody wrong in 1985.

From 1972 onwards, there had been a steady trickle of new professionals simply because the professional game was starting to offer more opportunities. The world championship was on a firm footing; the Benson and Hedges Masters started in 1975; Pontin's, the holiday-camp chain, started a spring festival of snooker at Prestatyn in 1974; the UK Championship was launched in 1977. Prize money was made permissible in amateur events in 1971, so professionalism came to be defined simply by membership of the WPBSA. There were full-time and even part-time amateurs who could earn more than the lesser professionals. There was more money in snooker generally.

Doug Mountjoy was briefly a miner, buried once for a few minutes in a roof fall. He played for Risca Colliery and for Abertysswg, a village club that could field a team of Welsh champions. He himself won the Welsh amateur title in 1968 and was perfectly happy as a foreman in a cardboard-box factory until he resigned in 1974 because the management wanted him to take a stricter line with 'his boys'. He had never considered that snooker would offer him anything more than enjoyment and trophies, but his severance payment enabled his wife to start a hairdressing business while he began to play full time.

That spring, Pontin's staged the first of their annual opens at Prestatyn with professionals giving 25 start. Mountjoy, far too good on this mark, won the £1,000 first prize. For someone who had been on £60 a week, this was a lot of money. It was obvious that the game was on the up and he decided to turn professional, preferably with a prestigious title to his name, but even to qualify for the 1976 World Amateur Championship he had to win his second Welsh amateur title earlier that year.

This seemed unlikely when Dai Thomas stood over the match-ball blue in their semi-final. 'He should have potted it, but a moth settled on the ball. He got up and down two or three times and obviously it had put him off.' Although Mountjoy was going to turn professional anyway, he would never have had a flying start to his career but for that moth. He would never have gone to Johannesburg, let alone been invited into the 1977 Benson and Hedges Masters as world amateur champion two months later. He beat Ray Reardon, the reigning champion, 7–6 in the final.

Anti-apartheid pressures of one sort or another had kept South Africa out of several world championships, so I was in two minds as to whether to go to Johannesburg as a journalist. I was glad I did because I saw for myself what an awful place Dr Vorster's iron-fisted apartheid republic was. When I walked from my hotel to the tournament hotel, I was struck by a chessboard with man-size pieces – black and white, of course – which seemed to be perpetually in use in Joubert Park. Just a little further along, there was an alcove at the side of the cinema where a couple of policemen were beating up a black man who may or may not have had something amiss with his papers. At the tournament hotel, an Afrikaner was about to get into a lift in which a black chambermaid was already travelling.

'Which floor, sir?' she asked.

'I don't want to travel in the same lift as you,' he replied.

A South African official, who would have been counted as almost a liberal, entertained one competitor and his wife to dinner one evening. His own wife, unable to eat all her steak, asked for a doggy bag so that she could take it home for her maid. This was her idea of kindness. Quite a nice bloke from the South African Press Association believed in all honesty that London's *Sunday Times* was an agent for the Communist Party so *The Guardian*, my other paper, would have been quite off the scale by this reckoning.

It disconcerted some players that a number of referees called the score in Afrikaans, and the South African television service did not strike me as a model of flexibility. They had set their timings for their Saturday equivalent of *Grandstand* and came to the snooker just as the players were disappearing for their 15-minute mid-session interval. The commentators – thankfully I was not among them – talked for the 15 minutes. Just as the players returned, the programme moved on to athletics.

Sri Lanka and India boycotted the championship, an absence that Bob O'Neill, the 75-year-old Australian building millionaire who had just been elected International Billiards and Snooker Federation (IBSF) president, chose to attribute to 'power-hungry politicians in other countries who do nothing to harm the tournament but merely prevent their players playing in an event like this'.

These sentiments were received with uproarious approval from the Afrikaner element who seemed, like O'Neill, blissfully unaware that it was the obnoxious racial policies of their own power-hungry politicians which had led several countries to decide not to play against representatives of such a regime. O'Neill did not like the accuracy with which I reported his speech and thus became another implacable enemy.

For Doug, of course, focused on his game, only the title was relevant.

'Winning the world amateur meant that I went straight into *Pot Black* as well,' he said. This BBC2 weekly series was a wonderful shop window for players who still made substantial slices of their livings through exhibitions.

'I started giving exhibitions in 1974 as an amateur. I used to charge a tenner, no win, no fee, giving club teams of seven 250 start – members only, no imports. I only lost two.'

By the time he turned professional, he had managed to increase his fee to £35 and a few years after that, he got it up to £50. Later, shows in town halls and theatres brought him fees of £1,000 a night, albeit when tournaments were by then limiting the dates top players could devote to exhibitions.

Arrangements did not always go smoothly. One promoter in Rhyl donned a monkey outfit to try to sell tickets on the promenade. Once, he found himself in Dartford, Kent, when he should have been in Dartmouth, Devon ('I even found School Road as well, but there was no club there, of course').

The 1979 world champion, though, was Terry Griffiths, who had been Welsh amateur champion in 1975 and English amateur champion in 1977 and 1978 – Welshmen then being permitted to play in both. He had been a miner, a blacksmith's apprentice, a bus conductor and an insurance salesman. He was 24 before he made his first century, unthinkably late by today's standards. In his first professional season, he was struggling to obtain the two £70-a-night club exhibition engagements he needed each week to keep his head above water. He lost his first professional match, in the UK Championship qualifying competition, 9–8 to Rex Williams after leading 8–2, and went into the world championship qualifying with no higher objective than getting into the 16-man field at the Crucible so that he could pay off what he owed on his car. He arrived in Sheffield in the ideal state of mind for a snooker professional: 'With no immediate worries, I felt I had everything to gain and nothing to lose.'

He quietly fancied his chances against Perrie Mans who, despite reaching the 1978 final, did not seem to have much breakmaking fluency. He beat him 13–8 and a 13–12 quarter-final win over Higgins, the third time in a row Higgins had lost by the odd frame at the Crucible, put him in the semi-finals against Charlton, who with his old nemeses, Reardon and

Spencer, already eliminated, believed that it might be his year at last.

The brilliance of Higgins had been met by the deadly counter-punching of Griffiths, who amply illustrated the importance in championship snooker of making clearances of 50, 60 or even 70-plus to snatch frames on pink or black. With Charlton, he found himself embroiled in a war of attrition.

Its final session ran 5 hours, 25 minutes and it was 1.40 a.m., with BBC's coverage still live, before Griffiths prevailed 19–17. 'I'm in the final, now, you know,' he exclaimed with pride and disbelief into David Vine's microphone in his moment of victory. It was a popular win, not least with BBC's cameramen and technicians, who in those more heavily unionised days went onto double rates if coverage continued after midnight.

Dennis Taylor came through the other half and the final was tight until Griffiths, from 17–16, won seven frames in succession. Doubling the transmission time from the previous year, the BBC created in him a new television hero as millions shared his battles and became emotionally involved in his aspirations.

'Terry winning this has been the greatest achievement the game's ever known,' said Fred Davis. 'The only thing you could really compare it with was Higgins in 1972, but the game was nothing like as big then and the championship was broken up over a whole season, not concentrated into a fortnight. For someone like Terry, with no experience of long matches, to come through and win is just remarkable.'

It had seemed almost magical that snooker had changed in only a couple of years from low profile folk sport to a major television attraction which could spearhead all sorts of commercial developments. New snooker clubs sprang up, table and equipment sales soared, sponsors wanted to be involved. There was new money in snooker, and once there was money there were middlemen and things to argue about.

Some players ceased to be merely players as political alliances started to be formed; some of them realised that they were not going to be top players forever but that snooker was all they knew and a living had to be made somehow. Managers now appeared on a scene on which previously there had been nothing much to manage. Snooker was about to lose what was left of its innocence.

6

GREED STARTS TO KICK IN

IF SNOOKER, OR ANY OTHER MAJOR SPORT, HAD EVER BEEN PLANNING a controlled expansion and headhunting the most credible chief executive, it is unlikely that it would ever have turned to Del Simmons, an affable, colourful East Ender with a chequered business background. Of course, snooker did not have a master plan but invariably adapted instead to a series of historical accidents.

As a young man, Simmons ducked and dived in the East End like many another, working the markets, becoming involved in the motor trade and with a number of nightclubs, including the Capabana in Ilford, where he enterprisingly employed a bogus French accent during his time as a croupier, and the Kinema in Redbridge. Sociable and likeable in a jovial, rough diamond sort of way, he refined his cockney affability into an asset and spent many a convivial hour in the company of Bruce Forsyth, Jimmy Tarbuck and others, some of it at Variety Club pro-celebrity golf gatherings.

His passion for golf was reflected in the name he chose for his second-hand car business, Wentworth Motors, which was located not in Surrey's leafy glades as its name might imply but on a former bombsite in Manor Park, East London. He knew Bobby Moore, England's 1966 World Cup captain, and became friendly with Sean Connery, one of filmdom's superstars. Moore, Connery and Simmons were among the directors of Woolston Hall, an ambitious country club in Chigwell, Essex. All did not run smoothly with this venture. There were threatening phone calls, an arson attempt and a shotgun attack on Simmons's home, shattering his lounge windows and chandelier, as he sat there watching a Western.

Woolston Hall, it seemed, was uninsurable and was dissolved by the registrar following a compulsory winding-up order. Wentworth Motors was also wound up, and it was not until July 1985 that Simmons was able to repay Connery all the money he owed him. His last cheque was overpaid by £29 and this amount was returned to him.

From Chigwell, Simmons decamped to Weybridge, where he ran an afternoon drinking haunt, the Tonic Club; when the 'c' fell off the illuminated sign, this establishment was thereafter known as the Toni Club. It had a gymnasium and a couple of snooker tables, and the members wanted to see the best players. When Simmons booked them, he was surprised how cheap they were. There were three big names in the '70s: Reardon, Spencer and Higgins.

'You could have them for £50 a night,' said Simmons. 'We gave them £200.'

Reardon and Spencer accepted his suggestion that they form a company, International Snooker Agency (ISA), to handle bookings for leading players. In 1976, after the Q Promotions debacle had left him managerless, Higgins became their first client.

'We were like father and son,' said Simmons. 'Alex always respects firmness. I had to slap him a few times to keep him in line, but we got on.' Reardon resigned in 1981 just before Higgins left but, even with Higgins, there was still no real money in such a venture. ISA's last return in 1986 showed net liabilities of £1,425.

In ISA's early days, Spencer had also introduced Simmons to David Fisher of Bristol Coin Equipment, a buccaneer who shook up the complacent, conservative equipment trade, which had been sleeping for longer than Rip Van Winkle.

Fisher's business empire grew from tiny beginnings. He supplied cigarettes for the workforce of his employers, a Bristol engineering company, through a vending machine. He gravitated to the amusement machine trade and set up BCE. One day, he suddenly needed 1,000 cues for pool tables in his pub and other amusement machine outlets.

'I went to a local wholesaler in Bristol. He offered me seven and said he'd do his best to get me some more.' Impatient at this, Fisher imported 1,000 from someone he knew in America. No hot cakes ever sold quicker.

'I didn't really want a distribution business, but I bought 28,000 cues from Taiwan to take to the Amusement Trades Exhibition in January 1975. I was just going to sell these and take the profit, but the response was overwhelming. I took orders for £250,000 and I thought: "Maybe there's something in this distribution business after all."'

He came to know Dick Helmstetter, an American cue maker who had set up business in Japan. He made lovely cues and when Fisher heard one day that Spencer was in Bristol, he knocked on his hotel room door with several in his arms.

'John had shaving cream all over his face. He said they were beautiful cues but no good for snooker and made several very useful suggestions. He thought I was out of my brains when I said I was hoping to sell at about £20 wholesale because at the time the top price for a cue was about £8 retail.'

With Fisher as the British distributor, Helmstetter's range of Adam Custom Cues was ready in January 1979 after a year's development work. Lively marketing with big-name endorsements, including Spencer's, was the keynote of the operation. Simmons took a 20 per cent commission for the player on each of these contracts. Soon, Fisher bought out a struggling firm of cue makers, Askrod, and became, as Billiard Cues of England, a manufacturer.

Fisher was already distributing the Belgian Aramith ball, a market leader in pool that could make no headway in snooker because, from time immemorial, the products of the Composition Billiard Ball Supply Company (Compo), first Crystalate and then, from 1973, Super Crystalate, had been the designated ball for professional and amateur championships. Of course, if this was the ball with which all matches of any significance, amateur or professional, were played then hardly anybody was going to buy another sort of ball for practice.

'Compo' did not suffer from an excess of dynamic management. Even with a quasi-monopoly, it was not very profitable. Fisher bought them out, somewhat to my relief, as Compo was suing me for libel at the time. They were *Snooker Scene*'s back cover advertisers, but I nevertheless believed that the snooker world was not being best served by a situation in which monopoly prices could be charged for a product which was not beyond criticism. One article in the latter vein bore the headline: 'Balls: Another Fiasco'.

Jim Cameron, the peppery little Scot who had become managing director, was furious, as he was when we published an analysis of Compo's balance sheet. Jim had tunnel vision as far as his company was concerned. Once at the Canadian Open, a Canadian trader asked him how things were going. Jim replied that his problems included the arrest of his production manager, who had murdered his wife.

'It's happened at a very bad time for us,' said Jim.

'What would have been a good time?' he was asked.

We were on rock-solid factual ground as far as the libel action was concerned, but it was still a worry because I had been advised that we might be awarded only two-thirds of the costs and that the other third, if the action was dragged out to trial, could be about £5,000, which in 1979 was a lot of money to us. Immediately he bought Compo, Fisher rang up to say what nonsense the action was. I accepted his suggestion that it be discontinued with each side paying its own costs.

Some years down the road, when Fisher went a bridge too far with his expansion plans, he sold Compo to Aramith, who thus became by far the worldwide pool and snooker combined market leader.

'In the meantime,' said Fisher, 'people started to ask us about tables. I went to a couple of table makers, but the terms I was quoted sounded like a rip-off. I asked my own chippy to make a few enquiries about mahogany and, from what he told me, I decided to go into the table business.' When the supply of slate for the table beds looked as if it could be a problem, he bought a slate company in Portugal.

Fisher liked Simmons. Their wives liked each other. Fisher needed a managing director for BCE's tables division who would also keep an eye on other aspects of the snooker business. There was also a revolution led by Simmons, with the backing of leading players, which installed him as contracts negotiator of the WPBSA. So from an office in Bristol on which Fisher held the freehold, Simmons was at one point operating for ISA, BCE and WPBSA.

The revolution arose from a ten-hour AGM on the day after Terry Griffiths won the 1979 championship. On the one man, one vote principle, the minnows forced through a proposal that for the 1980 championship only Griffiths and Dennis Taylor, the 1979 finalists, would be excused the qualifying competition. Neither the BBC nor Embassy liked the sound of this because it increased the possibility of the new personalities it had created being knocked out before television coverage began.

The star names did not like it either and signed up to Professional Snooker Association Ltd with Simmons at the helm. PSA's very choice of name hinted at its takeover ambitions. There were hawks, like Reardon and Spencer, who believed that too little of the game's new money was finding its way to the players; there were doves, like Griffiths, who nevertheless did not wish to be on the weaker side. PSA brought pressure on WPBSA, of which Rex Williams was still chairman, and almost immediately the new exemption system was thrown out in favour of extending the televised phase of the championship to sixteen exempted players and eight qualifiers. Meetings of PSA and WPBSA were often held on the same day, even in the same room, usually with most of the same people present because some PSA shareholders were also on the WPBSA board. Conflicts of interest were never considered, for this was a gold rush and snooker was the Klondike.

Those who had the power would, in the main, have the money.

It was resolved that only the twenty-one players who had reached the last 16 of the world championship within the last three years would have a vote and that the top ten in the rankings would automatically constitute the board, though as Alex Higgins, for one, was manifestly unsuited to corporate life, this provision was soon dropped as unworkable in favour of an elected committee. PSA believed, or at any rate stated, that Mike Watterson, who had not only taken the championship to the Crucible but had also started a UK Championship in 1977 and promoted various other tournaments, was making too much money out of these events. He became, in essence, a target of the players' acquisitiveness and PSA – Simmons and the leading players – had the muscle to insist that all key contracts with television and sponsors should go through a governing body controlled by the players.

The eventual outcome was that on 5 September 1981, PSA Ltd was wound up (with net assets of £544) and WPBSA was reconstituted as a limited company to organise the circuit and negotiate contracts in the manner expected of governing bodies. Simmons was taken on board at £13,000 a year as part-time contracts negotiator. Wearing ISA, BCE and WPBSA hats, Simmons had it made. More and more WPBSA business began to revolve around him and as the money flowed in from television contracts (a novel concept for snooker) and sponsors eager to participate in the growing snooker success story, no one closely questioned his effectiveness.

Even after Simmons left BCE in 1986 to work full time for WPBSA at £60,000 a year, other table firms tended to agree that BCE was still regarded as the favoured son in terms of being awarded contracts for televised tournaments.

A trawl through BCE's shareholders' register at Companies House was unlikely to have disabused them of this impression. On leaving BCE, Simmons held 747,821 shares worth £284,172 at the time of issue. The value of this tranche was set to fluctuate by £7,478 for every penny BCE's shares rose above or fell below the issue price of 38p.

His name did not actually appear in the register: some shares were held by nominees, others appeared to have been given to his wife, Audrey; their children, Gary, Julie and Laura; and Sandy Winter, who was engaged for several years to run the bar in WPBSA's hospitality room and for whom he left his wife. Simmons remained in charge of negotiating WPBSA contracts until 13 May 1991, when he departed with 323 days of his latest contract to run and a severance payment of £270,000.

Paul Hatherell, who had become WPBSA's number two executive, was another BCE shareholder, as were three WPBSA board members: Ray Reardon, John Spencer and Gordon Ingham. Carol Covington, who was to become Reardon's second wife, was another, as was Spencer's wife, Margot. If you were in the know, you had shares, and if you were smart, you knew when to sell them.

Williams first appeared in the shareholders' register in 1989, as did two associates, John King and Peter Pioli. Steve Davis Properties Ltd, which was owned 50/50 by Steve Davis and Barry Hearn, held 100,000 shares in 1988 and sold them all the following year at a loss. John Rukin, an accountant, subsequently struck off, who was for a year or two Joe Johnson's quasi-manager, held 25,000 shares in 1989 but none in 1990. Robert Winsor, a millionaire who managed Cliff Thorburn for a while, held shares at the same time as his brother, John. The then parent company of Strachan, the cloth manufacturers, held a tranche. Neil Mitton, an advertising agent whose clients included WPBSA, Strachan and, at one time, BCE, had one, too. By February 1992, long after the good days, these shares were hovering around the 5p mark.

Those at the centre of power, least of all Simmons, did not believe in themselves as an authentic governing body, setting unimpeachable standards of objectivity and impartiality in its dealings; it perpetuated instead an insidious form of cronyism of which Simmons was at the hub.

Watterson's contracts with Embassy; Coral, his UK Championship sponsor; State Express, under whose banner he had founded a

World Team Cup; Jameson and Yamaha Organs were allowed to run their course before he was unceremoniously squeezed out of the snooker picture. WPBSA set up a wholly owned subsidiary, WPBSA Promotions Ltd, in March 1983 to put on its own tournaments, a step which effectively put the governing body in competition with some and potentially all commercial promoters. Hatherell, a Watterson aide, was poached to become managing director, although his abilities were limited and he was totally subservient to Simmons, who had limitations of his own. Nor could its staff recruitment policy be described as unimprovable. The head girl in the secretarial operation at WPBSA was Simmons's attractive daughter, Julie, whose qualifications were discussed at a board meeting.

'Can she do shorthand?'

'No,' said Simmons, 'but she can write fast.'

The commercial coup that had taken place, a virtual takeover of the game, was held in place by Simmons's popularity with the players. He was good company, the life and soul of every party, many of them funded at the expense of the membership because the status of WPBSA Promotions as a wholly owned subsidiary meant that only the most abbreviated accounts had to be submitted to an AGM. In any case, it was to be a few years before a supine membership rose temporarily from its torpor. Meanwhile, the rank and file compared their opportunities to the wasteland of only a few years earlier and congratulated themselves that they were living in a land of plenty.

Simmons was not without the negotiating skills of a second-hand car salesman, for he had indeed been one, but snooker was such a hot property that he could hardly avoid bringing back some attractive renewed and new agreements, albeit not as attractive as they might have been had the likes of BBC, ITV and Embassy been dealing with a more sophisticated and soundly structured organisation. At WPBSA, he was in the enviable position that people had to come to him if they wished to become commercially involved in snooker. This was fine while it lasted, but when snooker's bubble of popularity burst it was a different story when sponsors were harder to come by.

When Simmons essayed a venture of his own outside the WPBSA's protective umbrella, it went spectacularly under with debts of £99,369. A 12-man league without television coverage or sponsorship was always on shaky ground. Most matches were well attended but astronomical expenses were incurred. Its brochure and other promotional material cost £19,450, nearly £16,000 over budget. The press launch, budgeted for £1,000, cost £6,500.

'If you're doing your brains in,' said Simmons picturesquely, 'who needs £50,000 of flowers round the arena every night?'

With financial disaster looming, WPBSA was invited to invest. The proposal was defeated only on the casting vote of Williams, who had been deemed surplus to requirements by the original PSA Ltd consortium but who, from his chairmanship of the rump of the original WPBSA, was taken on as chairman of WPBSA Ltd. He was, it was reasoned, snooker's most plausible front man. In the next 20 years, Williams was to do some dreadful things in the WPBSA's name, but in this instance, at least, he – and a few others – did recognise some fiduciary duty to the membership as a whole.

Simmons was to have a pivotal role at WPBSA for more than a decade. Its election system was to undergo various cosmetic changes, but essentially it continued to be run like a local golf club, by a relatively small number of players utterly lacking the kind of business expertise which could have given it the sound structural base and the kind of commercial vision that could have developed a genuinely worldwide circuit.

At the centre of snooker, some behaved as if the sport would be on honeymoon with television, sponsors and the public forever. Others assumed that it would flare and fade like a firework and that a good time should be had for as long as possible. It took a long time for unpalatable truths to dawn and even then those in entrenched positions of power and privilege were unwilling to surrender them.

Simmons was adept at interpersonal politics. Some believed him to be responsible for most, if not all, of the financial investment in snooker, but he either inherited sponsors set up by others, like Watterson and Benson and Hedges, or was dependent on sponsors or their agents approaching him. If they wanted to get into snooker, where else, in the late '70s and early '80s, could they go?

Between winning the 1979 world title and coming to defend it in 1980, Griffiths acknowledged that the PSA/WPBSA issue worried him more than any other. WPBSA, as it stood, was going nowhere; PSA Ltd was too narrow a takeover by leading players. WPBSA Ltd, an uneasy compromise, was the best that could be done, but the flaws were obvious from the outset and would eventually have cast the game into the shadows but for its saving grace: players and tournaments attracting figures excellent at best and respectable at worst. Faced with the direct television ban on advertising, the tobacco manufacturers spent their funds lavishly on sports that did not feel uncomfortable associating themselves with a product which was a clear health risk. Through historical accident, professional snooker came to rest on the twin bedrocks of BBC and tobacco.

7

THE NEW KIDS ON THE BLACK

IF IT WAS CLEAR AT THIS STAGE THAT STEVE DAVIS WAS A RISING FORCE, no one dreamt that he was to dominate the '80s with six world and six UK titles. He was not outstandingly blessed with natural talent. Arthur Baker, an amateur championship referee who was a member of Plumstead Common Workingmen's Club, where the teenage Davis used to play with his father, said: 'He was always going to be a good player, but you'd never have picked him as a future world champion.' What Davis did have was relentless determination, an insatiable appetite for practice and an intelligence which enabled him to learn quickly from experience. Neither had any leading player before him studied the mechanics of technique so minutely. Earlier champions had tended, broadly, to play with the techniques they had been born with apart from a few instinctive modifications along the way. Golfers were always checking and modifying their swings, but Davis was the first snooker player to scrutinise and adapt aspects of his cue action in this way. He travelled all over London to find the best practice opposition and was one day in the Lucania Club, Romford.

Lucania's chain of run-down snooker halls had been bought in 1975, not least as a property investment, by Barry Hearn, a sharp chartered accountant with a background in the rag trade. He located his office in the Romford club and had his attention drawn one day to a tall, gangling ginger-haired youth with an air of eerie concentration. It was like Mr Rolls meeting Mr Royce.

Hearn's career as one of Britain's most colourful sports

entrepreneurs was founded on his first sports management client; Davis acquired not only a manager to guide his career and maximise his commercial potential but also a surrogate elder brother. Davis was provided with championship class practice facilities at Romford and matches against all leading players who were prepared to go there for a fee, though some of these disappeared in sidestakes. On his home table, he was well-nigh unbeatable.

Davis's first significant showing on television was to bring down Griffiths, the defending champion, at his first fence at the Crucible in 1980. With Griffiths jaded from the year's pressures, Davis led 7–0 but was caught at 10–10 before prevailing 13–10. Not quite ready to seize the snooker world by the throat, Davis lost in the quarter-finals to Higgins, who contested a dramatic final with Thorburn.

This could hardly have offered a clearer contrast in styles, between Higgins – quick, edgy and impulsive – and Thorburn – measured, cool and calculating. So gripping was the television coverage that when it was interrupted to show the life-or-death drama of the SAS resolving the siege at the Iranian Embassy, many viewers telephoned irately to demand that snooker be restored to their screens.

Not many people hit it off with Higgins on a lasting basis, but Thorburn did not hit it off with him from his first day in England in 1973 when Higgins, who was world champion at the time, grandly offered him 40 start for £5 a game.

'Being the gentleman I am, I only took 28. I don't think he won a game,' Thorburn was to recall. 'All I remember is Higgins at the top of some stairs; I still haven't been paid and he's got a ball in his hand, threatening to throw it at me.'

A year or so later, they were in a card game together. 'Higgins went broke and asked me to lend him £50. I'm losing as well so I say OK, if he gives me his ring. He's with Cara, his first wife, so that night she comes down to my room and demands the ring off me. I said no, so Alex pretended to faint on the floor. I went to pick him up and the guy grabbed a bottle. I grabbed him and threw the bottle down. I got my left arm around him and just pounded his head until my hand got sore.'

There was aggro too in the world final. Higgins accused Thorburn (without foundation) of standing in his line. Thorburn accused Higgins (with foundation) of clinking ice cubes into his glass as he was about to play.

At 9–5, Higgins looked the winner but characteristically cast aside the element of restraint which had helped him to this lead as he started to play to the gallery. Thorburn won the four remaining frames of the day to level at 9–9.

This was the key passage of the match, although it was still close. At 16–15, Thorburn missed a very easy brown from its spot as he was clearing up to go two up with three to play: 'When I missed the brown, I nearly died. I felt as if my whole body had turned into one big heart.' Higgins levelled at 16–16.

The interface between long dreamt-of ambition and its imminent reality had been too much for Thorburn. In the 1978 championship, as Charlton was coming from four down with five to play to beat him, 'the feeling that I was going to lose came over me like a tidal wave'. This time, he brushed the setback aside, making 119 to regain the lead and playing another immaculate frame to win 18–16.

Leaving aside his natural grit, how had he held up so strongly? Perhaps, of all possible opponents, he least wanted to lose to Higgins. Certainly, because he was more secure in his personal life than ever before, newly married to Barbara, 'good to be with and yet very well organised at the same time'. Backstage, she was supporting Cliff just as vocally as Lynn was supporting Higgins.

At 16–16, Lynn walked into the players' room with a cake inscribed: 'Congratulations. Year of the Hurricane. Alex Higgins world champion, 1980'.

'I thought Lynn and Alex were just perfect for each other,' said Cliff drily. 'The cake was there when we all went to Napoleon's that night. I had about six pieces of it.'

Cliff was a droll, likeable if infuriatingly unpunctual bloke. When I came to write his book, *Playing for Keeps*, I made some fourteen appointments for sessions of tape recording and he was late for every one – even at his own house. Laconic and laid-back in private life, he loves the battle, either competing on the table or as a fan of other sports.

His early life was often a grim struggle for moral, even physical, survival, but he managed to harness to his advantage the kind of experience which would have crushed most. Abandoned as a baby by his mother and the victim of a custody struggle which kept him in an orphanage until he left it to be brought up by his father and his father's mother, he was an inwardly solitary soul despite the friends he made on the sports field in lacrosse and baseball, in both of which he excelled.

He could make little sense of the adult world and sought refuge in the world of sport where inequalities of birth and wealth are at least minimised and where the rules and codes of the game impose a sense of order not to be found in the incoherence of 'real life'. Perhaps, too, he had the rage of the abandoned, even if it took years for this to dawn on him in full.

At the age of twenty, he learned that his mother had not died when he was a baby, as his father's side had always told him, but in fact was alive and well and living with the four children of her second marriage. He felt betrayed by their reluctance to treat him as an adult by not telling him the truth. It hardened his resolve to make something of himself.

Cliff had been about ten when his father had taken him to a bowling alley. When he heard the click of pool balls, he wandered off in that direction:

It was a game for money, a crowd getting excited. In the end, there was a big groan when one guy banked [doubled] the 8 ball to the side pocket to win. I just knew then that I wanted to be part of it all, becoming a man and all that stuff.

He learned his trade in the poolrooms of Canada and North America, whether it was 9 ball against a fisherman who pulled a knife on him in Campbell River, pink ball in San Francisco in the days of flower power, the hippies and Sgt Pepper, or snooker in Deli, Ontario, on a red cloth with 15 yellows instead of reds. Excuses and self-pity had no currency in these places. He was prepared to lose his last $10 and not eat; he was prepared to take the other man's:

> I don't want this to seem that I had a real tough deal because I didn't. I was doing what I wanted to do. I was broke sometimes or hungry or freezing cold, but there was always another day.

He played eight to ten hours a day for ten years. Once, he played a redoubtable hustler, Cornbread Red, for 52 hours non-stop. 'I knew he had really come to play when he laid out two clean pairs of socks.' Something stronger than black coffee was needed to play this long without sleep.

In Montreal, in 1970:

> I was giving a guy called Legau 20 start, one red. I had lost all my money and I'm playing the next game on my nerves, so to speak. It goes to a re-spotted black. The fellow pots the black and goes in off and then I beat the guy for all his money. So, I've never had that fear of the last game. The 15th round or the last hole, or something like that, is what turns me on.

For Thorburn, the world title proved, as it had for Griffiths, a poisoned chalice. Apart from an initial burst of curiosity from the Canadian media, the public recognition, which he believed to be part of the prize, was denied him. Lacking astute managership, he had no offers of lucrative endorsement contracts and, also lacking a naturally entertaining style, was not as heavily in demand for exhibition engagements as a world champion might expect.

Recognising that much of his life would revolve round the

British circuit, he tried to settle in Walton-on-Thames but missed his Canadian friends and felt almost anonymous in a land which seemed to acknowledge that he was world champion only in terms of some aberrational departure from British dominance. Indeed, his morale became so low that two years after his world title win he was to return to live in Toronto, reckoning that he could do no worse by commuting when necessary.

On the other side of the world, Jimmy White won the World Amateur Championship at the age of 18 in Launceston, Tasmania, albeit not before he had been de-selected and reinstated as one of England's two nominations.

This championship was held every two years. Jimmy had won the English amateur title at the age of 16 years, 11 months in 1979; Joe O'Boye, one of snooker's all-time drinkers, who was to acquire a lengthy disciplinary record on this account, was the 1980 champion. Together, they were dynamite.

At the amateur home internationals at Pontin's, Prestatyn, they were having a quiet half of lager in their dress suits when England's team manager, Bill Cottier, a former police inspector from Bootle with a sponge cake haircut, came by.

'That's it. You should be ashamed of yourself, Jimmy White. You won't be playing today,' said he.

It seemed as if he meant it, so, on the assumption they would not be playing, these young bloods started getting stuck into the vodka and orange. A couple of hours later, Jimmy was told he was on next against Wales.

'Wales, do I know him?' he mumbled, as he stumbled towards the table.

It was Wales in the person of Steve Newbury, whose 3–0 win gave Wales the match and, as it turned out, the championship.

Cottier was puce with pomposity. 'That's it. You're definitely not going to Tasmania now. You're out.'

Jimmy staggered to his chalet and passed out, still in his dress suit, as indeed he was when his burly manager, Henry West, arrived hotfoot in response to this emergency a few hours later. By this time, Jimmy was recumbent in an overflowing bath using his cue as a paddle. He was, he told Big H, canoeing to Tasmania.

Extremely well educated at street and snooker hall level, Big H had become Jimmy's manager when he was primarily a supplier of pool tables. His marketing style was refreshingly direct. He would lift existing pool tables bodily into a pub's backyard and replace them with his own. 'I've just taken over,' he would say, 'get on the blower and tell them to come and take their tables away. You won't be needing them, will you?'

Determined to look after Jimmy after he had won his southern semi-final of the English Amateur Championship, he allowed him to visit the Gents, only to realise a little later that he had absconded through a window. Wearing the same suit – as was natural because he had not been to bed – he showed up ten minutes before the off the next day and duly won to put himself within one match of becoming the youngest ever amateur champion. Henry's brother, Wally, who had a keen sense of tradition, asked him in the car, driving home, how he felt. 'OK, mate. Got a bit of a cold,' he replied artlessly.

He lived, and continued to live until it was too late in his career to make any difference, for the pleasures of the moment. He always practised because he loved to play, but there were no concessions to any other conventional ideas of preparation for matches. This created a fundamental tension with his pursuit of a tantalisingly elusive heart's desire, the world title, which would enduringly relieve the insistent ache of opportunities lost, particularly two defeats from winning positions by Stephen Hendry in the 1992 and 1994 world finals. He was to lose six world finals in all and win only one Masters and one UK: an underweight delivery on his exceptional natural talent.

Too busy living to have much time for retrospection, living not only as if there was no tomorrow but no yesterday either, he admitted that 'my only discipline has been snooker and the competitions' but, on the whole, it was not discipline enough.

Even before he fell in love with snooker, he was a serial truant.

One day, he and a mate were scrapping on a Tooting pavement with two other ragamuffins when reinforcements – for the other side – were sighted. At that providential moment, the door of Zans Snooker Club opened. Jimmy and his friend dived in to hide amidst the dust and fag ash under a table.

'The place fascinated me long before the game did,' he said, for this was real cowboy territory, full of villains and hot gossip. It was nine months before he played. From that moment, snooker consumed him.

When he was 13, he and Tony Meo, who was 15 and who also became a leading professional, were approached by 'Dodgy' Bob Davis, a taxi driver who proposed setting up money matches and giving them 10 per cent of any winnings. They ventured all over London and further afield to the badlands of Herne Bay, Bedford, Brighton and Aylesbury.

These two kids saw some remarkable things – a man shot in the legs in a club in Wimbledon – and heard at first hand about others – a 'grass' lured to a club in Windmill Street and then, with the doors closed, stoned to death with snooker balls. Frequently, Jimmy and Tony would be up all night. When they kipped at one mate's house, there were invariably off duty bunny girls from the Playboy Club relaxing.

They were involved in legit competition, but it was the high life, winning and squandering, which entranced them. One morning, this heroic duo won £1,500 at snooker. By 4.30, they had lost the lot at the bookie's. There was always more where that came from.

In many ways, it was more fun being skint, hurdling barriers at Underground stations or pillaging fruit machines with a coin on a length of cotton. Jimmy's little gang was once arrested in possession of a mountain of two bob (10p) bits. The police could not find a meter to fit the crime and eventually let them go.

Jimmy's first girlfriend, Maureen, quickly pregnant, became his much-put-upon wife, although their marriage was to survive for many years a series of epic bust-ups, albeit not by a wide margin, before they were divorced in 2003.

But how could marriage possibly compare with two 'free as a bird' kids flying about all over the country: Maureen holding his money and his coat in many a seedy dive by day, ready to run if he gave the signal, snuggling up in a bed and breakfast by night.

Along the way, she taught him to read and write for, as he reasonably remarked of Ernest Bevin Comprehensive, Tooting, 'They couldn't teach me if I wasn't there.'

Barry Hearn summed up Jimmy's education: 'He could work out a yankee, but he couldn't tell you the capital of France.'

For him and O'Boye, it was child's play to wheedle out of Cottier, the team manager, their entire £1,500 expenses for the Tasmania trip long before arrival. Straight off the plane in Sydney, they headed for the Randwick racetrack, where they promptly lost it all. This left them to get through ten days in Tasmania on no money.

Big H hung on to his wallet in the deluded belief that, without money, Jimmy could not get drunk. Jimmy remembers winning the championship easily. Actually, Newbury missed match ball against him in the quarter-finals, but it seems that he did not take much notice.

While Jimmy was living it up, Steve Davis was knocking them dead in the Coral UK Championship at Preston Guild Hall. Partly in genuine tribute to his efficiency, partly to underline the mechanical air he brought to demolition, Terry Griffiths, whom he beat 9–0 in the semi-finals, dubbed him the 'Romford Robot'. The same treatment was meted out to Higgins in the final, 16–6.

Suddenly, despite a lowly ranking of 13th, Davis was favourite for the Embassy World Championship at the Crucible. His first round victory, 10–8 over White, who turned professional on his return from Tasmania, was his closest. Thorburn was still in it at 12–10 in the semi-finals but lost 16–10. In the final, he won the first six frames against Doug Mountjoy and this was the margin at the end, 18–12. Hearn, unable to contain himself, came charging across the arena and lifted him in the air.

Together, they had pursued a dream. With its fulfilment, Hearn knew how to turn it into gold. He was to market the new world champion as no snooker world champion had ever been marketed before and they would have a lot of fun doing it, for snooker was still on the crest of a wave. The BBC's musical item from the championship, 'Making your mind up' by Bucks Fizz, encapsulated its *joie de vivre*.

Hearn started to book Davis for exhibitions at £1,500 a night; a contract with Leisure Industries guaranteed him £100,000 over three years from sales of miniature tables; there was an equipment contract with E.J. Riley, and promotional contracts with the *Daily Star* and Coral, the bookmakers. The money rolled in. Top snooker players were in demand for everything from game shows to the God slot.

Davis's confidence, already high, seemed armour plated. He annihilated Dennis Taylor 9–0 to win the Jameson International on ITV; he retained the Coral UK title by beating White 9–0 and Griffiths 16–3 in the last two rounds. This was excellence to an intimidating degree, although it was to be undermined by a schedule of exhibitions, travelling and personal appearances, which his mind could not withstand. Hearn was to learn the hard way one of management's most underestimated arts – that of refusing lucrative engagements to maintain tournament performance as his client's unyielding priority.

Even so, Davis's constitution withstood many challenges. Heavily jet-lagged from a round-the-world trip with Hearn, who realised the commercial importance of starting to build Davis's name overseas, he began 1982 by making the first televised 147 maximum against Spencer in the Lada Classic in Oldham.

This was a moment of some poignancy for Spencer. It was all very well to be involved in the first televised maximum but after the Thames meal break had left his 147 at Slough unrecorded three years earlier, it was not quite the same sitting in the non-striker's chair. Davis was too tired to be nervous on the verge of making history and even in the final against Griffiths was still jet-lagged, even falling asleep in the pressroom during a mid-session interval.

From 8–3 down, he came back to 8–8 before Griffiths won 9–8 on the final black. Griffiths summed up the psychological pressure Davis was exerting on his rivals: 'I should have won 9–3, and against most players I would have done, but against Steve you try that bit too hard. You get to think he can't be beaten. You have a mental barrier against him.'

Davis and Griffiths met in five consecutive finals on the circuit, Davis winning three, and were confidently expected to meet in the 1982 world final, but at the Crucible both lost in the first round.

Opening the championship against Tony Knowles, Davis's match was of two sessions, Friday evening and Saturday morning. Even on the Friday afternoon, he was signing copies of his hastily produced instructional book in a Sheffield bookshop. In the arena, he could hardly pot a ball. Knowles played sensibly, simply feeding off his opponent's errors, and won 10–1. Endlessly in motion, Davis had had no time for repose, to think or even to remain aware of who he was or what he was becoming. Exposed to a wider variety of experiences, he had compromised his standards of dedication and preparation. He never made the same mistake again.

More immediately, his defeat made Griffiths favourite, but perhaps unbalanced by this he lost to Willie Thorne: 'I expected too much. I should have known better. I thought I had adjusted my mind to Steve losing, but I look back on it and I realise that I didn't.'

The championship was wide open and Higgins, who had not had much of a season, realised he had as good a chance as anyone. Already facing disciplinary action after an altercation with the crowd at the Irish Masters, he now chose, while practising late at night backstage at the Crucible, to utilise a flowerpot as a urinal to save himself a walk of a few yards.

He assumed the other players present would have no objection and checked with the girlfriend of one, the only woman present, whether she too was in this category. 'As long as you don't waggle it about,' she stipulated in her refined way. The only discordant note came from a security man. There was a scuffle and the man's pullover was torn, thus generating another disciplinary action.

Higgins and White were both wild boys, kindred spirits save that White very rarely caused offence, but they really could play the game and the finish to their semi-final produced one of snooker's most treasured moments.

White, who was still only nineteen, was two up with three to play and, at 15–14, had two first class chances to nail down his place in the final. First in with 41, he missed a black from its spot. Second in as well, he added only 18. On the brink of a world final with a chance to supersede Higgins as the youngest ever champion, White simply could not cope with the enormity of what he was about to accomplish. Playing for posterity and his place in the record books was altogether more than playing for the moment.

For Higgins, it was the death-or-glory situation for which he unconsciously hungered. His compulsive urge to live on life's dangerous edge – stronger than any mere desire to win – was like an addiction to the thrill of turn of the card gambling. Hyped up by a potent cocktail of crowd excitement, media attention, a great occasion, drink, adrenalin and, in one of his pet phrases, 'what have you', Higgins was at his most dangerous in a situation of peak emotional intensity. He was the gunfighter down to his last bullet and from 0–59 produced a wonderful clearance of 69, the most often reprised item of BBC's snooker footage, to level the match.

This left White psychologically broken. Higgins ran through the decider as well and beat Reardon 18–15 for the title, striking his richest seam of form again in the closing three frames. With a 135 total clearance which was like a lap of honour, Higgins was champion for the second time.

Crying with emotion, he beckoned his wife, Lynn, and 18-month-old daughter, Lauren, to join him in a surreal but spontaneous winner's tableau. 'Winning this will set Lynn and Lauren up for life,' he had said earlier in the tournament. He was wrong, of course. Only three years later, he and Lynn were divorced.

On his first day as champion, Higgins sent champagne with his compliments to the WPBSA board, which was sitting in disciplinary judgement on him. Already well gone alcoholically, he perched himself to the immediate right of Rex Williams, the chairman, looking intently, unblinkingly, into his eyes. He was sociably fined £1,000.

The WPBSA was, incidentally, facing an unfamiliar money problem: they had so much they did not know what to do with it. Having been a low-key, low-income operation, it suddenly had money in the bank, notably a three-year £435,000 contract with the BBC. Rather than pay much of it away in tax, they preferred to redistribute it to their members in the form of prize money through a new world ranking event, the Professional Players Tournament. This itself was so successful in 1982 and 1983, even without television coverage, that Rothmans picked up that slot in the calendar. Nine days' television coverage was transferred to it from the World Team Cup, which was downgraded to four days later in the season.

But soon, having eased Mike Watterson out of his promotional and television contracts and set up its own subsidiary to run them themselves, WPBSA discovered that this was not quite the licence to print money it had imagined Watterson to hold. The association's constitution prohibited board members being paid, but they allowed themselves expenses with an ever more liberal hand. Having been run with admirable frugality by its part-time secretary, Mike Green, from his home in West Bromwich, the WPBSA now took luxurious offices in Bristol deemed more appropriate for its new financial status. Since snooker was so popular on television, it was assumed the good times would continue indefinitely.

8

SACKED BY THE BBC

STEVE DAVIS WON HIS SECOND WORLD TITLE IN 1983, ONE OF SIX HE secured in the '80s, although it was paradoxically his three defeats in this period, by Knowles in 1982 and by Dennis Taylor and Joe Johnson in successive finals in 1985 and 1986, which lingered in the public's collective memory.

Drama rather than excellence tends to stick more firmly in the mind. Similarly, in winning six UK titles in the '80s, it was his 16–15 defeat by Higgins in the 1983 final from 7–0 up which left the most lasting impression.

Occasionally, Davis lost but, in the main, his very aura was so very intimidating that he was in a class of his own until Stephen Hendry, who was to dominate the '90s just as thoroughly, came along to depose him from his no. 1 position.

Davis's 1983 world title was an anticlimax to everyone but him for in every respect other than winning it, the championship was to be remembered as Thorburn's through making the Crucible's first 147 and prevailing in three consecutive late night finishes: 13–12 over Griffiths, 13–12 over Kirk Stevens and 16–15 over Knowles. He was a mental husk by the time he lost 18–6 to Davis in the final.

Thorburn's 147, which earned him a £10,000 bonus, came in his opening session against Griffiths and made a huge television impact, but it was already receding into the past by the time their match reached a conclusion. These were the days for many players of long, grinding frames and these were two of the best grinders in the business. Thorburn led 8–6 after two sessions, but this still left a possible eleven rather than the appointed nine frames for the final session. Worse still, Charlton found it so difficult to nail Spencer 13–11 from 12–7 up that Thorburn and Griffiths did not enter the arena until 8.55 p.m.

At 2.18 a.m., Thorburn twice attempted the black that would have given him victory at 13–9, and at 2.56 another black which would have made him the winner at 13–10. At 3.26, Griffiths completed a 97 clearance to level at 12–12, but Thorburn's nerve held steady as he took the decider with a break of 75. The final session, which lasted a record 6 hours, 25 minutes, finished at 3.51, nearly two hours after the BBC had ceased recording. It was the first time they had missed a ball of the action since coming to the Crucible.

Some 200 souls remained until the end, though with the television cameras idle there was an eerie sense of a match behind closed doors. On top of it all, there were press conferences for the winner and loser. All this gave me an unexpected opportunity to see dawn rising over Sheffield as I walked back to my hotel.

Stevens had a kind of younger brother/elder brother relationship with Thorburn, whom he had challenged at the age of 12 with a painstakingly accrued $4. Having conceded him 50 points a frame, Thorburn refused the money, but Stevens insisted on thrusting it upon him. Nevertheless, it was already clear that Stevens was an outstanding talent. In 1980, when he was only 21, he reached the world semi-finals, losing 16–13 to Higgins. He was very popular, particularly with young female fans, although his trademark white suit was not conceived as an ingenious marketing ploy. He simply found one evening that he could not lay his hands on a pair of black dress trousers.

There was a dark shadow under his ready smile and engaging personality. This arose from the drug culture which no one in Canadian snooker could avoid. He had watched his sister's veins burst through drug abuse; when his mother died in a house fire caused by arson, he obtained a gun and lay fruitlessly in wait for several nights for whoever might have been responsible.

His own career and even his own life were to be almost destroyed by drugs. 'Have you taken cocaine?' he once asked. 'If you have, you'll want it again.' During their 1983 quarter-final at the Crucible, Thorburn's concentration was disturbed by noticing Kirk's pusher in the audience. He went to Mike Watterson and had him thrown out. Stevens led 12–10, but Thorburn won frames of 32, 53 and 61 minutes' duration to emerge the 13–12 winner at 2.12 a.m. after a final session of 6 hours, 11 minutes.

Thorburn also trailed Knowles by two with three to play in the semi-finals, but by the time he had wriggled out of that corner he had nothing left for Davis.

In the 1984 world final, Davis seemed to be heading for an even easier win over Jimmy White, whom he led 12–4 at the end of the first day's play. White, never one for excuses, told no one he was having a tip problem. This was dealt with at close of play and next day he put Davis under 'the most pressure I've ever felt'.

By the time White had reduced his arrears to a single frame, Davis was in a fine old state, but White, as is very often the way, started to miss a few himself when he no longer had nothing to lose and Davis staggered over the line, 18–16. Once more, it had been demonstrated that the most agonising pressure is that of a growing threat of having apparently certain victory snatched away.

Off table, the tabloids waged their circulation wars with their familiar weapons of tatty exclusives and ghosted columns. John Parrott was set up by the *Daily Star* as its clean-cut hero against Knowles, whom *The Sun* was projecting as a womanising reprobate. Knowles, egged on by *The Sun*, overstepped the mark. His three-part farrago of sexual boasting brought him a WPBSA fine of £5,000 for bringing the game into disrepute. Years later, he was to say, not without foundation: 'I felt that my game deteriorated from that point.' From no. 2 in the rankings, he slid gradually but inexorably downwards, deflected from snooker by easily available pleasures and by business ventures which never yielded their anticipated wealth. Among female followers of snooker there came to be a brisk sale of 'I said no to Tony Knowles' T-shirts and badges. Engaging professional management, Howard Kruger's Framework, did not solve his problems. Rather it was to add to them.

One seed of Davis's defeat by Dennis Taylor in the 1985 world final was his loss at the hands of Higgins in the 1983 UK final, not merely because he had been 7–0 up but because it was the first time that Higgins had beaten him in four and a half years. Another factor was Taylor's capture of his first major title, the Rothmans Grand Prix, which through a peculiar psychological shift seemed to release him from the tensions which had been appearing to inhibit him on the threshold of major success.

In October 1984, Taylor's mother died without warning. Shattered with grief, he withdrew from his Jameson International quarter-final next day and had no appetite for the Rothmans Grand Prix later that month but, once involved in the fray, his concentration was never better. It was a relief to concentrate on something to deflect his mind from his grief. His bereavement put snooker in perspective: he was never again going to regard winning or losing as the end of the world because only dying was the end of the world. Also, as the tournament proceeded, he acquired a sense that winning could offer a means of uniting his large and loving family in a joy which could relieve their sorrow.

Not every significant factor was in the mind. His adoption of the specially made type of snooker spectacles which became his trademark – his celebrated 'upside down' glasses – were worn so high on his face that he could look down the cue through the optical centre of the lens rather than downwards through slight distortion. The larger lenses also gave him better peripheral vision for pots in which cue ball, object ball and pocket were not more or less straight in line.

Davis also did him a favour. Thorburn's 9–7 win over him the previous evening was a draining affair and Taylor, who had had a day's rest, put Thorburn away 10–2 in the final. The tears flowed and the title fortified Taylor's confidence when he found himself in with a chance in the Crucible final six months later.

This seemed extremely unlikely when Davis led 8–0. Taylor's immediate priority was simply to avoid annihilation but, in such a situation, unwelcome as it was, he had everything to gain and nothing to lose. Davis's expectation of victory had grown so large in his own mind that he, on the other hand, now had everything to lose.

Once Taylor had won a couple of frames, he found himself cueing more freely. Davis led 13–11 after three sessions and was within a frame of victory at 17–15 only to find himself floundering like a swimmer a few yards from the shore but held back by the tide.

Had their epic 68-minute decider been an early frame, it would never have been transmitted in a highlights package but context is all and the mistakes, the nerves, the near misses and the atmosphere in the arena all contributed to a drama which kept 18.5 million BBC viewers enthralled long after midnight. Its climax, with Davis overcutting the final black at short range and Taylor potting it to become champion, will forever be counted as one of the great moments in sport.

Paradoxically, it also became a cross snooker had to bear as sportswriters with no love of snooker were to become fond of pointing out a few years hence that snooker was not drawing audiences of 18.5 million anymore. Fairly or not, this figure came to stand as the high water mark of snooker's popular appeal.

It was quite an anticlimax to drive down a few days later to Abertillery to commentate on the Welsh Professional Championship, for which no other dates had been available in a crowded season. The Saturday afternoon semi-final had just finished and I flipped a switch in the commentary box to catch the football results. Instead, I saw horrific pictures of the fire at Bradford City's ground, Valley Parade, a stand in flames, men in agony with their hair on fire.

A year later, Joe Johnson, a Bradford man through and through, who had never previously won a match at the Crucible, produced an unstoppable surge of inspiration to beat Griffiths from three down with four to play in the quarter-finals and Davis 18–12 for the title.

Johnson had never sustained such form before and never sustained it again, although he did, after an otherwise poor season, also reach the 1987 final, in which Davis beat him quite comfortably 18–14. Two elements were key in the chemistry which had inspired his 1986 triumph. He was, he admitted cheerfully, 'besotted' with his new wife, Terryll, and had a sense, Bradford born and bred as he was, of what winning the title might mean to a city which had been in mourning for a year since the Bradford City fire in which many had horrifically died. In his off duty moments, he wore a 'Bradford's bouncing back' T-shirt.

Davis's defeats in consecutive world finals did not threaten his overall dominance of the sport or his top place in the rankings, which was consolidated by his 18–11 victory over Griffiths in the 1988 final and an 18–3 despatch of Parrott in the last world final of the '80s. Such was his dominance that it would have been impossible to predict with confidence that he would never win the title again.

The 1989 championship was overshadowed from the opening day when three miles up the road from the Crucible unspeakable scenes were unfolding at Hillsborough at the FA Cup semi-final between Liverpool and Nottingham Forest. Within minutes of the kick-off, a crush behind one of the goals began to develop into a staggering tragedy. That afternoon, I was commentating on Cliff Wilson v. Steve Duggan, not the day's top match and not one which was expected to be allotted much air time. This was just as well because from the moment someone else in the box switched on the 'feed' from Hillsborough, it was impossible to give much attention to a mere snooker match.

Alan Green, the football commentator, had been at the Crucible that morning and was again that evening, having had to deal like a war correspondent with scenes of chaos, death and devastation. He looked dreadful, though not as dreadful as some of the news reporters who sought refuge and oblivion in the pressroom bar after their harrowing day. The BBC reminded its radio and television commentators and reporters at all events not to use words which ordinarily figure all too casually in sports reporting – 'disaster', 'catastrophe', 'tragedy' and the like. Parrott, a Liverpudlian, wore a black armband for his match next day and happened to be playing the following Saturday, the midpoint of the championship, when the afternoon session was delayed in order to observe a minute's silence at 3.06, the precise time of the tragedy. The silence was moving and for Parrott disturbing. 'That first frame I just wasn't there because of that,' he said. In fact, he lost the first three frames but nevertheless beat Dennis Taylor 13–10, following this with wins over Jimmy White and Tony Meo before he collapsed against Davis in the final, the victim of a long and stressful championship after a long and stressful season in which he had reached the semi-finals or better in almost every tournament.

Very early in the BBC/WPBSA relationship, an inner clique formed which I could not bring myself even to attempt to join. As time had gone on, I had stepped up my criticism of the WPBSA's shortcomings in *Snooker Scene*. Del Simmons, with support from Rex Williams and John Pulman, tried to wind up Nick Hunter to sack me as a BBC commentator. I could sense that real trouble would come one day and to this end engaged an agent, Geoff Irvine, who represented David Coleman, Barry Davies and Michael Aspel amongst many others. This was to prove a very wise move.

There was also an attempt to persuade the Canadian Broadcasting Corporation to replace me as commentator for the Canadian Open. Simmons had become friendly with Bob Moir, CBC's head of sport. They were similar drinking, bantering types and had a good time together. Simmons persuaded Moir that Williams ought to replace me, but CBC's executive producer, Laurence Kimber, said that if Williams was imposed on him, Kimber himself would not work on the production.

At the 1985 UK Championship at Preston, there was a press conference one morning after which Hunter beckoned me over and began very aggressively: 'You going to Canada hasn't done us any favours.'

'What do you mean?'

'You're talking too much.'

Canadian television requires a commentary with fewer pauses than the BBC's laid-back style, but I was well aware of the difference and had no trouble adapting either way. I therefore knew Hunter's criticism to be unfounded. Even if it had been justified, this was not the way to put it to someone who was supposed to be a valued member of this team.

I cast caution aside. 'No, I'm not.'

'Well, I'm the producer and I say you are.'

'I know you are and, of course, I listen to what you have to say, but I've not had a word of praise from you ever since I've been working for you. You've been deliberately holding me back and I'm fed up with it.' I turned and walked off.

Later that night, I was tipped off by a sympathiser that Hunter had gone morosely into the WPBSA room and told Simmons and his other cronies what had happened. They had again encouraged Hunter to get rid of me and he said he would. I worked normally for the rest of the tournament, including a part of the final, in this knowledge.

Hunter did not have the courage to sack me face to face but walked into the BBC sports office in Manchester on the morning after the final and informed everyone, before he had told me, that I would not be working for the BBC again. He dictated a letter, which I received the next day, but by then I had informed Geoff Irvine of what was in the wind and he was ready for it.

Immediately, Geoff rang Jonathan Martin, BBC's head of sport, who happened to be on a mountain in Austria. He knew nothing about it, so there was an immediate question mark over whether Hunter had exceeded his powers in sacking a contract artist without permission.

This was early December and the matter dragged on until early January when Geoff, Hunter and I assembled in Martin's office. Martin opened the meeting by saying that the BBC wanted to terminate my contract because I was too difficult to get along with and not a team man. Hunter spoke along these lines. Geoff and I said, in different ways, that this was untrue and that the trivial instances that Hunter had managed to drag up were not grounds for dismissal. We went round the room again, reiterating pretty well the same arguments that we had used in the first round. I apologised for using direct language to a (supposed) superior but explained my frustrations and asked whether it was the first angry exchange ever to have occurred within BBC Sport.

'Far from it,' said Martin.

We departed with ritual handshakes. Martin, a shrewd cove, would have been aware that it would not pass unnoticed in the press if I was sacked without just cause. This would not exactly bring the BBC down, but it would be better for the BBC not to be shown in a poor light. Obviously, he felt there were no grounds to sack me and rang Geoff not much more than an hour later to say that Hunter would be ringing me.

He took his time. He told Williams and Pulman, who were at Warrington for the Lada Classic, that I was to be reinstated before he told me, although by then Janice Hale, who was working there for the *Daily Telegraph*, had gleaned this intelligence and relayed it to me.

I therefore continued with the BBC. Not long afterwards, Martin seemed to identify Hunter's sporting empire in the north as some sort of threat to his own hegemony. Hunter was grandly invited to London to become assistant head of sport, a position he was soon to discover had a large title but no power. The sports for which Hunter had responsibility, except for rugby league, were brought under direct London control. He departed to British Satellite Broadcasting, an epic fiasco which was swallowed by Rupert Murdoch's Sky in the nick of time to enable Sky itself to survive. Hunter then went to Meridian, a relationship which soured so badly that it ended up in legal action. Soon afterwards, I noted, he was accepting freelance jobs as humble as directing camel racing on two cameras in Dubai.

9

THE KING OF THE PLAYGROUND

WHILE SNOOKER'S GLITTERING TELEVISION SHOP WINDOW OF THE '80s had shown Steve Davis winning, winning and only occasionally losing, cracks were appearing in snooker's fragile infrastructure. The lunatics, in the guise of players, had taken over the asylum, running the game, or at any rate the WPBSA, like a club or, perhaps more accurately, a club within a club. No thought was given to structures or the future; almost all thinking was commercial and in the here and now. Snooker's insiders did very well out of it, as did players good enough to win serious amounts of prize money. It was soon obvious that a board of directors on which, constitutionally, players had to outnumber non-players could not run WPBSA to its full commercial potential. Even the non-players on the board had their own agendas in the game.

Barry Hearn could have taken over snooker if he had felt like it but temperamentally he preferred being king of the playground to headmaster or head prefect. He did, from time to time, sit on the WPBSA board but, from within or without, mostly manipulated it. It would be simplistic to say he was wholly motivated by money; certainly, this was a powerful motive, but he was also driven by the need for action, the buzz of breaking new ground and, not least, by a love of the limelight. He liked to be a star and, in snooker's relatively small world, he was.

Even at Buckhurst Hill Grammar School, Hearn had the predator's instinct to identify a weak part of the market and exploit it. When entries were invited for the Essex Schools Athletics

Championships, he dreamt of glory but lacked an event. His eyes fell on the two mile walk, the least glamorous in the programme. He resolved to train for it and on the day found himself doing well, comfortably second but an appreciable distance behind the leader. It would have been easy to coast in for second, but he resolved instead to try to win.

'I was so far behind that there was no way I could catch the guy in front, but I pushed myself to go faster and faster. What happened? I was disqualified almost on the line for "lifting" [breaking into a run], so I didn't even get second. At school assembly on the Monday morning, the headmaster said how terrible it was that anyone from the school should have been disqualified. I could have been second easily, but this was his attitude.'

In adult life, Hearn remained prepared to wage war against the world's headmaster figures in any of the various establishments with which he had dealings. The son of a bus driver, living almost literally in the shadow of the Ford works at Dagenham, he had working class roots and an instinctive understanding of what may be called, for want of a better expression, working class pleasures and values. He always loved sport but readily admitted that he lacked the dedication, in terms of commitment and time investment, to be more than a dabbler as a participant. Nevertheless, for a couple of years, he did train daily to compete in marathons, running to work behind his chauffeur-driven limo. The splendid Robbo, head minder and driver for Matchroom, Hearn's group of companies, was apt to turn up the theme tune from *Rocky* full blast on the speakers to encourage him.

He could not have been so successful in sportsbiz if he had not understood sport and sportsmen. He would barely have reached first base if he had not understood the workings of the worlds of business and finance. At 21, he was a chartered accountant; at 26, he could add accountancy's highest qualification, FCA, to his name. In his 20s, as financial director of Kensal House Investments, he was heavily involved in the world of fashion and textile design. He talked Kensal House into buying a down at heel chain of snooker clubs, Lucania, which did, however, hold the freehold of all their operational sites. He increased his own holding from 5 per cent to 33 per cent. In June 1982, the clubs – indeed the whole of Kensal House Investments – were sold to Riley Leisure for £3.1 million.

Hearn himself retained the Romford club as an office base for his burgeoning Matchroom empire and as a practice base for Davis, who was the foundation of his credibility in the sports world and who, in time, became a director of several of the companies in the Matchroom group. Initially, he managed only Davis and those days of the two of them against the world were in some ways the time of his life in terms of fun and excitement. Inevitably, as his business grew, life became more complex.

First, he signed up more players to give himself more group strength: Tony Meo, Jimmy White's boyhood buddy; Terry Griffiths, who remained a top player without ever winning a major title after the 1982 UK; Dennis Taylor, whom he signed immediately after he beat Davis in the 1985 world final; Cliff Thorburn, who won three Benson and Hedges Masters in four years; Willie Thorne, Neal Foulds and finally White, who was notoriously difficult to manage.

Davis was invariably given first bite at any contract that was going, but there was plenty of other work to go round and a stable of players needed to be on tap for the tours which Hearn took to uncharted snooker territories in the Far and Middle East and mainland Europe. Although his own motives were commercial, the effect of such pioneering ventures was to give snooker a significant impetus in several countries, notably Thailand and China. He built up international contacts while WPBSA dozed on.

James Wattana, a future world no. 3, first came to prominence through the Hearn tournaments in Thailand. His mother had opened a snooker club in a rough part of Bangkok and the teenage Wattana soon had a syndicate backing him for money. A Thailand snooker association was founded and developed by two sport-loving British expats, Maurice Kerr and Tom Moran. When Wattana won the 1988 world amateur title in Sydney, he became a national hero and immediately established himself as a significant presence in the professional game. When Davis and Taylor made their pioneering trip to China in 1985, even the best of the few Chinese players were scarcely of 30 break standard. Ten years later, it was snooker's greatest growth area, with millions of players, including some of professional quality. In 2005, its standard bearer, Ding Junhui, won two world ranking titles; in 2006, another.

Socially, the snooker world found Hearn a cheerful, engaging fellow, very good company with a ready supply of witty one-liners. Even clients who left him with unresolved grievances, justified or not, were apt to confess that they liked him despite it all. He was a bright, lively, original energiser, the scourge of a champagne-swilling establishment which he almost invariably outwitted. These aspects of his personality mitigated the impression he could also give of embodying a spirit of ruthless enterprise emblematic of Thatcher's Britain, a cynical world of prices rather than values, which he came to epitomise.

In tournaments, his players were so successful that the money list tended to be divided into Hearners and non-Hearners. In the 1986–87 season, for instance, his players won all six world ranking events between them (Davis three, White two, Foulds one) and aggregated £1,076,680 in prize money, on which Hearn took a 20 per cent commission, as he did on all other sources of his clients' income. He believed that snooker was 'on the verge of a global breakthrough, the like of which no sport has seen for a hundred years' but noted that Davis's £80,000 cheque for his fourth world title in 1987 had been only about half Wimbledon's first prize. In 1981, the prize for Davis's first title had been about the same as John McEnroe had received for winning Wimbledon that year.

The key figure at WPBSA's Bristol headquarters remained, of course, Del Simmons, by now the WPBSA's £65,000 a year contracts negotiator, whose skill at interpersonal politics made him a formidable internal powerbroker. Even when he was voted out of one of the non-players slots on the board, his influence continued unabated. Nor was it one of Hearn's best ideas to propose that the vacancy he created should be filled by Howard Kruger, who had met Tony Knowles on a beach in Marbella and decided to go into snooker management. His Framework group of companies was to mushroom, collapse and leave several players, including Knowles, Alex Higgins and Joe Johnson, with severe financial bruising.

The WPBSA badly needed men of vision who could assess its shortcomings, tackle the problems inherent in its constitutional and disciplinary systems and work out long term policies. Instead, it seemed steadfastly determined to keep power within an inner group, reacting issue by issue on a contingency basis.

Hearn, content with exploiting the system as it was rather than seeking to reform it, which he perhaps reasonably did not see as his responsibility, made a cautious alliance with Mark McCormack's International Management Group, which was dipping its toe in snooker waters with a straight pool/snooker/9 ball triathlon featuring Davis and the American pool star Steve Mizerak. IMG's television arm, Trans World International, promoted and recorded this at the Palace Hotel in St Moritz and sold on the package internationally. Indeed, as producers, packagers and salesmen of sports programming, TWI were and remain a very formidable act indeed.

Had Hearn and TWI's head of European affairs, Bill Sinrich, been able to unite on the snooker front for their common benefit, the WPBSA could easily have been reduced to some kind of organisational shell. As it was, they soon fell out and Hearn declined to allow TWI a piece of World Series, eight linked events in Tokyo, Hong Kong, Toronto, Las Vegas and four other cities which were never, in fact, decided upon.

The WPBSA board had abandoned its hopes of building up an international circuit by resolving in December 1986 to work with individual promoters, like Hearn, rather than promote any more overseas events itself. This board also voted a £50,000 WPBSA subsidy for the Toronto leg of World Series. Hearn then felt obliged to resign from the WPBSA board on the grounds that his private promotion of World Series was in conflict with his responsibility to the WPBSA's world championship contract with Embassy, which expressly precluded the WPBSA from sanctioning the use of the word 'world' in any other singles competition.

His resignation was immediately followed by the remaining directors passing a vote of no confidence in the chairmanship of Rex Williams. Some did not like his style, but the chief complaint appeared to be that he had allied himself too closely with Hearn, who had invited him to commentate on the Tokyo and Hong Kong legs. He had also joined Hearn's players on a visit to Peking, ostensibly on the grounds that the Chinese premier, Deng Xiaoping, had a sentimental attachment to billiards because he had played it as a young man. Williams, a former world billiards champion, played a billiards exhibition with Davis but Deng did not attend.

In opposition, Hearn ran rings round the WPBSA. In managership, overseas promotion and obtaining high profile publicity, snooker had never seen anyone like him. He had chanced upon a commercially unexploited sport at its point of maximum growth and had found it almost too easy to become king.

IMG, rebuffed by Hearn when they wanted to be involved in World Series, concentrated on an alliance with the WPBSA, who were nevertheless fearful that this smooth, well-connected octopus of an organisation might acquire too much influence in the sport. Amazingly, WPBSA therefore rejected IMG's offer of £925,000 prize money for four overseas world ranking tournaments. In due course, no one came to be more relieved about this than the IMG executives responsible for making the offer.

World Series crashed. Hearn released a story to the Press Association's wire service – timed for 4.30 on a Saturday afternoon, just before the football results, to ensure minimal impact – saying that World Series would not be completed in 1988 but might be re-launched in 1989. He cheerily stated that clashes with the Olympic Games and the World Cup, which he might have been expected to foresee, had made it too difficult to sell television packages.

The killing thrust, apparently, was that Kruger, with his own management stable, had undercut the Hearn promotion with the sponsors, British American Tobacco. Hearn rubbished the Kruger venture, not without justification as it turned out, and struck at the WPBSA by allying himself with Frank Warren (who wanted quality events for the London Arena in Docklands) and TWI (rebuffed by the WPBSA and still seeking an angle of entry to snooker) to announce a World Matchplay Championship and World Open Championship.

The latter was never staged and the former involved dislodging one of the four elements of WPBSA's ITV contract, that for the world doubles, the weakest in viewing terms. Trevor East, a friend of Hearn and at that time ITV's executive producer in charge of snooker, liked the sound of an eight-man world matchplay. None of the WPBSA's other 120 professionals liked the loss of an earning opportunity this would entail.

ITV pulled the plug on the doubles and told the WPBSA that they would be interested in a Masters-type event for the top 16. However, ITV's contract with WPBSA stipulated that thirteen of the top 16 must enter whereupon Hearn intimated that four of his top 16ers would not. The WPBSA had to cave in to avoid losing a plum ITV slot for snooker.

It was Hearn's first foothold in terrestrial television – despite the myth widely propagated subsequently that he had pioneered snooker as a television sport. A field in which he was, however, well ahead of WPBSA was satellite television. He promoted a tournament for his own players at Southend in 1987, which was shown on Super Channel, and syndicated its highlights. With innumerable satellite and later cable stations about to come into play all over the world, he appreciated that there would be a much expanded market for sports programming. He was determined to have his slice of this cake. Some of this programming was pretty low budget because high budgets were not sustainable, but he was in on the ground floor.

Reluctant to forego income from its tournaments, Hearn did not want to put WPBSA out of business but did consider, on the boxing model of several world title sanctioning bodies, each allied to powerful television interests, a parallel body with Williams as chairman. Hearn, Warren and Sinrich admitted they 'went a long way down that road'. Ian Doyle, holding a key card in managing Hendry, declined to join them. If he had, WPBSA would have been in deep trouble. Even without him, had the Hearn–Warren–Sinrich alliance been a little more interested in structure and a little less in commercial opportunism, it could have relegated the WPBSA to an insignificant role as a players' trade union. As it was, the moment passed.

Sponsors were still attracted by snooker's viewing figures but several stayed only a year or two. Tennent's, the brewers, twice sponsored the UK Championship but then withdrew, pointedly thanking everyone in snooker except the WPBSA. The Canadian Masters, twice staged in CBC's Toronto studio at a modest profit, was recklessly put into a cavernous out of town venue, the Minkler Auditorium, and bombed spectacularly. CBC executives, noting the acreage of empty seats, decided forthwith that they did not want any more snooker.

A projected Australian Open in 1989 somehow ended up in Hong Kong. Regarding snooker, IMG and the Australian Broadcasting Commission were dealing with an Australian-man-about-snooker, Ian Robertson, who presented himself as a more substantial figure than he actually was. He stated that he had business premises in the Sydney suburb of Parramatta although the address he gave turned out to be that of the municipal bus station. Several blue chip sponsors that Robertson had named failed to materialise as it became embarrassingly clear that the event was a non-starter.

'It seems unbelievable to me that with only six weeks to go, the WPBSA have switched continents,' said Hearn of the re-routing to Hong Kong. This event provided Mike Hallett with his one and only world ranking title. Generous to a fault, he celebrated by buying some expensive trinkets for his wife, several suits and no fewer than 72 shirts. Ian Doyle, his manager, pointed out that by also taking into consideration such trifles as travelling and hotel expenses, tax and his own modest commission, he could not afford to win another £40,000 first prize for some time and threatened to nail his credit cards to his desk. The WPBSA admitted a loss of £120,000 on the event.

This fiasco came only a few months after IMG had staged the inaugural European Open in the out-of-season French gambling resort of Deauville when it did strike even the more unreflective competitors that it was somehow disproportionate to undertake journeys of several hundred miles by various combinations of air, road, train, ferry and bus to perform for a tiny audience consisting almost entirely of each other.

Promoting a snooker tournament in Deauville was like putting cricket in the Yankee Stadium and hoping for the best. John Parrott, who won the title, was fortified by having crosswords faxed in each day to help him fill his non-playing hours in this foreign land. Another player, Eugene Hughes, emerged from the arena in his dress suit only to be mistaken for a waiter. Doug Mountjoy was charged £25 for a plate of sandwiches with chips, his coach, Frank Callan, £2 for a room-to-room phone call. 'Colditz with carpets' was the description of one incarcerated player.

Guerrilla warfare between Hearn and the WPBSA intensified. When Rothmans decided not to renew its sponsorship for Hearn's snooker league, his reaction put his players in line for retribution: he sued Rothmans and his players agreed not to give press interviews during the WPBSA's Rothmans Grand Prix.

This legal action was eventually settled to Hearn's satisfaction, but he had put himself in a bad light with the interview boycott – which was in any case ineffective – and his players were hit hard in the pocket. Taylor, who declined five press and two television interviews, was fined £8,000; White and Griffiths £4,000 each; Foulds £3,000, Meo £2,000 and Thorne £1,000. Davis, who declined five press and two television interviews, the same as Taylor, was fined £4,000 more – £12,000. This looked suspiciously like fining on the principle of the offender's wealth.

With Hearn and WPBSA at war, bridges were rebuilt between WPBSA and IMG, who became its representatives in sponsorship and television negotiations for overseas world ranking tournaments. Soon, Hearn, who had promoted the Dubai Duty Free Masters for his players, was outraged to discover that IMG had persuaded the sponsors to switch their support to a WPBSA event the following year. In protest, Hearn pulled Davis out of the European Open, the first ranking event under the new IMG/WPBSA arrangement, and none of his players, to the detriment of their finances and world rankings, competed in the new Dubai Classic.

An unlikely and, as it proved, temporary alliance was formed between Hearn, an unapologetic elitist in his approach to snooker, and Geoff Foulds, father of Neal, who was himself a solid professional for whom the snooker boom and the possibility of earning a living from the game had come a few years too late. Geoff became leader of a Peasants Revolt dedicated to a better deal for the lesser lights. Both asked several awkward questions at the 1988 WPBSA AGM, the answers to which reluctantly disclosed that the annual dinner at the Park Lane Hotel had made a loss of £47,000, a disastrous public relations operation had cost £15,000 and a junket to Goodwood races £6,300.

In what was tantamount to a vote of no confidence, the board narrowly survived because of the votes wielded by Kruger's players and those of Doyle, who believed, ironically in view of what was to happen a few years later, in defending the established governing body against disruptive private enterprise.

Hearn, of course, was characterised as 'wanting to take over the game', just as Doyle was to be towards the end of the '90s. IMG, back in alliance with WPBSA and fearing the voting power of Hearn's players – nine in a very small electorate – acquired the contracts of Kruger's six to obtain voting muscle of their own. This availed them nothing politically and proved a pig in a poke commercially as Kruger's labyrinthine empire began to receive extensive press scrutiny.

The 1989 AGM was again, in essence, a vote of no confidence in the board. This time John Virgo was ousted from the chairmanship 30–11 and the auditors, the distinguished city firm of Coopers

Lybrand, were ousted by voters who perceived them more as tools of the board than servants of the membership. The profligacy of the administration of which Simmons was still at the centre could not be concealed. By now, he was being paid £80,000 a year. A new £23,000 Toyota had been purchased for his exclusive use and there was an electrifying moment when Foulds, still playing the Wat Tyler role in the peasants revolt, elicited the information that Simmons's previous company car, a Mercedes, had been sold to him for £1.

Under hostile questioning, it was revealed that £80,000 had been spent on new marketing aids without conspicuous success, £57,000 on a misconceived WPBSA supporters club and £42,000 on the annual dinner. These and other items contributed to an operating loss for the year of £553,408 compared with a surplus of £429,553 the previous year. So far was WPBSA on the skids that £17,983 had been paid in overdraft charges, although Martyn Blake, WPBSA's company secretary, insisted that there was no overdraft, only 'a temporary borrowing facility'.

So obviously was WPBSA heading for the rocks that the only practical solution was to co-opt Hearn and Doyle to the board. As snooker entrepreneurs and managers, they had an inherent and admitted conflict of interest, but the need for immediate action was so urgent that there was no obvious alternative. At least they knew how the snooker world operated and had enough commercial nous to prevent WPBSA vanishing down the plughole. Doyle's objective, as it always had been, was reform from within; Hearn's was to keep WPBSA afloat and preserve the BBC and tobacco contracts which brought in good money for his and indeed other players.

Foulds, who had been elected to the board at the AGM, was full of reforming zeal. He was asked to produce a report on the activities of the previous administration, although it might have been more fitting if he had not engaged his own accountants, Kingston Smith, to assist him. However, the concept of conflict of interest was poorly grasped both then and subsequently by most people involved in WPBSA.

Discovering 'a dreadful state of affairs', Foulds urged that the guilty should consider their positions on the board. He recommended the winding up of WPBSA Promotions Ltd, whose status as a wholly owned subsidiary had assisted WPBSA's inner circle to withhold certain financial information from the membership, and that the services of Paul Hatherell, number two to Simmons, 'should be dispensed with as quickly and as cheaply as possible'. He described Simmons as 'a very good contracts negotiator on his own account. It is a shame he does not do such a good job for WPBSA.'

On the provision of arena sets and programmes for tournaments, Foulds said: 'The more I hear about these, the more I am convinced that we are being ripped off by these bastards. Programmes should cost us virtually nothing and this item in our budget stinks. Who monitors the sale of programmes and makes sure that the money ends up where it should do?'

Foulds described the WPBSA supporters club, Cuecall, its phone information service, and *Newsbreak*, the association's vertiginously slanted house magazine, as 'three more fiddles which should be stopped as soon as possible'. He considered 'an investigation into the accounting system' as 'a priority'; he noted that the £1-a-mile travelling allowance was 'open to abuse' and indeed had been abused by certain individuals. Amongst this number was Gordon Ingham, a pie manufacturer from Halifax, who had been introduced to the association by Ray Reardon as the kind of businessman who could bring outside expertise, although no evidence of this ever became apparent.

Pointedly, Foulds said that the drug testing budget for the following year should not exceed £15,000 and that the draw for which players should be tested in various tournaments should be done 'in one hit'. It had been Ingham's practice to drive from Halifax to Bristol, claiming £250 each time, to make a draw for each tournament separately. It had been deemed prudent to have an independent witness and Hatherell's vicar had been recruited for this role.

Ingham was always prepared to drive – for £1 a mile – to any function, reception or committee meeting on association business but, as Foulds commented in his report, 'used his position with the board to his own benefit with little or no advantage to the association. I feel that we should get as much information from him as we can about certain people's activities and then decide on what part he has to play in the future with us, if any.'

Foulds accused other board members of 'neglecting their responsibilities' and advocated that one should be 'pursued relentlessly' and 'an example made as a warning to others'. However, no action of this nature was taken. Writing as a new board member himself, Foulds concluded: 'We must show our members that we are beyond reproach and put an end to the comments and rumours that attach themselves to the board of the association once and for all.'

Unfortunately, neither these practices nor well-founded rumours ceased. There was no doubting the authenticity of Foulds's commitment to the game and to WPBSA, whose dominant figure he became first as vice-chairman and briefly as chairman before his own scandalous abuse of the expenses system brought about his downfall. He was to attempt to restore his reputation with a libel action against *The Mirror*, which had detailed some of his abuses, but the jury found for *The Mirror* and left him facing costs of around £800,000.

Time after time, likeable chaps changed once they became part of a WPBSA administration. Few could resist exploiting the system for their own ends and if policies were criticised the response tended to be not to answer the criticism but to try to retaliate against the critic. Often, too, the board became a repository for players who knew only snooker and therefore had to scramble some kind of living from the game once their skills faded. Exploitation of the £1-a-mile travelling allowance, free meals, hotel accommodation and various other perks helped provide this.

Following the 1990 AGM, John Spencer became chairman because there was really no one else. Neither Hearn nor Doyle, as managers, could feasibly hold this position; Foulds had only just been elected to a board of which Spencer had been a not always enthusiastic member for 21 years, a period in which his attendance record had been patchy. His six years as chairman until December 1996, he was to admit, included several periods in which he was clinically insane. This arose from the side effects of drugs he had to take to combat the career ending onset of double vision he suffered in 1985. This condition, myasthenia gravis, stemmed from a deterioration in his eye muscles which could be kept in check only by taking steroids. These produced ungovernable spasms of aggression and deep depressions.

'Once, I went into my kitchen, grabbed a chair and smashed the place up. I dashed out to my car and crashed it into a tree,' he was to recall. When he was prescribed antidepressants, he became 'obsessed with suicide'.

Leaving aside natural sympathy for such suffering, this is not the corporate stuff of which a governing body chairman needs to be made, but WPBSA simply stumbled on.

10

REX, DRUGS AND SHOCK 'N' ROLL

FEW SPORTS COULD ENTIRELY ESCAPE DRUGS AND MATCH FIXING incidents. The WPBSA's structure and personnel were ill equipped to handle either.

Snooker's first drugs story arose from the 1985 British Open final at Derby between Kirk Stevens, who was hooked on cocaine, and Silvino Francisco, who was vehemently anti-drugs.

Stevens had reached no. 4 in the rankings without winning a major title. He had made a 147 in losing the 1984 Benson and Hedges Masters semi-final to Jimmy White; he had led White 12–10 going into the last session of their 1984 world semi-final but lost 16–14. He had been a professional for six years but had been playing for a living in one way or another since going on the road as a money player when he was fifteen.

'When I was 15, I looked like 12,' said Stevens. 'So when this little wimp went up to somebody and said "Like to play for $500?", they thought they couldn't lose.'

Unlike Paul Newman's character in *The Hustler*, he never had his thumbs broken by irate losers, but his car was once pursued out of Dayton, Ohio, by a hail of bullets. He did not stop to collect his winnings of $10,000. 'I was beaten up a couple of times, black eyes and stuff like that.'

He was 18 when his mother died in a fire caused by arson. Grief-stricken and angry as he was from his mother's death, it had a peculiar effect. 'As soon as I started playing again, I became a top class player overnight.'

It is impossible to be certain why this was but Freudians regard such symbolic severings of the umbilical cord as significant. Their theory is, in essence, that this at first creates a new sense of freedom and thus of new energy but then tends to provoke feelings of insecurity until the man accepts in his heart total responsibility for his whole life.

The circuit, for all its superficial bonhomie, is essentially a lonely place in which players alleviate their isolation by gathering groups round them which are at best supportive but at worst hangers-on. Stevens pointed out that for overseas players the difficulties were even more pronounced: 'There's not much family continuity or stuff like that.'

He ran up massive phone bills keeping in touch with his father, who had played professional gridiron football with the Toronto Argonauts. Snooker caused the break-up of a long-standing relationship: 'I took snooker over her. That's what it came to.' He did not get over this in five minutes and felt even more pressure upon him because success alone could justify the choice he had made.

His younger/elder brother relationship with Cliff Thorburn became, as it grew more rivalrous, more distant. 'It used to be important to me to have the approval of the older players. Then I realised they would never give it to me.' Of course not. Why make him feel better about himself and thus become more of a threat?

There would have been much unresolved grief, loneliness and inward pressure for a psychiatrist to explore but, on top of everything, Stevens liked drugs as an alcoholic usually likes drinking. Snooker insiders, including the WPBSA hierarchy, knew that Stevens was on drugs and were afraid that a police search would one day create a scandal.

'The board is mindful of the necessity of preserving the good image of snooker and in particular to illustrate to millions of young people all over the world that these illegal substances will not be tolerated in our sport,' ran the pompous official statement.

Drug testing had not been introduced in time for the British Open final but was to make its bow at the Embassy World Championship a few weeks later. During that final, though, Francisco became convinced that Stevens was on drugs, a possibility to which he might have been alerted by living in a flat near the one that Stevens had in Chesterfield. He was desperate to win and angry that he might have his first major title snatched away by someone who was benefiting from an illegal stimulant. He protested to the tournament director, Paul Hatherell, after the second of the final's three sessions. No action was taken, so the following afternoon, between frames, he followed Stevens to the toilet and confronted him. The match proceeded and Francisco's 12–9 win gave him a first prize of £50,000.

Nevertheless, his sentiments, privately expressed, came to the attention of Neil Wallis, the *Daily Star*'s chief news reporter, who went on to become editor of *The People*. He turned up on the doorstep of Francisco and his wife, Denise, and talked his way in. He was cheerful and charming; naively, they told him the whole story. Wallis was, as they say, wired by means of a tiny tape recorder in his breast pocket. If asked whether he was recording a conversation, he had the skill to turn the device off, as he extracted it from his pocket, thus demonstrating that it had been apparently harmless.

As it happened, the device malfunctioned after only a couple of minutes, but he could later claim, with at least a modicum of truth, that the conversation had been recorded. He also took notes and – a master touch – asked if he could take a cup of tea out to his photographer, who was freezing in the car. Hospitably, the Franciscos invited him in, thus unthinkingly facilitating a picture. Money was never even discussed.

On the morning of Francisco's first round match at the Crucible against Dennis Taylor, Wallis's piece led the front page with Francisco quoted as alleging that Stevens was 'as high as a kite on dope' in the Derby final. Francisco had had no deliberate hand in the story, still less been paid for it, and the timing of its publication left his concentration in tatters as he lost 10–2. Pulled in by WPBSA bigwigs, he unconvincingly stated at a press conference that the story was '95 per cent untrue'. The story did not help Stevens play any better either as he went out 13–6 to Parrott in the second round.

The board closed ranks round Stevens, fining Francisco an unprecedented £6,000 and docking him two world ranking points for 'not adhering to the tournament rules in speaking directly to the press . . . and by his conduct bringing the game into disrepute. The fine also takes into account his admitted misconduct when he physically and verbally abused his opponent [during] the final session.'

Six weeks after the championship, Wallis delivered another front page exclusive from Toronto in which Stevens admitted that he was 'helplessly addicted' to cocaine and had been since he was 19. He told Wallis that he was spending $200 a day on it and had once got through $30,000 in three months. He estimated his total expenditure on cocaine at £250,000 over six years.

As he was 'helplessly addicted', he must have been under its influence when he played Francisco. Therefore, what Francisco had alleged was true. The WPBSA had done nothing to investigate his complaint but had tried to prevent him from speaking out.

The extent of the cover-up was prodigious. John Virgo, WPBSA vice-chairman at the time, said that he and his then wife, Avril, had tried to keep Stevens clean of drugs when he was staying with them in the early part of the 1984–85 season; Stevens said that Del Simmons, who was at the heart of WPBSA dealings, had obtained a hospital appointment for him in connection with his drugs problem as long ago as 1981. Stevens stated: 'I don't believe anyone high in the game, either player or administrator, is unaware that I have a serious drug abuse problem.'

Simmons put the standard defence: 'If you have a complaint, you put it to the board. You don't take the law into your own hands. Whether an opponent is on drugs or not, it doesn't give you the right to verbally and physically abuse him.'

But, of course, by the time Francisco could have filed a complaint – other than the one he made to Hatherell after the second session, which was ignored – the match would have been over and the board, by their actions, showed in any case that their sympathies did not lie with him.

Francisco threatened legal action after this kangaroo court had given its judgement. WPBSA were advised that they had breached principles of natural justice so thoroughly that their decision was legally unsustainable. He had not been given proper notice to prepare a defence; nor allowed to call witnesses. And some of the players sitting in judgement had vested interests because forfeiture of world ranking points had implications in terms of the ranking list. My *Snooker Scene* editorial asked: 'How can it be an offence for Francisco to be quoted in the *Daily Star* without payment and without his permission, while it is not an offence for Stevens to co-operate in an interview, possibly with payment involved, comprising much of the same material?'

Presumably, on the grounds that helpless addiction does not operate on match days, no disciplinary action was taken against Stevens. WPBSA accepted that he had never taken drugs while competing in any of their events! Stevens did not test positive at the Crucible that year, the first tournament at which WPBSA drug testing was in operation. He may not have been tested at all. WPBSA, in control of who was tested, certainly did not want any positives.

Farcically, though, what WPBSA overlooked was that analysis of urine samples would reveal the presence of other drugs, notably beta blockers, which were not on the International Olympic Committee's banned list at that time but were due to be added to it that summer. Beta blockers decrease muscle tremor for long periods and had been used in top level competition by marksmen and archers. People achieve maximum co-ordination between heartbeats and beta blockers slow the heartbeat. They could not make a poor player into a good one, but they did have the effect of reducing nervousness so that a player taking them had more chance of producing his best form.

There are clear advantages to be had for the snooker player and the Sports Council's world championship tests revealed that a number of players were using them, including, very embarrassingly, Rex Williams, the WPBSA chairman. His explanation was that he was prescribed them to reduce the stress he felt from a combination of factors, including professional snooker. When the *Sunday Times* asked him whether WPBSA intended to follow Olympic guidelines by banning beta blockers, he did himself no favours by blustering: 'We do our drug testing according to the rules of the association and we have not banned beta blockers. It is nothing to do with you, the *Sunday Times*, or the Olympic committee. It is my association which makes that decision.'

Williams naively stated on television that WPBSA drug tests were intended only to detect illegal drugs, such as heroin and cocaine, and not drugs capable of enhancing performance, such as beta blockers. The chairman of the governing body was the last person who should have been perceived as taking a substance which informed judges in sports medicine believed to fall into the performance enhancing category. As a player, it suited him very well to take beta blockers. Indeed, at the outset of the following season, he reached the final of the Rothmans Grand Prix at the age of 53, beating Alex Higgins, Steve Davis and Neal Foulds before losing to Jimmy White. He tended to be an edgy, nervy match player but that week he coped with the sustained pressure of a series of matches as well as he had in his entire career.

Francisco remained in bad odour with WPBSA because he had unwittingly brought the drugs issue into the open. His £6,000 and ranking points were returned to him. It was recognised at last that players sitting in judgement on fellow players had an inherent conflict of interest, but WPBSA remained determined to nail him and convened an independent tribunal – or at least more independent than the one which had originally tried him – under Gavin Lightman QC, who later became a High Court judge.

No action had been initiated against Francisco in the six weeks between the British Open final and the appearance of the first

Daily Star article on 15 April. Lightman accepted that the 'damage done' had occurred through the reporter quoting Francisco's 'unguarded remarks'. Nevertheless, he judged that the 'interview [*sic*] and consequent article' had brought snooker into disrepute. Francisco admitted that he had shaken Stevens by the shoulders to make him listen to what he had to say, an admission which was enough for Lightman to find that physical and verbal abuse had taken place. Stevens never made a complaint and the charges were those laid by Hatherell as WPBSA's all-purpose number two executive. Francisco was fined £2,000 and ordered to pay £1,500 of Hatherell's (*sic*) costs.

Francisco's lawyers asked Lightman after the hearing to consider two matters arising from it. Had WPBSA acted unconstitutionally in funding a non-member's complaint? And why had a written complaint from Geoff Lomas, Stevens's manager at the material time, not been acted upon instead? Lomas had not considered the original incident at the British Open final to be serious but had written in response to the allegations of drug taking published on 15 April. All this strengthened the argument that the hounding of Francisco was nothing to do with the incident at the British Open final but with highlighting, albeit inadvertently, the drugs issue in the newspapers.

Lightman said that his remit had expired and he would consider these matters only if both sides agreed. The WPBSA did not agree and because it was financially unrealistic for Francisco to pursue it further, the matter rested there. Francisco was able to recoup his fine by suing Williams and Virgo for libel for remarks they had made in the run-up to the tribunal. The WPBSA shelled out in a pre-trial settlement on behalf of their chairman and vice-chairman.

It was a particularly inappropriate time for the WPBSA board to yield to Williams's suggestion that his own solicitors, Edge Ellison, also be appointed WPBSA's. John Wardle, its senior partner, was chairman of Rex Williams Leisure, which was producing and leasing pool tables. The obvious potential conflict of interest was ignored.

Stevens failed to appear for his first round match in the televised Benson and Hedges Irish Masters in March 1986 and in June was on a life-support machine in St Stephen's Hospital, Fulham. *The Sun* said that he was in a 'cocaine coma'; the *Daily Star* said that he was suffering from an infected collapsed lung caused by high blood pressure. Whether cocaine was involved or not, he was abusing his health by smoking and drinking to excess and keeping late hours.

WPBSA accepted at face value his explanation that he had simply missed the plane to Dublin for his Irish Masters match, ignoring the obvious fact that there were many London to Dublin flights. He was fined £500. Amongst his history of non-appearances was one for the Jameson International, a world ranking event, when Stevens claimed that his passport proved to be out of date when he attempted to check in at Toronto airport for a flight which would allow him to play next day. The High Court took a less amenable view when it ordered him to pay £5,000 to the promoters of an exhibition in Jersey for which he did not appear.

In the meantime, a list of beta-blocker users was emerging. There was Williams; there was, for a time, Alex Higgins; there were two Scots: Eddie Sinclair, a world class drinker, and Murdo McLeod, a baker who believed and for a time proved that he could make more dough from snooker; and John Dunning, a veteran Yorkshire pro with a heart condition.

Neal Foulds did so well in 1986–87 that, going to the Crucible, he had earned even more ranking points that season than Steve Davis, but the accumulated stress of playing so many pressure matches plus the stress arising from a disintegrating marriage undermined his health. As he lay in bed one night, his heart began to beat alarmingly rapidly. For the soundest of medical reasons, he was prescribed Tenormin. The then Minister for Sport, Colin Moynihan, was to describe this and indeed all beta blockers as 'tantamount to cheating'. Foulds was not the sort to seek an unfair advantage and indeed had been playing so well that he did not need one, but this did not prevent a furore when he disclosed at the 1987

Embassy World Championship that he was taking Tenormin. He reached the semi-finals and was ranked no. 3 at the end of the season, but this proved to be the high point of his career.

Bill Werbeniuk's dependence on beta blockers was altogether more fundamental and eventually drove him out of the game. Like his compatriot and contemporary, Cliff Thorburn, he had developed his game as a money player. Travelling together by train, Bill had once bemused Cliff by practising his cueing into a Coca-Cola bottle – the tip not touching the sides even on the follow-through – and had on one journey even earned a few dollars coaching a fellow passenger in this way.

Bill had an uncontrollable tremor in his right arm. This may have been genetic; a car accident may have been at least partly responsible. One genetic peculiarity certainly came in useful: no matter how much alcohol he consumed, he never appeared to be drunk. This was immensely helpful to a man who habitually drank 40 pints of lager a day. His theory was that this intake helped stabilise his right arm. While the rest of us were on coffee and cornflakes, Bill would on match days start drinking lager with his breakfast to get himself ready to practise; a few more would get him ready for his match; a pint per frame would get him through it. He would down a few more pints out of sheer sociability afterwards. The Inland Revenue famously allowed the cost of all this as a business expense but subsequently reversed this decision. I never once saw him the worse for drink but, so his story went, he needed Inderal, the form of beta blocker which Williams was also prescribed, to help his heart cope with all that alcohol. My own view was that any stability of his cue arm was due to the Inderal rather than the lager.

When WPBSA attempted the compromise which led to excommunication from the official Sports Council testing system, banning non-cardio selective beta blockers but allowing cardio selective, those specifically for heart conditions, Bill could not find one suitable for him. With his game consequently in tatters, he was forced into retirement. He vanished from the scene and was next discovered a few years later with waist-length hair playing cards for a living in Vancouver. In January 2003, he died in hospital from heart trouble.

Prior to this, there had been uproar when Thorburn tested positive for cocaine at the British Open in February 1988. Barry Hearn, who was his manager at the time, obtained a High Court injunction so that he could play in the Embassy World Championship, following which Gavin Lightman QC, again as a one-man disciplinary tribunal, fined him £10,000, docked him two world ranking points and suspended him for two tournaments.

Rival managements pronounced Thorburn's punishment too lenient; Williams, who suggested an investigation into how the information had been leaked, declared that Thorburn had fallen into 'an unfair trap' but said that John Virgo, who had succeeded him as chairman in September 1987, should resign after his admission that he had smoked cannabis some ten years earlier.

Ian Doyle, manager of the rising Stephen Hendry, perhaps sowed the seed of Williams's subsequent enmity when he declared that 'he should quit snooker and go off to Disneyland. He'd be a bigger attraction than Mickey Mouse because nothing he says can be taken seriously. He wants his friend [Thorburn] excused for failing a drug test in the last few weeks, but Virgo booted out for something he did years ago.'

Personal friendships and enmities, alliances and conspiracies on the inside of the game showed how WPBSA could degenerate into a morass of conflicting self-interests. The group of insiders at the heart of it did not really want to run snooker properly but simply reacted issue by issue according to their own interests and preoccupations.

Abandoned by the Sports Council because they would not toe the line that other sports toed, WPBSA's drug testing and policies spiralled into farce, unwittingly assisted by me.

In the summer of 1988, I was engaged by the Canadian television channel The Sports Network to commentate on the final of the Canadian Championship in Toronto. I was surprised to discover that the commentary box was entirely encased in black cloth. Somehow or other, a remark of mine on the importance of the box being soundproof had been misinterpreted. Apart from that, it was a routine engagement until the morning after the final when I awoke with what felt like an excessive dose of jet lag.

At breakfast, I almost passed out. I was attended in my room by the house doctor, who diagnosed that my sinuses were not functioning as they should. This seemed to be because they were not sufficiently adaptable to the violent change of temperature between a scorching heatwave outside and ice-cool air conditioning within.

The doctor prescribed me some painkillers, which I took only that day, and some decongestant tablets called Triaminic, each of which contained, according to the label on the packet, 50 mg of phenylpropanolamine, about the same as could be found in the cold cure Contac which, like Triaminic, was available over the counter without prescription. My tablets were sent by taxi, as I was too ill to fetch them. The doctor did not tell me what was in them. I did not ask because I was interested only in feeling better. In a few hours, I did.

Five weeks later, shortly before playing in a qualifying competition in Blackpool, I had some minor sinus difficulty and took a few more of these tablets, never realising that phenylpropanolamine was, like 300 other drugs, on the IOC banned list. When I was called upon to take a random drug test, I declared on the appropriate form that I had taken some of these tablets.

I lost 5–0 that afternoon and 5–0 in another competition the following afternoon, so it would have been difficult to argue that my use of a banned stimulant had been performance enhancing. Nevertheless, it was an unpleasant surprise to be notified that I had tested positive for a substance I had never even heard of.

Amongst the many sports journalists hot in pursuit of drugs stories at that time was Ian Stafford, then of the *Mail on Sunday*. Very frequently, journalists who are not specialists ring me up when they are considering writing something about the snooker world and one such call from Ian enquired whether I had heard of any 'positives' which might be in the pipeline. I did not want to tell a colleague an outright lie. I said that I had heard of one but that the name should come from WPBSA. They should not have disclosed this but, within five minutes, Ian phoned me back. It had been too good a chance for my old adversary, Del Simmons, to miss. Without compunction, my name was leaked and there I was in the *Mail on Sunday*: 'TV man fails drug test'.

After commentating that night, I was solemnly interviewed on BBC TV by David Icke, number two snooker presenter to David Vine. This was before he claimed to be the Son of God but followed a previous career as reserve goalkeeper to Fred Potter at Hereford United. I found it hard to take seriously, but the BBC felt that they had to cover themselves once one of their own was linked with the magic word 'drugs'.

Next day, there were follow-ups. 'Snooker ace dope shocker', screamed the *Daily Star*. Heroin or aspirin, it seemed as if it was all the same to the tabloids. The *Daily Express* asserted confidently that I was 'to undergo a second drug test at King's College, Chelsea, later this week'.

How I could 'undergo' a test for a banned substance some two months after the match in question must remain a mystery. What in fact had happened was that I had nominated King's to test the B or 'defence' sample from the original test, the urine sample having been routinely separated into A and B bottles.

Some of the circuit's more raffish characters, such as Jimmy White and Alex Higgins, thought it was a huge joke that I had been linked with drugs. I thought it pretty funny myself and knew that I had ingested only a miniscule quantity of a banned substance and that any breach of the rules was technical and inadvertent. On the other hand, I knew that my many enemies at WPBSA were itching to get even with me.

I wanted King's to test my B sample because it was the IOC's accredited drug-testing laboratory in Britain. I knew they would do the job properly. Their reading (85 parts per million) was so dramatically at variance with the reading from the A sample (48 parts per million) as to make any case against me legally unsustainable. Kevin Mitchell, then working for the *Sunday Times*, wrote that WPBSA's drug testing at Homerton Hospital 'is suspect, could lead to serious injustice and any penalty imposed would be open to legal challenge'.

This did not stop WPBSA libelling me in their self-congratulatory house magazine *Newsbreak*, alleging that I had 'disregarded' their drugs regulations 'by not informing the doctor before play that [I] had taken medication'. Sheepishly, they were forced to admit there was no such rule. Players were required to notify the doctor before giving a urine sample after their match and I had done that.

It was alleged that I had 'refused to accept the findings' when all I had done was exercise my right to have the B sample tested; that I had 'repeatedly' pressed for King's College to be used because I 'apparently suspected [their] usual facilities at Homerton Hospital'. Actually, I made only one such request and my misgivings about Homerton were amply justified. Finally, they alleged that I had 'cost the association approximately £3,500 and put many people to a great deal of trouble, including [their] legal and medical advisors'.

It was unclear how it could be deemed unnecessary for a player to defend himself, entirely within the rules of his association, in such a potentially damaging situation.

This attack on me was signed Drugs Committee Report, but its chairman, Gordon Ingham, disclaimed all knowledge of it. I therefore asked who was misrepresenting himself or itself as the Drugs Committee in WPBSA's own publication. There was no answer to that.

I settled for my costs and a grovelling apology. I should have taken them to the cleaners. I did not make the same mistake again.

Demand for drugs stories subsided. Occasionally, there would be a positive for marijuana or some stimulant accidentally taken in a cold cure. Jimmy White aroused suspicion – but no action

– by leaving the building a couple of times without producing a sample as requested. It was easy to gain the impression that the drug testing programme had become almost entirely a public relations exercise. Certainly, without Sports Council supervision, it had no credibility.

There were moments of farce. One Canadian player tested positive for marijuana, but his explanation – that he had inhaled passively because his girlfriend was smoking it in their small car – was accepted; another Canadian attracted the suspicion of a supervising doctor who noticed a sound less consistent with urine being passed into a bottle than it being poured from one into another.

In 1997, WPBSA eventually went back to official Sports Council testing, although detection was one thing and punishment another. It became standard for players simply to forfeit any prize money or ranking points they had earned from the particular event at which they had tested positive, as Paul Hunter, Ronnie O'Sullivan and Stephen Lee from a younger generation of players all did for marijuana, which no one regarded as performance enhancing but which was on the list simply because it was an illegal drug. As the average age of top players fell, there were no beta-blocker cases.

Silvino Francisco was the innocent catalyst for snooker's drugs saga and the cover-ups, blunders and bungles it produced. He was also, perhaps not so innocently, the catalyst of the match fixing scandals which attracted many more acres of press coverage to the game.

11

FIXERS AND FALSE ALARMS

ALMOST AS SOON AS SNOOKER HAD BECOME A MAJOR TELEVISION SPORT, there were excitable stories in the tabloids about match fixing. It was obvious that most were entirely without foundation and even in the very few cases there was smoke, no one could locate a fire.

For the tabloids, simply reporting snooker tournaments whose matches were contested with scrupulous integrity was too boring. To conjure with the possibility that fixing or fraud was taking place before the very eyes of millions seemed much more exciting.

Brian Radford, a journalist who was to achieve infamy in snooker circles 15 years later, wrote a snooker-fixing story for *The Sporting Life* during the 1985 Embassy World Championship, quoting the 'fear' of William Hill and Mecca that players 'may prearrange results in major tournaments, especially frame scores'. Hill and Mecca may indeed have been fearful, but Radford was unable to establish any justification for their fears.

The chairman of Surrey Racing was quoted as saying: 'Players can stake up to £20,000 or more on a match easily.' The reaction of the snooker world was that there would have been a big problem in getting a bet of anything like that amount accepted in those days.

The *Sunday People* carried a front page story in September 1985 with the headline: 'TV snooker sensation: big final was bent, says ex-manager'.

The ex-manager in question was Geoff Lomas, proprietor of Potters, Salford, who had been involved in the management at various times of Tony Knowles, Jimmy White, Kirk Stevens, Alex Higgins and John Virgo.

No names were named, but the WPBSA took legal advice on behalf of its members. A six line formal apology therefore appeared in February 1986, accepting that there was 'no truth in the allegations of fixed snooker matches'.

The journalistic problem was to 'stand the story up'. Enter indignant bookmakers, knowing less about snooker than horse racing, prepared to make claims unsupported by documentary evidence. The next move was to ask for a quote from the 'other side', usually the governing body, which could be relied upon to say – what else could it say? – that it would investigate any evidence laid before it. Inevitably, players protested total innocence – well, they would, wouldn't they?

All this facilitated stories along the lines of (1) bookmakers suspend betting – which they are entitled to do at any time without giving a reason, although their credibility would be at risk without one; (2) governing body will investigate; and (3) players deny match fixing. All true in their way, but in the absence of specifics, simply a haze of suspicion.

An alleged coup at the 1987 Irish Masters was exposed as absurd by John Martin in the *Irish Independent*. One bookmaker, Alan Weinrib, had taken a bet of IR£7,100 at 5–6 for Tony Meo to beat Tony Knowles. Weinrib realised that he had probably overpriced Meo, even at 5–6, and with even longer odds available elsewhere, laid off at evens. This produced a chain reaction through the Irish betting fraternity and an allegation of suspiciously heavy betting on Meo to beat Knowles which, to the surprise of few snooker insiders, he did. Knowles had been struggling at the time; Meo had just won the English Championship.

The WPBSA immediately issued a statement. It had 'no reason to suppose that any of its members are involved with any unlawful betting coup' and had 'every confidence in Tony Meo and Tony Knowles'.

However, no such statement had been issued in relation to two previous allegations relating to Knowles's 5–1 first round win over Silvino Francisco in the 1986 Benson and Hedges Masters and Francisco's 5–1 win over his nephew, Peter, in the 1987 Mercantile Credit Classic.

The WPBSA took the former so seriously that they called in Scotland Yard, but the men in blue found no evidence of any coup, much less of any malpractice contributing to a coup and neither the police nor the WPBSA ever went so far as to interview the players. Most neutrals at the time thought that the WPBSA establishment was going out of its way to make life difficult for Francisco because he had let the cat out of the bag with the drugs issue and had also had the temerity to successfully sue the WPBSA chairman and vice-chairman, Williams and Virgo, for libel.

The Manchester bookmakers, Done Brothers, had taken three bets, each staking £100, for Silvino to beat Peter 5–0, 5–1 or 5–2 but, bearing in mind the odds available on these scores, they were in effect asking WPBSA to consider that collusion had occurred between these two players for a net profit of £600. WPBSA rejected the complaint from Done Brothers but never issued a statement to this effect or even notified the Franciscos.

These betting and match-rigging stories came and went relatively quickly, but the 1989 Benson and Hedges Masters, a very high profile event in that it was held at Wembley and covered in its entirety by BBC TV, produced one with much more impact. Again, it involved Silvino Francisco. Again, any evidence that was actually produced was sketchy and inconclusive and, of course, Francisco was so thoroughly hated within the WPBSA hierarchy for other reasons that the dispassionate observer could not help but suspect an element of stitch-up or at any rate eagerness to believe that allegations of match fixing against him were true.

When Francisco lost 5–1 to Terry Griffiths, the *Daily Mirror* splashed a betting coup story all over its front page. It was quickly revealed that one punter or a group of punters had placed £90 bets at seven closely grouped Ladbrokes shops in North London within a few minutes of each other. Some guile was used in that the gamblers clearly knew that bets of £100 or more had to be cleared with head office, but it was far from unknown for a punter wanting a substantial bet at advertised odds to find only part of the bet accepted at those odds or that lower odds were offered for the whole bet.

Ladbrokes, who apparently stood to lose around £10,000, became so nervous at the pattern of betting that they unsuccessfully attempted to contact WPBSA at Wembley shortly before the match. They also suspended betting some 40 minutes before the off. In Ireland, Adrian Eastwood, who had done his own credibility no favours through his insinuations of match rigging at the Irish Masters two years earlier, took £540 in bets and rang *The Sporting Life* shortly before the off to predict a 5–1 result.

It was wildly claimed that a coup had netted £50,000, but John Martin in the *Irish Independent* threw a bucketful of scepticism over the allegations: 'That suggests that at least ten individuals were involved in placing the bets and that's an awful lot of middlemen requiring a cut of the action. It leaves very little for Francisco – hardly enough to make it worth his while jeopardising his entire career should the allegations be proved.'

Virgo, no friend of Francisco, expressed full confidence in the integrity of the match: 'I watched it and, if anything, the players seemed to be trying too hard.' He added: 'I'm quite interested in betting, but I don't see where the value comes in.' To Griffiths, Francisco's opponent, it felt like a hard match.

This time Scotland Yard did investigate allegations of match rigging very rigorously. Francisco was even arrested, albeit released on police bail. There was suspicion, even grave suspicion, but no documentary or other form of proof.

Years went by without another match-rigging story, although there was some suspicion in retrospect about Francisco's 5–1 defeat by Steve Davis in a tournament in Plymouth in 1994. Davis gained the impression, rightly or wrongly, that Francisco was not trying to win the third frame. In turn, he deliberately left frame ball over a pocket so that Francisco had to pot it. Davis went on to win 5–1, although there had been more bets placed for 5–0.

Peter Francisco, like his uncle Silvino, was ranked in the top 16 at his best. Less than two weeks before coming to the Crucible in 1995, he had beaten the world no. 11, Nigel Bond, in reaching the last 16 in the British Open at Plymouth. Up to 2–2 against Jimmy White, whom he had a reasonable chance of beating, Francisco again played pretty well, winning the second frame after needing a snooker. White's game had been patchy and erratic up to 2–2 and did not improve. Nevertheless, he won the five remaining frames on the Saturday evening and the first three next day to win 10–2.

I commentated on the entire match with Virgo as my summariser in the first session and Dennis Taylor in the second. All three of us were puzzled at times by Francisco's shot selection. Dennis said: 'I can't figure out what's going wrong with Peter' and 'His thinking doesn't seem to be there. He hasn't got his thinking boots on today.' I said: 'He's just not thinking straight.'

I was so used to players trying their hardest, particularly at the Crucible, that the explanation took some time to break clear of my subconscious. This happened in a peculiar way when Francisco was 4–2 down and therefore on course for the 10–2 scoreline in favour of White.

As the diagram shows, White went in-off to go 21 behind with only one red remaining in the seventh. That red was unmissable; the pink lay over one middle pocket, the black near the other with position available for either in such a way that it was easy then to obtain position on yellow. Even red-blue-yellow would have been a not unreasonable shot choice.

Instead, Francisco chose the only possible way he could go wrong: red-yellow-yellow. In taking the yellow, he ran some risk of snookering himself (when it was replaced on its own spot) behind the brown. He actually left himself bridging over the black.

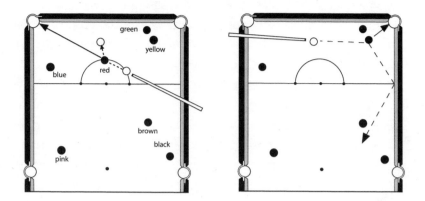

Even so, his attempted yellow should at least have hit the jaws. Instead, it missed by what I described as 'a vast margin'.

I was literally struck dumb by his choice of red-yellow-yellow. My brain would not inform my voice of the thinking behind this because I instinctively shrank from recognising that the thinking was corrupt.

There were several other highly suspect shot choices and a committee of former players – Geoff Foulds, Bill Oliver and Mike Watterson – was set up to consider whether any malpractice had taken place. No one could deny that this trio knew the game, in terms of what was happening on the table, inside out. Francisco was banned for five years.

His lawyers made the usual protestations and threats of appeal to a higher authority, but it is almost unprecedented for a court of law to overturn a decision made on a field of play issue as long as its proceedings have been seen to be fair. For instance, if the stewards at a racecourse decide that a race has been unfairly run, their word is law.

The whole foundation of snooker – and of betting upon it – is that a player does his best to win every frame he plays. The bookmaking fraternity was content with the outcome and happy to accept that this was an isolated incident which did not warrant an overreaction.

Since then, there has been no whiff of suspicion at the Crucible.

There have been matches in which the losing player has become so demoralised that it was obvious, long before the end, what the result was going to be – in some cases, with a high probability that the loser is not going to win another frame – but match fixing can only be defined by a player not only ceasing to try his utmost but also ceasing to try his utmost because of a financial incentive.

Only one televised match in a world ranking event – in a last 16 – attracted intense suspicion. In a best of nine, player A was leading player B 4–0 at the intermission, during which a punter (who turned out to be a friend of player B) placed £7,000 at 4–7 on player A to win the next frame, a very unusual and sizeable bet in such circumstances.

He may have known that player B, playing poorly, was so demoralised that he was extremely unlikely to win a frame; it may have been that player B wanted to supplement his prize money as a last 16 loser by not trying and thus being sure to share in the profits of a winning bet.

In the latter stages of tournaments, prize money differentials, round by round, plus the large number of ranking points at stake, militate strongly against losing on purpose but early rounds offer more temptations, particularly in the last, or last but one, tournament of the season, when it can already be clear in which ranking band – top 16, 32, 48, 64 or 96 – a player is going to finish. These ranking bands determine the number of rounds from which a player is exempted in ranking events the following season.

Impending retirement can be a factor in a modest betting coup, with or without a player's complicity. Before the Regal Scottish Open in April 2000, Chris Scanlon was already certain of relegation from the world ranking circuit, not a situation which would have motivated him to practise. Two years earlier, most bookmakers had ceased betting on first and second round matches – qualifying competitions, in essence – partly because they lacked sufficient depth of information, so the only market available was spread betting. The way this works in this instance is that the greatest margin of victory gives the greatest profit.

Normally, an obscure first round match between Scanlon and David McLellan would have attracted negligible interest but so many punters swarmed in for McLellan between the morning opening of business and around eleven o'clock that both IG Index and Sports Index suspended betting. McLellan won 5–0; IG Index lost £15,000.

No suspicion ever attaches to the winner in a case like this. Indeed, it may put him off if he knows something crooked is afoot. Unless a match is televised, no visual evidence remains. There was at the time a buzz that a coup had taken place, but it could be argued that everything could be explained by punters having knowledge of Scanlon not having practised and thus not having any motivation. Was it the case that he simply did not try – as has happened with other players on their farewell appearances – or did he have a financial motive for not trying? The spread betting firms inclined towards the latter interpretation.

The name of the bustling Pontefract professional Jimmy Michie featured in two matches with which bookmakers were not entirely happy.

His first round match against Mark Gray in the April 1998 British Open would never have emerged from obscurity but for William Hill, Ladbrokes and Stanley all suspending betting the day before the match after Gray had been supported with bets potentially worth £30,000.

Hill's shut up shop on the match after Gray had been backed down from 11–10 to 1–3; Stanley's did likewise after shortening his price from evens to 1–2. Hill's initially said they were withholding payment but reversed this decision after receiving assurances from WPBSA. Their spokesman, Graham Sharpe, said: 'We will not be withholding payment. We suspended betting because by that point, from a bookmaking stance, it had become impossible to balance the book. In any snooker match, there's a winner and a loser and here it looks as if a lot of punters have picked the right one.'

Michie, who had not won a match all season, lost 5–3. He flatly denied any involvement in a betting coup: 'If I hear anyone slagging me off, I will sue them for defamation of character.' Asked why bookmakers had taken such an unusually large amount of money for this type of match, he said: 'I honestly have no idea. I practised hard before the match to try and win it, but the whole thing got on top of me. I had it all day yesterday and people kept winding me up. I tried to put it out of my mind, but I couldn't. People were virtually saying I was implicated in it all.'

Had Michie won the match, he would have increased his first round loser's cheque for £1,200 to £2,100, assuming a second round defeat. Having started the season 55th in the rankings, he finished 81st but still not in the relegation area. When Gray was asked whether he saw anything suspicious about Michie's performance, he said: 'Not at all. He was getting aggravated out there. He'd have to be a good actor.'

Two years later, Michie was named again when two matches at the Regal Scottish Open in April 2000 aroused suspicions from bookmakers as large bets were placed on Sean Storey to beat Michie – as he did 5–3 – and on Patrick Wallace to beat Darren Clarke – as he did 5–2.

The WPBSA, informed of these unusual betting patterns by the Betting Office Licensees Association (BOLA), sent experts – whom they declined to name – to view these matches but concluded that: 'There is no evidence that the disciplinary rules of the association have been breached.' Whatever suspicions there may have been, there were no television pictures to argue about.

Nick Jones, a spokesman for Done's, the Manchester bookmakers, outlined the sequence of events as far as his own firm was concerned: 'A client came into a Manchester office to ask for a price for Wallace to beat Clarke. Our price was 5–6, but I asked the office to give me a ring if the client wanted more than a three-figure bet. He wanted £6,000 at 5–6, which was a very substantial bet for snooker. It was a size we wouldn't expect to see outside the world championship. We laid him a token sum and put out warnings to our 120 shops. Another shop in Manchester had an enquiry on the same match and two other shops in Castleford and

Hull had enquiries fifteen seconds after we opened for business at 10 a.m. the next morning, which was also fifteen seconds after the match started. They were customers not known to us, who didn't seem to know how the betting world worked. It was really naive to expect to put £6,000 on a match like that without causing alarm bells to ring.'

Alarm bells also rang at IG Index, whose phones came alive at ten o'clock with bets worth £15,000 to support Wallace. In the ordinary way, these would have been accepted, as a 10 a.m. match would be unlikely to start before 10.05.

'A client in Castleford asked for £10,000 for Storey to beat Michie at 11–10 when Hills had him 5–4,' added Jones. 'This was ten minutes before the start of the [afternoon] match and was declined.'

BOLA advised their members not to pay out, although, as always, this decision ultimately rested with the individual bookmaker.

The WPBSA said that it would pursue the case further only if the bookmakers could provide any evidence. This seemed to imply that the association was satisfied with the opinion of its 'experts' without deeming it necessary to speak to the players.

Michie, who had started that season 63rd in the rankings was to end it at 41st, although he would have needed to reach the Scottish Open semi-finals to finish in the top 32. He expressed anger that he should be named: 'It's all been dragged up from two years ago. I've had this before and I'm sick of it. I've been full of flu, so maybe someone found out and bet against me. Why would I want to throw a match? My career is taking off. I've done nothing wrong. I can sleep tonight – no danger.'

Clarke earned £800 as a first round loser, Michie £1,350 as a second round loser. Losers in the third round received £2,400.

Again, without television pictures, any case would have been difficult to prove, however grave the suspicion, but it was also difficult to escape the impression that WPBSA, far from having any will to stamp out malpractice, simply wanted to gloss over any temporary embarrassment as swiftly as possible.

This also appeared to be their attitude when Gerard Greene faced thinly veiled but, in my view, unjustified allegations of match rigging in autumn 2004 after he had broken his cue shortly before the Totesport Grand Prix at Preston, a factor which may have encouraged some fairly heavy betting by opening match standards on his opponent, Nigel Bond, who duly beat him 5–2.

The bets came predominantly from Greene's neck of the woods around Bexleyheath, Kent. Some £7,000 was staked on a Bond win with one high-street bookmaker, for instance, and about £8,000 paid out.

Despite Greene's defeat, betting on Stuart Bingham v. Greene opened a month later with Bingham as a slight underdog. There was strong support for Bingham then, again with both of them quoted at 5–6, and still with Bingham at 8–11.

The respective rankings of Greene (26) and Bingham (37) suggested on the face of it a not easily predictable outcome but, throughout the day, support for Bingham intensified until one leading bookmaker declined a wager of £8,000 at 8–11 and suspended betting. William Hill declined one of £10,000.

The prevailing opinion within the game was that Greene, largely because of his cue problems, was known to be severely lacking in form and confidence and that no malpractice could be inferred. The amount of money staked on a Bingham win (or Greene defeat), very large for such an early round encounter, was attributable, it was argued, simply to knowledgeable folk believing that Greene's pre-tournament poor form would continue and that he would not, as eventually tends to happen, get used to his cue one fine day and start to perform better.

Nevertheless, after Bingham beat Greene 5–1 several journalists and bookmakers seemed eager to believe the worst. WPBSA confirmed that it had been aware of the suspensions of betting and suggested that it was 'extremely likely that [some punters] were aware that Greene broke his cue earlier in the season and that his chances of winning the match were therefore diminished. There has been no suggestion from bookmakers that there was any other reason for betting to be suspended.'

The spokesman stated that WPBSA has 'procedures in place to monitor matches in order to guard against match fixing. These procedures are an internal matter.' In reference to Bingham v. Greene, WPBSA was 'entirely satisfied that there was no suspicion of match fixing and that both players were making every effort to win the match'.

Comforting as it may have been that procedures were in place, why be so secretive about what they were? These can only be (1) appointing an appropriate observer to watch the match closely and/or (2) instructing the match referee to keep an especially keen eye open for any hint of malpractice. A roving observer would be unlikely to be fully effective. In the case of televised matches, there would also have been a videotape to rely on, but Bingham v. Greene was not played on the television table. No special observer was appointed in this instance. The referee, Peter Williamson, was aware of the circumstances but reported nothing amiss.

The winner would have no motive to be involved in anything untoward, while Greene's circumstances make it seem unlikely that he would have been party to a fix. At 25th in the rankings, 36th provisionally after Preston, 41st after Brighton, Greene would have been keen to safeguard his top 32 ranking – and the financial guarantees which go with it – and would certainly not have wanted to slip too far towards the abyss of relegation from the world ranking circuit.

Of the leading 16 bookmakers, 14 did not offer odds on the Greene v. Michie first round match in the Travis Perkins UK Championship at York, the only match of the round they ignored. Continuing uncertainty over Greene's capability with his new cue might have been one reason for this. Another might have been that Michie had twice lost matches on which bookmakers reported a betting pattern towards that outcome of which they were suspicious.

As it transpired, Greene trailed 4–0, led 7–6, but lost 9–7. Afterwards, he told me 'these stupid rumours are doing my head in'. The betting patterns, he insisted, 'are nothing to do with me' and angrily spoke of consulting his manager to discuss legal action if suggestions to the contrary were made. He confirmed that 'two inches snapped off the end' of his cue four days before he had played Bond. John Parris, the cue maker to whom many players turn in this kind of emergency, added two inches to the butt.

'It's the same cue, only fatter,' said Greene, who was only to be expected to take some time to get fully accustomed to it. He also revealed that he had been banned from Gillingham Snooker Club, his practice base for many years, after what he described as 'a clash of personalities with the owner'. Apart from a few games against players in their clubs, he had been unable to practise properly. 'Not enough practice,' was one reason he cited for his series of early season defeats.

Reiterating his emphatic denial of any malpractice, he said: 'I've got a girlfriend, a little boy and another on the way. The last thing I want is to be losing matches and dropping out of the 32.'

Indeed, financial anxiety, by putting Greene under further pressure, might not have done his form any good either.

Defeat by Michie, not as good a player as Bond or Bingham, when Greene could have had no financial incentive to lose, supports the view that he had been trying his best. It is not surprising that a huge wave of money running all one way in the betting market on two matches, involving the loser on both occasions, could arouse suspicion but, by and large, snooker's inner core of knowledgeable gamblers tend to know more about snooker and its players on a day to day basis than bookmakers do.

Another match about which bookmakers were suspicious was the 5–3 first round win for Marcus Campbell, then the world no. 63, over Quinten Hann, then ranked 18, in the first round of the 2004 Totesport Grand Prix.

Around Hann's practice base in Ealing, the word was that he had been practising very little but, even so, wagers of £8,000 or £10,000 for a first round match are extremely unusual and not everybody would have been confident that, even without practice, it was impossible that he could beat Campbell, who had not won a match for nearly a year.

Opening at odds of 7–4 with Stan James, for instance, Campbell was rapidly backed down to 13–8 to 5–4 to evens while still attracting support right up to the off. On the exchanges, Campbell was backed from 2.74 to 2.38 while Hann drifted from 1.54 to 1.7.

Some students of the market, though, thought it odd in this context that it should be a comparatively limited player like Campbell, with a poor recent record, who should be the one to set the pulses of some punters racing so fast, even after he had been backed down to 5–4. Some observant punters may simply have been following the money, the trend of betting. The confidence of other, more suspicious souls may have been boosted by believing, rightly or wrongly, that something unusual was afoot.

The Association of British Bookmakers considered all the circumstances interesting enough to spend a day or so collating betting information but decided not to call for the WPBSA to examine the BBC tape of the match or take any other further action.

'The number of bets and who they were coming from suggested that some people knew something that we didn't,' said one bookmaking source.

Amongst those whose suspicions were aroused was *The Sun*, which was also tipped off by someone close to Hann that he might be prepared to fix matches for money. Two undercover reporters posing as front men for a betting syndicate arranged to meet him in chalet 147 at Pontin's, Prestatyn, where world championship qualifying was taking place. The meeting, in which Hann expressed his readiness to throw a match, was secretly filmed and recorded.

First, Hann had to win his opening match against a Chinese wild card in the China Open but then said that losing his next match to Ken Doherty 'could be a moneyspinner'.

Hann was told he would receive £5,000 upfront and a further

£45,000 if he lost 5–0 to Doherty in Beijing. The undercover reporters agreed to Hann's demand for £20,000 upfront although *The Sun*, of course, was never going to conspire in the commission of a felony by actually paying this money. Hann was therefore informed that the deal was off because it had proved impossible to lay enough bets to make it worthwhile.

The match was played honestly; Doherty won 5–2 and Hann told *The Sun*'s reporters to 'give me a call in September'. Of his Grand Prix match against Campbell, Hann was recorded as saying: 'I know a few people had big bets on Campbell to beat me and they collected £40,000 odd. Betting was suspended and they watched the match, but it was all sweet.'

In a subsequent story, *The Sun* quoted Hann's fellow Australian, Neil Robertson, as saying that Hann had tried to suborn him to throw a match for £30,000. Robertson was appalled and quite certain that Hann was serious.

The Sun's stories coincided with Hann's acquittal on four charges, including two of sexual assault, after a five day trial at Isleworth Crown Court. Three years earlier, he had been acquitted at the Old Bailey in a high profile rape case. Innocent as he was in the eyes of the law, the circumstances of both cases were extremely unsavoury and depicted Hann in a poor light.

WPBSA's disciplinary process was so sluggish that five months later Hann sent a doctor's note excusing him from participating in the 2005 Grand Prix. This entitled him to £3,000 as a first round loser, which WPBSA duly paid. After submitting another sick note to excuse himself from a disciplinary hearing, he was sent further prize money, £1,625, covering his first match in the China Open qualifying and £2,500 as a first round loser in the UK Championship. Without hitting a ball, he was paid £7,125 in all.

Finally, in February 2006, the Sports Disputes Resolution Panel found in his absence that Hann had 'knowingly entered into an agreement to join in an unlawful enterprise to fix the results of certain snooker competitions in return for financial gain'.

Notwithstanding his resignation from WPBSA three days prior to the hearing, he was suspended for eight years and ordered to pay £10,000 costs.

Betting coups sometimes do have an innocent explanation. The classic case was John Parrott's win over Doherty in the 1996 Regal Scottish Masters when a few knowledgeable insiders knew that Parrott's cue had been lost and that he would be using one with which he was unfamiliar.

So great was the flood of money for Doherty that betting was suspended. Willie Thorne, heavily in debt and hardly able to wait to collect the £35,000 he was confidently expecting, spent an agonising afternoon in the commentary box as, to the amazement of all, Parrott won 6–3. Very soon, he was declaring his new cue better and quipping that he was thinking of offering a reward to whoever had stolen his old one.

12

HIGGINS IN A TAILSPIN

WHEN STEVE DAVIS LOST 9–4 TO JIMMY WHITE IN A POOR FINAL OF THE Canadian Masters in Toronto in November 1988, he described it as 'the day the rubber band came off'. He was not delivering the cue through as straight and true as he had been. He could no longer take his technique for granted and concentrate solely on the match.

Working hard on the practice table, he at times put everything right, winning the 1989 world title with an overall frames tally of 70–23, but in August 1990 he invited me to his room in the Hong Kong Hilton to explain his problem. He did not expect any answers but I was, apparently, 'one of the few people who'll know what I'm talking about'. In essence, he was tending to overcut when he was potting to his left and undercut when potting to his right. He was to go 27 months without winning a world ranking title. At his worst, his problem was even influencing his choice of shot.

As it happened, I did know what he was talking about because, at my far lowlier level, the same problem had visited itself upon me. My back injury had forced me into a squarer stance. Somehow, I believed I was addressing the centre of the cue ball when I was, in fact, hitting across it. So was Steve.

Many a great sportsman has spent the first half of his career playing in his natural style and the second half of it trying to unpick the instinctive machinery, discover how it worked and put it back together again. For the rest of his career, there were times when Steve looked very good, almost as good as ever, but he could never recapture the imperious form and immense confidence arising from the implicit faith in his technique which had characterised his greatest days.

On top of it all, the emperor of the '80s was coming under threat from Stephen Hendry, who was to be the nonpareil of the '90s. Hendry was not quite 18 when he won his first ranking title, the Rothmans Grand Prix, in October 1987. He was clearly going to be world no. 1 and in the 1989–90 season won three ranking and two major invitation titles on his way to the Crucible. At twenty-one years three months, he superseded Alex Higgins as the youngest ever world champion by beating Jimmy White 18–12 in the final.

White had beaten Davis 16–14 in the semis but no sooner was he in a position to achieve parity or better with an opponent who had so often blighted his progress in the '80s than Hendry was emerging as the force with which neither he nor anyone else could consistently cope in the '90s. Hendry v. White was to be the decade's great rivalry, but it was Hendry who won all four of their world finals, two of them from positions from which White should have won.

Of course, White was the hero of the drinking and wild living classes and those who admired such a lifestyle. Hendry, Scottish amateur champion at the age of 14, again at 15, and Scottish professional champion at 16, had always been cool, professional and focused on his ambitions. If ever he needed any reminding of how focused he had to be, his manager, Ian Doyle, never shrank from telling him.

Doyle, a Scot born in 1941, originally made money out of hardware, property and leasing businesses. He became involved in Scottish snooker as a sponsor of the amateur game and opened a club in Stirling. Hendry entered his life out of the blue on 16 November 1983 when the club received a visiting junior team from Edinburgh.

'I'll never forget the first time I saw him,' said Doyle. 'There he was in his little leather jacket, carrying a cue case which was taller than he was. You could have cut your finger on the crease in his trousers. He happened to be playing my son, Lee. He made 47 first shot as sweet as you like and I just knew he was something special. Lee said afterwards that there was somebody who was going to be world champion. I agreed with him. My wife, Irene, said: "Och, he's only a wee boy."'

Hendry was not originally managed by Doyle but by Ron Clover of, yes, Four Leaf Promotions, but once Doyle did take him on, his affairs were managed with painstaking attention to detail. In due course, Doyle assembled a stable of players, starting at roughly the same time as Hearn was losing interest in snooker generally and snooker management specifically. Hearn, fitful, inspirational, impatient of detail, was the direct antithesis of the meticulous Doyle, a workaholic, who was loquacious, forthright, outspoken, even hectoring at times, never troubling to conceal his low opinion of this or that aspect of a brother manager's ability or performance. Doyle and Hearn co-operated from time to time, but their approaches to snooker management and entrepreneurship were so different that compatibility tended to be fleeting.

Hearn and Doyle were easily the most capable in their different ways, but Hearn's failings included an entrepreneurial restlessness and a wish to be a star himself. When he moved into boxing to promote Frank Bruno v. Joe Bugner at White Hart Lane in 1987, it was not long before his players, griping that his priorities had shifted, began to move away. Soon, only Davis remained, a blood brother and a business partner in that he was a director of several Hearn companies. This was to leave Doyle, soon exerting through Hendry the clout Hearn had had when Davis was world champion and world no. 1, as indisputably snooker's leading manager, but his remaining rivals grew so resentful and envious of his status and success that they were prone to form conspiracies of mediocrity against him.

Though managed by Howard Kruger, Higgins was essentially a loose cannon, unpredictable even to himself. Regardless of results, he remained a prime box office attraction. His marriage to Lynn, patched up several times, came irretrievably apart as his off-table life became ever more turbulent.

In January 1985, he beat Dennis Taylor in the Mercantile Classic on ITV sporting a black eye, which he claimed had been sustained through a kick from a horse called Dreadnought. He later admitted that he had received it in a fistfight with one of his regular practice opponents, Paul Medati. Beaten by Rex Williams, then the WPBSA chairman, in a quarter-final which reminded pressroom wags of naughty pupil and headmaster, his frustrations boiled over into backstage conduct which brought him for the umpteenth time before a disciplinary hearing. Amongst his heinous offences, he had referred to Gordon Ingham, the Halifax pie maker and WPBSA board member who had shamelessly exploited its £1-a-mile travelling allowance, as 'that fucking limping cunt'. In the pressroom, Ingham thereafter tended to be alluded to, for short, as the 'FLC'.

At the 1986 UK Championship at Preston, there was an incident extraordinary even by Higgins's standards. Having just beaten Mike Hallett 9–7 to reach the quarter-finals, he was asked by Paul Hatherell, the tournament director, to give a urine sample. Higgins never failed a drugs test, but those close to him attested that he knew everything about drugs that there was to know. At 7–7 against Hallett, he had left the arena and returned a couple of minutes later to play two stunning frames. This might simply have been his talent, but the guvnors wanted to be sure. When Hatherell began to hurry him, Higgins simply head-butted him. The ensuing scrimmage spilled out into the corridor, witnessed by journos who had descended from the pressroom at speed when a breathless informant had apprised us of the essentials: 'Higgins has nutted Hatherell.'

Higgins, demented and flailing, was being restrained, though not before kneeing Frank Baker, the WPBSA's security man, in the genitals. At Preston Magistrates Court, he was fined £200 for assault and £50 for criminal damage to a door. Hauled before Gavin Lightman QC, now Mr Justice Lightman, at a disciplinary tribunal, he was fined £12,000, easily a record for snooker, and suspended for five tournaments.

Shortly after his return from suspension, he initially refused to give a urine sample at a non-ranking event in Glasgow. Eventually, he agreed to do so only in the public toilet, not the test cubicle, on the further condition that the press should also be present. 'The photographers were all in there flashing,' Doyle stated. Notably, Higgins sported a black eye following his first match and two black eyes following the second. 'According to Alex, he had an accident in a revolving door, twice,' said Doyle.

Struggling for form, Higgins recaptured the limelight in unorthodox fashion. An epic row with his girlfriend, Siobhan Kidd, a psychology graduate he had met while she was working as a waitress, ended with her locking him inside her flat. Attempting to crawl round the building on a ledge, he sustained broken bones in his foot in plunging 25 feet to the pavement.

'Fortunately, Mr Higgins was not hurt as he landed on his head,' was one imaginative quote attributed to the first policeman on the scene.

A couple of weeks later, on crutches, unable to put any weight on his left leg and with his weight distribution therefore all awry, he showed farcical courage in winning a match in the European Open in Deauville and in much the same condition a few weeks later, battling against mounting exhaustion, the Irish Championship. A few weeks after that, no longer hopping but limping, he won the Benson and Hedges Irish Masters, beating Cliff Thorburn, Neal Foulds, John Parrott and, in the final, Hendry 9–8 from two down with three to play. It was the last major title of his career. At two o'clock the day after this emotional and exhausting triumph, he had to be in Preston for his Embassy World Championship qualifying match against Darren Morgan, a hungry young Welshman who had won the 1987 world amateur title. Morgan beat him 10–8, so Higgins did not play at the Crucible that year.

Siobhan was the love of his life, but inevitably Higgins wore out his welcome with her just as he did with everyone else. She departed finally with a fractured cheekbone for her trouble. Out of his mind with rejection, deserved as it was, and his sense of loss, Higgins was to sink to a new low at Bournemouth in February 1990 at the World Team Cup.

In many sports, a player who, even outside the arena, had grabbed a referee by the neck and threatened him would long since have been banned but such an incident involving Higgins and the referee John Street at the 1987 British Open qualifying was glossed over, as were many more. However, it had reached the stage where Higgins's presence in any hotel foyer or bar late at night, especially when he had lost, spelt trouble. Incidents in the 1988–89 season included one at the Rothmans Grand Prix when he grabbed one journalist round the neck and threatened another with a heavy glass ashtray. At the Dubai Classic, he behaved so provocatively to journalists that Dave Armitage, the amazingly tall reporter from the *Daily Star*, punched him; also in Dubai, Higgins's unfriendly rubbishing of Danny Fowler provoked Fowler's manager, Tony Goulding, killed in a car accident a few weeks later, first to throw Higgins fully clothed into the swimming pool and then duck him until he apologised; in the hotel nightclub, aggravation reached such a pitch that Jim Chambers, a player endeavouring to act as peacemaker, sprained his ankle falling down some steps and was carried away to hospital in agony.

The underlying trouble was that Higgins had reached the age of 41 with a set of emotional needs scarcely modified since infancy: an insatiable lust for the limelight, an imperious wish to have his own way and a yearning for unconditional love expressed as an assumption that he would be forgiven no matter what he did. He claimed a child's licence to say the most hurtful things he could think of yet sought adult refuge in alcohol and denial of unpalatable realities.

At Northern Ireland's semi-final victory press conference in 1990, he hinted at what might be to come when he mumbled: 'If I'm not captain tomorrow, I'm not playing,' the sort of childish threat he had uttered so often in his career that it had tended to be ignored. He insisted that he, Dennis Taylor and the other member of the trio, Tommy Murphy, a former apprentice coffin maker, hold a meeting in the women's toilet because they might be overheard in the men's. At this, Higgins suggested that after they had each played two frames in the final Taylor would play the remaining two of the afternoon session.

Taylor was in no doubt that this arose from Higgins 'glory hunting as usual' because this would give him more frames in the evening. 'I was supposed to be captain, but we went along with Alex just for the sake of a bit of peace.' However, when Higgins lost his second frame the following afternoon, he insisted, despite Taylor being dressed and ready to play, that he play the next two himself. Higgins lost them both to leave Northern Ireland 6–2 down.

A furious row ensued in the players' room. 'I come from the Shankill. You come from Coalisland. The next time you're in Northern Ireland, I'll have you shot,' said Higgins amidst his torrent of abuse, some of it directed at Taylor's late mother. This was to reduce Taylor, as sturdy a character as he was, to tears of hurt and frustration.

Publicly, Higgins tried to defend himself by attacking Taylor, whose 71 was still the front-runner for the £6,000 highest-break prize. If it stood, Taylor said that he did not intend to share it: 'When this first came up years ago when we played together, Alex's own words were "There's no way we share it."'

At the press conference, after Northern Ireland had lost 9–5 to Canada, Higgins said: 'In my estimation, Dennis Taylor is not a snooker person. He is a money person. The more he gets, the more he wants. He will never be sated. He puts money before country. He belongs back in Coalisland. He's not fit to wear this badge, the red hand of Ulster.'

In reality, there was nobody more interested in money than Higgins and one of the most distasteful aspects of the whole affair was the unpleasant whiff of religious bigotry he injected into the situation, sport having been one of the few elements to bind the

Northern Ireland community together rather than intensify its divisions.

Taylor originally wished to say nothing for publication but changed his mind after Higgins's press conference. He first deplored Higgins's remark after the semi-final: 'In front of a few people, Alex told Tommy that he had played like a cunt. That's a good way to get him into shape for the final.

'I've known Alex since 1968. When he came over to Blackburn, I found a flat for him to stay in. I got a television put in for him. I did my best to help him. I was literally shaking when I went out to play tonight. I wanted to win this for Tommy. But everything was shaking. At the height of the troubles in Northern Ireland, I brought all the top players over. Two days after I won the world title, I had the best reception I have ever had in my life in the Shankill Leisure Centre. I've never got involved in the politics.'

To some, Higgins remained a loveable scallywag, but Taylor's view was that 'the majority side with him because they don't realise the sort of person he is'.

Fatefully, Higgins and Taylor were drawn together in a first round match in the Benson and Hedges Irish Masters some 12 days later. Snooker is so cerebral and delicate a game that it is not designed to withstand the level of emotional tension and sheer aggro involved in what Steve Davis succinctly described as 'the grudge match of all time'. The standard of play was not up to much, but in the circumstances it was surprising that it was up to anything at all. It was an evening, regrettably, when only the result mattered. The contrast between Northern Ireland's two former world champions was poignant.

Taylor's father, Tommy, had driven down from Coalisland; his eldest brother, Martin, had flown over from Preston; his then wife, Trish, revised her intention to stay at home, away from such an unpleasant level of emotional tension, to sit in the audience. It was not the way she would have chosen to spend their 20th wedding anniversary. Taylor must also have felt the warmth and good wishes not only of friends but also of those neutrals who felt that Higgins's conduct at Bournemouth had been an affront to snooker's good name and everything that sport stands for.

Higgins, give or take minders and hangers-on, was spiritually alone. Siobhan had fled and when he called on his former wife, Lynn, a few weeks earlier, with presents for their children, she would not let him in. His sense of rejection and his uncontrollable rage allowed him to demonstrate his love for them only by throwing a skateboard through the window. He was fined £50 for criminal damage. Between his world qualifying match on the Tuesday and this match on the Friday, Higgins had maintained his defiant front, even undercutting an apology issued by his manager, Doug Perry, by saying on BBC's *Sportsnight*: 'I'm not really bothered about what happened last week.'

The venue was Goff's sales ring at Kill, County Kildare, some half an hour out of Dublin, which was mostly used for auction sales of bloodstock. With all seats taken and standing accommodation full on all three tiers of what is at the best of times a cockpit of an arena, the atmosphere would not have been out of place at a bare-knuckle prize fight. When, as promised, Taylor cursorily shook Higgins by the hand to conform to accepted snooker etiquette, it was like boxers touching gloves before trying to maim each other. The roar was that of a crowd roaring for blood.

At the intermission, Higgins remained brooding in his player's seat, talking to anyone who would listen. When he finally left the arena, he reassured the first person he bumped into: 'Don't worry, I've thrown away the first four frames.' It was, in fact, 3–1 to Taylor at the time.

On the resumption, Taylor was kept waiting in the arena while Higgins, rather than walk the extra few yards to the toilet, urinated in a drain. He again availed himself of this facility after reducing his arrears to 3–2 and at a key stage of the 47-minute sixth frame, the drain came into play again before Taylor secured the 4–2 lead which he was to convert into a 5–2 victory.

Higgins's press conference was both pitiable and threatening.

Here was a man whose self-control appeared to be hanging by the finest of threads.

Early in the match, with no hint of irony, Higgins had admonished the crowd: 'Ladies and gentlemen, this is the Irish Masters. Let's have a bit of decorum.' Now, just outside the arena, seated on a chair brought to what is normally a mustering yard for horses about to be auctioned, Higgins declined to begin until he had been furnished with an ashtray, so fastidious was he about dropping ash on the concrete floor – only a few feet from the infamous drain.

Slurring at times to the point of incoherence, wild eyed, heavy with drink, he regurgitated slights real and imagined. He was 'disappointed for the people'; losing early would give him time 'in Dublin's fair city where girls are so pretty', or for some rounds of golf. But his immediate response to questions of a more probing nature was counter-attack. He rose from his chair towards Dave Armitage of the *Daily Star* – 'who put one on me in Dubai'. One of his minders placed a hand over the BBC microphone. Minders hustled Higgins to his dressing-room.

He emerged for an interview with RTÉ in which he said: 'I would like to apologise to Dennis one more time.' As to his chances in the world championship, he took refuge in omnipotence fantasy: 'It's a foregone conclusion.' Indeed, it was, though not in the sense he intended.

Trailing Steve James 8–5 at the mid-session interval, he sat in his chair in the arena rather than in his dressing-room. When he had lost 10–5, he stayed several more minutes as if reluctant to relinquish even the last vestiges of limelight while the table was being covered and the lights dimmed. In a gesture reminiscent of a child attacking his teddy, he ripped off the head of Antrim, his leprechaun mascot.

But we had seen nothing yet. On the way into his obligatory press conference, apropos of nothing, he punched Colin Randle, the WPBSA press officer on duty, in the stomach. It was an unprovoked, motiveless attack, not personal but against a symbol of the authority that WPBSA represented. This inevitably became the subject of an official complaint with several witnesses going on the record.

Ascending the podium, he did not wait for a question: 'Well, chaps, the current events over the last few weeks have not been very good, this way or the other. So I would like to announce my retirement from professional snooker. I don't want to be part of a cartel. I don't want to be part of a game . . . where there are slush funds for everybody, where the players are mucked about. I do not want to be ever again in my lifetime to get less than job satisfaction.'

He searched, though not with success, for a parallel to his own situation: 'If Derek Jameson can leave the *News of the World* and go to Sky TV, then there has got to be a place for me in this life. I'm not playing snooker anymore because this game is the most corrupt game in the world. It needs to be brought to the attention of the Department of Trade and Industry. There are an awful lot of people running about this world who put their kids through certain schools, feeder schools, grammar schools and you get absolute tossers doing jobs for exorbitant money.

'Well, I don't really want any part of it, so you can shove your snooker up your jacksey. I'm not playing no more and it's not sour grapes, nothing. It's the truth. I wish Cecil Parkinson and Maggie Thatcher would do a probe into snooker, then we would actually find out the real truth. The Hurricane doesn't want to be part of this tripe anymore. No disrespect to the Northern people because I like tripe.

'There's a thing called job satisfaction. I don't want to be part of a cartel, corruption, whatever. That is the end of the story. I hate it. I abhor it. I'm not going to break the cue because I like the cue, but it's a corrupt game. Excuse me, I've not finished, I've not finished . . . rock on, Tommy.

'The people who work within the game appal me. I won't be using a cue again. I've had all sorts of shit thrown at me by the media in the past six or seven years. I was supposed to be a stalwart of the game, the guy who took all the brunt. The kid who took all the brunt is absolutely sick up to here. I'm not prepared to take it any longer. I might do overseas trips and teach kids from Amsterdam. I don't like the WPBSA – the way they do things, they can throw me out, shove me out, I couldn't give a damn. I cannot handle some of the untruths. I am going to the law courts. I'm going to fight the newspapers. I have got plenty on my plate. One of the first papers I go for is *The Star*, *The Sun* and what's the other one?'

There were a few traces of truth in this tirade, although his language lacked forensic precision. There was no cartel for Higgins to belong to, whether this was his desire or not; there were no slush funds; his unspecific allegations of corruption amounted to no more than that some players were closer than others to the game's Establishment, which was inevitable since the WPBSA board of the day consisted entirely of players. His threat to retire was viewed as a pre-emptive strike – forestalling WPBSA disciplinary action – a veiled request to beg him to stay, or simply the action of a little boy who doesn't want to play anymore if he can't win.

'Snookered by birds, booze and brawling' was the *Daily Star* analysis in an article in which Ms Liz Kendall might have been surprised to see herself referred to as one of his former wives. Most papers contented themselves with stringing together a list of his past misdeeds. Some read almost like obituaries. Nancy Banks-Smith, the *Guardian*'s peerless television critic, wrote:

> Higgins actually looked ill. He seemed a juddering succession of twinges and twitches, like a video running [in] reverse. 'I would like to congratulate . . . who is it . . . my opponent . . . Steve. He's a nice lad. He means well and all the rest . . .' hardly suggests he knew who he was playing, let alone what he was saying.

Frank Curran in the *Daily Star* asserted 'Top actor John Hurt is tipped to star as fiery snooker star Alex 'Hurricane' Higgins on screen.' Hurt had previously starred as Bob Champion, the Grand National winner who had recovered from cancer, Quentin Crisp, the celebrated transvestite homosexual, and the Elephant Man, but nothing more was heard of any role for him in any biopic of Higgins.

In the same paper, Tony Brooks stated after nearly a week's patient research that 'snooker bad boy Alex Higgins knocked back 27 vodkas before announcing his retirement from the game'. He quoted an unnamed member of the catering staff as saying: 'The word is that he got through nine treble vodka and oranges – about a bottle in bar measures.'

Higgins himself co-operated for a sizeable fee with the *News of the World* in presenting his broken romance with Siobhan Kidd as the reason for his current spate of bad behaviour and asserted: 'I am determined to be a stabilised, understanding person again.' A few days later, Higgins was observed spending a few days as the guest of Oliver Reed, a notoriously thirsty actor, in Guernsey. It was concluded from this that Higgins did not envisage abstinence playing any immediate part in the resolution of his problems.

By the time the final had taken place, Higgins had been forgotten, albeit temporarily. Hendry superseded Higgins as the youngest ever champion and remained utterly self-possessed. His was not the joy of a man who had won the pools but the satisfaction of one who had believed with all his heart that he was well capable of winning the world title and that he was now where he should be.

13

KRUGER: THE FIZZ GOES FLAT

NEXT UP: THE PUBLIC CRUCIFIXION OF HOWARD KRUGER, WHO WAS neither the first nor the last snooker manager to impress gullible players with flash trappings only to do them grievous financial harm.

In 1985, Kruger was on a beach in Marbella, fresh from a £250,000 rock video debacle. So was Tony Knowles, who was just about to have a problem: a former girlfriend had kissed – well, actually, more than kissed – and told. *The Sun* was about to publish her claims that Tony liked dressing up in women's underclothes in a sexual context and that he had treated her violently and meanly. A public relations counter-offensive was organised but only made matters worse.

When *The Sun* ran the story during the Goya tournament in Stoke, it provoked some unseemly levity amongst snooker's regular hacks. One quipped that Tony was so maddened by the story that he rushed downstairs to phone his former girlfriend only to ladder his stockings in haste. Another queried whether Janet Reger might be about to sponsor a tournament.

Flanked by a London public relations outfit, he called a press conference. Poker-faced and in all seriousness, Tony read a statement in which he denied that he had 'at any time sought sexual pleasure through wearing women's underwear or lingerie' although he did admit that he 'once attended a fancy dress party with my ex-girlfriend, the outfit for which incorporated some of these items. This party was a one-off and I have not attended anything similar since. The party was not in any way perverted or kinky.' He went on to deny that he had ever 'deliberately physically abused my ex-girlfriend' and to state that 'the primary reason for our relationship breaking down was my single-minded approach to snooker'. Naturally enough, he lost to Neal Foulds that evening.

Kruger became Knowles's manager and formed a company, Framework Management, with offices first in Belgravia, then in Brighton. Knowles put up half the money to become a 50/50 partner. Later, ill advisedly, he sold Kruger a further 1 per cent. He was later to claim that the Kruger experience had cost him a good £200,000.

Knowles signed a guarantee for £120,000 with the Midland Bank, Brighton. This was soon up to £144,000 with interest and a county court judgment against both him and Kruger for £157,000 each eventually followed.

Other players – Alex Higgins, Joe Johnson, Dean Reynolds, Peter Francisco, Martin Clark and Eugene Hughes amongst them – were recruited to the stable. Even John Parrott, who spent his entire career with one manager, Phil Miller, allowed Framework to act on a commission basis for work actually obtained, thus enhancing their credibility through his name being featured in their advertising. Some of these players were signed to associated companies, such as Framework Exhibitions, Kruger Holdings and Homestage, which were part of Kruger's labyrinthine activities. There was considerable trading between companies, all of which seemed to have different year ends. In reality, as an employee summarised: 'The whole operation was robbing Peter to pay Paul. It was all leases, hire purchase, double mortgage.'

Even on day one, something did not quite add up. An archetypal spoilt rich kid, Kruger lived in a mansion in Hove named after the Flamingo, the Soho jazz club run by his father, Jeffrey, a well-known character in the music world. His cars were high performance and he flaunted both a helicopter and a yacht, though whether he actually owned them, no one was ever quite sure. When they were trying to persuade David Roe to sign, staff were instructed to take him out on the boat and tell him about the helicopter and all Kruger's other supposed possessions.

Trusting, credulous, vulnerable players fell over themselves to sign up with him. So did Alasdair Ross, the *Sun's* bewhiskered snooker correspondent, much of whose Crucible coverage tended to originate from his vantage point in the Brown Bear nearby. Ally was taken on as press officer, with or without the knowledge of *The Sun*, for whom he continued to work, airily dismissing suggestions that this might constitute a conflict of interest.

The bewhiskered one was to the fore when, eager for rehabilitation, Framework set up an interview for Knowles with Noreen Taylor of the *Daily Mirror* although any hope that might have been cherished that this would produce a soft feature by a dewy-eyed woman writer accepting a superstar at his own valuation was dispelled by the unpromising intro to a nine-column centre spread: 'Since that Snooker Stud label has made him look such a buffoon, it is understandable that Tony Knowles and his advisors are deeply anxious to clean up his tacky, one-night slag image.'

Ms Taylor, who was shortly to be married to Roy Greenslade, then editor of the *Daily Mirror* and subsequently a prominent commentator on media affairs, was invited to Tony's house in the Lake District, an appropriate setting to interview a man wishing to present himself as 'at heart an innocent outdoors enthusiast, the sort of chap commonly found on the Duke of Edinburgh's Award Scheme'.

'Hey, Knowlsy! Couple of pictures of you fishing,' proposed Ally. 'Then you can go up and down the lake a couple of times, dry off and what about chopping up a couple of those logs? That would make a nice shot.

'Don't mention anything about sex stories. Tony will only be talking about waterskiing,' he stipulated.

However, Tony was in no mood to forget the allegations of his former girlfriend.

'That bloody bitch who told all them lies about me . . . if I saw her, I'd crack her one on the jaw,' he expostulated in a desperate attempt at exculpation.

On he went in similar vein with Ally, the press agent, valiantly trying to stem the tide of reminiscence.

Ms Taylor continued:

A calmer, more subdued Tony sits quietly for some moments. Then, just as the press agent thinks that the outburst is over, Tony perks up. He says the first thing that comes into his head when he is stuck for words and a female is in the room: 'Hey, why don't we go to bed? I'll tell you everything you want to know about them girls.'

Ms Taylor, perhaps concluding that she was unlikely to learn anything more about waterskiing, made her excuses and left.

Tony's notoriety brought him some bizarre offers of work. He rejected an invitation from Noel Edmonds to compete in a Jumping In and Out of Your Y-Fronts challenge on *The Late Late Breakfast Show*. Nor did he agree to co-operate with *That's Life*, which was running a consumer item about a full-size table delivered to a customer which had a rutted (*sic*) slate and, wait for it, no pockets or cushions. *That's Life*'s idea was for Tony to play a few shots, bringing the ball not off the cushion but the redoubtable bottom of Mollie Sugden, doyenne of the sitcom *Are You Being Served?*

Undercutting a tournament which had been set up by Barry Hearn, Kruger represented an event in Beijing in 1987 as a kind of diplomatic triumph. Prize money of £120,000, with a first prize of £35,000, attracted the participation of a decent field. Unfortunately, he forgot to say that the first prize was £35,000 only if one of the two Chinese competitors, neither of whom was much cop, happened to win it. Parrott won the tournament but received only his £3,500 guarantee. Martin Clark, a young player new to the professional ranks, was runner-up but received not the advertised second prize of £20,000 but only his £1,500 guarantee. By the time Kruger had deducted his contributions to gifts for their Chinese hosts and a share of the costs of making a video (which was never screened), Clark netted £120.12 from the trip.

Clark, who had signed for Kruger on the day that he had handed over his £3,300 first prize in the Everards Open, only to have it erroneously booked as a loan and be charged interest on it, was rescued from impending financial disaster by an accountant, Ian Beech, and by Ian Doyle, who became his manager. It transpired – a familiar story – that Kruger had incorrectly charged several bills against him, including one from a hotel in which he had never set foot. Between November 1987 and May 1989, he received no financial statement from Kruger. When one was finally forthcoming, it revealed that Clark was owed £12,000.

Tony Drago had an even more devastating experience. He borrowed £22,000 from the bank that Kruger used in Brighton, the Midland, to pay off a debt to his former manager, Neil Westfield. The loan was guaranteed by Framework Management, but the money was represented to Westfield as a payment by Kruger for taking over Drago's management. Drago ended up still owing money to his former manager and to the bank. Kruger had effectively acquired Drago as a client for nothing.

In the fullness of time, it emerged all too clearly that Kruger had betrayed the trust of several players who had given him total control of their financial affairs. Knowles's mortgage was not paid, neither was that of Hughes; Reynolds had his electricity cut off; Clark's car was almost re-possessed; and Higgins's alimony payments were not, in fact, paid. It was the complaints of Higgins that brought down Kruger's snooker empire. He claimed that Kruger owed him £51,356 and pursued those claims to the bitter end, Framework Management being wound up on his application with debts of £374,361.

Higgins also pursued Kruger through the disciplinary procedures of the WPBSA. A hearing conducted by Gavin Lightman QC ruled that he had brought snooker into disrepute and ordered him to be publicly reprimanded. There was nothing further that he could order since Kruger, who had amazingly become a board member of WPBSA, had resigned on the eve of the hearing.

On the evening of the judgement, John Virgo, who was then the WPBSA chairman, played an exhibition at the official opening of Kruger's snooker club in Brighton, Harry Potter's. (This was before J.K. Rowling published any of her books.) In due course, The Kruger Organisation wanted to turn it into a student nightclub. The proposed contract involved the Sussex University Students' Union sharing liability of a Harry Potter's brewery loan, investing £50,000 of its own and giving 60 per cent of profits to TKO. When the university's lawyers aborted the deal, TKO attempted to sue for £200,000. Grotesquely, Kruger had also received the WPBSA's Services to Snooker award in 1988 through the simple expedient of signing for votes as proxy to his players.

The International Travel Bureau of Worthing, a Kruger company which, in preference to thousands of others in the British Isles, was selected by his fellow board members as the WPBSA's official travel agents, collapsed with debts of £470,000. ITB, it emerged, was a wholly owned subsidiary of Kruger Holdings, of which Howard Kruger held 25 per cent and his father Jeffrey 75 per cent. It showed a net deficiency on its last accounts of £11,231, having shown a surplus the previous year of £33,592 through creating a 'revaluation reserve' of £138,000 for ITB. Contrary to accepted accountancy practice, goodwill had been arbitrarily re-valued from within, but for which a deficiency of some £100,000 would have been shown.

Del Simmons was still very much at the helm of WPBSA at the time and his daughter, Julie, was by then working for Kruger. As the official receiver began to make enquiries into Framework Management and ITB, it was found that several documents had been damaged by a flood. He was also told that Kruger and an associate had been observed pouring water into the office computer.

A public examination by the official receiver in Brighton had to be twice postponed because Kruger claimed that he was suffering from nervous anxiety and depression, the chief symptom of which was said to be a constant grinding of the teeth. This necessitated him wearing a mouthguard at all times.

Kruger also made himself a nuisance outside snooker. To enhance his credibility, he claimed to be the exclusive manager of Mike Gatting, then England's cricket captain. In fact, this was the loosest of arrangements and Gatting even had great difficulty in extracting from Kruger payment for an advert for his benefit programme. Claiming to have introduced Chris Eubank to Barry Hearn, Kruger sued under the banner of Framework Exhibitions for half the proceeds of the Eubank fights that Hearn promoted. When Hearn won the case and pursued his costs, he found that Framework Exhibitions had been wound up, leaving him holding this particular financial baby.

Finally, in October 1991 at Brighton County Court, Judge David Jackson disqualified Kruger for five years from holding any company directorship: 'Today, we have seen the seedier side of sporting life where money is the driving issue and a lot of people are getting hurt by people who, like this defendant, are incompetent, reckless or worse. This is a clear example of the unhappier side of professional sport. When money comes into it, sport creeps out of the window. Kruger should certainly have looked after his businesses, but he certainly did not.'

Even then, Kruger surfaced a little later when he tried to muscle in on the world of muscle. Operating from Iceland, Kruger attempted to persuade several competitors in the World's Strongest Man competition to reassign their contracts to him. Only when details of his snooker career, previously unknown to them, were drawn to their attention did they withdraw from this intention.

Of the snooker players who were under Kruger's care, he dealt no one's career an immediately fatal blow, but Higgins never got over it financially and none ever entirely recovered the ground they had lost under his mismanagement. In the short term, the affairs of Johnson and Clark were sorted out by Doyle. Knowles, whose game was in decline, survived for a while but various business ventures intended to restore his finances merely added to his problems. Peter Francisco, who had been carried away with new-found wealth and glamour, was soon skint and in 1995 was shamefully revealed to have been guilty of match rigging. Roe, who never recovered his best form, never got out of financial difficulties including, finally, bankruptcy; Drago staggered from one crisis to another; Reynolds, who already had a drink problem, plummeted down the rankings as this problem grew worse; Hughes, who almost lost everything, doggedly recovered by acquiring a snooker club in Dublin and making it sufficiently successful to start enjoying the game again.

Fate dealt Clark's snooker career a final blow unrelated to his Kruger experience. Having reached nine world ranking quarter-finals and spent several years in the top 16, he was forced into retirement as discs in his neck had gradually worn away through the repetitive strain of having his head down on his cue but with his eyeline elevated to the view of the shot. If he tried to play for any substantial length of time, he was in agony and the condition was inoperable without great danger.

Johnson played until past his 50th birthday and was for several years the oldest player on the world ranking circuit. The glory and the euphoria of winning the 1986 world title soon exacted its price, much worse than reporters shinning up the drainpipe of his house, much worse than the pressure, pressure, pressure to do this, do that, appear here, appear there, decide this, decide that. Nor did the rip-off artists neglect him. The JJ 986 number plate was for sale at £200 but the price went up to £2,500 when it transpired who wanted it. He paid it anyway.

Thinking he needed a high-powered big city manager, he signed for Kruger. He was never paid £10,000 from his BCE contract which was instead held by Kruger against future commissions. Prize money of £2,744 paid in New Zealand currency for the New Zealand Masters was shown only as £2,500 in his accounts and he was charged £1,500 for expenses even though the sponsors had, in fact, paid them. His bill at the Beverley Hills Hotel included, by an extraordinary coincidence, the exact amount that Doyle had had deleted from his own bill after it had erroneously been charged there instead of to Kruger. An exhibition engagement aboard the QE2 ended in farce. As the vessel was in dock, it was assumed a normal game of snooker would be possible, but when Johnson broke off, every single ball rolled to a side cushion.

But worse than the money, worse than the shattered hopes, worse than the missed opportunities, was the feeling that all he had gained was drifting away. As champion, more was expected of him on the table, but even if he had maintained the blissfully untroubled state of mind with which he had been blessed at Sheffield, he could never have maintained the inspiration. He was still only 10th in the rankings and even if he could have played to that standard he would still have suffered his fair share of defeats. In fact, the on- and off-table pressures soon enveloped him so comprehensively that he could hardly win a match until he somehow mustered his best form of the season to reach the 1987 world final.

He tried his best but could not escape the thought that he did not again want to go through some of the experiences which had followed from winning in 1986. He was quite happy to lose to Davis 18–14. His wife put it neatly: 'Joe loves snooker, but he's the kind of player who wants the lights and the TV cameras to be switched off when the last ball goes down. And then he wants to go home.'

Two years after winning the title, he was financially back at square one – but now with an expensive house to run. He still loved the game but did not love everything that went with it. His results were not so bad by most standards but not very good by the standards by which he now had to be judged. Pressure had crushed some of his spirit. Playing in the UK Championship at Preston, he had his first heart scare. Taken to hospital in the interval, he came back to win. Even in pain, his sense of humour had been unaffected. Offered a beta blocker of a type that was on the banned list, he quipped: 'No, thank you. I'd sooner die.'

At the start of the 1990–91 season, he told Mary Riddell of the *Daily Mirror* that he was:

> broke, humiliated and depressed. The strain was really growing inside me. If I wasn't going to start winning, what could I do with my life? That was when I decided to get fit, live my life correctly and start being a snooker player rather than a celebrity.

Nine months of this and he came to the Crucible in April 1991 three stone lighter to play Dennis Taylor. He lost 10–6 and it seemed as if his colossal efforts had been for nothing.

'I fell back into my old ways, eating not practising,' he said. He smoked like a chimney and, abandoning all dietary constraints, ballooned out again. He was consumed by inertia until Terryll pushed him into going to the fitness club. Foolishly, he went straight into his full-peak fitness workout. He collapsed in the shower in unbearable pain.

Within ten minutes, thanks to the trainer of the fitness centre and the prompt arrival of an ambulance, he was in intensive care, fighting for his life. The doctors told him his career was over. He could have collected over £100,000 in insurance and, in addition, £3,000 a month for life. With an overdraft and his £200,000 house on the market with no takers, this made, on the face of it, financial sense. But how would he have felt when snooker came on television?

He cut his smoking from 30 to a handful a day. He had a proper holiday. Tests told him a few weeks later that his arteries were clear. He wanted to play. What else could he do with his life? Doyle got his affairs in order and Johnson survived on the circuit, not setting the world on fire with his results but not doing too badly. Once he was out of the wood, though, he embarked on certain business ventures about which he kept Doyle in the dark. Doyle said that he could not continue to manage him on this basis. Johnson spoke of Doyle's 'bullying ways'. They parted and were never again on good terms.

14

HEARN: TOO CLEVER BY HALF

FOR BARRY HEARN, JANUARY 1991 WAS THE WORST OF MONTHS AND the best of months.

WPBSA, still under the direction of Del Simmons, had been unable to land a sponsor for the 1989 UK Championship. Hearn provided one, Stormseal, on condition that he took over that part of the BBC TV contract in a back-to-back deal and that he kept the whole of the gate money. WPBSA was also lumbered with the costs of the qualifying competition.

It looked like a mighty coup for Hearn. All went well with this arrangement in 1989 but just after the 1990 tournament Stormseal went into receivership. On arriving home from his Christmas break in Florida, Hearn learnt that he would have to make good a £299,000 shortfall in prize money. Hendry, for instance, had earned £110,000 for beating Davis 16–15 in a dramatic final.

For all his flamboyance, Hearn was not carrying £299,000 around in his back pocket and it was a large amount to extract from the cash flow of any but the mightiest of businesses. Everyone was eventually paid but, no doubt about it, it was a setback.

Hearn had also been forced to reduce the prize money for his Coalite World Matchplay Championship on ITV in December 1990 from £250,000 to £200,000 but omitted to tell the press, who thus unwittingly colluded with him in deceiving the public.

One remarkable stroke of business enabled him to recover his lost ground. Rupert Murdoch had just launched Sky TV, of which Eurosport was then part, and Hearn had persuaded him that a £2.5

million event, including £1 million in prize money, on the model of Wimbledon's tennis championships, with men's and women's singles and doubles, a mixed doubles and a junior event, was just what he needed to drive sales of satellite dishes. It did not do so to any very significant extent, but Hearn certainly staged a lively tournament at the National Exhibition Centre, Birmingham.

There was some preliminary unpleasantness. In 1988, Hearn, Frank Warren, the boxing promoter, and Bill Sinrich, representing Mark McCormack's Trans World International, had formed a triumvirate to promote the World Matchplay Championship, which ITV preferred to the WPBSA's World Doubles, and the World Open Championships. However, when it became clear that Hearn proposed to promote this alone, Sinrich threatened legal action and the event was re-branded as the World Masters with Sinrich picking up the production contract for TWI.

A roving crane camera captured action on 'outside' tables to supplement traditional coverage from the main arena. Unfortunately, it was parked two tables away when James Wattana embarked on a 147 break. Short of charging heedlessly across those two matches, it could not be moved in time. Eurosport dealt with this misfortune by simply not mentioning that a maximum had been made although newspapers, of course, reported it next day. It also transpired that for all the £1 million prize fund, no provision had been made for any bonus for a 147. 'I was thinking of a big money,' said Wattana wistfully at his press conference.

With Hearn determined to whip up maximum international content, there were some unusual characters in the field, including Rui Chapeu, a Brazilian who played in all white from shoes to cap. Juan Castaneda, carrying the hopes of Panama, had never seen a snooker table prior to his arrival and had played only a Latin American cue game in which flukes are fouls. Very creditably, he made a 50 break but could only express his consternation fruitlessly to the referee as his opponent fluked virtually every colour in the clinching frame. Some were puzzled by the disparity between the encyclopaedic knowledge of angles and the poor potting of an

Austrian, Gerfried Kotzinger. This turned out to be because he mainly played three-cushion billiards on pocketless tables.

These colourful characters flavoured the early stages of the event but, in the end, class told as the familiar faces dominated the later stages and Jimmy White beat Tony Drago 10–6 for what was then a record first prize of £200,000. White had also won the two previous tournaments on the circuit, pocketing £70,000 from the Coalite World Matchplay and £60,000 from the Mercantile Classic, in the final of which he ended Hendry's 35-match winning streak in ranking events, so this was the best-paid month of his life.

The junior event introduced three players who within ten years would each win a world title: John Higgins, who won the £5,000 first prize on this occasion; Mark Williams, whom he beat in the final; and Ronnie O'Sullivan, whom he beat in the quarter-finals and whom Hearn was shortly to sign to a five-year contract. Quinten Hann, who was to achieve some fame but more notoriety, became at 13 the youngest player ever to make a century on television.

Karen Corr, who won the singles, and Allison Fisher, who won the doubles with Stacey Hillyard and mixed doubles with Steve Davis, dominated the women's events and made sizeable contributions to Hearn's coffers in management percentages, but Hearn's high hopes for the women's game, based on this stable and a contract to promote the women's championship for ten years, failed to come to fruition. He boasted that he would make Fisher, seven times women's world champion and the best woman player snooker had ever seen, its first millionairess, but their association was to end in discord: 'All he ever got me was some free clothes from Dorothy Perkins,' said Fisher. As women's snooker failed to take off, Hillyard joined the police force and Fisher departed to the United States, where she was joined later by Corr. They swiftly became the best two players on the much more lucrative women's 9-ball pool circuit.

Boxing and events linked to television became Hearn's priority. His own production company, Matchroom TV, was able to sell countless packages, many of them low-key, to a multiplicity of broadcasters. The growth of satellite and cable TV meant there were many more potential buyers. Annually, he ran a league, which he initially sold to Eurosport, and a World Mixed Doubles championship, for which he selected the four pairs it comprised, which he also sold to Eurosport. His World Seniors Championship was aired on Screensport in 1991; the World Trickshots Championship had various buyers.

But this did not add up to all that much, or threaten to do so, until Hearn decided to offer Sky the World Matchplay Championship, which had been in abeyance for two years, the World Seniors and the World Mixed Doubles, with the further prospect of offering them his league. He did so while WPBSA, on whose board he and Davis were serving at the time, was still negotiating its own Sky contract for three world ranking events. The WPBSA board refused Hearn's application for sanction of the World Matchplay, the World Seniors and the World Mixed Doubles and deferred those for the Trickshots and the league, as they had no substantial objection to these continuing on Eurosport.

Once the application for the Sky package was refused, it was clear even to Hearn that there was an irresolvable conflict of interest between his own project and his fiduciary duties as a WPBSA director. The starting date for the World Matchplay Championship was particularly contentious: 12 May, only a week after the conclusion of the Embassy World Championship on BBC. Worse, with WPBSA sanction, Sky would have had the clearest possible incentive to hype the World Matchplay as an alternative world championship, as was common practice in the world of boxing. Hearn and Sky did exactly this when the Professional Darts Council (in reality all the best players) split away from the British Darts Organisation and the BBC to organise a rival world championship.

In the High Court, three companies that Hearn controlled, Matchroom Snooker Ltd, Matchroom TV Ltd and World Matchplay Ltd, sought injunctions against WPBSA's refusal to grant sanctions to his companies. An initial hearing limited the scope of the trial to the World Seniors and Judge Robin Jacobs ruled for WPBSA. The thrust of his judgment was that WPBSA was an appropriately recognised governing body for the sport and that unless it made a clearly unreasonable decision it was not for the court to intervene. Costs were awarded against Hearn and he took the matter no further. (The law was not in his favour at the time but would have been after the passing of the 1998 Competition Act.)

Meanwhile, Hearn signed a £10 million deal with Sky to promote eight world title fights in a year. Since Chris Eubank was the only world champion he was managing – and he only under the World Boxing Organisation banner – he could not afford to be careless in his choice of opponents. He had seduced Eubank from ITV and negotiated the deal personally with Kelvin MacKenzie, the flamboyant editor of *The Sun*, who had moved to Sky but was not an expert on sport.

Subsequently, MacKenzie finished on the wrong end of a power struggle with Sam Chisholm, then Murdoch's right-hand man, and departed from Sky, leaving Hearn to negotiate future boxing deals more on the credibility of the contests he was offering and less on the supposedly promotable qualities of the principal combatant. In a way, boxing suited him because it is a world in which a manager's talent for manipulation has fullest scope – in contrast to those sports which have open-to-all tournaments, impracticable in boxing admittedly.

Despite previous disagreements, Hearn did re-sign Jimmy White and, with Ronnie O'Sullivan signing a five-year contract on his 16th birthday and Steve Davis, of course, remaining firmly in the camp, maintained a snooker management stable of sorts. Most of his former clients had expressed various disappointments but either went quietly or resolved to write off any grievances, justified or not, in the interests of getting on with their careers.

Hearn made his attitude to any dissatisfied former clients plain: 'If they believe there was mismanagement, take the necessary action. Sue! Don't talk about it. Any child can whisper behind corners. Be a man! Sue! Because there was no mismanagement. Now I'm into boxing, I deal with proper men – men who stand up to be counted every day of their lives.'

One boxer who did stand up to be counted, far preferable in that profession to lying down to be counted, was Steve Collins. Actually, Collins did not do the suing but mounted a successful defence when Hearn did, claiming 25 per cent of his earnings from three fights under a management agreement which Collins argued had already lapsed because Hearn was in breach of it. Hearn wanted £550,000.

Defeat in the High Court would have cost Collins more than he had: not just the £550,000 but around £1.5 million in costs. Instead, it left Hearn facing a seven-figure bill. It is one of Hearn's more endearing qualities that he takes defeat gracefully: 'A bad day at the races . . . these things happen. I shall go home and lick my wounds and see where I am going from there.'

In terms of major boxing promotions, Hearn was going nowhere as the Collins affair virtually finished him at this level. He continued to promote at the York Hall, Bethnal Green, and other small halls, largely to provide low budget material for Matchroom TV to sell television packages, mostly abroad, and reverted to his early instincts in exploiting underdeveloped markets, effectively taking over professional 9-ball pool and professional darts worldwide. He also became big in tenpin bowling – or as big as it would allow – and continued to promote a day long anglingfest for Sky, *Fishomania*, besides applying his effervescent energies to Leyton Orient.

Exemplifying the triumph of hype over experience, the cheerful, gregarious Barry had ignited a mood of initial optimism and community involvement at Brisbane Road following his purchase from Tony Wood of a 76 per cent holding in the club for £5. Orient's opening match of the 1995–96 campaign against the mighty Torquay United drew 8,221 souls through the gate, about eight times the average attendance of the previous season. Such was the congestion that the kick-off was delayed by ten minutes, as was, by extension, the on-pitch wedding at half-time of two supporters with the Revd Alan Comfort, a former Orient player, conducting the necessarily short service. As if to illustrate the power of prayer, Orient prevailed 1–0 through a goal in the 77th minute. Playing the grants system astutely, Barry kept the club alive but survival was the only ambition he could afford as Orient sank into the sediment of the Football League's lowest division before rising triumphantly to promotion from it in 2005–06.

15

WHITE AND HIGGINS: TRAGICOMEDIANS

JIMMY WHITE AND ALEX HIGGINS BOTH BEHAVED AS IF THEY HAD THE secret of perpetual youth. Snooker was the glue which precariously held their undisciplined lives together. In decline, White kept his dignity, his good humour and his love of the game; Higgins existed in a state of paranoid denial, looking back in anger and bitterness and forward only to an abyss to which he was perpetually drawn with only a weakening instinct for survival as protection.

White was a top class player whose career came to be defined not by winning ten world ranking titles and twenty-three in all but by his defeats in six world finals at the Crucible. 'The greatest player never to be world champion' was to be his professional epitaph. His was a life which encompassed innumerable pleasures of the moment but not the true fulfilment of his talent. He embodied the Keatsian aspiration to live a life of sensation rather than of thought.

In 1984, against Steve Davis, he gave himself a chance to win from the unpromising position of 12–4 down but lost 18–16; in 1990, having beaten Davis in the semi-finals, he left innumerable safeties well short of the baulk cushion as Stephen Hendry, with deadly potting from distance and heavy scoring once he was in, beat him comfortably 18–12. When Hendry unexpectedly fell to Steve James in the 1991 quarter-finals, it seemed as if it was going to be White's year at last. Unfortunately for him, John Parrott produced a superb opening session to drub him 7–0 and nursed that margin until victory arrived at 18–11.

In 1992, White was flying again, having won the British and European Opens, but from 14–8 up against Hendry in the final, lost 18–14. This was not entirely his fault. Hendry kept his nerve and his resolve in the face of daunting arrears, but there were mistakes from White also. The first frame of the last session – when he was still leading 14–10 – should have been his, but he did not make sure of the last red which, barring two snookers, would have put him 15–10 up. He seemed strangely unfocused, as if he could not identify a key shot and apply himself to it with just a modicum of extra care. He seemed to want to take everything in his natural stride and it probably did him no good to have so many friends and hangers-on around him, even in his dressing-room, when what he needed was at least a few moments of reflection and repose. As it was, Hendry built up an unstoppable momentum.

Early in the 1992–93 season, White won the Rothmans Grand Prix and UK Championship but was not to win another ranking title until April 2004. By the end of that season, he was starting to struggle. Somehow he reached the final at the Crucible but was overwhelmed 18–5 by Hendry. His best and last chance for the title came the following year. After a poor pre-Christmas season, he reached a couple of semi-finals on the run-in to the Crucible. In the final there against Hendry, the title was his for the taking in the deciding frame of 35. In play, 13 in front and with enough open reds to secure the trophy, he was undone by missing a simple black from its spot that he will remember to his dying day.

'When he got in, I was delighted for him,' said Hendry, reflecting on the camaraderie of their rivalry. 'Anyone else and I would have hated it. I was ready to shake his hand and really congratulate him because he deserves the title.' All this was forgotten when White choked on the fateful black and Hendry rose from his chair to make 58 for frame, match and championship. The following year, White reached the semi-finals but after that he was fighting an increasingly arduous battle against decline.

As the loser of six world finals, he tended to spend his summers getting over winters which had culminated in grievous disappointment at the Crucible. It took him longer and longer to get into gear the following season until eventually there came a season when he could not get into gear at all. There are always more tournaments but, even in a career as long as his, only so many Crucibles and even fewer realistic chances of the title. To have been so near and yet so far from consummating his heart's desire in 1992 and 1994 gave him anguish which could not be assuaged by headlong pursuit of transient pleasure. As he grew older, some of life's more uncomfortable realities caught up with him as well. He never lost his love of the game, which offered all he needed to maintain the lifestyle to which he had become accustomed, and he began to live a little more moderately, but by this time he was hanging on around the fringe of the leading group of players.

Perhaps the right management could have mitigated his propensity for unwitting self-destruction, but he never wanted the kind of manager who would give him advice he preferred not to hear.

It might have seemed a good idea in January 1995 to appear in an advertising campaign for Cover Up, 'a cosmetic breakthrough' which would replace bald spots by 'enhancing the hundreds of minute little hairs that still remain on bald or thinning patches'. To lend authenticity to the necessary 'before' and 'after' pictures, he agreed to undergo a 90-minute operation under general anaesthetic at the grandly named National Centre for Cosmetic Surgery in Warley, West Midlands.

The operation involved inserting a plastic extender under the skin of the scalp and dragging together the remaining hair. Later treatment was expected to involve transplanting hairs one by one from one part of his head to another. The pictures were indeed impressive and may have prompted some of the follicly challenged to send £15.95 to EMG Medical Group, based at the same address in Warley, West Midlands, for a hair activator pack.

This promotional literature understandably made no mention of the horrendous facial swelling which White suffered, so painful that he could not even rest one side of his face on a pillow. He was in such a state that he had to withdraw from the European Open in Antwerp, which had serious implications in terms of ranking points since he had not progressed beyond the last 16 of any of the season's preceding three world ranking events. Together with the 1989 British Open, the 1990 Mercantile Classic and the 1993 International Open, this gave him a more extensive record of withdrawals than that of any other prominent player.

White's bald patch did recede after a visit to a Paris clinic but, a few weeks later, the National Centre for Cosmetic Surgery was raided by the police. Four years earlier, EMG Ltd had been prosecuted for advertising an anti-wrinkle cream which proved to have ingredients which caused skin cancer. They were fined £3,500. The Medicines Control Agency, who had instigated that prosecution, were alerted by the White adverts and, armed with council warrants and with police on standby, smashed down the doors of its premises. There had been allegations that thousands of prescription-only drugs had been illegally manufactured and sold from the premises. Hair restoring and anti-wrinkle creams were seized amidst suggestions that drugs and other substances had been poured down drains.

Moving from farce to potential tragedy, White noted in April that year a testicular lump. This was a test of nonchalance even for him: 'Oh yeah, they took it away. They sort of lifted it out. But I can still have children and things. I can still function. You know, function.' The arrival of a son, Tommy Tiger, to join his four daughters bore this out.

In the previous summer, 1994, still raw from losing the deciding frame of his world final against Hendry, which was his for the taking, he had allowed his drinking to spiral out of control and was caught driving while four times over the limit. He acknowledged humbly and sincerely that he had been grossly at fault. He could have gone to jail but was sentenced instead to 120 hours' community service and turned even this into a means of increasing the sum total of joy in the world.

Harry and George, both in their 80s, became particular favourites of his in the old people's home where he was putting in his community service time. They enjoyed their days out with him at Kempton Park or similar haunts – too much on one occasion.

'He had a couple too many of the Guinness, didn't he? Couldn't take his medication that night. They put me on cleaning kitchen floors after that.'

As for his own imbibing, he took it steadier, most of the time. 'I'm not drinking as such,' he tended to say.

Real life kept catching up with him, far more often than when his future as a top player was unrolling endlessly in front of him. Bereavement hit him hard. When his eldest brother, Martin, died at the age of 52, this close family appropriated his body from the undertaker's, dressed him in his best suit and hat, set a drink in front of him and dealt him in as they played cards, as they so often had. On his way to the cemetery, a short detour was taken to Wimbledon dog track, where Martin had spent many happy if not always remunerative hours. His mother died shortly afterwards.

Gambling was another of Jimmy's addictions and it was only late in his career – too late – that he discovered the benefits of moderation. Quite without irony, he invited Alan Fraser of the *Daily Mail* to Kempton Park to inform him that he had given up gambling and proved this by staking only £100 on the first race, a winner as it happened.

This, of course, was not gambling – obsessive, thousands every race gambling – but having a bet, one of life's pleasures. He also revealed that he had been cheated of £55,000 some 15 years earlier by a business associate and supposed friend. The Inland Revenue sent him bankrupt.

'It's me own fault. I was probably stoned at the time. It was during one of my states of JD [Jack Daniel's] and Coke.'

Drink was certainly one of his ways of dealing with pre-match pressure: 'I used to be put to bed the night before a match and

I'd sneak out down the fire escape to a nightclub. The pressure seemed to disappear after the fifth drink.'

Given to many forms of excess as he was, Jimmy was quick to play down parallels sometimes drawn between him and Alex Higgins: 'I'm more of a flyer than a tearaway. The difference between me and him is that he's out to beat the system, always has been. If you try to beat the system and you haven't got the right kind of back-up, you'll end up completely fucked. I'm different from Higgins. I've never gone out to fuck the system. I'm more interested in playing the system.'

While Jimmy had an engaging personality which encouraged forgiveness of his misdemeanours, Higgins adopted an unapologetically confrontational stance with the world which encouraged authority to do its worst.

Higgins accumulated a notoriously lengthy disciplinary record, conviction and punishment well deserved in most cases. The exceptions were when the WPBSA overreacted, as when he was fined £500 for one unguarded expletive – 'I'm fucking back' – which was picked up on a table microphone in the very moment of his dramatic victory over Steve Davis in the 1985 Benson and Hedges Masters, or when it tried to improve the case against him with a stitch-up.

The worst of these followed an incident backstage at the Crucible in 1994, his farewell appearance there as it transpired. He had lost 10–6 to Ken Doherty and was asked to give a urine sample for a drugs test.

Dr David Forster, a Sheffield neurosurgeon who had become WPBSA's medical advisor almost by chance because he happened to live locally to the Crucible, where snooker drug tests were first conducted, alleged that Higgins had failed to provide a sample under the regulations. In fact, he had and it had duly been divided according to customary practice into two bottles, designated the A and B samples. The B sample is analysed only if the A sample proves positive.

Higgins was not in the best of moods. He and Forster had words and as Forster wrote in his complaint: 'One of the sample bottles became broken.' He did not specify who had broken it, although Higgins had, in fact, thrown it against a wall.

When the A sample was later tested, it was found to be negative and there was no need of the B sample. However, with one bottle broken, Forster told Higgins that failure to provide another sample would contravene the WPBSA's regulations and that refusal would be considered to equate to having given a positive sample. This position was supported by Ann Yates, the WPBSA's tournament director, who stated to the ensuing disciplinary tribunal that she had pointed out the relevant rule to Higgins in the WPBSA's handbook.

Embarrassingly, when Mrs Yates was invited by Higgins's lawyer, Robin Falvey, to point out this rule, she was unable to do so, perhaps not surprisingly as no such rule existed. Mrs Yates believed it did and perhaps it should have done, but in fact the rules were silent on this matter.

So the situation was (1) Higgins had given a proper sample; (2) there was no justification for any request for a second sample; and, amazingly, (3) that even if Higgins had refused the first request to give a sample, there was nothing in the rules to say that this should be construed as tantamount to a positive. That was how amateurishly the rules had been drawn.

The tribunal, comprising three members of the WPBSA board, had no alternative but to accept Falvey's submission that there was no case to answer but on the spur of the moment said they wanted to consider two other matters: the throwing down of the sample and the flourishing by Higgins in a subsequent press conference of a packet of Marlboro cigarettes when the tournament was sponsored by a rival brand, Embassy.

Falvey immediately argued that these matters had not formed part of the original complaint and that no proper opportunity had been given for the gathering and rebuttal of evidence. All this was eight months after the original incident and one key piece of evidence, the broken bottle, had disappeared. Despite Falvey's protests, Higgins was found guilty, the WPBSA declining to specify either then or later on what charges. He was fined £5,000 and suspended for a year, both punishments suspended for two years conditional on his future conduct.

Falvey responded by filing 17 complaints against Dr Forster, Mrs Yates, the WPBSA, their solicitor, Matthew McCloy, and all members of the board involved in either this disciplinary fiasco or the one in 1992 when five of the seven charges against Higgins had been dismissed. On that occasion, Higgins had been fined £500 after being found guilty of verbal abuse of Mrs Yates and 'failing to accord the match referee, John Street' proper dignity and respect.

Among the complaints dismissed was one by Ian Doyle, Stephen Hendry's manager, that Higgins had used gratuitously foul and abusive language to him about Hendry and one from Hendry himself, who complained of remarks Higgins made to him after their match in the 1991 UK Championship. There was certainly a striking difference of recollection about what Higgins had said after Hendry had completed his 9–2 victory. Higgins remembered his remark as: 'Well done, Stephen, you were a little bit lucky.' Hendry heard this as: 'Up your arse, you cunt.'

Snooker insiders formed their own opinions as to which of these two versions carried the greater ring of truth, but when it eventually came to the day of the hearing, much postponed, neither Doyle nor Hendry made an appearance to give evidence and these charges were dismissed.

The WPBSA had been notified three weeks earlier that it was unlikely that Doyle or Hendry would give evidence, but this information was not passed on to Falvey, who therefore incurred much needless work and expenditure of time in preparing an appropriate cross-examination. There were also many instances of lack of even-handedness in the pre-trial proceedings which revealed the absurdity of WPBSA attempting to act as both prosecutor and judge.

The WPBSA's rules did not allow for appeal against disciplinary decisions. Neither did it seem at all likely that it would find its own board or appointees guilty of any offence whatsoever. Falvey's 17 complaints remained indefinitely on file.

Higgins could have had no more valiant fighter on his side than Falvey, but this did not prevent him, a few years down the road, unceremoniously ditching him and leaving him to whistle for his money, some £50,000.

Growing progressively more obnoxious and argumentative, Higgins freely insulted referees and opponents as he plunged down the rankings, but numerous official reports of misbehaviour were not proceeded with because this would have brought into play the 17 complaints he had instituted against WPBSA and its functionaries. In this respect, there was an impasse, an armed truce.

Many were prepared to befriend him but with all he wore his welcome out, even, eventually, Dave Moorhouse, a former policeman with 30 years' service, who twice had him in long term residence at the Pymgate Lodge, a small hotel of which he was the proprietor.

'I feel desperately sorry for Alex, but I can't help him anymore. He needs medical advice,' said Moorhouse when he finally gave up the struggle.

'He's a real Jekyll and Hyde. When he's good, he's charming. On Christmas Day and Boxing Day, he helped us serve guests and tidy up. I just feared it was too good to be true. I am genuinely fond of him and so were the guests, but then he snaps. Alex suffers from great highs and great lows. He has sung love songs outside my window at three o'clock in the morning, woken me up and asked me if I want a sleeping tablet.'

A late night fracas at the Pymgate ended with the police arresting Higgins as he cried: 'I'm a British spy. You can't do this to me.'

Stockport magistrates bound him over to keep the peace although he seemed incapable of keeping it for very long. Any lingering spark from the embers of any injustice ever done to him was likely to ignite an ungovernable rage, but any sympathy he might have aroused tended to be reduced by his wholesale rubbishing of the current top players as 'soulless, boring people', not a category into which Ronnie O'Sullivan, Jimmy White or even the quieter sorts like Stephen Hendry and Steve Davis would be placed by fair-minded folk.

'None of them were ever good enough to lace my boots,' he raved. 'I was the Tiger Woods of snooker.'

He had sunk to 156th in the world rankings by the time he lost 5–1 to the world no. 182 in the first qualifying event of a new season in August 1997. Truculent and troublesome, he was involved in a considerable amount of backstage bickering, some of which impinged on a public area. Police were summoned and he was escorted from the premises. Some 12 hours later, at 4 a.m., he was found by police sprawled on the ground outside a Plymouth nightclub. He said that he had been the victim of an 'unprovoked assault' with an iron bar.

He was taken to hospital with contusions to the side of his head. His right wrist, feared fractured, was found to be badly sprained, as was his right ankle. He was discharged after a few hours and sent word that he was unfit to play in the next qualifying event.

On his return to Manchester, he made his way to the house of Holly Hayse, a self-admitted former prostitute, who sometime earlier had told *The People*: 'I loved him. I still do, but I don't want to be with him anymore. He's too frightening.' She estimated – accurately or not – that she had spent £50,000 on him in the course of their relationship, in the first two years of which he had allegedly hit her frequently before she hired a boxer to hit him and warn him as to his future conduct. She had nevertheless allowed him to live in a caravan in her garden.

On his return from Plymouth, there was a row. Responding to a 999 call, police broke the door down. Ms Hayse (née Laura Croucher) was found hiding under a table. Higgins left after talking with police. An hour or so later, Higgins was back. There was another row. Neighbours noted 'a lot of shouting' and 'blood all over the place'. The police returned and discovered Higgins hiding behind a hedge in a nearby garden. An ambulance took him to hospital. He discharged himself before staff judged that he was fit to leave. Ms Hayse was arrested and released on bail, charged with stabbing Higgins.

At Salford Magistrates Court, she was cleared after the prosecution admitted that it faced 'evidential difficulties'. Higgins had been stabbed three times in his right arm but had made no official complaint and had declined to give evidence. As she left court, Ms Hayse said: 'Of course I stabbed him. I have admitted it from day one. But I still love him deeply. I want to marry him and put his life back on the rails.'

She gave her fullest account of the incident to John Stapleton on *The Time, The Place*. Asked why she had originally been attracted to Higgins, Hayse drawled: 'Well, it certainly wasn't his overcoats.' She has a droll sense of humour rather similar to that which Higgins can exhibit on his better days.

She admitted that she found 'his way of life quite stimulating'. At first, she did not know who he was: 'I thought he was a jockey, he was so skinny . . . After four dates, he turned up on my doorstep . . . After six months, I noticed his anger and aggressiveness. I never knew where he was. He would always have friends to buy him a drink because Alex never buys a drink. He would be very drunk when he returned home.

'Love is blind. It overlooks the other necessities of the relationship. I had to keep my valuables in the safe. I've only loved two men in my life. I still love my daughter's father. He's horrible, but I still love him. I'm still in love with Alex.'

On the night of the stabbing, Higgins arrived drunk. She gave him supper. 'I brought a knife in with me to cut up the chicken fajitas.' He started 'ranting and raving' and 'slapped me around'. She dialled 999 when he was distracted for a moment.

The police arrived, breaking down the door. They took Higgins to a taxi rank. A couple of hours later, he returned through the broken door and began assaulting her again. 'In a split second, I'd picked up the knife. That's all it took. It was as if I was in a dream and then I saw the blood all over my clothes.'

Many a fracas made the newspapers, including one at the Citywest Hotel, Dublin. Higgins had left a champions dinner held just before the Irish Masters after pouring two glasses of wine into the pocket of Jim Elkins, tournament director of the Benson and Hedges Masters, not an action likely to guarantee an invitation to a similar function at Wembley the following year. At 6 a.m., the police were called to the Citywest after an incident which had left Higgins with a black eye.

Twice, he was struck by cancer. In 1996, he had an operation for cancer of the palate and in 1998 the disease returned in his throat. The *Daily Express* rang Jimmy White to see if he had his latest phone number. In his helpful way, White said that if there was an interview to be done, Higgins could do with a sizeable cheque. Subsequently, a £10,000 fee was agreed.

However, when Anna Pukas of *The Express* contacted him, his response was not encouraging: 'I have no interest in talking to you or anyone else in the press. Why are you ringing me?'

This proved not to be his final word but, even so, he objected strongly to being photographed. Gaunt and emaciated as he was, this was understandable.

Doug James, a faithful friend of Higgins for 25 years, became the intermediary for arranging the details of the meeting in Manchester. These were complex enough for a John Le Carré novel.

First, Higgins vetoed the suggested hotel in favour of a wine bar, The Square Albert. James met Ms Pukas there and explained that Higgins was on the other side of the square. 'In the rainy gloom,' she wrote, 'I saw a red-capped figure hopping about between bollards and parked cars.' Her mobile rang. It was Higgins, furious that she had brought a photographer. 'Eventually, he agreed to let me walk across to him alone. We were barely 200 yards apart, but he wanted me to call him on the mobile to recite my movements. Suddenly, there was no sign of Higgins. My phone rang. There was some slack-mouthed muttering about not trusting us bastards.'

Higgins then spoke to his friend James and fixed another venue, a café round the corner, to whose toilet Higgins took the contract to read.

Apparently satisfied, he seized Ms Pukas by the hand and walked her at speed down a series of alleys.

'When you grow up in Belfast, like I did, you've got to know how the secret services operate. It's in your blood,' he said.

Eventually, at 11.45 p.m., they sat down in Pearl City, a restaurant in Manchester's Chinatown.

'Five minutes later, he had another of his mood swings,' wrote Pukas. 'He was standing up, croaking loudly, his face so close to mine he was showering it in spittle. He didn't like newspapers.'

With which, he flung the contract away and stormed off.

Next day, Doug James rang Pukas to attribute Higgins's behaviour to his illness. The day after, Higgins called to say he would talk about this if *The Express* would also pay his tax on the £10,000 fee. A photograph would be 'a grand in cash up front'. Pukas had 15 minutes to be at a pub called The Seven Oaks, 'where you will be collected and brought to me'.

They eventually met in a pub called The Circle. From there they adjourned to the Allied Irish Bank around the corner, where Higgins wanted to have his cheque examined: 'I'm Alex Higgins and I need to see the manager about this urgent enquiry.' The manager confirmed that it was a perfectly ordinary cheque.

'How long does it take to cash?' croaked Higgins. 'Seven days? I haven't got seven minutes.'

The cheque was never banked and *The Express*, quite legitimately, got its story.

Pukas remarked: 'Higgins has for years been dependent on the kindness of friends or fans who take him in. There can't be many of either left. He treats strangers like lackeys and friends like slaves. I've never heard him say "thank you" once to anyone.'

He always did have an unpleasant streak in his nature and it often did not take much to bring it out. In his best years, he had the capacity not only to play to an exceptionally high standard but also to do so in a unique, indeed inimitable way. At times, he even played well enough to give himself the illusion of the omnipotence he craved to keep at bay the vulnerability he feared. Even when there was, through age, a natural decline in sheer natural ability, he had the knowledge, the grit and the temperament to stay in the top flight. Whenever he was involved in a major match, he had a way of raising the emotional temperature of the arena.

His downfall was mostly his own fault, caused not merely by his failings but also his reluctance to address them, or admit them, even to himself. He had some injustices perpetrated upon him, particularly by the WPBSA, but fed so ravenously on this sense of injustice that this itself became a need. He obtained legal aid to sue WPBSA in the High Court; he joined with some 200 other smokers in a lawsuit against Embassy and Benson and Hedges, two prominent snooker sponsors. Both actions lapsed. Rather than press realistically for realistic compensation through realistic methods, he seemed to prefer a grandiose fantasy in which somehow everything would be made just as he wanted. No one could ever help him enough and there always had to be someone else to blame.

On the table, he was addicted to the death or glory situation with all eyes upon him. Sometimes self-preservation intervened but usually he was prepared to stake all even when he did not have to. It was a ghastly irony that his return to peak-time viewing in August 1999 should be in BBC's *Tobacco Wars* in the harrowingly real situation of his life-or-death battle against cancer. His eyes, flashing angrily, seemed uncommonly large, like pools of despair. His ears seemed enormous in relation to his gaunt, wasted face.

A few months later, relatively well recovered from surgery, some 50 gruelling radiotherapy sessions and still taking 38 prescribed tablets a day, he was due to record an interview for a video – for which he would have received a fee and royalties – at RTÉ's studios in Dublin. I had warned the independent producer, Freddie Madden, that the project would come to grief, but he was determined to press ahead with me as interviewer. Negotiations were conducted with a Dublin tailor, Louis Copeland, one of his long-standingly loyal supporters. The video was simply to celebrate his playing career. No awkward questions.

He had been observed two days earlier smoking long roll-up cigarettes and drinking cider as he hustled pool for £10 a game in the Gladstone Bar in Skerries, just outside Dublin, on whose premises he was believed to be living. Of course, he did not show up for the interview, thus costing Freddie his own and my airfares, my daily fee and various other expenses. A month later, Higgins met Freddie in a bar in Chelsea and charmed £200 out of him on the basis of some vague promise which was never fulfilled.

16

THE CIVIL WARS COMMENCE

IN THE '80s, BOTH BBC AND ITV HAD CONTRACTS WITH WPBSA TO cover four events annually. BBC's portfolio was the Grand Prix, the UK Championship, the Benson and Hedges Masters and, the jewel in the crown, the Embassy World Championship.

The first difficulties with ITV emerged in the late '80s and led to them pulling out of snooker in 1993, not because viewing figures were unsatisfactory but because snooker could not be satisfactorily scheduled. It was at this time difficult enough persuading a dozen or more regional controllers to stage the same football match, a one-off slot of two hours maximum, let alone a snooker tournament running afternoon and evening for nine days.

In 1987, ITV transmitted 89 hours of snooker. Channel 4 helped them fulfil their WPBSA contract for the requisite number of hours by transmitting a further 51. Michael Grade then moved from BBC to become Channel 4's controller and immediately terminated this arrangement.

'Snooker helps boost our viewing figures, but it damages the image of our channel,' said Grade. 'We will replace it with programmes for people who hate snooker.'

Without Channel 4, there was no way ITV could make good the shortfall in hours. MIM Britannia declined to renew its sponsorship of the British Open for this reason and over the next five years ITV's coverage was steadily eroded. The Hofmeister World Doubles had given way to the World Matchplay, which Everest and Coalite sponsored in turn, but this disappeared in 1990.

The Fidelity [Unit Trust] International was dropped in 1989; the Mercantile Classic survived until 1993, as did the British Open. The end was surely in sight when scheduling in most regions became insolubly tangled. Viewers in all but a couple of regions left the British Open semi-final between Steve Davis and Jimmy White with the score at 3–1 and an invitation to tune in again to the following day's final. The writing was on the wall and in the 1993–94 season there was no ITV snooker at all.

The newly emergent Sky picked up the British Open and one other event, but its audience for everything except football was well below the million mark and in many cases not even into six figures. Sponsorship, even part sponsorship, was therefore difficult to come by so events tended to be funded by a modest television rights fee and WPBSA membership funds.

Even sponsorship of BBC events became erratic. When Rothmans sponsored the Grand Prix from 1984 to 1992, it was one of the highlights of the season. The sponsors spared no expense and the event exuded class. When Rothmans withdrew from all sports except motor racing, Skoda became the sponsors from 1993 to 1995, but their hearts never seemed completely in it and they would not have continued into their third year if it had not been almost as expensive to cancel. Despite its nine days' guaranteed BBC coverage, WPBSA could not find a replacement until LG Electronics began a three-year involvement in 2001 and re-named it the LG Cup.

The UK Championship was sponsored by Coral, the bookmakers, from 1978 to 1985, then for two years by Tennent's, the brewers, for a year by Stormseal and then in 1992 by Royal Liver, who would have continued with a small increase only for WPBSA to insist that the event was 'worth' more. Of course, it was worth only what a sponsor was prepared to pay. After a couple of sponsorless years, Liverpool Victoria, who had originated their own event, the Liverpool Victoria Charity Challenge, which ran for three years on ITV, were persuaded to sponsor the UK for seasons 1997–99. When they pulled out, there was no replacement until PowerHouse made an eleventh hour contribution in 2002. Travis Perkins, the builders' merchants, took over for 2003-5 and were succeeded by Maplin Electronics.

There was no problem about retaining Benson and Hedges for the Masters since B&H had originated the event and owned it, but its run from 1975 to 2003 ended when the government, after a period of due warning, banned tobacco sponsorship except, very controversially, for Formula One and for snooker's Embassy World Championship, which was therefore able to count on this support until 2005.

Embassy's sister brand, Regal, sponsored the Welsh Open on BBC Wales and from 1998 the Regal Scottish Open on Sky, though only after WPBSA had bungled a deal with Highland Spring, the water suppliers. Ian Doyle revived the Scottish Masters under the sponsorship of Regal in 1989 and obtained coverage on BBC Scotland.

The circuit had always relied on tobacco money, but in the '90s non-tobacco sponsors became even fewer, further between and short-lived. Suspicion hardened that the business and sponsorship world had little or no confidence in WPBSA, who paid various sponsorship consultancies lavishly to insubstantial effect.

Largely through the power of television but also through the growth of the amateur game, which in less than 20 years increased the number of national associations affiliated to the International Billiards and Snooker Federation from a handful to more than 60, it was clear that there was an overseas market for snooker, but WPBSA seemed to have no idea how to exploit it. Their strategy did not seem any more sophisticated than to arrive like a travelling village, play the tournament – largely financed by membership funds – and depart.

This had been a successful strategy for Barry Hearn's self-financed tours. He had kept the field small and mostly restricted to the players he himself managed, plus a few local heroes. The WPBSA, a members organisation, could not do this because it was committed to providing tournament opportunities for as many players as possible. This meant not only large fields at main venues but also extensive and costly qualifying competitions.

Thailand was snooker's greatest growth area in the '90s although, without Thai audiences wanting to see James Wattana, their only world class player in top class competition, world ranking events would never have been staged there. As it was, there was one every season, sometimes two, from 1989 until 2002. Wattana won the Thailand Masters twice and reached third place in the world rankings, but as his form deteriorated these proved less viable as local sponsorship became more difficult to obtain.

Through a combination of reduced sponsorship and wasteful spending, snooker was habitually living beyond its means. The WPBSA tended to shrug off criticism, notably from me in *Snooker Scene* and from Doyle, who ran his management company with demonic efficiency and could not restrain himself in his acerbic criticism of other managers and anyone else who came within his arc of fire. The 1995 AGM, traditionally held just before Christmas, was not notable for its festive atmosphere as it focused on the mood of growing discontent.

Doyle arrived bearing gifts, not of gold, frankincense or myrrh but ten proxies and a long list of awkward questions. I was another traveller from afar, following several signs to Bristol Zoo but deciding to defer the attractions of the monkey house to another day by making a left turn down the hill into upmarket Clifton and a day's sport at WPBSA HQ.

One of the board resolutions which the membership was being invited to approve was not only that board members should be paid but that they should also be allowed to fix their level of fees without consulting the membership. To some of us, this seemed that the board, having mismanaged the association, now wanted to be paid for mismanaging it at a rate that they themselves deemed appropriate. If there were going to be payments at all, they would need to be transparent and at rates fixed in advance, was Doyle's line.

The most forceful advocate of payments for board members was the vice-chairman, Geoff Foulds, who since his election six years earlier had made himself into its central figure. No one questioned his effort or commitment, but he was inclined to take personally any criticism of ideas or practices which he supported. The way Foulds saw it, he was working full time for WPBSA and was entitled to be paid. When this proposal was defeated, he set about shamelessly exploiting the expenses system to create an income in that fashion. Doyle, initially friends with Foulds, even to the extent of lending him money, believed that WPBSA should have a proper management structure with executives of appropriate quality.

The more Doyle criticised any aspect of WPBSA's conduct of affairs, the more Foulds became his mortal enemy. It was through Doyle's ten proxies that the proposal to pay board members was defeated and Foulds did not forget this.

As at 30 June 1995, WPBSA was in a relatively solid financial position, a profit of £579,940 on the year's trading contributing to reserves of £3.372 million. Profits were not necessarily the object of the exercise, as WPBSA was in business primarily to re-distribute money to its members (i.e. the players) in the form of prize money. Even then it was prudent to keep substantial reserves in case of a downturn in television or sponsorship income. There were already warning signs in sponsorship: of the £4.605 million distributed in prize money that year, £1.410 million had come from the membership's own funds.

The players tended not to be voluntarily favoured with anything but the most basic financial information. To one query, Foulds answered: 'We can supply an answer on a private and confidential basis, but we don't want to read it in *Snooker Scene*.'

'Why not?' I piped up.

Foulds responded that there was 'no sinister motive'.

Just as I had at several previous AGMs, I queried the propriety of the £1-a-mile travelling allowance, which had been introduced to circumvent the constitutional ban on board members being paid for their services. Foulds appeared less worried by this than he had been in 1988 when, as leader of the so-called Peasants Revolt, he had been loud in his calls for curbs on board over-spending, particularly on inessentials.

He pointed out that the £1-a-mile was limited to 250 miles and highlighted the tragic case of one of his henchmen, Bill Oliver, who lived in Plymouth, having sometimes to drive to Blackpool for a meeting for a paltry maximum travelling allowance of £250. Foulds also considered it inequitable that he should have to spend several hours in a meeting in Wembley and be able to claim only £3 each way from his home in nearby Perivale. 'You want us to work for nothing and eat corned beef sandwiches,' Foulds suggested to me. Actually, my point was that £1-a-mile was: (1) a circumvention of the constitution; (2) open to abuse; and (3) inequitable within the board itself in relation to work done.

It was much later to emerge that Foulds, dissatisfied with £3 x 2, Perivale to Wembley and back, invoiced and was paid £150 because he claimed to have gone via Colchester.

Even without the benefit of hindsight, it was evident that Foulds was determined to be paid one way or another. Several other board members were quite happy to play the system, though not perhaps quite so blatantly. Forceful board members, such as Foulds, could cow WPBSA's executives into going along with abuses in order to ensure their own continued employment.

Foulds objected to 'every mistake made by a member of staff being pounced upon and broadcast through the pages of *Snooker Scene*'. I confirmed that where there was incompetence, it was in the best interests of the game and its players to expose it and that this was therefore our policy.

Doug Perry, the then manager of Alex Higgins, asked Foulds, chairman of the disciplinary committee, amongst other functions, why no action had been taken on the 17 complaints submitted by Robin Falvey on his behalf.

'We discuss between ourselves whether there is foundation for complaints and decide from that whether to take action,' said Foulds, a response which did nothing to increase confidence in the impartiality of WPBSA's disciplinary processes.

The skirmishes at this AGM prefaced the first of snooker's two major civil wars, with Foulds and the establishment on one side and

Doyle and me on the other. Our main weapon was information; theirs was the ingrained power and status of government.

Both sides wished the sport well, but for most people at the heart of WPBSA snooker was all they knew and somehow it had to provide them, in whole or in part, with a role, a lifestyle and a living. The clash between the ancients and the modernists was epitomised by a letter sent to *Snooker Scene* under the name of John Spencer, but actually written by Foulds, in response to Doyle publicly questioning the board's business credentials and its capacity to run the game properly.

Spencer's (Foulds's) letter asserted:

To be a director of WPBSA requires no business experience, qualifications, previous directorships of a plc or the like. What is required, however, is a love of snooker and a willingness to work very hard for the game and the members and be prepared to be a target of those who profess to support snooker but in actual fact are only interested in personal gain.

Incredibly, the letter was approved by the entire WPBSA board. Having no idea how to put underlying problems right and at times motivated by no higher purpose than simply to stay in power, the Foulds administration simply lashed out at its critics, Doyle and myself chiefly, impugning our motives and trying to get even with us by various underhand tricks.

BBC Scotland mounted a discussion during the Regal Scottish Masters of which the starting point was the lack of a sponsor for two events receiving nine days of BBC TV coverage: the Grand Prix and the UK Championship. The association claimed to have rejected an offer of £250,000 for the UK on the grounds that it was 'too cheap', but this rejection did not make a higher offer more likely and no such offer came. The two events were funded with prize money of £1.37 million from the membership's cash reserves.

I told BBC Scotland: 'The WPBSA has outgrown its administration.

It started as a players' trade union when there was just a handful of players and maybe it was adequate for that, but the game has spiralled out of all recognition. It's run by the players – it has a board of seven – so players (someone who has been in the top 128 at some time or other) have got to be in a majority on it. You're immediately limited in terms of people you can have on the board.'

As history was to show, it was not easy to choose the right person and things were to go from bad to worse.

Meanwhile, in an atmosphere in which anyone showing any sign of believing that criticism of the board was justified was at risk, Stewart Weir, who had been appointed WPBSA's press officer 16 months earlier, was dismissed, accused of being, amongst other things, 'too friendly with the press', an odd charge to level at a press officer.

Weir wrote in *Snooker Scene*:

I found a poorly directed, inward looking organisation which, because of its own insecurity, adopts a hands on approach to everything. I found a staff so frightened to make a wrong move that they had become totally scared of doing anything constructive.

He crossed swords with Rebekah Ayres, a marketing lady then in her 20s, who had been headhunted from Royal Liver, the previous sponsors of the UK Championship. As tends to be the case with people whose knowledge of the sport into which they are plunged is superficial, Ms Ayres was hot on the cosmetics of its appearance.

After 'media evaluations' – though not apparently by the BBC, who were televising the event – she commissioned a re-design of the UK Championship set which made it look as if the players were performing in an oversized paddling pool or a ring on hire from the Moscow State Circus. This cost WPBSA £84,542 – more than £25,000 over budget. Tickets went on sale late and had to be flogged off at £1 each. This was presented as a thank you to the people of Preston. Money was squandered on advertising, programmes, media folders and an array of consultants whose roles were vague to say the least.

A leaked internal memo revealed that, contrary to publicly optimistic noises, there were actually projected losses on nine of the current season's tournaments, ranging from £117,000 to £504,000 for the UK Championship, with three more in excess of £400,000.

One marketing masterstroke was to send Terry Griffiths, then a board member, together with Ms Ayres and her assistant, on a four day businessmen's cruise around the Isle of Wight on the good ship *Oriana*, carrying marketing men from many companies though not, unfortunately, those responsible for sponsorship budgets. This produced no substantive leads and cost £35,000. Having signed up for the following year as well, the WPBSA had to pay the cancellation fee of £21,000.

However, the reporting of unpalatable facts tended to rouse WPBSA to fury, as its kingpin, Geoff Foulds, proved on his first visit to the Grand Prix pressroom at the Bournemouth International Centre in October 1996.

'I expected to see shit all over the walls, the amount that's been flying about the last few hours,' he began elegantly to the room at large. 'Who's responsible for this crap? I can't believe it. It's a disgrace. It's doing nothing but harm to the game.'

It was possible to infer that he was none too pleased with my piece in *The Guardian* enumerating some of the WPBSA's more spectacular own goals of recent months, although Phil Yates had also written a piece in *The Times*, reporting in his usual scrupulously fair fashion, if with some understatement, that there was 'a groundswell of dissent' against the board.

Phil queried whether there had been any inaccuracies.

'Don't get funny with me,' snarled the board's leading diplomat. 'It's gutter journalism and whoever's written it is a gutter journalist,' Foulds told the man who through newspapers and various radio outlets provided tournaments with more column inches and airtime than any other journalist in the press corps.

Foulds and his cohorts were determined to get even and it was not long before Bill Sinrich of Trans World International rang me with bad tidings. TWI had engaged me to commentate on the World Cup in Bangkok but now informed me: 'The WPBSA, who are providing the funding for the television production of the World Cup, do not wish to use you in that regard.' Bill told me that he had 'received [his] instructions from the chairman of the board, John Spencer', who had added that this was 'the wish of the board'.

There is never any point in shooting the messenger. I calmly said that I considered this action to be an outrageous abuse of power but accepted that Bill's 'hands are tied'.

My first reaction was that this had cost me quite a lot of money. My second was a sense of loss in not being able to commentate on the most exciting new development in snooker for a decade. Many countries were taking packages that TWI were producing and BBC was transmitting the semi-finals and final. The BBC listed me, Dennis Taylor, Willie Thorne and Spencer as the commentators and I thought it pretty rich that I had been sacked by a member of the same commentary team.

There was no point in taking this up with the BBC. They were buying packages from TWI, who were selecting the commentators. The BBC needed to know in advance who they were and had a right of veto but as long as the commentators were of an acceptable standard that was about it. But because WPBSA was paying the production costs this meant they had a right of veto as well for reasons that were nothing to do with professional competence. Indeed, they tried to have Phil sacked as well until TWI protested that they could not properly cope with all the work without him.

I told *The Guardian*, whose snooker correspondent I had been since 1976. Neil Robinson, a colleague, accurately quoted my description of the WPBSA's action as 'an act of petty revenge'.

He also allowed WPBSA, as the phrase goes, a chance to give 'their side of the story', an invitation sometimes bawled through letter boxes at fraudsters who have gone to ground.

There was no immediate response, although the WPBSA's dirty tricks operation clicked into gear in the form of a tip-off to Sinrich that *The Guardian* was planning to run a story quoting me and showing TWI in a bad light. There was no truth in this. I had already made up my mind to sue WPBSA for inducing TWI to break their contract with me and several months later I was paid in full.

Meanwhile, WPBSA came back to *The Guardian* with a short statement:

> The WPBSA has until recently had a good working relationship with Clive Everton. Unfortunately, this relationship has now deteriorated to such an extent that we do not feel it is in the best interests of the sport for him to be involved in an official capacity at our forthcoming World Cup and we very much regret that this decision has had to be taken.

This obligingly confirmed that I had been dismissed from doing a match commentary for criticising their administrative shortcomings. There was more to come. A few days into the Grand Prix, I returned to my hotel room to find a hand-delivered letter informing me that WPBSA was not prepared to allow me to travel with the official party of players, press, officials, board members and their wives. They would not even offer me the concessionary rate of £500 available to all other press.

Since WPBSA's avowed policy was to maximise media coverage of snooker, particularly of prestigious events like the World Cup, it seemed a remarkable strategy to alienate in one fell swoop the three outlets the game's senior journalist was contractually obliged to serve: BBC Radio Five Live, *The Guardian* and the *Independent on Sunday*. All three were duly outraged not only on my behalf but their own: why should they be disadvantaged in relation to their competitors?

Simply to get to Bangkok, I asked Ian Doyle whether any of the players he managed had spare guest allocations. I was thus booked onto the flight as Nigel Bond's guest. The WPBSA welcomed this like an attack of leprosy. A WPBSA minion was instructed to ring Doyle's office to bring to Bond's attention that under their rules of discipline, so they claimed, Bond would be responsible for anything his guest (i.e. me) said or did in Thailand and that I would be expected to remain in the players' room and would not be allowed in the pressroom.

The Guardian's sports editor, Mike Averis, rang WPBSA to demand that its correspondent (me) be afforded the usual facilities. A minion rang him back to say: 'There is no problem with that, but why has he chosen to go as a guest of Nigel Bond?'

Self-evidently, it was because I had been kicked off the flight and must therefore get to Bangkok as best I could. This magnificently irrelevant query merely underlined the depth of anti-Doyle paranoia at Bristol.

Haplessly, the WPBSA's then company secretary, Mike Veal, said there was 'no problem with *The Guardian*. It's all to do with *Snooker Scene.*' 'In that case,' responded Averis, 'why has this happened, when he's writing stuff which is critical nearly every month, but the moment he writes about it in *The Guardian* you are doing mean and spiteful things like this?' Grudgingly, the board climbed down, possibly fearing action for restraint of trade, and I was allowed in the Bangkok pressroom.

The morning after the Grand Prix finished, I was hovering round the Thai Airways check-in desk at Heathrow when I fell into conversation with Eric Gold and Ricky Tobias of Clubnet, who had been responsible, so Gold told me, for all the WPBSA's official travel, hotel and pension arrangements for the previous two years.

'It all came through Geoff Foulds,' said Gold artlessly, in reference to Clubnet's association with WPBSA. 'I've known him for years.' Both had habitually played in the same club in Neasden. Clubnet's effectiveness was to be questioned at a later date.

Steve Davis in play against John Spencer in the 1982 Lada Classic match in which he made the first televised 147 break

But for Steve Davis, Terry Griffiths would surely have won more than one world title

Alex Higgins and Dennis Taylor exchange the frostiest of handshakes prior to 'the grudge match of all time' in the Benson and Hedges 1990 Irish Masters

Alex Higgins (left) in his prime and (right) suffering the ravages of cancer of the palate and throat

Cliff Thorburn gives a relaxed
press conference

John Virgo in his finest hour as
1979 UK champion

Doug Mountjoy, twice UK champion

Jimmy White: six times runner-up
at the Crucible

Del Simmons made himself into the godfather of snooker as it was transformed
from folk sport to major television entertainment

Mike Watterson, seen here receiving the Services to Snooker award, took the
World Championship to the Crucible and through promoting other tournaments
played a major role in bringing the modern circuit into being

Stephen Hendry is awarded the original Benson and Hedges trophy after winning the tournament on five consecutive occasions

Lord Archer launches his brief career as WPBSA president, with Ken Doherty, against the backdrop of the Houses of Parliament

August 1988: Barry Hearn had his own commercial motives, but on the whole his influence on snooker was beneficial

August 1989: The Australian Open ends up in Hong Kong. Signposts satirically refer to the WPBSA board's notorious £1-a-mile travelling allowance

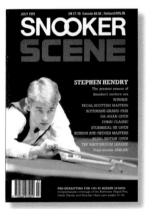

July 1991: This cover illustrates Stephen Hendry's dominance and the high level of prize money at that time

August 1996: Images of triumph at the Crucible

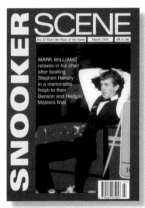

March 1998: Mark Williams relaxes after his dramatic 10–9 tiebreak black victory over Stephen Hendry in the Benson and Hedges Masters final

December 2001: Exposing some of the shortcomings of the Rex Williams regime at WPBSA, we could not bring ourselves to wish all our readers the compliments of the season

June 2002: Peter Ebdon enjoys his
2002 world title triumph with one
of his four daughters

September 2002: The rejection of
the Altium proposal left *Snooker
Scene* imagining a bleak future for
the sport

October 2003: Richard Dormer
depicts Alex Higgins in symbolic
pose during a performance of his
play, *Hurricane*

June 2004: Ronnie O'Sullivan
defeats Graeme Dott to win his
second world title

June 2005: Shaun Murphy wins
the 2005 world title as 150–1
outsider

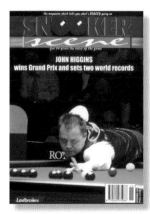

November 2005: John Higgins sets
two records at the 2005 Grand
Prix – centuries in four consecutive
frames and 494 unanswered points

Barry Hearn (centre) at the peak of his involvement in the snooker world, with his seven clients: (clockwise) Jimmy White, Steve Davis, Neal Foulds, Dennis Taylor, Willie Thorne, Tony Meo and Terry Griffiths

In Bangkok, the tournament began quietly in the ballroom of the Amari Watergate Hotel. Alan Hughes, who had been flown over to give the introductions a touch of pizzazz, made his entrance only to discover not a single living soul in the arena for Belgium v. Iceland apart from TWI's cameramen, Chas Lewis and Tony Apps.

Six gleaming new paybox phones awaited us in the pressroom, although we were informed that there was a snag: they would not receive incoming calls. Soon, we discovered another snag: outgoing calls could not be made from them either. There were two phones on the press officer's desk which did work. Things picked up gradually, but there were still problems with the commentary team.

Once my fellow BBC commentator, Ray Edmonds, had made it clear at Bournemouth that he disagreed with the ethics of the decision to sack me, he himself was effectively ruled out. Desperately, Spencer rang up Ted Lowe, who had retired from BBC commentary the previous spring, and offered him and his wife two business class flights to Bangkok, plus a fee, to cover two quarter-finals, both semis and the final. This compared with the economy fare plus a fee originally offered to me to cover the whole event.

Farcically, no sooner did Ted arrive in Bangkok than he was rushed to hospital with stomach and back pains. Fortunately, these turned out to be attributable to nothing more serious than a short-term virus. He recovered just in time to fly home at the end of the event, not having uttered a word of commentary.

At the end of it all, even with the sponsorship of Castrol and Honda negotiated by Sindhu Pulsirivong, the WPBSA's wealthy and well-meaning man in Bangkok, the event cost WPBSA some £500,000. No expense was spared and even the reserves for the three-man teams were flown out business class. Canada's reserve, Ben Reicker, arrived from Calgary at almost exactly the moment Canada went out of the competition, 10–6 losers to the Republic of Ireland. Young Ben's trip cost about £2,800.

As ever, the on-table entertainment was of a high order, but the

WPBSA, having lost so much money on this World Cup, did not stage another. WPBSA's rapidly diminishing credibility was already holed below the water line commercially and the next five years were to see an inexorable decline.

Spencer resigned the chairmanship of WPBSA in November 1996 shortly after the World Cup. Terry Griffiths and Jim Chambers also resigned from the board. Civil war raged. The rump of the board resorted to every trick in the book to cling onto power; snooker people who did not like Doyle, for whatever reason, supported them. Searching desperately for an alternative – not easy because the structure and constitution of the association demanded a former player – Doyle decided that he would support Rex Williams in a return from the political wilderness on condition that a new board under his chairmanship would set up a proper management structure, complete with a suitably qualified chief executive.

Williams and Doyle met me in my office. Williams said that he would like me to be his vice-chairman were he to be elected chairman. I said that I would prefer to remain independent. I warned Doyle that Williams had certain attributes but that his ego and vanity were formidable. Surely a Williams regime could not be any worse, Doyle and I believed naively.

The immediate priority was to bring down the administration that was dominated by Foulds. This did not appear a difficult task, as there was then a 'yes' or 'no' system of voting. If a candidate's 'no' votes outnumbered his 'yes' votes, he was not elected.

The ruling junta then had a bright idea. Candidates would be voted upon singly in an order which it had itself determined – by lot, so it was claimed – so that if all seven places on the board were filled before all candidates had been considered, this was simply hard cheese for those drawn low on the list.

'It's damn bad luck that Rex Williams, who everyone knows has my support and is the biggest threat to the status quo, has been drawn last,' was the reaction of Doyle, who managed 11 players with full voting rights in an electorate which then numbered 48. 'To even suggest such a system of election in which all the candidates do not receive simultaneous consideration and therefore an equal chance is outrageous.'

The AGM of 19 December 1996 had to be adjourned because a procedural irregularity meant that the vote could not proceed. There was, though, four hours of trench warfare on the accounts. These showed that WPBSA, on a £9.7 million turnover, had made a profit of only £234,861. This was roughly the amount that had accrued in interest, largely on money already in the bank at the start of the year. With three sponsors dropping out after that financial year, there was clearly going to be a more severe drain on the association's reserves. At the time, these were £3.587 million.

The accounts revealed that Foulds had been reimbursed £21,873 in travelling expenses under the £1-a-mile arrangement and £3,272 in telephone and sundry expenses. Travelling expenses referred to 154 meetings he had supposedly attended. Spencer had claimed £22,795 (travelling) and £2,561 (phones and sundries) for attending 155 meetings. Foulds had also been paid £9,000 at £250 a day for 'consultancy services to the association on a temporary basis following the sudden death of the former company secretary'. This £9,000 covered the period between Malcolm Hulley's death in early April and the end of the financial year on 30 June. Foulds disclosed at the AGM that he had been paid another £9,000 for services rendered after 30 June.

Since Nigel Wren, WPBSA's in-house accountant, had acted as company secretary after Hulley's death, it transpired that Foulds had been paid these amounts for such trivial tasks as helping to organise hospitality at tournaments, the awards dinner and the golf day, tasks within the competence of virtually any member of staff.

Through the coaching committee, of which he was chairman, he was also charging £500 a day for services on coaching business, including conducting exams, although the standard daily rate for WPBSA coaches at the time was £100. He defended his charges on the dubious grounds that he worked long days and had an international coaching reputation.

It emerged that the Benevolent Fund had not been audited for three years. Bill Oliver, its chairman, said he did not realise that it was one of his responsibilities to see that this was done. The activities of Clubnet, introduced by Foulds, were discussed. Their work as discount agents in such areas as travel and hotel bookings, health insurance and cars aroused more curiosity than was satisfied.

The resignations of Spencer, Griffiths and Chambers left a board of three consisting of Foulds, Oliver and Pulsirivong, key to any snooker activity in Thailand but entirely out of touch with the squalid realities of snooker's political turmoil.

Fighting to the last, the Foulds regime issued an edict banning players from airing any complaint or grievance in the media, even over playing conditions, and holding players responsible for any statements made by their managers or agents. Even after an EGM resolution calling for his removal from both the chairmanship and the board had been passed 30–9, Foulds declined to resign 'on the strength of a meeting at which I believe the members were misled'.

Barry Hearn had also attempted in vain to intervene on behalf of Foulds, proposing a three-month adjournment and an independent review committee on which he himself would serve, together with his longest standing client, Steve Davis, a lawyer and an accountant from the City. No one could work out why Hearn was defending Foulds in this way unless there was some doubt about his Premier League being sanctioned by WPBSA.

These four musketeers, he proposed, would produce 'a scrupulously fair report without any conflicts of interest', a pretty rich assertion from someone who had taken WPBSA to the High Court three years earlier, an action which, for all the WPBSA membership had been told, was still active.

Nevertheless, Foulds had to bow to the inevitable when a further meeting was requisitioned to remove him under section 303 of the Companies Act. Oliver, who unlike Foulds was due for re-election, was voted off 33–13. Williams (41–5) and two hand-picked supporters, Bob Close (34–12) and Jim Meadowcroft (29–17), were elected. Mark Wildman and Jim Chambers were co-opted at the new board's first meeting. When the special meeting was convened to remove Foulds, he did not appear and was ousted 4–0 on a show of hands.

Doyle and Williams were agreed that the way forward, after an investigation into all aspects of the association's affairs, was to have a properly structured management with a chief executive at the helm to run it on a day to day basis with the board, meeting every month or so, taking a merely supervisory or watchdog role.

'I think the first task of the new board is to conduct a thorough inquiry into every aspect of the company,' said Williams. 'I think the members deserve that and deserve to see a report of that inquiry. There has been a lot of wastage.'

Indeed, there had, but as history had shown, fine words buttered no parsnips. An inquiry was commissioned, but its findings were determinedly kept from the membership because, a few months on, the Williams regime needed the support of some of those who were being investigated in order to stay in power.

Channel 4 News sniffed out that there was a story in snooker's mismanagement about which the public might be interested to hear but I was nevertheless shocked, on the eve of the 1997 Embassy World Championship, to hear the trailer for the programme in which it was to appear referring to 'the dying days of a corrupt regime'. This, however, turned out to be a reference to the last days of President Mobutu's rule in Zaire.

It emerged that Neal Foulds, a former world no. 3, who had earned more than £1 million in prize money, had received interest-free loans of more than £35,000 from WPBSA when his father, Geoff, had been the dominant figure on its board. Geoff insisted that the Benevolent Fund was 'completely independent' and emphasised that he was not a trustee. Nevertheless, the trustees were all friends of his and had voted unanimously on 3 July 1995 to 'accede to a request from G. Foulds' to loan his son £15,000 to assist with the settlement of a debt owed to the Inland Revenue. Reference was made to the balance of an earlier loan and also to WPBSA underwriting the costs of a libel action by Neal Foulds against *Golf World* over unfounded performance enhancing drug allegations, which netted him £25,000.

It all went to show that when the same group is in power for a long time, cliques form and a culture of complacency and defensiveness develops. Leaked documents were to give rise to suspicions that Benevolent Fund loans and advances against prize money had been used by the establishment to help secure votes at AGMs and EGMs. The faction in power was then – until *Snooker Scene's* successful campaign to secure confidentiality through the Electoral Reform Society – able to see whether the players they had helped financially had voted the way they were supposed to by scrutinising their proxy forms and/or their completed voting slips.

17

LORD ARCHER ENTERS THE FRAY

'**THE WPBSA IS ENTERING A NEW ERA OF PROFESSIONALISM AND WE** are building a high calibre management team to make a step change into the future,' said Rex Williams after concluding negotiations for the appointment of Jim McKenzie as chief executive. 'Jim is the cornerstone of this new team.'

However, McKenzie, a former managing director of E.J. Riley, the table and equipment firm, was not afraid to stand up to Williams's formidable ego and lasted only five months. He successfully sued WPBSA for breach of contract, the settlement on the last working day before the court action was due to start incorporating that of a libel action arising from Williams's reckless attempts to justify his dismissal.

The events leading to McKenzie's downfall arose from Williams's bizarre invitation to Lord Archer, the much disgraced Tory peer, to become WPBSA's non-executive president. It was an appointment made possible only by a change in constitution at a low profile EGM the previous day, the membership being entirely unaware of its purpose or who it was intended to accommodate. This meant that the presidency was in the gift of the board rather than electable by the membership.

The WPBSA had never had a peer as president although one of its forerunners as the game's governing body, the Billiards Association and Control Council, had several, notably Lord Alverstone, who sentenced Doctor Crippen to death a couple of days before he presented Melbourne Inman with the World Billiards Championship trophy in 1919.

Inman's semi-final opponent, Tom Reece, interrupted the noble lord's speech on the final night with the words: 'Excuse me, my Lord, but if you knew as much about Inman as I do, you would have given Crippen the cup and sentenced Inman to death.'

Archer professed huge love for the sport, particularly the quality of its sportsmanship. 'I hate cheating of any sort,' he said. He declared his intention of attracting celebrity spectators and indeed a start was made at a tournament at Bournemouth a few weeks later. Max Bygraves arrived one afternoon and the late Buster Merryfield – Uncle Albert from *Only Fools and Horses* – on another although he left precipitately when it became clear that he had partaken all too enthusiastically of WPBSA's hospitality.

'I am not a president who will appear once a year. I have a purpose. That is to take the sport to its next stage,' said Archer.

He certainly helped to do this, albeit it in a downward direction, but far from attracting celebrity spectators, he not only commandeered the best seat in the house for the final night of the world championship from its occupant of several years, Ken Renwick, but also had to be given players to sit alongside him so that the adjoining seats would not be empty.

Following his investiture as president at a House of Commons press conference and photo call, Archer was also in characteristically cheery form at the WPBSA awards lunch the next day.

'Can I just say,' he began, 'that I've just come down from the Conservative Party Conference and how nice it is to see a crowd.' A little later, deflecting an interruption, he quipped: 'I worked with Margaret Thatcher for 15 years. I'm used to being interrupted.'

But snooker's brief respite from internecine strife was over. There had been a row the previous day between Williams and McKenzie, with Williams resolved to show who was boss and McKenzie determined not to be treated like an office boy. Williams did not mention McKenzie's appointment in his chairman's speech at the awards dinner and several sponsors grumbled about lack of recognition in comparison with fulsome acknowledgement of Embassy. The negligible acknowledgement of Sky and Eurosport gave representatives of those broadcasters the impression that their support was little valued in comparison with the BBC's. It was a party at which some partygoers felt more welcome than others.

Williams's first attempt to sack McKenzie was defeated 4–1 by his own board, but he quietly persuaded two henchmen, Jim Meadowcroft and Bob Close, to his point of view. Williams also played on the vanity of Archer by involving him in the strategy of McKenzie's dismissal. Drawn to meddling in a world of which he knew little and instinctively, it seemed, backing the more morally dubious side, Archer hosted a meeting at his famous London penthouse on 21 November 1997.

Those present were Williams; Mark Wildman, his vice-chairman; Matthew McCloy, the WPBSA solicitor; and Martyn Blake, its secretary. Wildman was growing increasingly uncomfortable because his conciliatory attitude, in the face of Williams's raging dislike of McKenzie and determination to dismiss him, was clearly not working.

Prior to moving on to Archer's penthouse, this quartet assembled at McCloy's London office. 'There was an A4 sheet of paper on McCloy's desk in Rex's handwriting listing about a dozen reasons for sacking McKenzie,' said Wildman. 'They were things like "bumptious", "full of himself", "big-headed", "criticised Martyn Blake to Ian Doyle" and "late for meeting".' It seemed ironic to some that Williams was attributing to McKenzie traits of character that others frequently observed in him.

'On the other side, there was a note in McCloy's handwriting which said, in effect: "All these points are serious but whether individually or in sum total not enough to dismiss McKenzie."'

This did nothing to reduce the resolve of Williams, Blake and McCloy and when the meeting moved to Archer's residence, Archer demanded of Wildman: 'Are you with us or against us?'

Williams's approach to Wildman was abrupt and vicious. Only a few weeks earlier, the billiards committee had wanted to honour Wildman at the awards lunch for his ten years' work in that capacity only for Wildman to demur because he believed that such an award might look as if the game's inner circle was rewarding itself with little presents.

The billiards committee respected his wishes, but Williams, as WPBSA chairman, insisted. Wildman duly received a pair of silver candlesticks paid for by the membership. A few weeks after that, Williams was doing everything in his power to oust Wildman from the board – and indeed succeeded.

On 1 December 1997, in the most mean and spiteful manner possible, McKenzie was sacked. Williams alleged, quite without foundation, that McKenzie 'chose to prefer a secret agenda with other connected persons', a clear reference to Doyle and more obliquely to Doyle's friend, Joe Beeston, chief executive of Highland Spring, who a couple of months earlier had accepted a consultancy to help WPBSA search for sponsors.

'We will,' said Williams, 'over the course of the coming weeks show how your association was in danger of being hijacked and was being mismanaged by McKenzie.' Williams could demonstrate no such thing and the immediate result was that Highland Spring, who were on the brink of putting £200,000 into the Scottish Open, a not insignificant sponsorship for a Sky tournament since Sky's viewership was but a fraction of the BBC's, tore up the proposed contract. Beeston also made public his low opinion of an old Williams crony, Terry Crabb, who had been appointed WPBSA's marketing manager. Beeston had been asked to interview him on WPBSA's behalf and was just searching for the right words to tell him he was not up to scratch when Crabb cheerfully informed him that Williams had already appointed him – with a starting date.

Williams had also looked backwards to another old crony in his appointment as company secretary of Martyn Blake, first appointed in 1984 but invited to resign in 1994 amidst allegations of costly mistakes and long, liquid lunch hours. Blake had originally been selected as the ideal man to conduct an inquiry into the activities of the Geoff Foulds regime. Then, after minimal consultation with his board, Williams restored him as company secretary.

His experience of that position gave him an intimate knowledge of the association's systems: he knew either where the bodies were buried or where to look for them. Since Foulds had instigated his dismissal, Blake could have been said to have had an axe to grind, but his findings, when they eventually came to light, were upheld by independent scrutiny.

But it was some time before Blake's findings did come to light because Williams, as soon as McKenzie had been fired, knew that he required every single vote for his regime to survive the 19 December 1997 AGM at the Café Royal. He knew, for instance, that he needed the vote of Neal Foulds, which was effectively controlled by Geoff Foulds, so there was no way Blake's report could be published.

In essence, this had been ready on 7 August 1997. Williams claimed on 12 December that it was incomplete. His vice-chairman, Wildman, said 'it seemed pretty complete to me' and that it appeared 'to raise very serious matters indeed'.

This was the first major battle of the Williams regime. Doyle was incensed at the manner of McKenzie's dismissal; Williams was determined to impose his will. Two directors of his choice, Wildman and Chambers, had opposed and still opposed McKenzie's sacking; Williams was determined to be rid of any dissident opinion in the boardroom and to discredit anyone who opposed him. He suggested that Doyle wanted to take over the game and formed a natural alliance with the acerbic Scot's not inconsiderable number of enemies. It was also easy to lean on various players for their support, as there was no confidentiality of voting at the time. The ruling junta knew in advance how a player would be voting from his proxy form – few attended meetings of this nature in person – and also knew from the completed forms subsequent to the meeting how players had voted.

Anthony Davies, for example, first supported the Williams camp, voting by proxy against Wildman and Chambers. He was then persuaded the other way and cast a second proxy accordingly. However, as soon as the establishment became aware of this, an envoy was despatched and Davies voted for a third time. This was a mockery of democracy but in several cases players were afraid of upsetting the rulers of their sport. Players were also induced by various promises, including that of coaching work or Benevolent Fund loans and even appearances on the television game show *Big Break*, for which one of Doyle's rival managers, Troy Dante, was the booking agent. For a player not in the top flight, an appearance fee of £800 for the show was not to be sneezed at.

In the end, the voting was 25–23 against Wildman and 24–24 in relation to Chambers, against whom Williams added a casting vote of dubious legality. Williams also broke with previous practice in disqualifying the votes of Wildman and Chambers themselves because they were serving as co-opted directors and not elected by the membership.

'Well done, Rex,' Foulds called out cheerfully at the end of the meeting, clearly in a better mood than when Williams, Doyle and others had been asking him all sorts of nasty questions at the previous year's AGM.

Barry Hearn, controlling the vote of Steve Davis, had proved himself a vociferous supporter of Williams at a meeting of managers on 16 December. His support came in the context of imminent consideration of his application to WPBSA for a sanction for his Premier League to be shown on Sky TV and he clearly approved of the way Williams had handled the AGM.

'Shall we call you God after today?' he quipped, as Williams brought it to a close. WPBSA sanctioned the Premier League and Williams told the AGM that all legal disputes between Hearn and the association, some going back almost four years, had been settled. He declined to say on what terms.

Archer sat through the meeting, accompanied by his lawyer, contributing nothing except a platitudinous opening address containing such bromides as 'nothing more important than the game' and 'no individual more important than the game'.

Contrary to previous practice, proxy holders were not allowed to speak, thus spiking the guns of managers like Doyle who were better equipped than their players to ask searching questions.

Wildman and Chambers engaged Doyle's lawyer, Gerry Sinclair, to apply for an injunction, effectively freezing the result of the AGM and preventing WPBSA entering into contracts. This was granted on Christmas Eve but, four weeks later, WPBSA's application to lift the injunction was unopposed, Williams having indicated that the question of voting rights would be addressed internally. It was not. Several more months into this conflict, it was clear that the Doyle side had cast away a valuable advantage.

I was incensed by Williams's bulldozing tactics and could envisage the future of the game being compromised by his petty vanity and cronyism. 'I've had my differences with Clive Everton over the years, but he has been the game's watchdog and thank goodness we have had him,' Williams had said during the AGM of February 1997, which had led to his return from political wilderness. However, he did not seem to think that in discharging this role I should scrutinise his actions and those of his new board in quite the same way. As was common in snooker, he seldom attempted to rebut criticism but merely tried to attack the critic. *Snooker Scene*'s February 1998 issue burnt my boats with him with a long section, 'Tales from the Rex files', which reviewed various incidents in his career and drew attention to his intolerance of opinions other than his own. I had always seen him as 90 per cent Jekyll, 10 per cent Hyde, but it was clear that I had not assessed these proportions accurately.

Even though his regime narrowly survived the December 1997 AGM, it was soon clear that there was a resistance movement against him which would not go away and he grew more vicious and more paranoid. He was aided and abetted in this regard by Brian Radford, a disreputable tabloid hack who was then freelancing for the *News of the World*, by McCloy, who proved a satisfactorily pliable tool of successive boards, and by Blake, his habitually crapulous company secretary.

McCloy had arrived at WPBSA when it needed a replacement for Richard Alderson of Edge Ellison, who had been embarrassingly shown not to have been even-handed in the preparation of the 1992 Alex Higgins disciplinary case. David Harrison, the WPBSA's chief executive at the time, met McCloy at an Institute of Professional Sport gathering; at around the same time, Geoff Foulds was looking for a solicitor to represent his son Neal in his libel action against *Golf World*. Foulds was friendly with Radford, who lived at Newbury, as did McCloy, and knew him quite well because they often travelled on the same train up to London. Radford therefore introduced McCloy to Foulds.

McCloy thus came to act for Neal Foulds and also became the WPBSA's solicitor. The WPBSA board was persuaded to underwrite this libel action, which was soundly based and yielded £25,000 in an agreed settlement. McCloy also acted for the WPBSA chairman, John Spencer, in another libel case, again successfully.

The first dent in McCloy's credibility arose on an American Airlines flight to New York in October 1995 to attend the Breeders' Cup as part of the British Horseracing Board (BHB) party. Flight personnel radioed ahead that he had become intoxicated, had created a disturbance when refused more alcohol and had been handcuffed on the orders of the captain because he was considered a danger to passengers, crew and aircraft.

On arrival in handcuffs, he was involved in a scuffle in which a New York Port Authority policeman broke a rib. McCloy claimed to remember nothing of that until he woke up in a police cell. Next day, said the WPBSA's solicitor, 'I was moved into the prison system and into a dormitory with criminals of all shapes and sizes. I was lucky because I fell among some very nice people.' He claimed to have no recollection of how he had come to be cut and bruised.

McCloy pleaded guilty – to avoid delaying his return to Britain, so he claimed – to a charge of disorderly conduct. Charges of assault and resisting arrest were dropped. When he appeared at the Breeders' Cup, he looked like a boxer who had just gone ten exacting rounds.

There was an initial attempt to spin the story in British newspapers as one of farce rather than misdemeanour. Its thrust was that his arrest at JFK airport was attributable to him being mistaken for an internationally sought Jamaican criminal of the same name. This suggestion had some comic potential as McCloy was of Caucasian hue and spoke with a pronounced public school accent. The NYPA denied any confusion.

McCloy weathered the immediate storm of this incident but resigned from the BHB in June 1998. On his departure, he was described by David Ashforth of the *Racing Post* as 'one of the cleverest but least trusted members of the BHB'.

But at WPBSA, McCloy had his feet well and truly under the table. As at 30 June 1997, his outstanding billings to WPBSA stood at £100,600. Some believed that much of this work did not really require specialist legal expertise; others argued that if there really was this amount of legal work, an in-house lawyer would be more economical.

Blake – he of the long liquid lunch hours – quickly demonstrated his old tendency of insobriety, Benson and Hedges banning him from their tournaments because of two instances of offensive behaviour fuelled by drink.

Jim Elkins, who co-ordinated B&H's sponsorships, complained in the strongest possible terms of Blake 'abusing and embarrassing' him in front of his wife and guests, insulting a senior tournament organiser and drunkenly gatecrashing their private dinner table.

'Throughout this whole unsavoury incident, Mr Blake was incoherent in his speech . . . Various inarticulate attempts to have a conversation ensued over the next 15 minutes or so before he decided to leave.' At another dinner party during the Embassy World Championship, there was another incident fuelled, according to Elkins, 'by an obvious excess of alcohol'.

Blake, effectively branding important sponsors as liars, denied any such incidents had taken place. An 'internal inquiry' was 'absolutely satisfied' that he was 'totally innocent'. Benson and Hedges, Benson and Hedges (Ireland) and Highland Spring then boycotted the WPBSA awards lunch. Blake also showed up at one meeting smelling of either drink or an extremely unusual aftershave and arrived 20 minutes late, without apology, for the start of the billiards AGM, spending several minutes in the early part of the meeting apparently asleep.

Another old friend Williams gathered round him, if that is quite the right phrase, was Sandy Simmons, the statuesque widow of Del Simmons, who had died of throat cancer. Sandy originally appeared on the WPBSA scene serving drinks in its hospitality room. There she attracted Simmons sufficiently for him to leave his well-liked wife, Audrey, the mother of their three children, after twenty years of marriage. After six years' absence, Williams brought her back to run the bar within WPBSA's inner sanctum at tournaments not only near her Sheffield home but also travelling with him to events as far afield as Aberdeen and Plymouth.

Radford had first surfaced in snooker as the biographer of Steve Davis but subsequently fell out with his manager, Barry Hearn. Geoff Foulds, unhappy with some aspects of Hearn's management of his son, Neal, also fell out with Hearn. Foulds and Radford became friendly enough to exchange information, some of which was used journalistically. Radford was once frisked in Hearn's office and discovered to be wearing a secret recording device. This left him with a rabid antipathy to Hearn which was to be matched by one equally rabid for Doyle and myself. As a rule, our enemies were his friends.

In the *News of the World*, Radford reported that Williams had had WPBSA's Bristol HQ 'scoured for surveillance bugs' and that he had 'ripped the office apart to uncover evidence of computer hacking and searching of waste bins'. Despite his failure to expose 'a spy in the camp' or industrial espionage, Williams alleged: 'Doyle had access to confidential material so the source or sources had to be found.' Of course, they never were.

Williams did not show comparable concern in investigating who had leaked a WPBSA letter of 2 January 1998 which was the basis of a Radford piece in the *News of the World* headlined: 'I'll ban Hendry and all his team, vows boss Williams'.

It could not have done Hendry's peace of mind or thus his game any good that successive WPBSA regimes had tried to attack

Doyle through him, as had a Foulds counter-offensive which had taken the form of a Radford *News of the World* piece on 24 November 1996 alleging that Hendry had 'wrecked New Year for hundreds of deprived kids by refusing to spend a day with them for nothing'.

The context was the upcoming Liverpool Victoria Charity Challenge in which players competed for prize money not only for themselves but also for a designated charity. There was also some public relations activity, mostly in the form of pictures. Radford's piece was headlined 'Scrooge Hendry delivers Xmas snub to deprived kids'. A picture was mocked up to depict Hendry as Scrooge. However, no such children had been selected. Radford's piece was a malicious fiction.

Now, the 2 January 1998 letter stated that a disciplinary rule introduced in the last desperate days of the Foulds regime to attempt to silence criticism would be implemented. It made players responsible for any remark made by their managers and provided for fines, suspensions or deductions of ranking points. Doyle had indeed been extremely critical and Hendry himself had said: 'The game is poisoned from top to bottom.'

Venomously, Williams stated: 'In the case of Doyle, we have rules which can be used to prevent him from entering a venue where this association is running a tournament. He will be banned or ejected just like any member of the public who causes a problem. We have security people who would do this for us – these are not idle threats.'

This bullying strong-arm approach would have been more appropriate to a raging drunk than to someone – the game's leading manager – who simply did not share Williams's opinions. Radford reported that Williams was 'seething at the way Doyle has tried to undermine his control of the sport' – yes, Williams's control.

Doyle, who had introduced two ranking event sponsors to the association, was duly banned from WPBSA venues although Benson and Hedges, Benson and Hedges (Ireland) and Liverpool

Victoria, who ran their own invitation events, said that he would continue to be welcome. Benson and Hedges in turn excluded WPBSA personnel from their pressroom and players' room.

Soon, Williams was using WPBSA money to initiate legal actions to stifle criticism or to further personal vendettas. His conduct also prompted legal actions against the association, two of them from me.

First up, *The Mirror* obtained a copy of the Blake Report in which Blake had listed more than 50 questionable expense claims by Foulds. *The Mirror* alleged that non-publication of the report was a cover-up. Later, it was to emerge that the object of issuing the writ for libel was simply to deter *The Mirror*. The accuracy of its information was never internally challenged.

WPBSA also issued a writ against Doyle over critical but innocuous remarks he had made in *Scotland on Sunday*. The paper was not enjoined in the action, so the costs of defending it fell entirely, as Williams wished, on Doyle. In response, Doyle's players, led by Hendry, requisitioned an EGM, scheduled for 4 March 1998, to remove Williams and his two closest henchmen, Close and Meadowcroft. Williams counter-attacked with a motion for that same EGM to extend voting rights from the top 40 in the ranking list for the two previous years to the top 64, an obvious attempt to dilute Doyle's voting power.

Terry Griffiths resigned as WPBSA's director of coaching with £50,000 left on his contract, describing the association's institutionalised muddle as 'a hopeless set-up with no one giving the staff any direction at all. Nothing constructive, just going round in circles.'

Despite his frustration, he remained one of snooker's most fervent evangelists and attempted the daunting task of brokering a truce between Williams and Doyle. His plan hinged on proxies he had gathered between his resignation on 23 February 1998 and a meeting of the warring parties at Derby on 28 February. He told both Williams and Doyle that he held enough proxies to hold the balance of power and threatened each that he would support the other if terms were not agreed. He enlisted the support of two other former world champions, Dennis Taylor and Steve Davis.

The deal was that Doyle's side would not go through with its attempt to remove Williams, Close and Meadowcroft at the 4 March EGM and that WPBSA, in return, would drop disciplinary action against Hendry for his remark that the game was poisoned from top to bottom, rescind the ban on Doyle attending venues and drop its attempt to extend the franchise to the top 64.

On 28 February, all the right noises were made. Handshakes were exchanged. Smiles were glued on with Bostik. WPBSA said that for legal reasons the 4 March EGM could not actually be cancelled, but Doyle was assured that this was a mere formality and did not even send a representative. The resolution to remove Williams, Meadowcroft and Close was not proceeded with, but Williams and his supporters nevertheless proceeded with the motion to extend the franchise to the top 64.

This very significant change to the constitution and to the game's political balance of power was spirited through an EGM which almost everyone assumed had been aborted in the sense of transacting any meaningful business. This EGM achieved a bare quorum of eight, comprising six board members plus Bill Oliver, the erstwhile chairman of the Benevolent Fund and no friend of Doyle, and Andy Hicks, whom Oliver managed. The extension of the voting rights to the top 64, which would have been a highly contentious issue, went through on a show of hands by the farcical majority of 4–0, Williams and some of his supporters abstaining in an attempt to show that their hands were clean of any betrayal of the Griffiths truce.

The four votes were those of Hicks and three board members co-opted at the wish of Williams a few weeks earlier: Ray Reardon, a former world champion, Jim McMahon, a Glasgow driving instructor, and David Taylor, a former player and Williams crony of long standing. McMahon's only previous connection with snooker had been as the manager of his nephew, Alan McManus, who had lost a great deal of money in a previous management entanglement. McManus rejected an offer of management from Doyle in favour of his uncle, who then became an enthusiastic gatherer of AGM and EGM votes in causes to which Doyle was opposed.

In the immediate aftermath of the EGM, Doyle's office received a letter from WPBSA saying that there would be no charges against Hendry but that he would still be required to appear before the disciplinary committee. In other words, he would be expected to inconvenience himself and grovel. When Doyle protested, it emerged that Close, chairman of the disciplinary committee, knew nothing of this. A fundamentally decent sort despite his unquestioning devotion to Williams, Close saw to it that the request was dropped.

Doyle also received a fax from WPBSA saying that although the banning order against him had been lifted, he would be liable to a life ban if he subsequently criticised the board. He was also given the impression that WPBSA had dropped its *Scotland on Sunday* libel action against him although this was in fact re-activated the following Christmas Eve.

There was no longer any semblance of a truce and another EGM was requisitioned which sought to remove Williams and his entire board and replace it with an interim board consisting of Griffiths, Dennis Taylor and Davis. This was to be set for 4 June but in the run-up to it, the Williams regime plumbed new depths.

Radford, whose Rottweiler style had been amply displayed to the approval of Williams in the *News of the World* over the preceding few months, was engaged as a freelance editor of *In the Frame*, a house newsletter designed to give the players a rosy impression of the ruling junta and to attack its critics. A little later, he was recruited as WPBSA's head of media relations, an appointment which left press, sponsors and journalists aghast. They could hardly have been more shocked if Mad Frankie Fraser had been appointed principal of the British School of Dentistry.

Williams admitted that Radford had been 'a consultant for the association' even when he was writing articles in the *News of the World* under his own name. He was, to put it bluntly, being paid with the membership's money to attack members or their managers whom the ruling faction did not like.

In *Snooker Scene*, I pointed out that Radford had cost *The People* £250,000 (reduced to £110,000 on appeal) plus a six-figure sum in costs for libelling Esther Rantzen in 1991. In an article headlined 'Esther and the sex pervert teacher', Radford had alleged that this prominent television presenter, who had founded Childline to combat child abuse, had herself protected an alleged child abuser. Nevertheless, the Williams regime, confident of Radford's willingness to attack its enemies and blinded by this, appointed him to this sensitive position.

He needed little encouragement. In February 1997, when he was maintaining a close association with Foulds, who was desperately attempting to retain control of the WPBSA, he had prepared an article which began:

> Snooker great John Spencer is undergoing special psychiatric treatment after allegations about his gambling activities. Insiders are blaming Stephen Hendry's manager, Ian Doyle and magazine editor, Clive Everton, for his chronic condition. Both have maintained a continual campaign against him.

The article ended: 'One senior insider said: "What's happening to John Spencer has been caused by two people, Ian Doyle and Clive Everton. They've made his life an absolute misery."'

Snooker Scene had certainly criticised aspects of Spencer's chairmanship of WPBSA, as it had all WPBSA regimes, but Spencer, whatever his shortcomings, had a strong sense of fair play and faxed a copy of the intended article to me. My lawyers immediately warned Radford that he and any newspaper publishing such an article would be sued for libel. Radford blustered that it had never been intended for publication – though the purpose of it was unclear if publication was not intended – and no such article was published.

Some of Radford's efforts were incredibly petty. In the *News of the World*, he attempted to present Hendry as some sort of pariah amongst his fellow professionals by alleging that 'some managers and players are even booking into different hotels to avoid the six times world champion and his supporters'.

What actually happened was that Tony Drago, John Higgins and Alan McManus, who had all checked in elsewhere originally, checked out and booked into the Swallow, where Hendry and the rest of Doyle's players were staying for the 1998 Embassy World Championship. Peter Ebdon did not stay at the Swallow, as he had the previous year, but Hendry was not inconsolable to be deprived of his company.

Radford reported Williams as baffled by the new demand for an EGM because a £660,000 profit was being forecast for the year ending 30 June 1998. What he did not say was that this had been achieved by cutting the number of world ranking tournaments from ten to eight.

Comically, Radford reported in *Sport First* that John Higgins had become a 'video fanatic' in the run-up to the championship.

'A whole room at his parents' home has been turned into a studio packed with films of his matches,' including, said Radford, the 'horror movie' of his 9–4 defeat by Gary Ponting in the UK Championship in November 1997.

'His mother taped it,' Radford reported, 'in case he'd like to analyse it when the shock and anger had worn off.'

This could not have been easy, as this match had occurred in the pre-televised stage of the competition.

Radford's targets also included Terry Griffiths, who had volunteered to work out three months' notice as director of coaching only to be pointlessly and vindictively told to cease all activity as soon as he was identified as wishing to remove Williams and his board. Now, the Blake Report, having been kept under wraps in so far as it related to Foulds, was leaked to Radford in order to smear Griffiths in the *News of the World* under the headline: 'Griffiths fraud squad sensation: snooker ace in expenses probe'.

Radford wrote: 'The sport's governing body has asked the fraud squad to investigate hotel bills and air fares submitted by the former world champion.' This was in conflict with an Avon and Somerset Police spokesman, Keith Jones, saying next day that they were not investigating 'any organisation or individual'. The WPBSA never did ask the fraud squad to investigate anything. The only request of this nature had been made in the preceding January by the solicitor representing Wildman, whose concerns were entirely reasonable but not related to Griffiths.

Radford claimed that 'an internal investigation' by the WPBSA had revealed that 'Griffiths broke their rules by claiming expenses for his wife, Annette, on an unauthorised trip to Hong Kong in November 1996.' Griffiths broke no rules. The trip was authorised. Next day, he produced the documentation to prove it.

A round trip, Bangkok–Hong Kong–Bangkok, had been made on official coaching business during the 1996 World Cup in Bangkok. The very same trip had been made at the same time by Geoff Foulds and his wife, who were not mentioned in the Radford article. The bill included £319 for the extra airfare for both wives. If there had been any objection to either or both wives making the trip, the correct procedure would have been to approach Griffiths and/or Foulds personally to suggest that the association be reimbursed £319. What happened, of course, was that the expense was deemed acceptable until it was decided much later to imply that Griffiths had somehow gone beyond his authorisation and fiddled his expenses.

Then came the dead giveaway as to the purpose of the article: 'The news could not have come at a worse time for Griffiths,' Radford commented. 'He is trying to remove the current board and has offered himself as a replacement director and possibly chairman.'

Griffiths was advised that he had ample grounds to sue for libel, but his attitude was that everyone who knew him, either in snooker or outside it, would know that the *News of the World* article was nonsense and that he did not want to go to all the bother and initial financial outlay of raising an action. I thought he was wrong and had no such compunction myself when the Williams regime moved to attack me.

Williams and his board survived the 4 June 1998 EGM to remove them by the precarious margin of 38–34, Williams having failed in his legal duty as chairman, it was to transpire, by not casting two proxies entrusted to him in the manner in which he had been directed. Griffiths, leader of the opposition, knew of 34 voting forms which had been lodged in favour of his side, though possibly some later countermanding proxies had been submitted or otherwise reversed by voting in person on the day. Waverers were uncomfortably aware that the board would know if they had ultimately voted for anti-board forces but not vice versa. The press, with the exception of Williams's pet Rottweiler, Radford, were excluded from the meeting.

Williams described the 38–34 margin as 'a pretty resounding victory' and expressed the pious hope that 'all this bickering will now stop, we will get some unity and harmony in the game and we can all work together'. Of course, he was interested in unity only if everyone agreed with him and, in the meantime, moved to strengthen his position and punish his enemies.

18

WILLIAMS UNLEASHES THE DOGS OF WAR

THE WILLIAMS REGIME'S FIRST COWARDLY, UNDERHAND AND PETTY retaliation against my critical coverage of its activities was to deprive me of my billiards membership of WPBSA. Having long since retired from snooker, this was my one remaining commitment as a player. My best days were many years behind me, but I still liked to play when I could and there was certainly no incentive to practise unless there were matches to play, even irregularly.

My expulsion without trial was activated by a cunning application of the rules. In January 1998, in common with several WPBSA members who had reached the age of 60, I received a letter informing me that I had been granted honorary membership. This gave us over 60s free entry into tournaments in addition to the normal rights and privileges of membership. I must confess that, at the time, I did not pause to consider the difference between 'life' and 'honorary'.

If I had, I would never have accepted honorary membership because article 2.8 of the constitution stated that it could cease if 'being an honorary member his annual membership is not renewed by the board'. No such membership had ever been revoked in this way, but Martyn Blake, the WPBSA secretary, wrote on 3 June 1998 to say: 'The board recently considered renewal of your honorary membership under rule 2.8 and decided it should be not renewed.'

Applying a similarly strict reading to the rules governing committee membership, I was still entitled to be a member of the billiards committee, but Rex Williams and his minions circumvented this inconvenience simply by excluding me from meetings.

This was a way of Williams himself running all aspects of billiards in which he was interested through a quisling committee. Williams promised the billiards players entitled to vote – many young, most none too bright – that if they stuck with him and not with me, he would see them all right. In fact, billiards soon began a descent to its lowest point for 30 years.

Some pretty heavy journalistic guns boomed out on my behalf. Donald Trelford, a former editor of *The Observer*, described me as 'the sport's leading evangelist for 30 years' and identified WPBSA's actions as 'a crude attempt to silence and punish' me. Alan Hubbard, sports editor of *The Observer* at the time, described WPBSA's action as 'spiteful'; Peter Corrigan, chief sports columnist of the *Independent on Sunday*, spoke of my 45 year career as a competitive billiards player ending without charge or trial and called, not for the first time, for an independent adjudication body under the supervision of the Sports Council to which examples of apparent injustice could be referred.

Steve Davis described it as 'another part of the pettiness that's really dragged our game down. The problem with snooker has always been that we have professionals on the table and amateurs in the boardroom, and Clive Everton has always sought to point out the weaknesses in the game. In a way, he has championed the cause in a way that other people couldn't, the ones who had no voice.' He added that I was 'one of the few people to stand up and say what's wrong with the game and all credit to him – against his own self-interest really. He felt, really, that he couldn't do anything else because he's loved the game all his life, similar to myself, and where he's seen injustice, he's had to speak out.'

Williams, drunk with power or sometimes simply drunk, let loose his dogs of war on me, particularly Brian Radford, who was explicitly instructed to attack me. He did so in such terms that I was to receive from WPBSA some two years down the road damages and costs for two libel actions amounting to £115,000.

An uninhibitedly inaccurate character assassination of me by Radford in the WPBSA newsletter, *In the Frame*, was to cost the association £50,000 in damages plus £15,000 costs. Radford alleged a breach of confidence and duty in that in the brief period about ten years earlier that I had been a WPBSA board member, I had leaked confidential information to the media. He alleged that I had 'held a number of secret meetings with executives of a Sunday tabloid newspaper and was in constant contact on the telephone'.

Radford was too shy to disclose that he was the journalist in question. There were no secret meetings. Once, at his invitation and because I then had no reason to distrust him, I had lunch in the executive dining room of Mirror Group Newspapers with him and the then sports features editor of the *Sunday People* he brought along, Alan Ridout.

At a pinch, Ridout could be defined as an executive, but I met no others. The lunch was no more secret than any other lunch. Both seemed obsessed with the idea that matches were being fixed. I disagreed. It was not even strictly accurate to allege that I was 'wined and dined'. As a virtual teetotaller, I drank no wine. *In the Frame* mentioned that this was 'where Robert Maxwell entertained guests' apparently to suggest a linkage between me and that master fraudster and pillager of pension funds.

Radford initially came across to me, as he did to many others, as a smooth, affable operator with a harmless hobby of singing in his local church choir. As many journalists would testify, I tend to answer their queries unless there is an obvious reason not to. Much more occasionally, they tell me something I do not know. For a while, this was my relationship with Radford.

In the Frame alleged that 'on at least one occasion, which involved a top left-handed player, he [I] was definitely paid. This story ended up in a popular daily tabloid. The exact cheque number for this payment has been passed on to the WPBSA.' Some readers might have deduced from this that I had been selling stories about players' sex lives, not a practice in which I have ever indulged.

In fact, four years earlier, Everton's News Agency had banked one small payment (£40) from Radford, who again was the journalist referred to. Just after he had left *The People* to go freelance, he asked for my help in steering him towards stories. He rang up one morning on which I had just learned that there had been a panic at a *Pot Black* recording for which Jimmy White and Alan McManus had not turned up. This was interesting but innocuous. I told him about it and his story appeared under a pseudonym in the now defunct *Today* newspaper. It was for my help that he sent me the cheque, an arrangement very common in the world of newspapers and freelance agencies.

Any relationship I had with Radford ceased at the 1993 UK Championship when in the course of a conversation on another subject he asked me why White had lost 9–7 to Darren Morgan after leading 6–2 overnight. Unguardedly, and assuming we were talking journalist to journalist, I remarked that White had not assisted his own cause by staying up all night playing cards. Without my consent and certainly without payment, Radford presented this in a Sunday tabloid in aggressive terms along the lines of 'BBC man accuses White'.

In the Frame claimed that:

The board have also been told about a specific event in May 1990 when a Sunday tabloid newspaper editor sent an investigator to the home of Silvino Francisco in Chesterfield. It is claimed that Francisco had offered to tell his story about gambling in snooker for a five-figure fee, but when the reporter arrived at Francisco's home he found Clive Everton sitting there advising the South African on what to say and what to be paid. The board will be deeply concerned about this claim not least because the WPBSA had already been involved in a lengthy legal battle with Francisco. Everton was also aware that he was about to be co-opted to the board, which he was, just three weeks later on 18 June.

Again, Radford was too shy to clarify that the investigator was himself. Francisco wanted me there because he was suspicious of tabloid reporters and did not want to be stitched up. I was also, on behalf of *Snooker Scene* and the *Sunday Times*, following all aspects of the Francisco situation with interest.

The legal activity Radford referred to was either Francisco's successful battle to overturn the findings of a WPBSA kangaroo court or his successful libel action against Rex Williams and John Virgo, which cost the membership some £20,000 in costs and some £5,000 in damages. This 'lengthy legal battle' had been concluded a full year before the 'specific event in May 1990'. WPBSA had been involved in a legal battle only because Williams and to a lesser extent Virgo had said something damaging which they could not substantiate.

It was untrue to suggest that I advised Francisco on negotiating a fee. I was unaware that a fee was involved, if indeed it was. My understanding was that this particular tabloid newspaper had gone a little further than was wise in the match-rigging allegations against Francisco which arose in the late '80s and that Radford was there to write a story very much from the Francisco point of view. Certainly, this was the sort of story which appeared under Radford's byline on 27 May 1990.

I declined WPBSA's invitation to explain myself in front of the board. I had nothing to explain and this was going to be a kangaroo court anyway. It was the WPBSA who were going to have the explaining to do.

The Williams regime's assault against me, though, had only just started. More than a week before I sloshed up the M6 to Preston to commentate on the 1998 Grand Prix, I was tipped off that I was to be banned from all tournament venues. Sure enough, as soon as I touched down in the pressroom, I was handed a faxed letter to inform me that I was 'banned from all premises owned or controlled by the association, apart from the BBC TV commentary box during such time as you are actually on air. For the avoidance of doubt, this covers all other areas at

WPBSA tournament venues, including the auditorium and the pressroom.'

The sheer malice of this latest effort from the department of dirty tricks was immediately apparent. The letter was dated 14 October and there I was, at 6.50 on Friday, 16 October, being informed by fax, past the hour when lawyers tend to shut up shop for the week, thus making a legal response over the weekend virtually impossible. The same letter was delivered by special courier to my home late on the Friday afternoon after I had left and my office received the letter on the following Monday morning.

It soon transpired that Blake and Radford had also been to BBC to try to get me fired from the BBC commentary team. Quite apart from any issues of fairness, there was no way that the BBC, paying a rights fee to WPBSA with public money, could allow itself to be seen to have its choice of commentators vetoed by a governing body, sponsor or anyone else.

BBC Radio Five Live, who immediately dropped my tournament preview in favour of interviewing me about my ban, took a dim view of WPBSA's attempt to interfere in their contract with me. Radio Five was due to give the event extensive coverage but, with their reporter of choice denied access to the radio broadcasting point in the pressroom, took the principled decision to carry no voice reports at all.

This would have come as no surprise to anyone who understands anything at all about the media. Give way in one instance and football managers would be insisting that the commentator should be Mike Ingham not Alan Green, or vice versa. The net effect was that the snooker public was denied a valuable source of information and the event itself denied free publicity which just might have improved the generally dismal level of attendances.

The two newspapers to which I was contracted, *The Guardian* and the *Independent on Sunday*, protested against the withdrawal of press facilities from me but carried reports I managed to compile through watching live coverage in my hotel room, on monitors in BBC production cabins or the Guild Hall restaurant.

The *Independent on Sunday* sports editor, Neil Morton, wrote to WPBSA: 'Surely snooker, with its damaging infighting, requires a more conciliatory approach, rather than conflict. Is the sport so vibrantly popular that it can afford to alienate those that do most to promote it?'

All this as another acrimonious AGM loomed. Four Williams loyalists – Ray Reardon, Jim McMahon, David Taylor and Jim Meadowcroft – were challenged by ten anti-establishment candidates – Terry Griffiths, Steve Davis, Dennis Taylor, Jason Ferguson, Mark Wildman, Jim Chambers, Mark Johnston-Allen, Malcolm Thorne, Roger Lee and Tony Knowles. Under a sane system, this would have meant fourteen candidates for five places, and the five with most votes elected. WPBSA's constitution provided for 'yes' and 'no' for each candidate but, even so, the greatest number of 'yes' votes or possibly the greatest number of 'yes' minus 'no' votes should have decided.

Instead, the Williams regime stipulated not only that all candidates would be considered singly but in an order it had itself determined until the board's full complement of seven was achieved. This was the system that Williams and his supporters had attacked when he was opposing the Foulds regime. Now that he was in power, the system did not seem such a bad idea at all.

First up, Reardon, Williams's vice-chairman, was returned 37–34 after a 55 minute count. After another 35 minutes, so was McMahon, 38–34. Reardon was assisted by some residual goodwill from his distinguished playing career; McMahon was supported by those who swallowed the Williams party line that Ian Doyle wanted to take over the game.

With neither Williams nor his acolyte Bob Close having to put themselves up for re-election until the following year, the re-election of Reardon and McMahon meant that there would be a Williams majority of at least 4–3 on the new board. At this point, realising the cause was lost, Griffiths withdrew.

It may well be that player voters did not fully appreciate that votes for either Reardon or McMahon were effectively votes for the continuation of the Williams regime. Some showed their dissatisfaction by rejecting David Taylor 43–30 and Meadowcroft 40–32.

Dennis Taylor, first up for the opposition, was elected 39–33 and the pace of the count accelerated against the background of a raucous Christmas party in the next room, Steve Davis and Jason Ferguson being elected by a show of hands. This gave the board its complement of seven members, so nobody knew how many votes would have been cast for the other candidates.

Williams made his customary call for unity at the end of the meeting and immediately, without telling his new boardroom colleagues, re-activated the WPBSA's legal action against Doyle.

However, the trio of newcomers did scupper Williams's wish to buy for snooker purposes an old tyre warehouse, Bridgestone House, at Oldbury immediately below an exit off the M5 and on the roundabout of the notoriously busy Birmingham–Wolverhampton road; so busy in fact that the Highways Agency was expressing reservations about allowing the public into the venue for fear of ensuing traffic jams.

An official inquiry into the stewardship of the Williams regime was later to find that together with the costs of conversion, loans and mortgaging, not to mention running costs, offset by only the most minimal gate money or other income, this grandiose project would probably have bankrupted the association.

Even Reardon joined the newly elected Davis, Taylor and Ferguson in expressing scepticism and the project was aborted. A bulletin to members stated:

> The board was on the verge of signing contracts . . . a tremendous amount of work and expense had been involved . . . we regret to inform you that the board were not unanimous in wanting to continue with the project.

Williams was incensed that his pet scheme had been blocked and within a few days one of his staunchest supporters, Willie Thorne, was trying to elicit support to remove Taylor and Davis from the board by seeking to inflame ill-informed criticism of those who had judged the scheme to be a massive potential loser.

The Snooker Writers' Association, an amiable lot on the whole, was appalled by the Williams regime's high-handed attitude to the press and decided to delete sponsors' names from their reports on WPBSA tournaments.

Two perennially thirsty members of the press corps, Tony Stenson of *The Mirror* and John Hennessy of *The Express*, bought a drink in the players' room at the UK Championship without realising that the press, contrary to the practice of friendlier eras, was not supposed to be there. An exchange with a junior member of staff ended amicably, but Radford, relishing his power, wanted to make an issue of it and told Stenson that he would be faxing *The Mirror*'s then editor, Piers Morgan, about his 'behaviour'.

Perhaps Radford did not realise that Stenson and Morgan had been friends for many years prior to Morgan's rise to eminence.

'Tell Radford that if I have any fax from him, I'm going to drive down to Bournemouth and personally stick it up his arse,' was the uncompromising response of Morgan, who then recalled Stenson and another *Mirror* journalist to base, thus terminating *The Mirror*'s coverage of the tournament, albeit not before Stenson had run a funny piece about my continuing ban. A line of stickers, each carrying a cartoon representation of a chicken, ran from the back entrance by the television scanner vans, up a staircase and through a foyer to the commentary box. As part of my ban, I was supposed literally to toe that line. Stenson christened this the 'chicken run'.

I thought all this to be as petty as it was hilarious. Radio Five Live still would not carry voice reports as long as I was barred; I again worked for *The Guardian* and the *Independent on Sunday* from either one of the BBC trucks or my hotel room.

'Sponsors snookered as press stands by Everton' ran the front page headline of the *UK Press Gazette*, reporting the Snooker Writers' Association ban on sponsor mentions. A WPBSA spokesman, too timid to identify himself, said that the reasons for my ban were 'secret and not that simple'. It was denied, albeit without any credibility, that my ban had anything to do with my criticisms of the Williams regime.

The ban on sponsor mentions affected Liverpool Victoria, Regal and Embassy. It did not make Imperial Tobacco feel any better that while two of its brands, Regal and Embassy, were getting no mentions, there was no restriction on mentions of their competitors, Benson and Hedges, who ran their Masters tournament without any input from WPBSA.

The WPBSA's intransigence was costing its sponsors most of the print media and radio exposure they could reasonably expect. Liverpool Victoria, whose sponsorship of the UK Championship had been undermined in this way, then seized 'operational control' of the pressroom at their other tournament, the Liverpool Victoria Charity Challenge. This meant that I was allowed back in. Embassy, facing the unwelcome prospect of no print or radio mentions from its sponsorship of the world championship, did the same.

With snooker spinning ever more giddily out of control, Radford was dismissed. WPBSA could not even do this properly. In a process which took the better part of two years, he successfully sued for wrongful dismissal.

A 26 March 1999 memo from Radford to Blake surfaced in which Radford stated: 'I was employed by the WPBSA to write and edit this in-house magazine in a forthright and aggressive manner and encouraged to target specific people, including Clive Everton.' This obligingly established the element of 'malice' which would reduce WPBSA's capacity to defend my libel actions while increasing the scale of damages I was eventually to receive.

19

SPANISH PRACTICES

WHILE IT WAS OBVIOUS THAT THE REX WILLIAMS REGIME COULD not last indefinitely, the sports media at large was tiring of snooker politics. Except for people at the heart of snooker, the battle was seen as akin to two bald men squabbling over a comb, so *Snooker Scene* was on its own when I discovered that a Ford Scorpio, originally registered to WPBSA and driven exclusively until February 1998 by its tournament director, Ann Yates, had been parked for more than a year outside the villa in Spain used by Williams as a holiday home.

This was why Nigel Bowden, a freelance based in Malaga, turned up on Williams's doorstep to ask him to comment on this chain of events.

'This is absolute rubbish,' Williams blustered. 'I've been accused of many things and this is just another move in the campaign to discredit me. I have a good idea who is behind all this. I don't need to steal cars. I don't do things like that.'

Actually, Williams was not accused of stealing a car. However, what had become of an asset purchased with its funds was certainly of interest to the WPBSA membership.

The two most obvious explanations were: (1) that the governing body had sold its car to the chairman; or (2) that Williams had gained use of the vehicle on exclusive extended loan in a country where WPBSA had no discernible business.

Williams claimed that he had bought the car 'over a year ago'. He declined to say how much he had paid for it or to produce the car's papers but volunteered: 'It cost more to repair the automatic gearbox and the air conditioning than the car cost me.' This came as a surprise to Ann Yates, who in February 1998 had been told that she would have to give up the vehicle as it was to be used as a WPBSA 'pool' car.

'It was six years old and only had 40,000 miles on the clock. It was running perfectly. I wanted to keep it, but I was told that I couldn't. I asked if I could have first refusal if they wanted to sell it but got no answer. I wondered at the time if it was earmarked for a board member. I was given a new black Honda.'

Accepting Williams's assertion that he had bought the Ford Scorpio more than a year prior to April 1999, the question immediately arose: how much for?

Williams may not, standing at the front door of his holiday home in his dressing gown, have felt like telling a passing reporter but should he not have told the members, whose interests he was supposed to have been protecting? There had been no mention of any such transaction in the WPBSA's annual report and accounts as at 30 June 1998.

Obviously, while the purchase price remained undisclosed, the weight of speculation tended to lie towards a relatively low price and it did not appear seemly that the deal had apparently been negotiated with Blake, a company secretary who might not have felt comfortable in driving the hardest of bargains with his chairman. Neither was the transaction mentioned to his board. Two of his boardroom supporters, Ray Reardon and Bob Close, said they knew nothing about it.

When told that the car had been in Spain for a year, Reardon exclaimed: 'Good God!' Asked if he could throw any light on the transaction, he replied: 'I haven't got a clue. This is the first I've heard about this. It never came through at board level.'

Blake was unco-operative with journalistic enquiries: 'I don't know what car you are talking about. We do not have a Ford Scorpio on our books. If you want to ask Rex any questions about any private dealings, I suggest you ring him.' The point was not whether the WPBSA had a Ford Scorpio on its books, but what had happened to the one it had previously had on its books.

I ran the story, together with a picture of the car, number plate prominently displayed, into which Williams was loading some shopping, under the headline: 'Is this your car, sir?'

WPBSA sat tight on any further information but, within snooker, this was still a sufficiently startling story for some of the Williams camp to begin to ponder where all this was leading.

Reardon, who as a compliant vice-chairman had supported Williams in various dirty tricks against me, appeared in my office one afternoon at the instigation of Tony Murphy, who himself was to play a controversial role in snooker politics a couple of years later.

How would I react to Reardon becoming chairman rather than Williams? I replied that any change was better than none. Reardon was very anxious that his own reputation should emerge unbesmirched from any investigation which might follow the demise of the Williams regime. I said that if he had done nothing wrong, he had nothing to worry about. He did not seem entirely happy with this response but had already realised that his reputation might be damaged if he continued to be wholly identified with the actions of the Williams faction.

It was customary for the WPBSA chairman to be elected by its board at its first meeting following the world championship. On 20 May 1999, the day prior to this meeting, Reardon decided to stand, believing he could count on the votes of the three 'opposition' board members: Dennis Taylor, Jason Ferguson and Steve Davis. He did not realise that while Davis and his manager, Barry Hearn, by now held a low opinion of Williams, they held a much lower one of Reardon.

So when Reardon, for what reasons only he could say, phoned Williams the night before the meeting to inform him of his intentions, Williams immediately rang Hearn to elicit the promise of support from Davis, which was to spell humiliation for Reardon next morning. However, a condition of Davis's support was the appointment at Hearn's suggestion of Peter Middleton, a high-flying City troubleshooter, as part-time chief executive. Hearn, chairman of Leyton Orient, had been impressed with Middleton's part-time chairmanship of the Football League.

In his youth, Middleton had spent five years in a monastery because 'it seemed more interesting than reading law at Liverpool University'. He left before taking full vows, graduated from Hull University and spent 24 years as a Foreign Office diplomat, several of them, it was to emerge, as an MI6 spy. In 1987, he was headhunted by the Midland Bank to revitalise Thomas Cook, its travel subsidiary. He became European head of the Wall Street finance house Salamon Brothers International, earning with bonuses a reported £1 million a year.

When he resigned in July 1998, colleagues within the company were quoted as saying: 'He never built a constituency; he just ploughed ahead.' Some of his proposals encountered resistance and he became frustrated. Amongst his priorities were the cutting of costs and the re-vamping of the executive team. Impressive as it was, his CV contained a hint that here was a man unafraid of abrasive methods, who tended not to linger long in one place. Even so, it could not have been predicted that he would last less than ten weeks at WPBSA.

'He has vast experience in the commercial world and we feel that he will guide the commercial development of the association over the next few years' was the welcome from Williams, which quickly turned to fury when he realised that Middleton intended to do in his own way the job for which he had been hired at the far from nominal rate of £50,000 a year for a two-day week.

Middleton set about with gusto the radical surgery required at WPBSA. He 'made a judgement about the competence' of two Williams cronies, Martyn Blake and Terry Crabb, who were swiftly on their bikes, albeit with a combined pay-off of £316,000 from the generous contracts Williams had awarded them. The official press release could hardly have been more emollient: 'Martyn and Terry have been very important members of the WPBSA team for a number of years. We are very grateful for the contribution they have made and extend to them our good wishes for the future.' Prior to the day on which their exits were announced, though, no one at Bristol HQ had an inkling – not even they, it seemed – that they would soon be departing.

This procedure was not applied to Crabb's assistant, Mike Trusson, whose trusty left foot had been crucial in amassing 69 goals for teams as various as Sheffield United and Brighton and Hove Albion. Unfortunately, this skill had not translated into securing new sponsorships, the purpose of the Crabb/Trusson department. Curiosity was expressed at HQ as to Trusson's whereabouts until, several days later, a note of resignation was unearthed on his vacant desk.

Williams, disturbed that his old sidekick Blake had been so unceremoniously cast out, convened a board meeting at the Heathrow Hilton on 9 August and his by now familiar 4–3 majority achieved the sacking of Middleton, who had been appointed only on 1 June. WPBSA claimed that he had not been dismissed but simply that terms could not be agreed. Reardon was quoted in the WPBSA press release as saying: 'Peter is a very busy man with many other interests and commitments. He has been helping us out on a temporary basis since the beginning of June, which we had hoped might develop into a permanent arrangement.'

There had been no mention that Middleton's appointment was temporary when his position had been announced, quite the reverse. If Reardon had been hoping that it would develop into a permanent arrangement, why did he vote to sack him?

'How can Reardon associate himself with such drivel?' asked Hearn. 'Where are his standards, his character, his respect for his own reputation?'

Middleton's dismissal was useful in that it sparked an EGM for the removal from the board of Williams and his staunch ally Bob Close. The end of the most pernicious regime in snooker history was in sight although, like a rat in a trap, Williams struggled to the last. A press release libellously stated that WPBSA 'no longer had confidence in Taylor, Davis and Ferguson to act in the best interests of the association and the game as a whole'. Williams's board cronies requisitioned another EGM to attempt to remove this trio; Davis demanded 'a complete forensic audit of the affairs of WPBSA'.

On 24 September 1999, well aware of the weight of the proxy votes that would have removed them three days later, Williams and Close resigned. Out of an electorate of 78, 50 proxies already stood against them. The EGM to remove Taylor, Davis and Ferguson failed abysmally.

Terry Griffiths and Mark Wildman were co-opted to replace Williams and Close, and Wildman, to his surprise, found himself elected chairman. Matthew McCloy, who had served the Williams dirty tricks campaign diligently as WPBSA's solicitor, was ousted; Middleton was restored as chief executive. Blake, having been briefly re-engaged by Williams, was sacked again, thus earning the distinction of becoming the only employee in WPBSA's history to be accorded three leaving parties.

20

ANOTHER FALSE DAWN

WITH REX WILLIAMS GONE AND PETER MIDDLETON RESTORED, optimism that the snooker world was now to live happily ever after was to prove unfounded, although there was an initial honeymoon with the new administration. There was a move to settle all outstanding libel actions. I received £65,000 in damages and costs for the *In the Frame* article. My playing rights were also restored. This was not easy money. It is no fun for an individual or relatively small business to carry the pre-trial financial burden of legal action against a much wealthier corporate body and there is always the faint chance of a perverse verdict in the face of all logic. Such is the detail demanded in pre-trial pleading and rebuttal of the opposing case that it requires an immense amount of time, which could be more progressively and pleasantly spent. A great deal of thinking time is also absorbed in this way, but the alternative to suing was to let the *In the Frame* article pass without challenge. Had I done so, people would have tended to assume that it had substance.

My second action against WPBSA, Williams, Brian Radford and Geoff Foulds related to an 'open letter' written by Foulds to *Pot Black*, the WPBSA's magazine, which was edited by Radford. WPBSA were also to brass up on behalf of all defendants another £50,000 in damages and costs.

Three libel actions, which Williams had instituted several months after my own had commenced, were dropped. One related to the 'Is this your car, sir?' article. The theory was that a negotiating position could be set up whereby I could be persuaded to drop my actions if they dropped theirs. There was never any prospect of this. They had also gone to the unpleasant lengths of serving these three writs on me at home on three separate evenings, knowing full well the address of my office and my lawyer.

All other legal actions emanating from the Williams regime, brought for no better purpose than to suppress criticism and intimidate its critics, were wound up. None had any hope of success if they had been taken into court. The re-appointed Middleton outlined a cost scenario of £1.6 million, covering all these actions. There had, he said, been no financial cost/potential benefit analysis prior to instigating any of this litigation. The forensic audit demanded by Steve Davis was instituted but, as is the way of the world, innumerable reasons were to be found later for delaying publication of its findings.

The probe was to concentrate on seven areas: (1) directors' expenses, particularly in relation to possible abuses of the notorious £1-a-mile travel allowance; (2) the content of the Blake Report with particular emphasis on financial and managerial controls exercised by the WPBSA; (3) the basis upon which grants had been made by the Benevolent Fund; (4) the reasons for, and principles behind the commencement and funding of legal actions by WPBSA; (5) the manner in which contracts for coaching, referees and officials were dispensed by WPBSA; (6) Williams's claim for commission on sponsorship attracted by WPBSA; and (7) WPBSA's offer to purchase Bridgestone House as a new venue for snooker.

Out of my libel earnings, I bought *Pot Black*. The association had paid £83,000 for it, well over the odds, as a mouthpiece for the Williams regime and to try to put *Snooker Scene* out of business, but it was costing the membership £80,000 a year with no prospect of ever making a profit. Williams's prediction at a players' meeting in October 1999 that 'it's going to make the members a lot of money' could hardly have been further wide of the mark.

It was not a smooth transaction. Ours was the highest bid first time round, but Middleton was nervous that if we bought *Pot Black* and merged it with *Snooker Scene*, as was our declared intent, the WPBSA might be left without an easily accessible and uncritical organ. He proposed a second round of bidding, excluding us. I got wind of this and talked to one of the more fair-minded board members. We were allowed to bid and won easily with our offer of £35,000, thus giving the membership a fair sale price on what remained, notwithstanding the appalling manner in which it had been run, a commercial asset.

It was no great loss that Lord Archer was forced to resign the WPBSA presidency after the *News of the World* revelation that he had asked a friend to lie in constructing an alibi to refute the *Daily Star*'s 1986 allegation that he had been to bed with a prostitute, Monica Coghlan. In the short term, this also led to him withdrawing as the Conservative candidate in the Mayor of London election; in the longer term, it led to him being sentenced to four years for perjury and another four concurrently for perverting the course of justice, and having to repay the *Daily Star*'s libel damages and costs with interest.

As is common with people parachuted into a sport of which they have little previous knowledge, Middleton put undue stress on cosmetics and not enough on uniting the various interest groups in a sense of common purpose. A Young Players of Distinction Scheme was launched, the theory being that those six players selected would attract boy-band type publicity by having their hair styled and wearing designer clothes. This tied in with the relaxation of the traditional tuxedo dress code. The idea that open-neck shirts and a variety of outfits might attract any measurable increase in viewing figures amongst the young evinced a farcical desperation. As it was to turn out, there was a torrent of protest from snooker enthusiasts, who liked the established formality of dress suits.

Middleton also adopted the motto: 'Thirst Amongst Equals'. Free bars backstage for players, managers, journalists and hangers-on had been costing WPBSA £20,000 per tournament – more at the Crucible. In abolishing these facilities, Middleton displeased those who looked on WPBSA as a private drinking club first and a credible world governing body a poor second.

Middleton brought in Liz Walker, whom he had met while he was at the Football League, a prettier face certainly than any previous WPBSA company secretary. Nevertheless, she was to play a role in WPBSA's further disintegration.

This process could have been reversed by what initially appeared to be a promising partnership between WPBSA and The Sportsmasters Network (TSN), a new Internet venture in which Warburg Pincus, the City finance house, invested an initial £10 million. TSN had close links with and was to take over Ian Doyle's Cuemasters management stable. It was also to be re-named 110sport, as confusion arose with the Canadian television channel The Sports Network.

In the glorious dawn of the dot-com revolution, the sky appeared to be the limit. Snooker's vivid colours, small field of action and leisurely pace gave it advantages on the net over sports providing quicker and more wide ranging action. The theory was to offer free coverage at first (originating from television coverage), with archive material available on demand, plus text information services and online betting and purchasing facilities. Through credit card technology, it was obviously going to be possible later to charge for live action on a pay-per-view basis.

Doyle, promoting the October 2000 Regal Scottish Masters, paid a fee to BBC Scotland to carry their coverage live on the Internet and also set up a TSN studio for interviews, inter-frame analysis and discussion items. An incredible 90 countries, including Taiwan, Brunei, Mauritius, Mongolia, Nepal, Lebanon, Uruguay, Saudi Arabia, Bulgaria, Ukraine and Bosnia, none of them by any stretch of definition snooker hotbeds, logged on. More predictably, there was heavy traffic in countries where snooker was more established, such as Australia, Canada, Holland, Thailand and, most of all, China, as Hong Kong's Marco Fu compiled a 147 maximum which was endlessly reprised.

BBC Scotland was happy. Broadcasting simply within Scotland, their viewing figures were unaffected. No doubt a few Scots logged on surreptitiously at work but, in general, no one with access to a television was thought to prefer watching an inferior picture on an Internet screen. As for those who logged on overseas, such Internet availability was obviously a potent agent of popularisation for the game and a means of enhancing the profile – and thus the commercial value – not only of the tournament but also the competitors.

TSN proposed a £3.3 million deal whereby they would sponsor four WPBSA events for three years and become their Internet partners, bearing all costs and giving them 45 per cent of the profits. On top of that, TSN were prepared to pay any necessary fees to BBC, ITV or Sky for the right to use their coverage. In the event of no such agreement being reached, TSN would have had the option of installing their own cameras and commentators.

In late May 2000, champagne corks were popping and backs were being mutually slapped at the WPBSA golf day at Carden Park. The deal had in essence been agreed and Middleton told the assembled gathering at dinner in the evening that he expected all tournaments to be sponsored in the 2000–01 season. Middleton told Doyle quite properly that other Internet deals would have to be invited because it would not do to have such a contract awarded on the nod. Doyle agreed.

No other substantive bids were received but, as the weeks passed, TSN sensed a lack of eagerness and demanded a yes or no from WPBSA. Deadlines came and went until TSN told WPBSA on 7 July that the deal was off. In characteristically peremptory style, Middleton replied on 12 July that if this was the end, then so be it.

A section of the WPBSA board did not share this view, even when Middleton suggested, entirely without foundation as it proved, that a better deal might come along. Here was a £3.3 million deal on the table right now. Could it be rejected in the hope of a better one at some indefinite future date with a party whose identity was as yet unknown and with whom no negotiations had yet taken place?

Unbelievably, it could, even though it would have been the better part of a year down the road before negotiations could have been opened and concluded with another party. By this time, one-third of the value of the TSN deal would have disappeared because the first season's four tournaments would have taken place.

All this suggested that Middleton could not be as effective as was desirable on a mere two days a week. Certain board members, angry that the TSN deal had slipped through their fingers with no apparent alternative on the horizon, opened their own lines of communication to TSN, thus making Middleton's position untenable. Middleton had so many consultancies to deal with that he simply did not have time to master the detail of the snooker world and nurture its constituent elements. After some steaming rows, he had retired from the chairmanship of the Football League in June 2000 but was a long-serving director of Royal Albert Hall Developments and a rather newer director of GTL Resources plc.

Within snooker, his style increasingly began to grate. Departing staff, regardless of quality or service, were refused references in case, apparently, this occupied too much executive time. Staff levels were cut so radically that there were not enough people left to do all the work and there was certainly not enough specialised knowledge in-house of how the snooker world actually operated.

There was a feeling that Middleton was more interested in exciting new projects than in grappling with some of snooker's more intractable problems. The Japanese finance house Nomura, whose bid for the purchase and development of the Millennium Dome was accepted in July 2000, recruited him to head up Dome Europe, only for Nomura, a few weeks later, to get cold feet about any involvement with this monumental New Labour folly.

In the corporate world Middleton knew so well, it seldom pays to have too retiring a nature, nor are robust exchanges of views uncommon. Nevertheless, the circumstances preceding the end of Middleton's chairmanship of Luton airport at this time caused a few eyebrows to rise.

Stelios Haji-Ioannou, the founder chairman of easyJet, asked by *The Independent* whether he would stop development at Luton because of a row over landing fees, commented:

> I think Peter Middleton took over with a desire to run things and soon realised that Barclays wouldn't let him get on with it. The first time I met him, he stormed out of the room. We then exchanged some very angry letters. In fact, I should publish the last one he sent. He said: 'I used to run Lloyds when it was turning over so many billions in fees, I used to run Salamon Brothers when it was turning over so many billions on the trading floor and I am not going to be intimidated by you and your little company.' It was a very arrogant letter.

While there are two sides to most arguments, some WPBSA folk who read this report felt that the allegations of arrogance chimed in uncomfortably with their own experience. When, for all his glittering record as a corporate bruiser, nothing of substance was being delivered in terms of deals, disillusion grew. When the TSN deal slipped through his fingers, his position began to be questioned.

It fell to Mark Wildman, the then WPBSA chairman, to tell Middleton, one to one, that the board had lost confidence in him and wished him to resign.

Wildman tried to resurrect the TSN deal, but there was indecision and a lack of urgency from the board. Liz Walker, Middleton's appointee, sent out many negative signals in her dealings with TSN, behaving as if it was simply one commercial company versus another instead of a governing body, committed to developing the sport, encouraging new investment in it and using its influence to reconcile factional disputes rather than setting itself up as a faction wishing to impose itself on all others.

21

THE CRUCIBLE OF THE HIGH COURT

WITHIN MONTHS OF MIDDLETON'S DEPARTURE, WPBSA JUMPED OUT of the frying pan into the fire, although it did not look like it at first. Jim McKenzie, sacked by Williams in December 1997, had set up a small equipment and servicing business, Titan, but was itching for a proper run as WPBSA chief executive. I thought he would do well. So did the influential Ian Doyle. We were both wrong.

The Sportsmasters Network, having once been rebuffed by WPBSA, still had a £10 million investment from Warburg Pincus in its pocket with which it had to do something. There was more scepticism about dot-com businesses than there had been a year earlier, even though the Internet clearly had a role to play.

TSN purchased the Cuemasters stable from Doyle and offered WPBSA an £8.8 million package to stage its circuit under WPBSA auspices. The package included £6.5 million in prize money, £300,000 in sanction fees and the rest in back-up costs. WPBSA were offered a 5 per cent equity stake in the company, controlled by TSN, which would promote and market the circuit.

WPBSA would have been required to put their BBC TV contract and the much smaller ones with Sky and ITV into the pot. This would have meant TSN's £8.8 million commitment, rising by 10 per cent in years two and three, being offset by about £5 million in television money each year. WPBSA would have been left with full disciplinary and regulatory jurisdiction.

In addition, TSN were offering a tobacco-free tour in contrast to a WPBSA tour heavily dependent on tobacco sponsorship, which was due to end by government decree in 2003 – only two years hence – apart from an exemption for the Embassy World Championship until 2005.

WPBSA's position was that, with tobacco money coming in for the next two seasons, it had no need of the TSN package, as two years was sufficient to bring in non-tobacco sponsorship to at least the same level to replace and possibly increase it.

How optimistic they were.

'With £300,000 a year from TSN in sanction fees and interest on the £4 million they had in the bank, WPBSA were looking at £500,000 a year profit without having to do anything except act as the rules and regulatory authority,' said Doyle. The problem of replacing tobacco sponsorship would also have been solved two years in advance.

The idea was that McKenzie would be tour commissioner, but the first stumbling block was that he was not in love with the prospect of running a regulatory body. He wanted to be doing deals at the centre of the game commercially. This unwelcoming attitude cost snooker dearly. TSN were rebuffed and ill advisedly announced a rival tour, which was clearly unviable without television exposure. There were no substantial outlets other than those filled with WPBSA tournaments.

TSN were bringing new money to the party, but the attitude of McKenzie, leading negotiations with WPBSA, was: 'We don't need you. You can't do anything that we can't do ourselves.'

The editorial line I set for *Snooker Scene* was to hope that somehow all parties could agree a negotiated settlement. Some hope.

TSN, by now re-named 110sport because of confusion with the Canadian channel of the same initials, were demonised as predators and rip-off artists. McKenzie banned TSN's website journalists from WPBSA tournaments. George Smith, chief executive, and Gerry Sinclair, managing director of TSN/110sport, travelled to the China Open but were denied access to the venue, although it was farcically clear that they could talk to whoever they wanted in the adjoining hotel.

WPBSA also hardened its anti-Doyle stance in January/February 2001 by signing up several players on what it said were promotional contracts but were in reality loyalty bonuses. These were designed not only to discourage these players from joining the alternative tour TSN/110sport was contemplating but generally to subscribe to their anti-Doyle effort. This widened snooker's fundamental schism between Doylists and anti-Doylists.

The players who signed were John Higgins, Peter Ebdon, John Parrott, Alan McManus, Matthew Stevens, Paul Hunter and Steve Davis.

These signings all had anti-Doyle history either personally or through their managers. Jim McMahon, a henchman of Rex Williams who somehow retained his seat on the board after the demise of that regime, once put it to Billy Snaddon, one of Doyle's players: 'You're Rangers and always will be. I'm Celtic and always will be.' John Higgins, and even more so his father, John Higgins senior, who was a close friend of McMahon, were long-standing enemies of Doyle; McManus was McMahon's nephew; Ebdon had remained close to his former manager, Ramsey McLellan, a former professional table footballer on the American circuit for whom Doyle's animosity was heartily reciprocated; Parrott was managed by Phil Miller, who never forgave Doyle for offering Parrott alternative management; Stevens and Hunter were managed by Wheels in Motion, where Brandon Parker, an anti-Doylist who travelled the circuit, was much more influential than Geoff Faint, its nominal principal; Davis was managed by Barry Hearn, who did not usually neglect substantial earning opportunities for his client.

Hearn secured Davis a three-year contract at £100,000 a year. Those for Ebdon, Hunter, Stevens and Parrott were for £75,000, and McManus £50,000. O'Sullivan, considered the jewel in the crown, was offered £1.2 million over three years, enough to woo him away from Doyle's management. Doyle considered these contracts to be an abuse of the membership's funds. O'Sullivan wanted to continue under his management, but Doyle refused to agree if O'Sullivan accepted the loyalty bonus. O'Sullivan at first signed and then requested his release from a new contract with Doyle, a release which cost him logo payments of £80,000 a year from BCE and £40,000 from Highland Spring. O'Sullivan never signed the WPBSA contract but did carry out work under its terms at £10,000 a day.

Of course, once the immediate need for the loyalty bonuses had disappeared, with 110sport abandoning plans for their rival tour, WPBSA were left still having to pay the contracted players. If, for instance, a newspaper wanted an interview, the player would do it under the terms of that contract. This tended to enrage those non-contracted players who habitually gave interviews without payment. As chief executive, McKenzie recruited several expensive consultants.

Hill & Knowlton, which recommended the association to 'think dirty' in relation to 110, was put in charge of public relations; Media Content, which was to go bankrupt the following year, was engaged to sell media rights and packages; World Sport Group, which had to be dismembered for financial reasons in 2003, was inexplicably engaged on a £28,000-a-month five year contract as event managers, a function which WPBSA's own staff on the ground had been performing perfectly adequately.

This involved getting rid of such long-standing figures as Jim Furlong, a popular and effective front-desk man who not only sued successfully for wrongful dismissal but also had the satisfaction of hearing an industrial tribunal characterise WPBSA's dealings with him as 'a charade'. Fortunes were spent, some quite needlessly, on legal and financial consultants; an expensive Accredited Centre of Excellence scheme was embarked upon just as WPBSA began to run out of money.

TSN/110sport's plans for an alternative tour would never have received such an enthusiastic reception from so many players – not just those Doyle managed – if there had not been so much dissatisfaction with WPBSA's stewardship of their livelihoods but, at the end of the day, a breakaway was seen as too radical and there was also a belief that, with McKenzie at the helm of WPBSA, things really were going to get better. To underline this, prize money was dramatically increased, albeit using the membership's own funds. The BBC gave the WPBSA its emphatic support and the TSN/110sport tour was aborted.

TSN's unfounded assumption had been that if enough players signed up for its tour, not the WPBSA's, the BBC would cover whichever tour had the preponderance of star players. However, the BBC's long established policy of supporting governing bodies, plus its contractual commitment to cover WPBSA's tour, even if payments were adjustable downwards if a significant number of top players did not participate, made TSN/110sport's project appear, in retrospect, snooker's equivalent of the Charge of the Light Brigade. The BBC was to admit quite candidly that its talks with TSN/110sport were designed simply to ascertain what they were up to.

WPBSA tried to consolidate its position with an attempt to smash TSN/110sport into the ground but clumsily went much too far and laid themselves open to a deadly counterpunch. It issued a set of tournament rules on 19 February 2001 whereby players were required to accept by 28 February conditions for the following season's circuit which would effectively have bound them hand, foot and finger. TSN/110sport resolved to challenge these new restraints on players' freedoms of movement and earning power in the High Court.

Its case was that, as matters stood, WPBSA could use its governing body function to disadvantage or even exclude other tournament promoters and thereby exclude players from certain sources of income. In short, it suggested that WPBSA was acting unlawfully as a quasi-monopoly.

Liz Walker had drafted the disputed set of rules with such legal overkill that they virtually invited challenge. Players were required to sign away their intellectual property rights to WPBSA for no payment; players were to be permitted only one logo of their choice on their waistcoats instead of two, with WPBSA having the right not only to veto any logo it deemed 'detrimental' to itself but also to impose one regardless of the players' wishes; players were to be required to give 14 days' notice of any exhibition or other engagement anytime, anywhere, with WPBSA having the power to insist that an engagement of its own took precedence; semi-final losers were to be required to attend prize presentations and in the event of an early finish on the final night to play an exhibition for no fee; players wishing to play in 8-ball or 9-ball pool tournaments – which were not games under WPBSA jurisdiction – were to be required to ask permission and give 14 days' notice.

Absurdly, players were to be required to act as unpaid public relations agents: 'Each player must refer to a tournament by its correct title, including a reference to the title sponsor at a press conference and at all other times.' Thus, if a player was asked what was his life's ambition, he was not to reply: 'To win the world championship.' The acceptable answer was: 'To win the Embassy World Championship.' Players were to be prohibited 'by word, gesture, writing or otherwise harming the reputation or questioning the honour or integrity of WPBSA, its directors, members, employees, referees, tournament officials and/or policies'. This was nothing more or less than a gagging order of the most outrageous kind.

When TSN/110sport commenced legal action, WPBSA immediately withdrew the restriction to one logo and tried to claim that the rules on the entry form were only a draft, although they were, in fact, legally binding.

Backing off in stages, it agreed to withdraw its prohibition on its member players competing in events which WPBSA had not sanctioned. The abandonment of this rule, a radical concession for an organisation with governing body credentials, meant that a promoter might now negotiate television coverage and sponsorship support without fear that WPBSA could effectively prevent the tournament from taking place by refusing to grant a sanction. The only trouble was that WPBSA was unwilling to undertake that it would not seek to reimpose such a rule. Had it made this undertaking, the case would never have come into court on 13 June 2001.

There were various postponements and skirmishes on the way to trial and WPBSA continued to use its internal communications to the membership to blacken the name of TSN and all who sailed in her. Doyle was pettily and vindictively banned from all backstage areas at the Crucible during the 2001 championship, thus denying him access to his players.

TSN/110sport wanted the High Court to order that WPBSA should be split into three elements, each independent of the other – (1) a promotional company; (2) a rules, regulatory and disciplinary body; and (3) a players' trade union – but on the first morning of the trial it became evident that TSN/110sport's original pleadings had been insufficiently amended.

Mr Justice Lloyd did not accept TSN/110sport's argument that divestiture by WPBSA of any of these functions was implicit in its claim and also ruled that even if WPBSA had mismanaged the sport it was irrelevant to the issue of anti-competitiveness. He also ruled that WPBSA's exclusion of TSN's website journalists from tournaments did not constitute anti-competitive behaviour.

The trial was thus left with specific alleged breaches of the 1998 Competition Act and Philip Shepherd, for TSN/110sport, made Liz Walker look foolish in the witness box.

Rule A5.1 stated 'Members are not permitted to enter, participate or play in any tournament match or game of snooker . . . [without the written consent of WPBSA]':

| Philip Shepherd: | Why did you include any game of snooker in rule 5.1? What purpose did that serve? |
| Liz Walker: | To make it clear; a tournament, in my view, is a game of snooker. |

Shepherd:	But, you see, read in the way it appears there, it meant that no member of the WPBSA could have a game of snooker without the written permission of the WPBSA.
Walker:	Correct.
Shepherd:	That is what was intended, was it?
Walker:	No.
Mr Justice Lloyd:	On the face of it, a member requires the permission of World Snooker to play an entirely private, entirely friendly, non-commercial game of snooker with a friend?
Walker:	On the face of it, yes.
Shepherd:	Was it also your idea to extend the ban on all sports requiring the use of a cue?
Walker:	I cannot recall. I think it was my initial view, but I obviously discussed internally . . .
Shepherd:	But you understood, did you not, that including cue sports would widen the ambit of the restriction very considerably?
Walker:	I did, yes, and there were good reasons for that.
Shepherd:	It was intended to do just that?
Walker:	It was.
Shepherd:	If there were good reasons for it on 19 February, how was it that those reasons had receded by the time the amended rule came into force on 16 March?
Walker:	Those reasons were, in my view, still there, but obviously we took a strategic decision in light of the pending litigation.
Shepherd:	It was a reaction to the litigation that 'other cue sports' was dropped?
Walker:	It was, yes.

Shepherd:	Otherwise, it would not have been?
Walker:	I do not believe so, no.
Shepherd:	There is no geographic limitation in this clause: was that deliberate?
Walker:	As far as I can recall, yes, I believe it was, on the basis that we are a world governing body and have and will be extending the game into all areas of the world.
Shepherd:	So, you appreciated fully, did you, that not including any form of geographical limitation would extend the ambit of this clause to a player who happened to be on the other side of the world who wished to play in a tournament which had no possibility of clashing with any tournament of the WPBSA, but he still had to obtain the WPBSA's prior written permission?
Walker:	Yes, or obviously it could be subject to the sanctioning policy we had adopted.
Shepherd:	But the answer to my question is that you did understand that, in those circumstances, players would have to make written requests for permission?
Walker:	Yes.

So, the situation was that if TSN/110sport had not instituted a legal action, all professionals would have been in the position of having to apply to WPBSA for permission to play in pool tournaments, one-day pro-ams or, strictly, any game of snooker whatsoever.

Even allowing that players would almost certainly have been allowed to practise together unmolested by the WPBSA, it is not the best legal principle to have a rule worded in one way if the intention is to enforce it in another. Nor could WPBSA argue that it would have taken an accommodating stance for any player wishing to take part in a pool tournament. The fact is that if a rule existed to prohibit a player from doing this, it could have been enforced.

Walker blamed time pressures for any shortcomings in her wording of the new rules: 'I have to say, these rules were prepared in a rush. I cannot say that I went through every line and fully appreciated every single consequence of every single line of the rules.'

Shepherd put it to her that in her ten years' experience as a solicitor, some of it in media and intellectual property law, she must have known that the rules would have to pass the doctrine of restraint of trade.

Walker said there was 'simply no time' to take advice from an expert competition lawyer and that since her 'training years' she was not 'fully up to date' with the doctrine of restraint of trade.

So, there it was. A High Court case was precipitated, at least in part, by the WPBSA's own in-house legal eagle who: (a) did not apparently understand the difference between 'game' (non-competitive) and 'match' (competitive); (b) drafted the rule in a hurry; (c) did not consult a specialist competition lawyer; and (d) did not consult with a specialist in restraint of trade, an area which she had not touched in the ten years since she had qualified as a solicitor.

Furthermore, Walker had drafted some highly restrictive rules with no formal appeals mechanism but simply an unwritten assurance that WPBSA would be jolly good chaps and not apply their own rules if they considered them unfair in this case or that. This stance left the judgement of this discretion with the WPBSA rather than with the player as a right.

Shepherd's cross-examination closed with an exchange over a proposed rule that a player had to notify WPBSA of any promotional activities 14 days in advance. Ultimately, Walker agreed that she 'did not think through the practicalities of that rule'. Asked whether it was completely unworkable and completely unreasonable, she agreed: 'It was unworkable, unreasonable; that is the reason we removed it.'

Yes, but would it have been removed – for the benefit of all players – if TSN had not instituted the High Court action? Of course not.

In law, there was only ever going to be one outcome on the main issue and Mr Justice Lloyd duly ruled that WPBSA had abused its dominant position and adopted an unlawful restraint of trade in the set of tournament rules it had issued on 19 February. The ruling meant that WPBSA could not reimpose rule A5 or anything like it.

This is what the trial was all about, but Mr Justice Lloyd's rulings on several subsidiary, almost marginal, matters allowed Hill & Knowlton, WPBSA's spin doctors, to claim that WPBSA had prevailed in five issues out of seven.

Even this was misleading because WPBSA had already backed down on the logo issue and Mr Justice Lloyd was content to let sleeping dogs lie. In arguing in the High Court that there should be no restriction on logos, TSN was simply hoping for a ruling that three would be acceptable, although they were quite happy with two.

TSN had challenged WPBSA's right to require players to do promotional work for no fee during tournaments, but its argument was one of degree. TSN fully supported players co-operating in the usual range of preview and post-match interviews but was nervous of WPBSA having too many enforceable rights. Mr Justice Lloyd's ruling was not in essence a victory for WPBSA but simply allowed existing practice to continue, leaving it open to TSN or any other player to refuse any unreasonable demand and allow a disciplinary hearing to rule – WPBSA having first to demonstrate that its disciplinary process was fair and objective.

At the conclusion of the *TSN* v *WPBSA* case, WPBSA could no longer delay publication of the report it had commissioned into the activities of the Rex Williams regime, which had fallen some two years earlier. The delay suited two members of the board, in particular Jim McMahon, the Williams disciple who had survived, and Joe Johnson, the 1986 world champion, who had been co-opted to it in January 2001, replacing Terry Griffiths, whose resignation had been demanded on the grounds that he was TSN's director of coaching.

To most of the incoming administration, it had seemed a good idea to expose the misdemeanours of its predecessors. However, the more time passed, the more reluctance was shown to publish the findings of Mark Gay, who headed up the sports law division at Denton Wilde Sapte. Like it or not, the new administration was always going to be to some degree tarred with the same brush as the miscreants, particularly as in some respects WPBSA was continuing much as before. Neither was it palatable that the report emphatically confirmed the criticisms Doyle and I had been making over how the game was being run.

22

FOULDS TAKES HIMSELF
TO THE CLEANERS

IN SOME AMAZING FASHION, EACH SUCCESSIVE WPBSA REGIME REPEATED the mistakes of its predecessors. If power corrupts, and absolute power tends to corrupt absolutely, the first sign of this at WPBSA was often arrogance from people truly appearing to believe that the sonorous ring of World – yes, World – Professional Billiards and Snooker Association gave them some kind of cosmic authority. In reality, it was simply a members' club, comparatively few of whom had voting rights, controlled by a committee calling itself a board, which was so ill qualified that it could neither run the sport itself nor adequately supervise those whom it appointed to do so on its behalf.

With arrogance came a resentment of criticism and a sense of entitlement which often involved abuse of the £1-a-mile travel allowance – the very existence of which was an outrageous rip-off of the membership's funds – and the formation of alliances within the game which, at its worst, was little more than a reciprocity of dubious favours. Resources which could have been spent on development were spent on demonising critics of the board or distributing self-congratulatory newsletters.

Despite WPBSA's unfavourable result from the High Court action, it propagated the self-contradictory canard that it had won but that, in some strange way, by having to pay £1.2 million in costs, it was TSN/110sport's fault that the membership's funds had been depleted. WPBSA kept saying they had agreed to withdraw the most serious of the anti-competitive restrictions complained of but were far less ready to admit that it was their refusal to undertake never to reimpose them which meant that the court case had to be fought to the death.

All the goodwill the new administration had behind it on ejecting the Williams regime in September 1999 was utterly gone by summer 2001. Mark Wildman was admirably resolved not to be a hands-on chairman in the Rex Williams mould but, in the process, too much power was given to executives and hired advisors. It was not to be very long before a circle of blamelessness was to be created. The WPBSA board would invariably say that they had taken some action or other on professional advice; the accountants or the lawyers would say they were carrying out the instructions of the board.

When the Williams regime had succeeded that of Geoff Foulds, an investigation had immediately been set up into the iniquities of the latter only for its findings – the Blake Report – to be suppressed because the Williams regime, only a few months down the road, needed the votes controlled by Foulds and his supporters to survive. This scenario was re-enacted at the fall of Williams and his henchmen when Mark Gay, arguably the leading sports lawyer in the country, was appointed to conduct an inquiry into its activities. However, in turn, only a few months later, this was not regarded as such a good idea since it was feared that his findings would tarnish the WPBSA's corporate good name – what was left of it – regardless of any change in personnel.

Therefore, inquiries into WPBSA misdeeds never quite caught up with new misdeeds by a new administration. The golden future which the early '80s had promised had been transmuted into an altogether baser metal. I was angry about this and the exposure of those who were responsible for it became a crusade. I thus became involved in assisting Mirror Group Newspapers to defend a libel action brought – ill advisedly, as it was to prove – by Foulds, who sought damages from *The Mirror* for two articles published in

January 1998. If a year and a day passes before action is instigated, it cannot be instigated at all. A week short of this deadline, Foulds issued his writ.

At the heart of the case was the Blake Report, which revealed wholesale abuse of the expenses system by Foulds, especially the £1-a-mile travel allowance. When the Williams regime suppressed it, *The Mirror* alleged a cover-up. WPBSA commenced proceedings on the basis of this allegation, although its own internal documents were to reveal that this was only to silence *The Mirror*, not to dispute its facts.

Perhaps Foulds anticipated that the documentation needed for a watertight defence to his libel action would remain, in large part, buried. Once it was clear that it would not, it seemed scarcely credible that he should have carried his case against *The Mirror* through to the bitter end. If he had never sued, he could have told the snooker world: 'Well, what *The Mirror* said was all lies, but I hadn't got the money to sue them.' Many would have believed him. Perhaps, beyond a certain point, it was a case of in for a penny, in for a pound. Defeat was going to mean ruin whether it cost him £200,000 or £800,000.

This consideration was not lost on MGN, which feared, at a comparatively early stage, that it was unlikely to recover its costs, which were running at about £10,000 a day at the trial. At the end of its third day, *The Mirror* offered to walk away, bearing its own costs if Foulds would discontinue the action and bear his. Foulds seems to have interpreted this as a sign of weakness. He rejected the offer and the trial ground on to what was for him a ruinous conclusion.

The case ran for 11 working days in the High Court with Ron Thwaites QC representing MGN and Tom Shields QC representing Foulds. The thrust of *The Mirror*'s two 1998 articles – 'Snooker is rotten to the core' and 'Snooker cover-up denied' – was, as Shields put it, that Foulds had systematically defrauded the membership 'of thousands and thousands of pounds by submitting both fabricated and inflated business expense claims'.

Shields said that readers would conclude from the articles that 'this chap is a serial and long term fraudster'. *The Mirror* maintained that its articles were true and fair comment. The onus was on *The Mirror* to prove its case. The proceedings were to expose to the full the insidious culture which had undermined snooker's health and development for two decades.

At its worst, abuse of the £1-a-mile travelling allowance for board members was tantamount to a fraud on the membership, but all calls to reform this system had fallen on deaf ears. It was viewed, to put it bluntly, as a source of income in clear contravention of the constitutional ban on board members being paid for their services as board members. The constitution stipulated that more than half the board should comprise players or former players but for most of them snooker was all they knew. Being on the board gave them a role in and an income from snooker.

An alternative to the £1-a-mile favoured by Foulds and others was to pay board members, the chairman and vice-chairman in particular, and resolutions were put before AGMs and EGMs to change the constitution to this effect. Others, believing them not to be up to the job, opposed this.

To people like me, such proposals were going further and further from what was needed: an able chief executive at the head of a sound management structure. If a particular chief executive was found wanting, it did not mean, as Foulds inferred, that the principle was unsound and that the business of the game was better left in the hands of players with very little relevant experience.

Thwarted in his wish to be paid, Foulds not only engaged in a systematic abuse of his entitlement to expenses but also secured a vastly overpaid appointment for consultancy services of an insignificant nature. He was determined to be paid one way or another.

This was not merely a matter of £1-a-mile. Flights and hotels could be booked through Bristol HQ as tournaments could be attended on any official pretext. Bills for meals, drinks and extras were signed to the WPBSA. This was a very pleasant lifestyle for anyone prepared to exploit his position. For Foulds, who was unable in the High Court to demonstrate any source of income other than WPBSA, the situation provided irresistible temptations.

Of all the expense claims Foulds made, it was one for £500 during the 1996 Irish Masters that probably caused most damage to his case. Such details as it had contained were, he admitted, misleading, but the claim had been accepted and paid simply on trust.

Foulds produced a letter from Malcolm Hulley, WPBSA's then company secretary, which he had received on the Monday morning he flew from Heathrow to Dublin. It was clear to him on reading it that Hulley was seriously ill. He claimed that he considered it imperative not only to see Hulley that week in Bristol but also to disclose this intention to no one. *The Mirror* investigated whether Foulds had ever made the journey from Kill, the venue for the Irish Masters, to Bristol that week and concluded that he had not.

For 27 March, Foulds had claimed £250 for miscellaneous meetings in Ireland, although the WPBSA had paid his return air fare to Dublin and a mileage claim was therefore inapplicable; for 31 March, Foulds had claimed £250 for attending in Ireland a meeting with representatives of Liverpool Victoria, who were there as WPBSA's guests, which he asserted had led to Liverpool Victoria becoming the sponsors of the UK Championship. In itself, this was a very large and dubious assertion, but as he was already in Ireland anyway no claim for mileage could be justified. Foulds therefore had to invent a journey or journeys with which he could justify running up these expense claims.

He maintained that he could not say at the time that he urgently needed to visit Hulley, as Hulley had asked him to keep such a meeting confidential. If, indeed, there had been such a meeting, the substance of any discussions might reasonably have required confidentiality, but it was difficult to accept that there could have been any valid reason for Foulds concealing from Bristol HQ and his fellow board members that there had been – so he said – a meeting with Hulley of an urgent nature. Instead, Foulds conjured up a series of explanations in an attempt to justify claiming £500 of the association's money.

Foulds first stated that on the Wednesday he had been driven from the tournament hotel to Dublin airport, flown to Heathrow, collected his car from the car park, driven to Bristol and met Hulley in a coffee shop near Temple Meads station just before lunchtime. They had talked, he said, for about an hour and Foulds had then driven back to Heathrow, flown from Heathrow to Dublin and been driven back to the tournament.

With no cheque stub or credit card receipt for his flight to support it, his initial version of events was exploded by the heated exchange he had had at breakfast in the hotel that Wednesday morning with Kevin Francis of the *Daily Star*, whose account of the incident, sparked by a Foulds tirade against the treatment of snooker by the tabloid press, had been published in *Snooker Scene*.

Francis was able to place the row between 9.15 and 9.30. Even some 15 minutes after its conclusion, he testified, he saw Foulds bearing a breakfast tray for his wife up to their room. Thus, on the basis of a 30 minute drive to the airport, at least another few minutes before he boarded a flight of an hour's duration, another 20 minutes minimum to disembark and get his car on the road and, finally, the better part of an hour and a half's drive to Bristol, he could not have met Hulley in the coffee shop, whose name and precise location he could not remember, around lunchtime that day.

Accepting this, after an exchange of witness statements embodying claim and rebuttal, Foulds filed another witness statement, a week before the trial, that he must have therefore met Hulley on the Tuesday. Obviously, Foulds had forgotten that around 1.15 that day he was templating the table for the tournament, which was to commence at two o'clock. *The Mirror* was able to produce a photograph of this very ceremony featuring Foulds himself, the chief referee, John Williams, and Andy Kennedy, the table fitter.

In response, Foulds adopted the 'black hole' defence. He regarded Hulley as such a good friend and was so upset by the seriousness of his illness, he claimed, that he could not remember anything that happened that week, not even the row with Francis or templating the table. But he was adamant that he had made the journey, as he had described it, that week. What was more, he now argued that the £500 expenses claim was not for this journey at all. He had paid his expenses for it out of his own pocket. No, the £500 related to drinks he had bought that week in his WPBSA vice-chairman role, entertaining representatives of sponsors the association had invited along for a jolly, and for unofficial payments to Benson and Hedges (Ireland) courtesy car drivers to ferry WPBSA guests hither and yon.

Although he might have hoped that the jury, having little or no understanding of the social workings of the snooker world, might have given some credence to this explanation, snooker insiders would not. The sponsor's hospitality was known to be wide ranging and lavish and its courtesy cars were invariably available not only for its own guests but for WPBSA's, who for the duration of the week were effectively guests of B&H(I) anyway. Nevertheless, Foulds contended that he had paid out £500 on drinks and bungs.

In investigating the feasibility of Hulley meeting Foulds on either the Tuesday or the Wednesday, *The Mirror* asked for medical records, which it could, had it been necessary, have obtained through subpoena. These disclosed that Hulley had been fitted with a Hickman Line, a central venous catheter, which had been inserted in his clavicle, and had been admitted to a ward at Bristol Royal Infirmary on the morning of Tuesday, 26 March to commence chemotherapy. He had undergone various standard admission practices that morning before his first date-timed procedure at 12.20. At 6.30 that evening, Hulley was given his pre-medication and an intravenous infusion commenced. The meticulously kept nursing records disclosed no interruption of this before he left hospital on Thursday, 28 March, on which the last date-timed entry for nursing care was at noon. The infusion was still running at that time and was probably completed around 1 p.m.

Dr Claire Vernon, a consultant oncologist with the highest credentials, testified that for Hulley to have left the hospital after 6.30 p.m. on the Tuesday 'would have necessitated taking with him the intravenous infusion that would have been on a wheeled drip stand some five to six feet in height. It would be possible to wheel this a short distance only.' In other words, the coffee shop meeting would either have to have been concluded about half an hour before 12.20 on the Tuesday – Hulley having somehow left the hospital to which he had only just been admitted – or have taken place on the Wednesday or Thursday morning, when Hulley was still attached to a drip he had somehow wheeled from the hospital to the coffee shop.

How could any jury believe this catalogue of lies, each version comprehensively disproved? And what did the jury make of Foulds's readiness to use the circumstances of a dying man – possibly on the basis that dead men tell no tales – to support his fictions?

There was also a series of inherently improbable explanations for £1-a-mile expense claims running into three figures when the distance involved was less than ten miles. This part of the case reminded me of Harold Pinter's comedy of menace, *The Caretaker*, in which the tramp, Davies, returns time and again to the phrase, 'I gotta go to Sidcup', a strange obsession carrying the sense of Davies believing, in some unspecified way, that the answer to all his troubles somehow resides in reaching that destination. Actually, he never leaves the house.

Foulds, in his ever more bizarre explanations of his expense claims, returned time and again to Colchester and towns in that area. Or at least he said he did. *The Mirror* said that it was inherently improbable that he had ever been to Colchester on the days that he said he had.

As he lived at Perivale, some 2.8 miles from Wembley, no one would have queried a charge of £5 or even £6 under the £1-a-mile allowance, i.e. £3 each way for a meeting there. In the absence of any note to the contrary in submitting his expense claim, it would have been a fair assumption that his own front door was the starting point of any journey to Wembley or anywhere else in the London area. Without appropriate explanation at the time, how could anyone at WPBSA's Bristol HQ, assessing the validity of a claim, assume otherwise? The truth was that Foulds was such a powerful figure at WPBSA's HQ that no one dared challenge him.

And so to Colchester. Or not, as the case may be.

Foulds claimed that in 1995 he was investigating in the Colchester area whether any premises were suitable for his friend, Ray Morris, proprietor of Ealing Snooker Centre, to open new snooker establishments. This was unpaid work which Foulds was doing as a favour to a friend, but he was, so his story went, so keen to complete this task that he several times drove the long road to Colchester at highly inconvenient times. For example, on 12 February 1995, Foulds claimed £150 at £1 a mile for attending the Benson and Hedges Masters final because, he said, he drove not directly from Perivale to Wembley (three miles) but from Perivale to Wembley via Colchester (76.8 miles).

The following morning, there was a board meeting at Wembley for which Foulds claimed the maximum travelling allowance, £250, on the basis that he had risen at 5.30 a.m., driven to Colchester, looked round the streets to assess suitable venues for snooker clubs and returned in time for the ten o'clock board meeting.

Colchester also figured in his explanation of his claim for £150 at £1 a mile for a meeting with Barclay/AZT in London that same week. This was, said Foulds, a late morning meeting. He had, he claimed, been to Colchester that morning, having risen again at 5.30 a.m. This would have put his arrival at Colchester at around 7 a.m. He said he had begun the return journey between 9.30 and 10.

The following exchange then took place in court 14:

Ronald Thwaites QC: What were you doing there for two and a half hours on that day?

Geoff Foulds: Looking round. Just driving round, surveying areas. I mean, you know, that's what you do. Or that's what I do anyway. You look for . . .

Thwaites: Was that your first trip to Colchester?

Foulds: I don't know. Think so, no.

Thwaites: So, where does that come in the eight or nine trips you made? You had been there two or three times before?

Foulds: I had been there before.

Thwaites: Yes. More than once?

Foulds: Probably.

Thwaites: And so, what was the objective you had on that day on your return visit?

Foulds: Well, you're looking for, as I was saying, the right population . . .

Thwaites: Were the population out on the streets . . .

Foulds: No.

Thwaites: . . . at a quarter to seven on 8 February 1995?

Foulds: By . . .

Thwaites: What do you mean by 'the population'?

Foulds: . . . the right kind of housing areas.

Thwaites: So, you are driving around council estates and private dwellings?

Foulds: Something like that, yes.

Thwaites: And making notes as you go?

Foulds: Mental notes, yes.

Thwaites: Why are you not writing down any promising estate or district that you drive through?

Foulds: Well, it's very hard to write when you're driving anyway, but I was just . . .

Thwaites:	I expect you stopped, did you not?
Foulds:	I was just looking for – when you're looking for a snooker club, especially out of London, you've got to find – it's no good opening a club where you've got the wrong, in the wrong kind of area, because you won't get the clientele in.
Thwaites:	No. But what progress are you making, making mental notes? If you are driving round and you see a promising area, you must make a note of it, must you not? Did you get out of the car, then, and speak to passers-by?
Foulds:	I would go to a particular area and sort of look round it.
Thwaites:	Did you get out and speak to the locals?
Foulds:	Not really, no.
Thwaites:	Did you see a postman on his rounds and get out and ask him: 'Are the people in this area snooker players, do you think?'
Foulds:	No.
Thwaites:	Well, is this a complete work of fiction, Mr Foulds?
Foulds:	No, it's – I'm an experienced person regarding this kind of work. I know what to look for and the kind of population, the kind of area, and then you see what competition there is in the area. What Mr Morris was looking for was a 12-plus-table club which could sustain a 24-hour business.
Thwaites:	Did you visit any snooker clubs in Colchester on 8 February?

Foulds:	I visited some clubs, but I'm not saying it was on 8 February because most of them aren't open . . .
Thwaites:	I was going to ask you that about quarter to seven – are there 24-hour snooker clubs in Colchester, Ipswich, Felixstowe?
Foulds:	I could not find a 24-hour snooker club open.
Thwaites:	What on earth is the point of testing the population, looking at the snooker clubs, trying to find a venue, of getting yourself there at quarter to seven on a Wednesday morning in February?
Foulds:	Well, in the snooker business, if you want me to explain, you're looking for three kinds of clientele. You're looking for daytime clientele . . .
Mr Justice Gray:	I think we have had this evidence before. I am not sure it is quite an answer to the question, is it?
Foulds:	Sorry, my Lord.
Mr Justice Gray:	The question really is: why did you drive to Colchester, arriving at quarter to seven on a Wednesday morning in February?
Foulds:	Because I wanted to survey a particular area.
Thwaites:	And, you see, that is on a day when you know that you are due in Chiswick, 5.6 miles away from your home, sometime in the late morning. Is that correct?
Foulds:	No. I think that meeting was at Wembley. I think.
Thwaites:	Well, that is even closer to your home, is it not?
Foulds:	Yes.

Thwaites:	So, you have got a meeting at Wembley, 2.8 miles away, on the morning of that day and just to make it as difficult as possible for yourself to get there on time you first of all drive off to Colchester, 76 miles away, to drive round the block a few times, looking for the population. Is that the best you can do, Mr Foulds, to justify a claim of £150 for mileage?
Foulds:	Well, I would have spent all day there but for the meeting.
Thwaites:	Did you go back there after the meeting?
Foulds:	Yes, I did.
Thwaites:	I see, the meeting is a short meeting, is it?
Foulds:	The meeting took about an hour and a half, I think.
Thwaites:	So, that takes us to when? About two o'clock, possibly?
Foulds:	Round lunchtime-ish.
Thwaites:	Then you go back on the North Circular or the M25, A11 or A12 and struggle down to Colchester again in the afternoon of 8 February, do you?
Foulds:	Well, I had a project to complete and I wanted to complete it as quickly as I could.
Thwaites:	Now, you see, so that the jury understand why you have to say you went back a second time was because if you were in Colchester on the morning of 8 February and you travelled back to London, you could only charge 76 miles on association business, could you not?
Foulds:	(No audible reply.)

Thwaites:	Because that is the mileage to the meeting. Then you could charge 2.8 miles from the meeting back home. And you have charged 150 miles, have you not?
Foulds:	Yes. Well, all this was explained . . .
Thwaites:	No, no. You explain it to us. Never mind who else you say you explained it to.
Foulds:	Yes, but this . . .
Thwaites:	First of all, do you agree that you have to say that you went back a second time to Colchester to justify the mileage?
Foulds:	I went back as often as I could to complete the project as quickly as I could.
Thwaites:	So, you are then driving around in circles again in the afternoon, are you?
Foulds:	If you want to put it that way.
Thwaites:	You see, this is the first time you said you went back on that day. You have not previously said that.
Foulds:	Haven't I?

In all, Foulds claimed that he had made eight trips to Colchester during that week although none of this wear and tear on the A12 to Colchester had led to his friend Morris opening a snooker club in the area. He was unable to produce a single petrol receipt to substantiate these journeys or any material from estate agents that might have been expected to furnish him with details of potentially suitable properties.

It was barrack-room lawyer versus an authentic QC and it was no contest, though Foulds, in his self-righteous arrogance and boundless sense of entitlement, may have been oblivious to the impression he was creating. Those of us who had known him for upwards of 35 years felt a sense of incredulity that it had really come to this, but it was a situation entirely of his own making.

As to expense claims during the 1995 Embassy World Championship, Foulds claimed £250 for travelling from Perivale to Sheffield on 24, 26, 28 and 30 April (i.e. every other day), maintaining that he had spent alternate days at home to help his wife care for her sick mother. *The Mirror*'s case was that Foulds had been booked into the Grosvenor Hotel in Sheffield throughout that period and was indeed there the whole time.

The hotel's phone records disclosed that on the mornings following the nights he claimed to have spent in Perivale, calls had been made from his room to his home around 7.30 each morning. His explanation for this was that he had risen at 5.30 or even earlier and phoned home on arrival at Sheffield. On the nights he was, as both sides agreed, resident in the hotel, he phoned home at around the same time the following morning.

Even the work he claimed to be doing was nebulous. On 24 April, Foulds claimed that he was helping with hospitality at the championship; for 26 April, he cited a BBC meeting albeit with no further details; and for 28 April, an IMG meeting. On 30 April, he was simply in attendance at the final and on 1 May he claimed £250 for attending a board meeting, having entered the maximum mileage claim of £250 the previous day and spent the intervening night at the Grosvenor.

On 28 June 1995, by invitation of IMG, who are big in tennis, Foulds was invited to spend a day in their hospitality tent at Wimbledon. Anticipating offers of alcoholic refreshment, he did not drive but submitted a claim for £110 without specifying any mileage. He told the court that he had engaged a chauffeur service, operated by a Mr Bowles, for the occasion although a taxi, easily available in either direction, would have been cheaper. He was unable to provide any documentary evidence of such a hiring either on that occasion or for 15 July and 21 July.

On 15 July, he attended the draw for the Benson and Hedges Masters at the premises of Karen Earl Ltd, B&H's sponsorship consultants, in Notting Hill. Thwaites reminded him that this was a short journey on the tube in daytime (eight stops with one change), but Foulds was affronted at the suggestion that he should have relied on such a humble mode of transport.

'Well, when you're talking to – when you're going to places where you are meeting sponsors, Mr Thwaites, where you're hoping to do millions of pounds of business on behalf of the association, when you're a director and vice-chairman, I think you have a standard and image to try and maintain and it is always nice to say to somebody who you may have got into contact with who wants to do some business with the association "May I drop you somewhere? May I do this? May I help you?" and I think it's all about image and I think that's why the association struggles so hard to get sponsors because one of its problems is a penny-pinching image.'

To anyone who knows anything about the snooker world, this was a classic of unctuous, self-important self-exculpation. How likely was it that a sponsor with millions of pounds would suddenly appear at the Benson and Hedges draw, which other sponsors did not attend? The B&H contract itself would have been unaffected by whether Foulds showed up in a limousine or on his pushbike.

Here again, though, Foulds said that he had hired a chauffeur-driven vehicle through Mr Bowles, whom the association had indeed used on several occasions. However, Foulds could produce no documentation to prove that he had been engaged on this one. Nor could he obtain documentation from Mr Bowles to confirm that he had been hired by Foulds for a 'review' committee meeting at a hotel in the Heathrow area on 21 July 1995.

These meetings were 'think tanks' at which issues of the day were discussed and a fine lunch consumed by a variety of invited worthies. Even I was once invited, all expenses paid, including a night's accommodation and, at lunch, a delectable Dover sole and a rather agreeable claret. I have no recollection, however, of anything useful being accomplished.

There was more, much more, in this vein. In December 1995, Foulds took to the air at WPBSA expense to be in Frankfurt for the German Open and on the 4th had a 'meeting' with Hans Kaufeld, who was running the German end of the operation. Foulds charged £250 without specifying any mileage. Thwaites nailed this one conclusively: 'But you are not allowed to charge for having meetings with people when you are already there and list them as expenses.'

Foulds claimed that he returned to England on the following day. He maintained that he had asked Bristol HQ to buy the ticket but had found on arrival at Frankfurt airport that he had to pay for it himself. He was unable to produce any documentation for this, even a receipt, having claimed to have paid in cash. His case was that he had returned to England on 5 December to attend a meeting at Bristol, although WPBSA could not confirm that such a meeting had taken place in Bristol that day.

The following day found him in Frankfurt once more, claiming £250 for attending a meeting with Nicola Cornwell, who was directing TWI's television coverage for Eurosport. This must have been a pretty urgent meeting as Ms Cornwell was there all week and would in any case have returned the following week to TWI's Chiswick headquarters, which any reasonable man would expect still to be only 5.6 miles from Perivale.

For the Liverpool Victoria Charity Challenge in January 1996, the WPBSA paid hotel accommodation for two nights in Birmingham for Foulds and his wife. And yet Foulds submitted two claims of £250 for mileage. This was because, he said, after the first night, he had driven his wife home to Perivale because of her commitments there and returned immediately to Birmingham. He thought more of his wife, he said, 'than to put her on a train'.

Thwaites: If you wanted to do that for your wife, what benefit was that to the association, that you were entitled to charge them for it? If you want to be a gentleman to your wife, which is your perfect right, why should the association pay for it, please?

Foulds:	Because we were in Birmingham on association business and I had to return to Birmingham on association business.

Foulds's claim was for 'two meetings', but one of the great metaphysical questions of our age is: what is a meeting? Is it a formal, full-scale assembly of the board? Or a conversation between two people of a non-urgent nature? Or something in between?

As the case of *Foulds* v *MGN* proceeded, the jurors constantly had to make their own assessments as to whether the meetings were on association business or simply a pretext for charging expenses. Or again, something in between those two extremes.

The Benson and Hedges Masters came round once more, but Colchester did not this time feature in explanations of Foulds's expense claims.

Perivale was still only 2.8 miles from Wembley, but this did not prevent Foulds from charging £50 x 3 (6 February, three meetings), £50 x 2 (7 February, two meetings) and £50 x 3 (8 February, three meetings). No mileage was specified.

'We had a hospitality week there,' said Foulds. 'I was backwards and forwards in my car, picking up people, running them around.'

Thwaites queried the whereabouts of Mr Bowles, the noted chauffeur, 'in this busy week at Wembley'. He highlighted the contrast between Foulds being chauffeured hither and yon at the association's expense on some occasions while this week, at Wembley, Foulds himself had taken on the role of chauffeur.

Thwaites:	How did that affect your dignity and standing as the vice-chairman of the organisation?
Foulds:	It just underlines the fact how hard I worked for the association.

Inexorably, Thwaites proceeded to two claims of £50 each Foulds had made in relation to activities in Malta on 25 and 28 February during the European Open for which his flight and hotel expenses had been paid direct by WPBSA HQ.

Thwaites asked Foulds whether having to make a short speech at the opening press conference on 25 February had entitled him to £50.

'No,' said Foulds, 'but you then go down and buy various members of the press drinks etc.'

Had the regular snooker press been present at the High Court in strength, there might well have been an outbreak of unseemly hilarity at this suggestion, Foulds's relationship with these gentlemen having worsened the longer he remained on the board. Foulds nevertheless maintained the necessity of courting their favour. 'You can see what happens if you don't. You get libelled,' he argued.

Thwaites also unfolded the saga of the loans Neal Foulds received from WPBSA and its Benevolent Fund, which is how Neal, with whom I was to spend many a pleasant hour in the commentary box, was drawn into this business through his father's attempts to help him.

According to a Benevolent Fund minute, which fell into the hands of Channel 4 in April 1997, its four trustees – John Spencer, Bill Oliver, Malcolm Hulley and Matthew McCloy – had agreed on 3 July 1995 to accede to 'a request from G. Foulds' to loan his son £15,000 'to assist with the settlement of a debt to Inland Revenue'.

There had been an earlier Benevolent Fund loan of £10,000 and further assistance of £15,000, comprising the return of the £4,911 repaid to the Benevolent Fund and a £10,089 advance against prize money from WPBSA's ordinary funds. Foulds told Channel 4 News in an interview broadcast on 18 April 1997 that it was 'absolute nonsense' that Neal had received a loan to help pay his tax bill. 'Anyone who says that Neal has received £30,000 from the Benevolent Fund is a liar.' Actually, he received only £25,000 in loans from the Benevolent Fund – but another £15,000 from the association's ordinary funds.

In cross-examination, Foulds said: 'I put forward a request to Mr Hulley on behalf of a member of the association. That member, according to the document you have just shown me, was my son.' A minute or so later, Foulds maintained that he 'had nothing to do with the Benevolent Fund. The decisions of the Benevolent Fund lie with the trustees and those decisions are strictly private and confidential. How on earth you got hold of a private and confidential document, I do not know.'

This was too good for Thwaites to ignore. 'That is what you would like it to be, is it not, so that the true position would not emerge in this court? That is your plea for confidentiality, I suggest, in the hope that the truth would not come out.'

Foulds supported two board-inspired resolutions at EGMs that board members should be paid. Both were defeated with the aid of the votes of players managed by Ian Doyle, a persistent campaigner against the assets of the association being frittered away, but Foulds had got himself into the position that the only way he could earn a living appeared to be through WPBSA. Certainly, according to any bank statements that came to light during the case, his earnings from other sources were negligible. Although he felt justified in charging WPBSA £500 a day for work in connection with the official coaching scheme, his outside work, despite his self-proclaimed international reputation, did not seem to be amounting to much.

On the death of Hulley in April 1996, Foulds had been engaged on board authority at a consultancy fee of £250 a day to take on some of his responsibilities. WPBSA's accounts as at 30 June 1996 showed that he had been paid £9,000 under this arrangement; under questioning at the December AGM, Foulds indicated he had received another £9,000 subsequently; Thwaites noted in the High Court that 106 days' work in all had been charged for a total of £26,500.

Debate about the detail of this was concluded by Mr Justice

Gray noting that even the payments for July, August, September and October 1996 amounted to £14,000. In short, whichever way it was looked at Foulds had received considerably more than he had admitted at the AGM.

As *Snooker Scene* remarked at the time, it was not unreasonable that Foulds, who knew the business well, should have been engaged as a very short-term stopgap for specific tasks, but this arrangement effectively turned into a job for a rate of pay equivalent to £60,000 a year.

The Mirror's case was that these tasks did not even come close to justifying the level of remuneration which Foulds received, even glossing over clause 30 of the constitution which stipulates that no player member of the board shall be entitled to receive any remuneration as an employee of the association. This was circumvented by Foulds not being an employee but a consultant.

Recurrently over the years and in the witness box at the High Court, Foulds revealed his resentment at board members having to work for nothing when, for example, players could be put on the standby fee of £500 to play an exhibition if a tournament match finished early and a fee of £750 if they actually played. In the incestuous world of WPBSA, this was another practice open to abuse.

The jury returned a majority verdict for *The Mirror*. With the evidence stacked so high against him, it was amazing to me that at least one juror, possibly two, was prepared to rule in his favour, thereby illustrating the unpredictability of libel actions. Foulds was left to pay over £750,000 in legal costs. He did not pay a penny. Ultimately, *The Mirror* had to bankrupt him.

The essential truth of the Foulds era was encapsulated by Martyn Blake when he originally presented his report to Williams in October 1997: 'The association fell into a one-man rule philosophy where you either did what G. Foulds dictated or you would be out. Major arguments took place internally where, particularly in M. Hulley's time, senior staff were told to do and pass items that in hindsight should never have occurred or been allowed to happen.

This board and any future board should never allow one director to have this power again.'

Of course, in next to no time, the one-man rule philosophy was soon to be in place again under Williams.

23

ROTTEN TO THE CORE

MARK GAY'S REPORT INTO THE WPBSA'S RUNNING OF SNOOKER FROM 1996 to 1999 illuminated the depths to which the Williams regime had sunk. It made the misdemeanours of Geoff Foulds seem trivial in comparison and amply justified Stephen Hendry's remark of 1997 that the game was 'poisoned from top to bottom'.

The system itself was conducive to the production of this poison. The seven man WPBSA board is voted in by the membership, or at any rate players ranked in the top 64 in the previous two completed seasons. Board members themselves also have a vote. At least four (or three if the board had only five members) board members had to have been ranked in the top 128 at some stage in their careers. This was supposed to keep control in the hands of the players.

What the system often did in practice was to put control in the hands of a clique who used the resources of the association – money belonging collectively to the membership – to pursue their own agendas, feed their own sense of self-importance and perpetuate their power and privileges. In the case of the Williams regime in particular, a network of patronage and favours helped insiders profit at the expense of the membership at large.

It would be simplistic to conclude that WPBSA's difficulties arose just because various boards of players and former players did not have the business expertise to run a multi-million-pound enterprise. It was not only successive boards that were not up to it. Neither were many of the players who elected them. Time after time at EGMs and AGMs, a significant element of an electorate of around 70 was so indifferent to what was happening to their own money or to the game from which they were trying to make a living that they allowed themselves to be manipulated so that the sitting administration could continue in power.

The system also allows for a management group – 110sport, for example – to sign up so many players that it could outvote the others. It would be difficult to defend this in principle, although in practice Ian Doyle and his colleagues were progressive forces for reform and new investment in the game.

All the abuses that *Snooker Scene* was reporting in the days of Foulds and Rex Williams seemed to pass over the heads of most players; the home truths that Doyle was delivering were conveniently ignored by those who did not happen to like him.

Doyle is not everybody's cup of tea. He can appear dogmatic, overbearing, even hectoring, but diligence to the point of obsession is the keynote of his business life and many also value his caustic wit and honesty. This number does not include those of whom he holds a low opinion he seldom bothers to keep to himself. Much of this comes from frustration. He has the business acumen to appreciate just how much bigger snooker could have been, not just in terms of his own interests but the game generally. Broadly, snooker's potential was undermined and its players betrayed for years by those busy guarding their own petty self-interest.

Whereas Foulds had been driven by venality – or at least his overpowering wish to earn a living from snooker one way or another – Williams's appalling stewardship sprang chiefly from vanity and arrogance.

Gay recommended that 'leading counsel be instructed to consider' whether legal action should be taken against directors who 'authorised or initiated' legal action which could have exposed the association to costs in excess of £2 million, no petty figure for a body whose annual turnover was between £11 million and £12 million.

Those most at risk in such a process were clearly Williams and his vice-chairman, Ray Reardon, who formed the legal committee with Martyn Blake, the then company secretary, and Matthew McCloy, the then company solicitor.

David Oliver QC, one of Britain's foremost practitioners in the field, recommended legal action for breach of fiduciary duty against both Williams and Reardon, whose mercenary instincts allowed him to be manipulated into supporting Williams in the dirty tricks with which he attempted to stifle criticism and strengthen his hold on office. A second opinion was sought. It supported Oliver's. No action was taken.

Gay found that the purpose behind the welter of libel actions instituted by WPBSA, particularly against Doyle and myself, 'appears to have been political rather than an attempt to serve the association as a whole'. The Williams board initiated seven libel actions, none of which it won, and through attacks on critics which it could not substantiate laid itself open to three more, none of which were ultimately defended.

The first new legal action in which the Williams regime had become involved was over the dismissal of Jim McKenzie as chief executive on 1 December 1997. WPBSA did not have a leg to stand on and hoped that McKenzie would run out of money if there was enough delay. It was forced to cave in two days before the High Court action was due to start. McKenzie received £68,000 in costs and damages for breach of contract and for the libellous remarks with which Williams had attempted to justify his dismissal.

The second legal action new to the Williams regime was one it instituted against Mirror Group Newspapers, which had alleged that the Blake Report had been covered up. As the Gay Report confirmed, so it had.

WPBSA had also served their libel writ in relation to Doyle's interview with *Scotland on Sunday* published on 14 December 1997. Forthright to a fault, Doyle had stated: 'I don't believe that any directors of the board are capable of running even a corner shop. We have to ensure that the men in grey flannels and black blazers are put to one side and the professionals are brought in. That is all I'm asking.' Indeed, this was a condition of the support he had offered Williams in the first place.

The board approved commencement of proceedings – thus making every party to that decision accountable – but WPBSA appeared in no hurry to pursue the claim, although its solicitor, Matthew McCloy, on its behalf, had instructed SAS, a firm of private investigators whose notepaper bears the slogan 'Who Cares Wins', to serve the writ at Doyle's home, a gratuitously unpleasant action WPBSA were to repeat in serving writs on me even though my solicitors were well known to WPBSA.

Doyle had been led to believe that the action had been discontinued, but ten months later it was reactivated in the spirit of the festive season when he was served with a writ on Christmas Eve. The best WPBSA could do was to reply that its agreement to discontinue the action was 'tied to good behaviour' – as defined by them.

Gay commented:

This is an astonishingly candid explanation for pursuing these proceedings. They were not being pursued for the proper purpose of protecting the association's reputation . . . but as a lever to silence Mr Doyle . . . and to punish him for his insolence in continuing to criticise the board. To issue or pursue proceedings for this purpose is an abuse of the process of the court. The board's conduct . . . also appears to be in breach of good faith on behalf of the board and possibly a breach of an agreement to settle proceedings.

Farcically, the action remains alive. WPBSA made an offer in January 2000 to pay £1,250 to Doyle in costs, but Doyle has simply let this matter lie.

Of two other actions against Doyle funded by the WPBSA in pursuance of the policy of trying to silence him, Gay commented that Jim McMahon, a board member since January 1998, had clearly endorsed this improper strategy.

It was in this context that WPBSA funded an action by John Higgins junior and John Higgins senior against Doyle arising from an interview he gave to the Scottish *Daily Mail* on 18 April 1999 in which he expressed the view that Higgins would have made more money under his management than that of his father. The Higginses might have been displeased to read this and it may not have been the most tactful remark Doyle has ever made, but it was not an unreasonable view for him to hold.

McCloy declined to allow WPBSA access to this file on the grounds that the Higginses were his clients – even though WPBSA were paying. Gay nevertheless was able to quote from conference notes with counsel:

MCM [McCloy] went to Scotland on Monday. Saw John Higgins senior. John Higgins junior is ranked number one. Board therefore needs his vote. Jim McMahon is also on the board and a supporter of Rex Williams. Equally as aggressive as Higgins senior.

McCloy predicted, inaccurately: 'Doyle will back off immediately.' Gay commented:

It is difficult to say how the allegation that John Higgins would have made more money had he been managed by Mr Doyle is defamatory of him. Mr Higgins senior is not a member of the association. Therefore, the WPBSA found itself funding litigation, which is essentially between two commercial agents, neither of whom are members.

McMahon also sued, backed by WPBSA funds, over Doyle stating in the Glasgow *Herald* on 17 April 1999, that McMahon's 'only claim to fame is that he is Alan McManus's uncle. He certainly did nothing outstanding as a manager but was invited on to the board by Rex Williams.'

In his particulars of claim, McMahon asserted that this meant:

(a) he was unqualified and unfit to serve as a director of WPBSA; (b) that he was not invited to join the board on merit but only because he was the uncle of McManus and willing to be 'Williams's stooge'; (c) that he believed he was capable of running an industry when he was not; and (d) that he is in consequence both self-deluded and incompetent. McMahon wrote to WPBSA on 23 June 1999 requesting WPBSA to take action against Doyle 'in relation to defamatory statements about myself. Should the WPBSA agree, I confirm that I will support that action.' In other words, this was not an action by McMahon against Doyle but in reality one by WPBSA against Doyle.

'Once again,' Gay commented, 'it is extremely difficult to see what damage the association as a company has sustained from the allegation that Mr McMahon had inadequate business expertise to be a director. This no doubt explains why WPBSA is not a claimant in this action, Mr McMahon is.'

Doyle's defence argued factual accuracy and fair comment. There the matter rested until Williams was forced to resign on 27 September 1999. McMahon remained on the board and to the surprise of some was re-elected at the December 2000 AGM, the vote being split between alternative candidates. He agreed on 26 October 1999 to drop the matter provided that he was 'not liable for any costs'. The WPBSA paid Doyle's costs of £2,862.50. The Higginses did not agree so speedily but were ultimately ordered to pay £4,000 costs, of which WPBSA subsequently agreed to pay half.

WPBSA also found itself defending a libel action from Dennis Taylor arising from the press release of 26 August 1999 after the Williams element on the board (Williams, Reardon, Bob Close, McMahon) had prevailed over the newly elected Taylor, Steve Davis and Jason Ferguson in a board resolution to call an EGM to remove Taylor, Davis and Ferguson.

The press release had stated: 'The board no longer has confidence in three of its members – Steve Davis, Dennis Taylor and Jason Ferguson – to act in the best interests of the association and the game as a whole.' Taylor settled for a withdrawal and an apology in open court plus £5,000 costs, 'generously abandoning his claim for damages'.

Gay summarised that ten libel actions had arisen during the Williams regime and that, on average, it took in excess of £100,000 to take a case to court. If they had lost all ten and had had to pay £100,000 each in costs to the other side, this was an exposure to £2 million in costs alone. In cases in which they were sued against rather than suing, there would have been damages too.

Gay concluded that the tactic of attempting to gag its prominent critics was not only improper but ineffective. Of the 'two highly defamatory and unjustifiable articles against the editor of *Snooker Scene*', Gay's view was that the board made a calculation that 'Mr Everton did not have the means or motivation to commence proceedings against the association. They were wrong. When Mr Everton not just commenced proceedings but proceeded with them promptly and efficiently, the then board took fright. This was particularly so in circumstances where it became clear that the factual basis for the libellous articles simply did not exist.'

Gay also found what would be widely interpreted as a culture of favouritism in the Williams regime's paid appointments to the coaching committee.

'Every member of this committee,' Gay reported, 'voted in favour of the Williams board at contested general meetings. Appointments were made without any advertisement or formal recruitment procedure; with one exception [Wayne Jones], no committee member had previously shown any interest in coaching; only one [Jones again] had a coaching qualification. One member of this committee [unnamed] voted against the Williams board prior to his appointment.' The Williams supporters favoured with such jobs were Reardon himself, Joe Johnson (who subsequently became a board member), Willie Thorne, Dave Finbow and Jones.

Gay concluded: 'There is always a danger of paid appointments being used as political patronage in circumstances where directors depend upon the votes of members to get or stay elected.'

Johnson, who had been inexplicably co-opted to the board in January 2000, even though it was aware that Gay's preliminary findings portrayed him in unflattering terms, told the *News of the World*, even before the Gay Report was published, that he believed it to be 'grossly unfair . . . one-sided . . . biased against genuine people'.

Williams and Reardon had set up a WPBSA coaching committee in May 1998, agreeing that Reardon would be its chairman at £12,500 a year on a three-year rolling contract. This meant that whenever it was terminated, as it duly was, following the ousting of Williams as WPBSA chairman in September 1999, Reardon had to be paid three years' money: £37,500.

Johnson and Thorne were on three-year rolling contracts at £7,500 a year; Finbow and Jones were awarded one-year contracts at £7,500. (It was far from certain that more than one year later either or both would have been eligible to vote.) It was Gay's view that 'the contracts as drafted are unduly favourable to those appointed as coaches. There is a close link between a pattern of voting in AGMs and EGMs to appointments to the coaching committee. Taken with the undemanding contractual duties and the little that was achieved by the committee, a clear impression is created that undemanding paid appointments were given by Mr Williams and Mr Reardon to known supporters of the Williams board . . . the appointments to the coaching committee gave the clear appearance of favouritism or cronyism.' The committee's activities amounted to six meetings and two coaching forums. Almost the whole of the coaching budget, £49,348, went in fees and expenses for these occasions.

It emerged that Jim Meadowcroft, a WPBSA board member who, unlike the entire committee – except for Jones – did have a WPBSA coaching certificate, was also sent a cheque for £7,500 before he was de-selected on the grounds that his appointment might look like jobs for the boys. Certainly, Meadowcroft was a very loyal Williams supporter, but he did have a coaching qualification. Quite why anyone should suppose that anyone should believe that the other appointments did not look like jobs for the boys – or at least jobs for Williams voters – was unclear.

In addition to their salaries, committee members were allowed to charge 50p per mile travelling expenses. Bizarrely, their claims for appearance money for a coaching forum at Croydon were also met. Johnson charged a fee of £350 plus £260 expenses, Thorne £350 with £120 expenses and Jones £250 plus £184 expenses. There was no authorisation for these payments in the minutes of either the board or the coaching committee.

If Johnson, Thorne and Jones thought they were entitled to claim appearance money, it is not clear what they thought they were expected to do to justify their salaries, although Johnson thought that his services had been obtained comparatively cheaply and told the inquiry: 'As a former world champion, there are special benefits. I was paid £20,000 a year merely to sit on the board of Auto Indemnity East Riding Ltd [1993–99]. When it eventually floated on the AIM, I received quite a number of shares. I was also given a Mercedes 500 SEL and £60,000 by Theakston Breweries to advertise their product on the car for two years.'

Gay commented tartly:

Mr Johnson either misunderstands his role on the coaching committee or identifies it precisely. Appointments to the coaching committee should have been based upon the work that each appointee was qualified to perform. Mr Johnson, however, clearly equates it with previous sinecures that he has received, whereby all that is sought from him is his passive endorsement. If this reflects the attitude the members adopted to serving on the coaching committee (and bearing in mind their achievements over the period maybe it was) it is not surprising that little was achieved.

No details were provided of the appearance fees or expenses claimed for the other coaching forum at Leeds, although Gay did state that four Yorkshire professionals – Paul Hunter, Peter Lines,

Jason Prince and Jimmy Michie – attended the forum and that Hunter and Lines were paid to do so. The four voted for the Williams regime at the 4 June 1998 EGM.

Johnson blustered that the Gay Report was 'directed at me personally and I deny vehemently its allegations or insinuations. It is a serious slur on me and I am looking at what action I should take.' Of course, he never did take any action because Gay's research was watertight. Thorne and Finbow huffed and puffed. 'It's nonsense. If I meet the guy who has written it, I'll stuff it up his nose,' said Thorne. 'It's a diabolical witch-hunt. I wasn't even asked to comment,' said Finbow. Williams himself, in characteristic brazening and blustering mode, dismissed the suggestion of cash for votes as 'absolute rubbish'. He had declined to co-operate in Gay's inquiries.

Shokat Ali was never on the WPBSA coaching committee; indeed, he failed its coaching examination. This does not, though, seem to have disqualified him from being offered coaching work at attractive fees.

Doyle reported to the Gay inquiry a phone conversation with Ali of 20 September 1999 in which he stated that Ali had claimed that he had been approached by John Parrott's manager, Phil Miller, a regular canvasser on behalf of Williams, and Williams himself prior to the December 1998 AGM in Birmingham. His voting intentions and coaching work were two of the subjects discussed. The conversation was corroborated by John Carroll, 110's road manager, who was listening to the call, which was made to his mobile phone.

Although this work did not immediately materialise, Ali did vote for the Williams regime and Martyn Blake subsequently wrote to him on 1 July 1999, offering him 'additional coaching and ancillary duties' for a 'guaranteed minimum payment of £5,000 over the next 12 months'.

When Ali met the Gay inquiry team in April 2000, though, he denied that he had ever been asked to change his vote in return for coaching and ancillary work. Instead, he said that he himself had approached Williams for work after winning the Asian Games gold medal for Pakistan in 1998. The following exchange then occurred between Gay and Ali:

Gay:	Who approached you about the coaching?
Ali:	About the coaching?
Gay:	Yes.
Ali:	I spoke to Rex. I spoke to Ray Reardon briefly and they said they would try and help me out.
Gay:	Were you approached by Phil Miller at any point?
Ali:	No, I had talks with Phil. Yes, we spoke.
Gay:	What did you speak about?
Ali:	Well, I said, I mean Phil, managing John Parrott, I said to Phil: 'Phil, what do you think? I've been approached by the governing body, no, I've approached them and they've come back. They have said we need somebody on the ethnic side in our sport, more to do with the coaching, because we don't have many Pakistani, Indian and Bangladeshi players coming through, so it would be nice, but we would have to consider your position with the other board members.' I asked Phil, I said: 'What do you think, Phil? I don't want to get too deep into it because I am still a snooker player and not at an age where I want to be a coach.' He said: 'I'll have a word with Rex.'
Gay:	We've got all the ballot papers from all AGMs and EGMs and we know from your ballot paper that you voted for Jim

	McMahon and Ray Reardon and what we wanted to know is whether originally that was your intention?
Ali:	Yes, yes.
Gay:	It was? No one approached you prior to that?
Ali:	Nobody approached me.
Gay:	Nobody said, or did anybody say to you: 'If you vote for us, then we may be able to find you a coaching job?'
Ali:	No, no.
Gay:	Was any connection ever drawn between a vote and coaching in any of the discussions you had with any of the officers with the WPBSA?
Ali:	No. I mean, I did go to a coaching test, which I failed.
Gay:	Now, have you ever seen this letter before? It is an undated letter from the WPBSA to you from Martyn Blake concerning coaching. As you will see, what it says is: 'Further to our earlier letter, I can confirm that there will be work for you in Preston in your capacity (it says) of gold medal winner of the Asia Games in full recognition of your tremendous achievement. Our office will send details to you of the work available, we shall ensure this will not be on days when you are playing.'
Ali:	Yes, I received that letter.
Gay:	Was that in response to your enquiry to Rex Williams?
Ali:	No, I just received this letter. I weren't even expecting it. I asked Rex, I said: 'When

> will I have the work?' right, and he said:
> 'It will be during the season and especially
> when you are not playing.' So, I received
> this letter and when the board was voted
> out, I never voted for Rex. I already spoke
> to other people that I don't think Rex was
> the man . . .

Gay commented that while Ali had categorically denied being offered coaching work in exchange for his vote – it would not have reflected well on his integrity if he had agreed to any such arrangement – he did agree that a vote for the Williams board made him more likely to obtain coaching work for which he had no WPBSA qualification.

'Well, I thought if I do vote for them, maybe they will give me the work, you know what I mean? But at the end of the day, I had this letter confirming that I will have the work, so I don't know,' said Ali, who voted in favour of the Williams regime at the 4 June 1998 EGM and the 23 December 1998 AGM. He abstained at the September 1999 EGM which brought the Williams regime to an end.

Regardless of what went through Ali's mind in considering how he would vote, the situation, said Gay, was 'indicative of the problems that are created where directors who have the gift of patronage depend upon votes of members in order to continue holding office'.

On the wider matter of directors' expenses generally, Gay's breathtaking conclusion was that 'as there were no sensible management controls in place, the directors could scarcely act in breach of them'. He recommended the abolition of the £1-a-mile travel allowance – a recommendation that fell on deaf ears: 'It acts as an encouragement to directors to make bogus claims as a means of bypassing the rules in the association's constitution prohibiting payment of directors.'

Gay reported 'widespread distrust amongst the membership

about the workings of the Benevolent Fund'. He acknowledged that there was no evidence which would stand up in a court of law of a link between grants from the fund and the pattern of voting at contested general meetings, but it remained obvious that, with a non-confidential voting procedure, a player's chances of receiving a Benevolent Fund grant, coaching committee job or other favour could be endangered by voting against the ruling regime.

It is unlikely that a piece of paper would ever exist on which a player solemnly promised his vote in return for this or that inducement. Indeed, even if such an inducement were on offer, a player who subsequently voted in line with it would wish to play down any such link for fear that this might reflect on his own integrity.

Even so, Gay found 'an interesting relationship between voting behaviour and receipt of grants in the case of voting members', Williams having proposed in June 1997 that Blake, the WPBSA's secretary, be given access to Benevolent Fund files, reporting solely to Williams.

An EGM was requisitioned for 4 June 1998 to remove the whole of the Williams board. It survived 38–34 but there were, Gay discovered, two irregularities. Williams was given a proxy by John Higgins with an instruction to vote for the removal of the Williams board. The proxy form was not signed by Williams and hence was invalid. Gay commented: 'Where the chairman of the meeting is given a proxy form and is directed to cast it in a particular fashion, it is a breach of his duty not to do so.' Jimmy White appointed Williams as his proxy to vote in favour of the Williams board. Williams signed the form but no vote was cast upon it either for or against. Yet this invalid vote was also included in the count on the Williams side. Take out these two invalid votes and the count would have been 36–34. Had the Higgins vote been cast as he directed, the result would have been 35–35.

Gay analysed the votes of players receiving Benevolent Fund grants at around the time of this EGM: Jimmy Michie, Jim Meadowcroft, David Roe, Steve James, Dean Reynolds and Neal

Foulds. All originally voted to retain the Williams board, although Michie and James, just before the vote, changed their minds and voted against it.

In Michie's case, he requested on 29 January 1997 an advance against prize money of £5,000 to pay off an overdraft. This was refused. When he made a similar request on 12 June 1997, he was advanced £2,000 against prize money with a 'handling charge' of 5 per cent, repayable in six months, although as at 1 July 2001 it was still outstanding. On 11 May 1998, Michie nominated Williams as his proxy to vote for the removal of the Williams board. On 18 May, he filed a second proxy, authorising Williams to vote however he wished. He attended the meeting in person and voted to remove the board. Meadowcroft's career was ended by a back problem, just the sort of situation the Benevolent Fund was designed to alleviate. He received a loan of £5,000 on 26 November 1993. On 3 May 1995, he was loaned a further £1,782 to cover mortgage payments for six months to prevent his house from being repossessed. There were three further loans, including one for £7,500 on 17 September 1998, by which time Meadowcroft was a member of the board.

Meadowcroft, who had a record of unblemished loyalty to Williams, was voted off the board in December 1998. On 17 July 1999, he unsuccessfully requested £30,000 to pay off his mortgage. The 1999–2000 Benevolent Fund accounts showed a total of £22,025.63 still outstanding from him.

Roe was facing bankruptcy and was loaned through his Individual Voluntary Arrangement with his creditors £12,500 from the Benevolent Fund; James was granted a £7,000 loan repayable at the end of the 1997–98 season through a third of his prize money; Reynolds received loans totalling £8,600: all gave Williams open proxies, although James countermanded his by voting in person at the meeting.

Foulds, easily the greatest beneficiary of the Benevolent Fund, had first applied for assistance in 1991. When he terminated his five year management contract with Barry Hearn's Matchroom, he owed around £200,000 to the Inland Revenue. Geoff Foulds blamed Matchroom for this state of affairs, but Matchroom did not accept this.

On 7 January 1992, by which time Geoff Foulds was on the board, Neal Foulds received £21,750, £10,000 of which was an interest-free loan and the remainder an advance against prize money. After various to-ings and fro-ings, his indebtedness to the fund stood at £19,526.50 in July 1995. In addition, he had had his legal expenses underwritten by WPBSA when he had sued *Golf World* for libel over serious inaccuracies in an article about drugs in snooker. Indeed, I immediately volunteered to give evidence for Neal. When *Golf World* offered £25,000 in settlement, Geoff Foulds phoned the Benevolent Fund trustees on various occasions to try to minimise the repayment from these libel winnings.

Eventually, with Neal Foulds still £100,000 in debt to the Inland Revenue and others, the Benevolent Fund agreed that he should repay only £2,500. On 26 November 1998, Neal Foulds was declared bankrupt, owing £134,793 to various creditors, including £10,567.50 to the Benevolent Fund. On 18 December 1998, the Benevolent Fund made a non-refundable grant to him (i.e. a gift) of £1,000.

Gay recommended that the charitable trust deed be amended so as to delete the power of the board to appoint trustees and that those trustees should be:

(1) the company secretary; (2) a member elected by a general meeting for three years and not to be eligible for re-election; and (3) an independent person selected by the above two, subject to the approval of the board. Board members and their families will be ineligible for grants.

A claim for commission by Williams for the 'introduction' of Regal as sponsors of the Scottish Open and Embassy for the world ranking list was given short shrift by Gay on the grounds that no such agreement existed and that, even if it had, 'any entitlement to commission would create a conflict of interest between the directors' duties to the association and their own interests and could be struck down on that basis'. Embassy had, in any event, been sponsors of WPBSA snooker since 1976 and Regal, another brand in the Imperial Group, was also a long-standing sponsor.

Gay was scathingly critical of the prospective purchase of Bridgestone House, a project strongly advocated by Williams. The intention was to convert this former tyre warehouse into a permanent venue for qualifying and amateur events, but Gay found that 'the board embarked on the project without undergoing the proper management processes necessary for an enterprise contemplating a project of this scale . . . The association could have found itself embarking on a project which was calamitous for its finances and hence for the income of its members.'

Initially, the board authorised an offer for WPBSA to lease it without taking a valuation of the property, and with no indication of the costs of conversion and fit-out or of running costs. Neither was there a business plan nor a cost/benefit analysis. Nevertheless, the mood moved to an intent to buy. On 15 September, Blake estimated WPBSA's assets at £4.5 million. With a purchase price of £2.6 million and fit-out costs estimated between £1.9 and £2.1 million, this would have virtually wiped out its assets. If the project had been funded by borrowing and had gone wrong, the effect would have been catastrophic, even to the extent of putting WPBSA out of business.

Mercifully for the membership, three new board members – Dennis Taylor, Steve Davis and Jason Ferguson – were elected at the AGM of 22 December 1999. Gay reported that neither their support nor that of Reardon was forthcoming and the project was abandoned. Even getting as far as it did with plans etc., its cost to the membership was considerable.

Turn in whichever direction one could, there was evidence of reckless spending either for sheer self-indulgence or for vote-winning, but Gay revealed that there were no clear guidelines as to what items board members could, or could not, claim on expenses. In one case, a claim was made for a novel bought at Manchester airport, although Gay reported that 90 per cent of the entertainment expenses incurred by board members during the Williams regime were incurred by Williams himself. On one occasion, he charged £711.50 to his credit card for the purchase from Wine Press, Stourbridge, of wine, port and cognac, 22 bottles in total. On the back of the receipt, this was described as wine stock.

Williams took umbrage at an August 1999 *Snooker Scene* story reporting a meal at which Williams and his Australian friend Ian Anderson had entertained Amanda Hann (mother of Quinten) and a friend. Mrs Hann gained the impression that one of the purposes of the occasion was to solicit the vote of her son at an upcoming EGM and reported that she had noted that the bill for the meal had come to almost AUS$1,000 (£450). 'Much to our amazement a bottle of red wine [£130] and a bottle of white wine [£120] were presented,' she said, querying whether the bill was met from WPBSA membership funds and, if so, how that expense could be justified.

Williams indignantly produced a copy of the bill from the Arrivederci restaurant, the venue of the meal. This disclosed that $300 had been paid for two bottles of wine and that the bill itself totalled $537. Mrs Hann's recollection was therefore incorrect in detail but not in essence. In any language, $150 is an expensive bottle of wine and the total bill cannot be called inexpensive either. Gay was scornful of a successful action for defamation being based on this discrepancy and Williams himself must have been advised against it as no writ was issued.

The Gay Report disclosed such a catalogue of mismanagement, incompetence and worse that the new regime might have been expected to give it maximum exposure and demonstrate how things had changed for the better. Unfortunately, this would have meant acknowledging that Doyle's (and my own) criticisms of how the association's affairs had been run were fully justified.

When the imperfections of the post-Williams regime also began to attract criticisms, its instinct was to draw the wagons into a circle.

Between commissioning and completion of Gay's report, the post-Williams WPBSA board lost its enthusiasm to publish it. It was kept under wraps for several months and even afterwards it was left to *Snooker Scene* to get its more interesting material into the public domain. The WPBSA said members could go to its Bristol office to read it but otherwise took no action to bring it in its entirety to its relevant audience. It was as if WPBSA wanted to claim that it had issued the report while doing its best to ensure that it was minimally disseminated.

24

MURPHY'S LAW PREVAILS

THE DECEMBER 2001 AGM AT THE BROMSGROVE HILTON WAS IN MANY ways typical of many other AGMs: sparsely attended with a low standard of debate and little clarification of basic information, the most interesting item of which in this case was that the association was plunging towards insolvency with an anticipated £2 million loss at its year end, six months hence. Through murky interpersonal machinations within the board, Mark Wildman had been deposed from the chairmanship the previous week in favour of Jason Ferguson, then a middle-ranking player who had a clean-cut image but was altogether too naive and inexperienced for such a position. Neither did it take him long to develop a grossly inflated idea of his own capabilities.

WPBSA was fond of claiming that it was a players' organisation, welcoming feedback and even constructive criticism, though history had demonstrated that it was not always easy to arrive at a commonly held view of what was constructive. This particular year, it was an unpromising portent that the AGM should be scheduled for noon at Bromsgrove, a few miles south-west of Birmingham and fully 150 from York, where the UK Championship final had finished the previous evening. Nor did it engender a large turnout that the chosen date coincided with the first day of a week of world ranking qualifying competitions. To the cynical, it appeared that the date and venue had been selected to ensure the lowest possible attendance and the least possible inconvenience to the current administration.

What those assembled most wanted to hear was some form of explanation for Jim McKenzie's second dismissal from the chief executiveship five days earlier. Encouraged by a WPBSA press release stating that 'the board will be providing further information to members at the AGM', players had journeyed from far and wide and in one case from Kirkby-in-Ashfield to be given the gen, but their hopes were to be dashed. Neither was Liz Walker, the in-house legal eagle and company secretary, who left WPBSA's employ shortly afterwards, in attendance for questioning.

'For legal reasons, we can't go into detail, but the board has lost confidence in Jim. A settlement has not yet been reached,' said Ferguson. It was difficult to disagree with the analysis that McKenzie's policies were involving too great an outflow of cash, but WPBSA had breached employment law in dismissing him, so any discussion of his activities in office did not arise. Wildman's fellow board members had been eager to dismiss McKenzie; Wildman wanted to wait two months until a review of his services was mandatory and he could be offloaded without financial penalty. Already, this raised the uncomfortable possibility that his dismissal had been mismanaged. McKenzie duly sued and pocketed £100,000.

Peter Ebdon, who was to win the world title six months later, spoke passionately in support of McKenzie and maybe not entirely because it was through him that he was enjoying such an agreeable loyalty bonus. A few days later, Ebdon and McKenzie convened a meeting at Glasgow airport also attended by Ronnie O'Sullivan, John Higgins senior and various other interested parties at which they stated their intention of restoring McKenzie and installing Sir Rodney Walker as chairman of a board which would include two other well-known figures from the football world: David Sheepshanks of Ipswich Town and David Richards, once of Sheffield Wednesday, who had become chairman of football's Premier League. Ebdon said that these non-executive directors would be paid £20,000 a year.

Doyle was also offered a seat on the board but declined to take part in the proposed coup, believing that WPBSA was heading for serious financial trouble and not encouraged by some scathing criticism in an official report of Sir Rodney's stewardship of rugby league. Richards's chairmanship of Sheffield Wednesday had left his club deeply in debt and even his own business had folded with debts of £3 million.

'On the face of it, neither Mr Richards nor, for that matter, Sir Rodney Walker appear ideally equipped to solve snooker's problems,' said Doyle. 'If they have been associated with foul-ups like these in the sports in which they have long experience, are they going to do any better in snooker, of which they have no experience?

'As for Mr Sheepshanks, I was interested to read a WPBSA press release of 27 September last stating that he had been co-opted to the board of WPBSA. This statement was never contradicted until it transpired last month that this was conditional on an amendment to the WPBSA constitution permitting directors to be paid.'

The WPBSA was in such dire straits that the only realistic move was to turn again to Ian Doyle's 110sport. This move was at first eagerly promoted by Tony Murphy, who had been co-opted to the board the previous October. He soon realised that WPBSA was heading for financial disaster and not the least of his concerns was that his son, Shaun, a very promising young professional, might not have much of a circuit on which to compete in his prime years. A fluent talker, as befitted his employment history in the motor trade, and energetic with it, Murphy made an initially good impression. This appeared to be characteristic – as did his failure to sustain it.

Living in Irthlingborough, Northants, he had become friendly with a neighbour, Max Griggs, the founder chairman of Dr. Martens, the shoe company. Out of this came a £10,000-a-year five year sponsorship for Shaun, which started when he was 12. Griggs also built and equipped a snooker room for him at the family home. Murphy's introduction of Griggs to Barry Hearn led to a three year sponsorship of Hearn's Premier League, which brought Murphy a 15 per cent commission of £115,000. When Hearn extended the deal, Murphy received a further payment. It was not long before his relationships with Hearn and Griggs soured, just as they did after Murphy had been appointed a director of Rushden Snooker Centre Ltd on 11 September 1997 only to resign in acrimonious circumstances on 31 December that year.

On 8 January 2002, a meeting took place in East Kilbride between Ian Doyle and his colleagues, and Ferguson, the new WPBSA chairman, Wildman and Murphy.

'They said that WPBSA was heading for bankruptcy without an investor partner,' said Doyle. What could 110 do? Could 110's backers, Warburg Pincus, help?

A Memorandum of Understanding was drawn up between the WPBSA, Doyle and John Davison, whose busy City life included a consultancy for Warburgs. On 8 February 2002, during the Benson and Hedges Masters, Murphy, representing WPBSA on this occasion, invited Davison, Doyle and Joe Schull of Warburgs to its private box at Wembley. During the evening, it became clear that Murphy expected a paid position within the proposed new set-up. He was rebuffed as politely as possible, but it soon became clear that he had lost his enthusiasm for the deal.

By 8 February, WPBSA had supplied very little of the information under the Memorandum of Understanding which an investor partner would require and this flow of information was to remain pitifully slow.

Murphy then asked for a meeting with Warburg Pincus the following week at which he told their executives that the reason the information had not been supplied was that Doyle was involved. If he could be removed, the information would be supplied. Warburg Pincus, loyal to Doyle, a valued associate, demurred and it was Doyle, not wanting a major investment into snooker to be lost, who withdrew. In that way, ABC Newco (later Altium Sport) came into being, with Warburg Pincus and Davison as the major shareholders.

Doyle had no shareholding but remained very keen that a deal guaranteeing the long term health of the circuit should be concluded. He wanted the satisfaction of having helped re-shape the game for the better and was well aware that the less the circuit was worth, the lower would be the earnings of 110's players and hence 110's commission on earnings. Even so, only a piffling amount of information was supplied to Davison, who was also concerned that John Wood of TLT, the WPBSA's solicitors, had effectively been appointed WPBSA's company secretary. Davison felt that any advice WPBSA was given should be totally independent rather than from a source already earning substantial legal fees from the association. Davison considered this a potential conflict of interest and also felt that the matter was sufficiently important to be dealt with by a senior partner.

Time passed. Hardly any information required under the MoU was disclosed. Ferguson, as WPBSA's chairman, put his name to a 27 March letter to members rubbishing Davison's proposal and promising that WPBSA would become:

> leaner, meaner, more effective and more commercially driven, putting us in a position to enter into productive relationships with real commercial partners. The board believe it would not be serving the best interests of its members if it were to present or recommend any proposal without looking at all the alternatives. With this goal in mind, it is still our intention to secure a partnership with a professionally equipped and established company.

Davison called WPBSA's bluff, waiving the rest of the exclusive negotiating period to which he was entitled under the MoU. TWI were not interested. Neither were Octagon, another powerful force in sportsbiz. Both signed up to support Altium exclusively. World Sport Group was the only other possibility, but its shares were suspended at 6.5p after its failure to file its accounts on time.

In early May, Altium were persuaded back into the contest. By this time, an EGM had been requisitioned to remove Murphy from the board. Ferguson tried to smooth matters over and wrote on 13 May that Murphy was 'considered by me and many others to be an asset to the business because of what he has achieved on behalf of the membership'. However, Doyle wrote to the board accusing Murphy specifically of stating on 8 February that 'unless he received a job within the new commercial arm' there would be no deal with 110.

The majority of the board, of which Murphy was still a very influential member, closed ranks around him, but when it was clear that he would not survive the requisitioned EGM, he resigned. However, such a resignation becomes operative only one month after it has been submitted, so Murphy remained on the board until 28 June, the day on which a players' meeting at The Tickled Trout, Preston, initially voted on the competing proposals of Altium and World Snooker Enterprises Ltd (WSE), a new concern which, with the encouragement of most of the WPBSA board, had sprung up a few weeks earlier with Richard Relton, of the about to be dismembered World Sport Group (WSG), at the helm.

WSG had run into trouble because it had overpaid, in a 50/50 partnership with Rupert Murdoch's News Corp in Global Cricket Communications, for the rights to the 2003 and 2007 Cricket World Cups and could not recover its investment through sales of sponsorships. WSG's 50 per cent had to be sold to News Corp for £1, the remnants of its European operation were acquired by Parallel Media and the founder of WSG, a Hong Kong-based Irish businessman, Seamus O'Brien, was left with certain contracts in Asia. Relton therefore needed a job and it was soon clear that he was the WPBSA board's preferred linchpin to take control of WPBSA's commercial rights even though his newly formed group could not contribute financially.

The board's philosophy was not only 'anybody but Doyle' but 'anybody but anyone on friendly terms with Doyle'. Snooker politics at their most sectarian were covered with a veneer of democracy. To this end, WPBSA did not call an EGM, which would have been legally binding, but a players' meeting so that, in the event of an unwelcome result, it could prevaricate.

At the Tickled Trout, Murphy at times sat behind the board's table – on his last day as a board member – and sometimes in the body of the hall, from which he asked questions helpful to the WSE bid, strengthening Altium's suspicions throughout the process, similarly to 110's two years earlier, that they were being strung along in order to smoke out virtually any other deal which would allow WPBSA to keep going without materially altering the way things were run.

The board said that WPBSA's resources allowed it to promote only six world ranking events in the 2002–03 season as opposed to the nine staged in 2001–02. This gave WSE's offer of £5.9 million for nine events – funded entirely from WPBSA resources! – spurious credibility, even though this nine included the conversion of two invitation events with limited fields, the Benson & Hedges Masters and the Irish Masters, into ranking tournaments for all 96 main tour players, an arrangement to the disadvantage of top players because prize money would be more widely spread. It was also overlooked that the B&H Masters was promoted by B&H's consultants, Karen Earl Ltd, so that WSE was in no position to promise anything about that event for 2003.

Altium guaranteed nine world ranking tournaments for five years (plus the B&H Masters, Irish Masters and two other invitation events), initially with £6 million prize money in the 2002–03 season, with a reduction to a minimum of £5.4 million in the following four seasons commensurate with the loss of tobacco sponsors. On any objective assessment of these proposals, Altium's guaranteed the players the most money and the most long term security.

From the point of view of winning a vote, though, Altium were suicidally honest in revealing that they would, after 2002–03, reduce the world ranking circuit from 128 players to 64 albeit with a better financed challenge tour. This was the board's cue to allow votes at the Tickled Trout meeting not simply to the top 64 in the rankings for the previous two years – the full voting members who would have been entitled to vote at an EGM – but to the top 128 during this period.

Regardless of financial considerations, all players want to be on the world ranking circuit. WSE were advised to maintain it at 128, come what may, thus ensuring massive voting support not only from those currently outside the top 64 but also from anyone in danger of dropping out of it. The WPBSA had always been there, reasoned all those players not old enough to remember when it had not, and there had always been tournaments with money to play for. Everything would be OK.

The support of the lower ranks, added to that of hardened anti-Doylists, scuppered a new start for snooker. Even then, the vote was 36–36. Another meeting was scheduled for 20 August 2002, but Altium withdrew at a few days' notice, claiming that WPBSA's summary of its proposals to the membership was neither accurate nor fair and noting that WSE had been allowed to amend aspects of their bid but Altium had not.

Many players seemed unable to grasp that by leasing WPBSA's commercial rights free to WSE for ten years, it was potentially placing no limit to the extent to which the membership might fund this arrangement. In contrast, Altium were guaranteeing not only larger prize funds for a longer period but also an assurance that the membership's money would be called upon to pay neither Altium's salaries, miscellaneous consultancies nor the expenses of staging the tour.

This was why Altium required WPBSA to transfer their remaining television and sponsorship contracts for a nominal £1 with a guarantee that every single penny of their worth would be redistributed to the players in the form of prize money. Altium also guaranteed that if sponsorship were to increase above the 30 June 2002 base level, 49 per cent of this would be added to prize funds, with 49 per cent going to Altium. A new independent regulatory body for whom Altium were already guaranteeing £400,000 a year funding would receive 1 per cent, and a new players' trade union with proper independent clout, for which funding was also guaranteed, would receive the remaining 1 per cent. Altium would also have been left to find not only the prize money but also all other costs – venue hire, tournament staff, security, referees and innumerable bits and pieces.

Unsophisticated managers, advisors and players eager to believe the worst of any proposal Doyle favoured obstinately refused to understand the notion of Altium purchasing WPBSA's rights for £1 and recycling them in prize money. Relton's proposal envisaged leasing these rights for ten years – with no payment – and amounted to almost the same thing, although it did not sound so emotive as a sale for £1. For what proved to be the aborted second meeting, Altium was willing to amend its proposal to make it the same as Relton's in this respect but was not permitted to do so despite alterations being allowed for the rival proposal.

No board member was a turkey who wished to vote for Christmas, thus illustrating that those who possessed power, great or slight, tend to be reluctant to surrender it, not least because it might imply an admission that their way of running things had not worked. It was easy to infer that the negotiating tactics of the board reflected a wish to alter as little as possible the way the game had been run for years.

When Altium withdrew, WPBSA quickly circularised the players with a letter whose tone was more indicative of satisfaction at repelling an interloper than regret at the loss of a prospective multi-million-pound investor. 'Wishing to focus on the bright future for WPBSA [sic]', the WPBSA accused Altium of ignoring 'detailed written responses to Altium's criticisms'. Davison, heading the Altium bid, maintained that his complaints still had not been seriously addressed.

Resentfully, the WPBSA letter alluded to 'factions in snooker that have consistently caused political mayhem in this sport'. Why was this so? Because one administration after another had proved itself inadequate for its role in running the game.

Even then, the players could have brought Warburg Pincus's money into the game when Steve Davis and Stephen Hendry were

among the requisitionists of an EGM to remove the board en bloc
and make a new approach to Altium to replace WSE, whose four-
man executive team were taking out £300,000 in salaries alone.
Davis and Hendry jointly wrote:

> Our accountants have examined the bids from information
> available and clearly Altium is worth millions – not thousands
> – more than the WSE bid. You advised the membership you were
> seeking an investment partner but, according to the information
> you recently provided, WSE are investing nothing.

Davis and Hendry were reluctant politicians. Neither had any
financial imperative. It was just that they could see that the game
they had helped to develop was heading for inevitable decline
without substantial outside investment. Wildman, who had fought
a lone battle within the boardroom in favour of common sense
and financial reality, resigned: 'I am unable to support the board
concerning the further processing of the WSE contract. In my
opinion, it lacks vital capital underpinning and carries undue risk
for WPBSA and its members.'

Ferguson, who had contributed to this debacle by backing several
wrong horses, also resigned, not now wanting to be associated
with any trouble which lay ahead. Jim McMahon, who less than
a year earlier had been asked to resign after being criticised in
the Gay Report, became chairman in all but name; Joe Johnson,
an anti-Doyleist who had also been criticised in the Gay Report,
remained on the board, as did Jim Chambers, a former middle-
ranking player, coach and landlord of a Walsall pub who was noted
chiefly for his long silences in board meetings. Gordon McKay, a
small-time manager, Edinburgh club owner and ally of McMahon,
was co-opted to the board, as was, to widespread incredulity, Tony
Knowles, who in several attempts to gain election had never
received more than a handful of votes, along with Paul Wykes, a
player just outside the top 64 who could also be relied upon to
toe the party line.

In the shadow of the approaching EGM, the newly appointed WSE announced two new tournaments, neither of which actually was. The Irish Masters was purchased for a staged six-figure sum of the membership's money from Kevin Norton, its promoter, with Norton retained on a £50,000-a-year management contract. Top players thereby saw the income they could expect from a 12-man invitation event subsumed into a 96-man ranking tournament. A European Open was announced but neither sponsorship nor TV coverage was obtained and it had to be funded by swingeing cuts in the prize money for the British Open and UK championships.

There were wholesale economies. Prize funds for the Challenge Tour were reduced; the billiards subsidy was cut to £25,000; the English Association for Snooker and Billiards was cast adrift with a £50,000 one-off payment; the Young Players of Distinction, coaching and Accredited Centres of Excellence schemes were abandoned. Everything was subordinated simply to keeping the circuit afloat.

Competitors arrived on the opening day of the 2002 British Open to discover that Stan James, the bookmaker, had rejected a last minute appeal to renew its previous year's £75,000 contribution to the prize fund 'in the light of previous dealings with WPBSA'. Much worse, the advertised prize fund of £666,800 had been reduced to £450,000, the first prize from £92,500 to £52,000. The cuts extended even down to players eliminated in the qualifying competition who had already been paid and were now informed that such reductions would be docked from subsequent earnings. Similarly, the UK Championship prize fund was reduced from £746,900 to £615,000.

WSE unsuccessfully requested Regal to maintain their contribution to the £597,000 prize funds for the Regal Welsh and Regal Scottish Opens whilst allowing WPBSA to reduce theirs by £97,000. Peter Dyke, consultant to Regal and Embassy, said: 'The prestige of these events is maintained partly by the level of prize money available to players and we would not wish to see this reduced.'

Most outside observers were convinced that, in the light of such ominous facts, the resolution to oust the board in favour of a new one under the chairmanship of Terry Griffiths would succeed. In fact, one lie, endlessly repeated, won the day for the board. The constant reiteration that Altium's previous interest, renewable if the board was removed, was nothing more than a front for Doyle to 'take over the game' produced a staggering majority of 48–26 in favour of the board – and WSE – remaining. Simple arithmetic suggested that ultimately even some of the requisitionists of the EGM had changed their minds.

The board crowed that this was 'a red letter day for snooker. A new era of stability and continuity beckons and it's up to all of us that it stays that way.' The players did not seem to realise that they had voted for an arrangement whereby the membership's income from contracts and other sources would be used, as it had been for years, to pay salaries, consultancies, professional fees – some of them very high – and expenses whereas, if Altium had prevailed, none of it could have been used for these purposes.

McMahon appeared on Sky immediately after the vote to say that his board's victory had been achieved 'despite a concerted and unbalanced media campaign' although some would have said that its policy of declining all media requests for interviews inevitably tended to show an articulate opposition in a better light.

Relton, now chief executive of World Snooker Ltd, the wholly owned subsidiary through which WSE managed WPBSA's commercial portfolio, proudly claimed to be delivering a total of eight world ranking events during the 2002–03 season, plus the Masters, with a total of £5.9 million in prize money. He did not point out that there had been nine such events the previous season, that what he was delivering was entirely with the membership's own money and that the Benson and Hedges prize money increase from £690,000 to £750,000 had been agreed years ago and was nothing to do with anyone but Benson and Hedges.

Had the Altium bid gone through, the guarantee would have been nine ranking events with an initial £6 million prize money, then £5.4 million for the following four years, plus the Masters, plus the Irish Masters retained as an invitation event, plus £416,000 for the Challenge Tour, plus £200,000 each for a new regulatory body and a new players' trade union. Even on a straight comparison between ranking events plus the Masters, the Altium offer was £850,000 higher in the first year alone. In the ensuing five years, players were to compete for £9.505 million less on the world ranking circuit than if Altium's proposal had been accepted.

Griffiths acknowledged that the board had campaigned more effectively than the opposition. If they were no good at anything else, they were good at winning elections albeit within the sort of 'rotten borough' that had been seldom seen since the accession of George III. Altium and Doyle reluctantly concluded that WPBSA was unreformable from within and resolved simply to stand back and see what happened. If WPBSA swam, it swam; if it sank, it sank, in which case they would review their position. The December 2002 AGM was uncontested. Tony Murphy, who only six months previously had resigned rather than face an EGM to remove him, was restored to the boardroom.

25

HALF A DOZEN DIAMONDS

OBLIVIOUS TO THE RELENTLESS INTERNECINE STRIFE WHICH WAS producing a progressively more poisonous backstage atmosphere, the public continued to enjoy the tournaments in large numbers as the age of Hendry gave way to a period in which titles were more widely distributed.

There were six world champions in the six years spanning the millennium: the cheerful, easy-going Ken Doherty, who had beaten a strangely lethargic Hendry 18–12 to win the 1997 world title; John Higgins, 1998; Hendry, 1999; Mark Williams, 2000; Ronnie O'Sullivan, 2001; and Peter Ebdon, 2002.

O'Sullivan, immeasurably the most talented, could at times make the game appear preposterously easy but was by far the most unpredictable. His dashing style, colourful off-table life and personality full of intriguing conflicts added up to star quality. As with Alex Higgins and Jimmy White before him, the question which constantly hung in the air was: will he self-destruct?

Higgins, Williams and O'Sullivan all played in the junior event in the 1991 World Masters at the National Exhibition Centre and turned professional later that year. Higgins departed from Birmingham with the £5,000 first prize, handed it to his then manager and saw no more of it. Doyle became his manager, although their relationship was complicated by the active role John Higgins senior wished to play in his son's career.

It was clear that Higgins could become one of the significant threats to Hendry's pre-eminence and this was not an ideal situation. Just as Steve Davis had been the foundation of the squad Barry Hearn managed, Hendry was the foundation of Doyle's. Diligent as Doyle was, it could not be denied that Hendry, like a firstborn, had a special status in the camp.

Having risen swiftly up the rankings to 39th, Higgins achieved his most significant victory thus far by beating Davis in the 1994 Dubai Classic. Naturally, he was pleased. So was Doyle, but among his various remarks it was tactless to say that it was a victory which kept Hendry top of the rankings at Davis's expense. The Higginses did not like this, but the breaking point came next day after Higgins had lost and had wanted to return home on the first available flight. He had lost his free ticket but a replacement would have been provided next day. If he was not prepared to wait, he would have to buy his own ticket.

Financial prudence was one of the disciplines Doyle incessantly instilled into all his clients, not always successfully and sometimes so unsuccessfully that he terminated contracts in exasperation. Whereas Hearn had taken the relaxed attitude that a client's money was his own and could be spent as he chose, even if it subsequently landed him in difficulties with the Inland Revenue and others, Doyle was a stickler.

Higgins paid for the new ticket; Doyle terminated his contract. Conflict had never ceased to bubble beneath the surface but this left Doyle the sworn enemy of the Higgins family. In all snooker's subsequent internal battles, Doyle and Higgins were to be on opposing sides.

As a player, maybe it was for the best that Higgins was no longer in the same camp as Hendry. Two weeks later, he won his first major title, the Skoda Grand Prix at Derby. In terms of off-table rewards, he would certainly have done better with Doyle than with his father, an electrician, who now became his manager.

Lacking flamboyance but not fluency, charisma but not class, Higgins proved time and again that every aspect of his game was very strong and that he had the temperament and application to go with it. There was little to criticise except when, for some reason, he was not fully focused. As a confirmed homebird, his overseas record was comparatively poor. Even at home, if his mental preparation was slack, he could give alarmingly sub-standard performances.

His commitment to family was total. He withdrew from the 2000 Grand Prix in the quarter-finals because the WPBSA's alteration of its original schedule brought it in conflict with his promise to be best man at his brother's wedding. His decline in form after winning the first three events of the 2001–02 season was attributed to his absorption in his newborn son.

There had been no signs of frailty when Higgins won the 1998 world title, beating Doherty in the final 18–12, a victory which enabled him to displace Hendry from the top place in the rankings he had occupied for eight years. During this championship, he became the first player in its history to make centuries in three consecutive frames and not when the result was a formality either but in the heat of his 13–11 quarter-final victory over John Parrott. His 14 centuries in the championship exceeded Hendry's previous record of 12 and his success illustrated that the hungrier a player can remain to practise, improve and compete, the less he is distracted by off-table issues and the more likely he is to perform at full capacity.

Williams, a laid-back, uncomplicated Welsh valley boy, a lover of dogs and motorbikes, was an outstanding potter and fine competitor, although his close control was not quite up to the standard of Higgins or O'Sullivan. A miner's son from Cwm, he was once taken down a pit when he was a boy: 'Once was enough. It was pitch black and very frightening. It made me realise how hard my father had to work to support us. I realise how lucky I am to be able to play snooker for a living. I try my best in every match I play.'

He climbed two mountains in the last two rounds to win the 2000 world title, beating Higgins 17–15 in the semi-finals from 15–11 down before his 18–16 victory over his fellow Welshman Matthew Stevens from 13–7 adrift in the final. This justified the sublime confidence of Kevin Bohn, a Llanelli factory worker, who had spotted him when he was 14 and been so impressed that he invested £140, a week's wages, with Coral at 300–1 to win the title by 2000. Ten years later, he collected £42,000.

Between the triumphs of Higgins and Williams at the Crucible came Hendry's seventh, an outcome which could not have been envisaged six months earlier when he lost 9–0 to Marcus Campbell, a useful but unremarkable Scot, in the opening round of the UK Championship. It was as if his game had had a nervous breakdown.

'This has been building up for ages,' said Hendry. 'There are one or two technical things that need tweaking but basically it's an attitude problem.' Campbell was 'dumbfounded. To me, Stephen seemed like he was strolling round the table with a million problems on his mind. As I pulled away, his head was hitting the ground.'

It was apparent that Hendry either had to resign himself to decline or bring maximum application to bear once more on honing the technique which underpins confidence, self-belief and the will to win. Between his November debacle against Campbell and coming to the Crucible in April, he won three events prior to beating Williams 18–11 to win the seventh world title which provided statistical confirmation of his status as the greatest player of the modern era. There is ultimately only one valid criterion for a player's greatness: what he has won. That Hendry could regain the title after such a troubled journey through the valley of doubt emphasised his core of inner steel.

Looking back on his November defeat by Campbell, he said: 'That night, I never thought I'd challenge for any title again, let alone be a realistic contender at the Crucible. Without doubt, this is my finest hour. After the terrible spell I went through, this means more to me than the first six titles put together. I've got nothing left to prove to anybody and that's a good feeling. This was my last burning ambition in snooker: I wanted to set myself apart from the rest.' It was difficult for him to maintain his finest edge of motivation after that, although his hatred of losing and his pride of performance in the arena remained as strong as ever.

Higgins, who had won five titles that season, maintained his position as world no. 1, with Hendry second, but Williams earned more world ranking points than either during that campaign and was himself to become world champion and world no. 1 in May 2000. During the two season cycle on which rankings were based, Williams won six counting events and reached four other finals.

It had always seemed to be O'Sullivan's destiny to become champion, but it was one which he might well have claimed sooner if his life had not been capsized by forces beyond his control. While Hendry, Higgins and Williams all rose to world champion and world no. 1 through steady progression, O'Sullivan reached these summits only after many a tumble, detour and retreat.

The O'Sullivans came from tough stock. Mickey O'Sullivan, Ronnie's grandfather, was a boxer, as were his brothers, Danny, British bantamweight champion 1949–51, and Dickie, known as 'The Toy Bulldog'. Boxing circles knew them as 'The Fighting O'Sullivans'. O'Sullivan's father, Ronnie senior, was a chef and his mother, Maria, a chalet maid when they met at Butlins. They were soon married and Ronnie's early years were spent in a high-rise block of flats on a notoriously grim estate in Dalston, East London.

Ronnie senior worked on the railway and as a car park attendant before he had the chance of an involvement in bookshops offering pornography. His increased income enabled the family to move to the more upmarket Ilford and, with growing commercial success, to a large house in Chigwell. When Ronnie junior was seven, his father built a snooker room for him at the bottom of the garden. He made his first century, 117, when he was ten but, no matter what the degree of hand–eye co-ordination or instinct for the game that a player may be born with, he has to work on his craft.

Virtually every moment he was not at school, Ronnie was in snooker clubs in Barking and Ilford. His father made it clear that he was not there to mess about. If he was going to make something of his life through his exceptional natural talent, he would not do so by playing cards or the fruit machines:

> I was inbred with, y'know, get up, go for a run, get down the club in the morning, bottle up and get on the table, because I wanted to feel I was putting my part in. When I had a bit of time and I could help brush tables, I did it. When the gels behind the bar needed helping out, I'd do it, so I started work a lot earlier than most people start. I started my career when I was eight.

For parents of talented children, there is often a fine line between keeping them focused on the field in which they excel and force-feeding them to the extent that they want to give it up. The O'Sullivans seem to have handled it about right and young Ronnie, of course, would never have persisted unless he had liked the game and the promise of what it could deliver, not only in cash but also in satisfaction.

His talent meant that he spent most of his childhood and youth in the company of older men. He won his first pro-am (events usually held in a single day, often with a late night finish, in which amateurs and lower ranked professionals competed) when he was 12. By this time, he was later to claim, he was earning £25,000 a year. Almost certainly it was not as much as that, but he was nevertheless earning. The best times were when his father, as fathers do, ferried him here, there and everywhere. At other times, he was with 'mates'.

'I was easily led and they threatened to knuckle my head if I didn't do what they said – like mooning to coaches on the motorway,' Ronnie said in an interview with Gordon Burn in *The Observer*. 'I liked being around with them, probably because I didn't have a big brother. They got me into a lot of trouble, though, and I had a little cry now and again, wondering why they were treating me like that. I wanted to bully them back by winning on the table. And I did.'

At 15 years, 97 days old, he made a 147 maximum in the

Southern final of the English Amateur Championship although in the national final he fell short of expectations by losing to Steve Judd, who in his subsequent professional career never broke into the top 100. He won the World Under 21 Championship in Bangalore, but when he was competing in the 1991 World Amateur Championship in Bangkok, for which he was favourite, his father was arrested and charged with murder. Young Ronnie was 'in bits' for two or three days and lost in the quarter-finals.

This was how his life turned upside down. Until then, he had not had a care in the world. His parents were happily married; he recognised their authority but knew he could ultimately count on their unconditional love and support. He was stable in so far as any genius can ever be stable.

In his first professional summer, while he was winning 72 matches out of 74 at the Blackpool qualifying school, his father was on trial at the Old Bailey for stabbing to death Bruce Bryan, the driver for Charlie Kray of the notorious East End criminal family, in a brawl in a Chelsea nightclub. Found guilty, he was sentenced to life imprisonment – with a tariff of 18 years which even professional deconstructors of hard luck stories might believe, in common with the O'Sullivan family, was excessive compared with other murder cases.

On any reading, killing a man is a terrible act, but there was a fight, and drink had been consumed. Ronnie senior and a mate were arguing over who should pay the bill. Two black men, signed in by Kray, misunderstood and thought they were refusing to pay.

Words were said. One man went to hit Ronnie senior over the head with an ashtray. It smashed as he fended it off and two of his fingers were severed. The other man hit him over the head with a champagne bottle. Ronnie senior picked up a knife that was on the side of the bar and stabbed Bruce Bryan several times. Ronnie senior was in hospital for four days. There had been no premeditation; he had not brought a knife with him; it was, he believed, 'me or him'.

Admittedly, this is the family's version of events, but its essential elements are not in dispute. As young Ronnie says: 'It was common sense to get up and say: "Look, I was attacked. He hit me first and I had to fight back. Unfortunately, I went too far and killed a man."'

At his trial, though, he was advised not to go into the witness box in his own defence. On being arrested, he had never gone beyond 'no comment', which was his standard practice when he was questioned by the police about anything. He never told his side of the story. He had the right to silence, but the judge and the jury were entitled to draw the conclusion that he was fearful of what might emerge from cross-examination and that therefore he was not only guilty but guilty in the circumstances that the prosecution had outlined.

Neither did he attempt to rebut the prosecution's allegation that his offence was racially motivated. No one who knows him believes this. He has always had black friends, many of whom, including Nigel Benn, the boxer, were prepared to testify to this. He was, says young Ronnie, simply 'too proud' to accept their help. In his summing up, the judge's reference to 'racial overtones', the family believed, added six years to the twelve which would have been considered the norm. Even so, an appeal against the sentence was rejected.

Although the details of the fatal incident may be disputed, the world in which Ronnie senior was moving and the business he had adopted always contained the possibility of serious trouble. During his trial, Ronnie senior was described as a 'porn baron'. Asked later if this was fair, young Ronnie replied: 'Dunno. If you want to call it that. It was more like a bookshop. It was more like a bookshop with an adults section there where you could buy stuff. He had a few in Soho and a few around the outskirts of London. But I was so young at the time that I wasn't really interested, to be honest with you. As long as I had me tenner for me taxi down the snooker club and me food money I weren't really bothered.'

Poverty and the urge to escape it can be a strong motivation, but it remains an unsavoury trade in which one is likely to find unsavoury people, and young Ronnie was inclined to fudge the nature of the merchandise on sale in his father's empire of 20 shops, an empire he continued to run even after he was jailed in 1992, chiefly through Maria passing on instructions to family and friends. It was Maria, in fact, who had originally identified a business opportunity, perhaps the only one realistically available, in the '80s.

'All the [porn] shops got shut down,' young Ronnie explained. 'My dad didn't have a job and Mom said: "Go and open that shop."' The business was run through a company, set up in 1986, which was known as Ronald O'Sullivan, trading as Ballaction. It turned over £360,000 in its first year. Maria took virtually no part in it until her husband was jailed but was then inevitably drawn in.

Much of the stock was kept in the garage at home. 'When I was 11, I'd be in the garage saying: "What's this then, this is great."' According to him, some tapes in luridly promising boxes were actually blank. These sold at £50 each, but it was correctly calculated that embarrassment would deter purchasers from demanding refunds.

It did not strike him that his was an unorthodox childhood: 'My dad wasn't breaking any laws. All he was doing was putting dinner on the table for his kids. He just wanted to be a family man.' The police, who had a long and wary relationship with Ronnie senior, interpreted matters differently.

Ronnie senior took his imprisonment on the chin. His son tried to use it as extra motivation, wanting to cheer him up by winning. They were able to talk on the phone at certain times and they had three or four conversations on the day, a week before his 18th birthday, that he beat Hendry to win the UK title, superseding him by nine months as the youngest ever winner of a world ranking event.

'He gave me very good encouragement,' he said of those conversations. 'He's the only person who says things that really go into my head. My dad never pushed me, but he said: "If you want to do what I did, and be a car park attendant for years and clean a few windows, then that's up to you. But if you want to have a good life, like Steve Davis, it takes a lot of practice and early nights and this and that."'

The practice, hour upon hour of it, was to fuse technique, fluency and feeling much as a concert pianist would. 'It's about ridding yourself of fear,' he said in reference to the theory that it is only self-erected mental barriers which stop players potting balls or completing clearances in matches as they regularly do in practice.

Barry Hearn, who had signed O'Sullivan to a five-year contract on his 16th birthday, remarked of O'Sullivan in particular and the rising generation of players in general: 'They've had ten years of watching Steve Davis on television. They've taken that TV knowledge and added to it the impetuosity of youth. They've removed the nerve ends and added more attack. The attack comes from the fact that they've got no mortgages, no wives, no children, no responsibilities. They just play. Apart from Davis, Hendry and Jimmy White, it's curtains on the old brigade because of players like Ronnie.'

It was nice to visit his father and show him the trophy, but once the pleasure of the moment had passed, the inescapable reality was that his father was still in prison and would remain there for many years. It began to dawn on him that he would never regain the quality years he expected to share with him.

O'Sullivan was inclined to blame the game for making him depressed, but it always seemed more likely that depression affected his game. His love for and loyalty to his father, who is even more of a hero to him than most fathers are to their sons, was touching and admirable and he loved talking about him as if this talking might, in a strange way, give him life separate from his tedious incarcerated existence.

'My dad had the sort of charisma of Al Pacino,' he said. 'He had a lot of style and a lot of class. He could put on a binliner and look good. I love visiting him, I love seeing him. I love talking to him, sometimes. Not all the time. We drive each other mad. He's always buzzing and positive . . . He's my guru, if you like. Someone I confide in and I ask his advice, and he hasn't done me wrong so far. So, y'know, I think he's done pretty well for himself. I know he's ended up where he's ended up . . . so have a lot of people. That doesn't make them bad people. It's just being in the wrong place at the wrong time. It could happen to anybody.'

Not everybody would rationalise it in these terms and, like any son and many before him, he idealised his father without realising that he did not have to do that in order to love him. Perhaps this was why – or partly why – in his bouts of depression he tended to blame others for nothing and himself for everything. The self-destructive way he lost certain matches looked like a self-punishing aspect of this.

Once the euphoria of winning that first major title had subsided, he became lethargic and unable to practise. On his Benson and Hedges Masters debut at Wembley, he could scarcely string three balls together and lost 5–1 to Dennis Taylor. On an upward mood swing, he won the British Open at Plymouth at Easter 1994 and was ranked ninth at the end of the season. The following year, he became the youngest ever winner of the Masters and finished that campaign ranked third.

He had just enough stability to cope until that summer when, in July 1995, his mother was convicted of evading £250,000 in VAT between September 1991 and March 1994. This was because, with Ronnie senior in prison, she was helping to run the family pornography business and signing documents as a director. The initial part of her sentence, which was served in Holloway, was hellish. As the mother of a wealthy celebrity, she became a focus for the pent-up rage of many other inmates. She was physically threatened, once with a razor, and was the object of unwelcome lesbian attention. It was her imprisonment which upset young Ronnie most of all.

During this period, Ronnie could not convince himself in a match, let alone in practice, that it was so very important to pot this red or that black. Before Christmas in the 1995–96 season, he made three first round exits in four starts. Mostly, he beat himself with shot selections beyond adventurous to the uncaringly self-destructive. He did not feel like playing and seemed to want to convince himself that if he lost without really trying, losing would not hurt. Briefly stimulated by the UK Championship, he reached the quarter-finals, but his heart still was not really in it and his mind not really on it.

There had been even more bad news. On her release, Maria potentially faced going straight back to prison on more charges connected with running the family business. The details were unpleasant. The seized material included bondage, flagellation, sex with animals, mutilations, torture and group sex. Then there was good news, albeit with a farcical twist. At Southwark Crown Court, the judge's attention was drawn to an article about snooker in *The Sun*, not something which happens every day. He ruled that some of the O'Sullivan family details in it were prejudicial to Maria receiving a fair trial. Two jurors had read the story. Maria was released.

In the midst of this, trying both for himself and the National Deaf Children's Society, he won the Liverpool Victoria Charity Challenge tournament early in the new year, thereby earning himself £30,000 and £100,000 for the charity, but it was on the back of a second round defeat in the Regal Welsh Open that he came to his defence of the Masters.

Maria's release and the dismissal of the other case had taken a weight off Ronnie's mind. Unfortunately, in circumstances on which he declined to elaborate beyond 'it's a long story, mate,' he injured his right foot kicking a concrete-mounted potted plant. He had had a row with his girlfriend. On a lesser occasion, he would have withdrawn but instead hobbled through his quarter-final against Darren Morgan and had to be virtually carried to a car. He took his foot out of an ice bucket to win his semi-final against Andy Hicks, demonstrating an application and caution frequently absent when he was fully fit.

'I've got a good safety game, you know. I just don't use it very often,' he said, disarmingly. He lost 10–5 to Hendry in the final, immediately relapsed into two more demoralising first round defeats and by the time he came to the penultimate ranking event of the season, the British Open at Plymouth, had lost often enough – for whatever combination of reasons – for opponents not to be afraid of him.

'I've got beat by some really bad players, as it happens, but they've played well, you know what I'm saying, and I haven't. And if I'm not playing well, these players aren't scared.'

He felt he was 'a little bit fresher in the mind . . . playing a little bit better' but could not help comparing this with how he plays when his mind and therefore his hand–eye co-ordination is stuck flush on the right wavelength.

'It's an instinct game for me. I get to the table and just know what to do but sometimes when I'm struggling it becomes a really hard game and that's where your Hendrys and Higginses are more clinical. I'm more of an "on the day" sort of player, which isn't really good.

'I know you've got to dig deep sometimes and I haven't done that. You've got to be up for it and, to be honest, I haven't been up for it. I haven't really practised at all. I haven't enjoyed it, you know. I can honestly say that there's no adrenalin flowing sometimes, and this game's all about adrenalin. I haven't been pumped up going out there. I wanna be nervous, you know, wary, and I'm not wary of anyone.'

I suggested to him that his lack of adrenalin might be attributable to the mind and emotions locking off and saying 'no more' to the pressures it might be prepared to take on board – those of competition on top of private ones. He responded with some interest: 'Is that it? Is that what it is? God, it's terrible.'

He was reluctant to go beyond the bare facts of his parents' circumstances, much less to imply any blame or even acknowledge that these may have made a difference.

'I'm a man now, so it doesn't make any difference. They can

take away what they want, but if you're a fighter, if you're a strong person, you can bounce back, and I'm a strong person so that hasn't affected me at all.'

At least he seemed to be enjoying snooker again. He lost 6–4 to John Higgins in the semi-finals but went to Sheffield in better heart for what was to prove an eventful championship for him.

His 10–3 opening round win over Alain Robidoux did not end with the customary handshake. The Canadian considered that O'Sullivan was mocking him through the number of shots he was playing left-handed – a skill he was to develop to an exceptional degree – and responded by not conceding a frame that was clearly beyond rescue. Even when the pink subsequently ran over a pocket, O'Sullivan perversely refused to pot it and the result was an embarrassing eight-minute impasse on live television.

Sympathy for him evaporated when he made a series of belittling comments about Robidoux in a BBC interview, describing his performance as 'useless . . . rubbish . . . I didn't give him any respect because he didn't deserve any.' By trampling upon the game's traditional professional courtesy, he put himself emphatically in the wrong, as he acknowledged with an apology a few days later.

This controversial interview had been conducted by Louise Port, who had been sent to Sheffield by Radio Five Live to help Phil Yates and myself. The theory was, as it had been with previous London-based general sports reporters who had fulfilled this function, that Louise would take care of all local radio requirements, assist Phil and me administratively and conduct post-match interviews. Instead, Phil and I found that we were helping her and that the dedicated BBC Radio phone was tied up for long periods while Louise was arranging her social life. It is standard practice for reporters to chat casually to players whenever they can to build rapport which might be useful later but, casting political correctness aside, young female sports reporters occasionally risk having friendliness misconstrued as flirting.

Thus it was that a couple of days later, according to Louise,

Ronnie attempted a seduction to illustrate the maxim: nothing succeeds like excess. Louise's account of this in a private telephone conversation – though media telephones in the pressroom are not all that private – was possibly the source of a story in the *Daily Star*. When a *Daily Star* reporter chatted to her, she somewhat naively confirmed the details.

Louise was quoted in the *Daily Star* that 'Ronnie kept attracting my attention' and asked 'Are you wearing a G-string under that?' as a preamble to offering her a private interview in his room at the Swallow Hotel. Finally, he was alleged to have invited her to 'come into the toilets and show me your G-string'. He did not avail himself of the opportunity to deny this version of events.

'I just think Ronnie is a spoilt, immature boy. This tournament has shown his lack of respect for his fellow players and the competition itself,' Louise was also quoted as saying.

The immediate result of this incident was that Louise, who turned down approaches to get her kit off for the readers of *The Sun* and the *Daily Star*, was ruled out as an interviewer of Ronnie after any of his subsequent matches, a task which thus fell on the already not underworked Phil.

Mindful that a good old-fashioned catfight never hurt the circulation of any tabloid, the *Daily Star* invited the views of Ronnie's girlfriend of long-standing, 17-year-old 'blonde stunner' Sally Magnus, who loyally found it difficult to understand why Louise had found his alleged remarks offensive: 'For a start, how did he know she was wearing a G-string? This girl should realise, he's just having a joke with her.' She added, optimistically as we all thought: 'Ronnie would never cheat on me.'

Next day, 'speaking from his plush hotel room', Ronnie told the *Daily Mirror*: 'Sally isn't my woman anymore. I finished with her a long time ago. I don't know why she makes out she's my bird.' It was to emerge that Sally was pregnant.

In the meantime, *The Mirror*'s article was a revelation to Helen Magnus, 43, mother of Sally: 'He's been saying he's dumped Sally, but he's round here quick enough when he wants her.'

The *Daily Star* was to reveal that after losing in the semi-finals:

Ronnie was knocking on the door of Sally's home, begging to be forgiven. The couple spent the rest of Saturday in his £750,000 house in Chigwell trying to salvage their romance. Sally then left to be with relatives and ponder her future.

Mrs Magnus went on to make it clear that if Sally took her advice, as daughters often do not, it would be a future without Ronnie:

That lad's an idiot. What he needs is a good kick up the arse. I keep telling her I'm going to take her for a brain scan for going out with him, but she doesn't listen. I suppose love is blind. That lad's going to get it from me. Even our dogs don't like him now.

To this, Ronnie was, as they say, unavailable for comment.

In another newspaper, Ronnie did admit: 'I really want a girlfriend, but there's just no time. I'm always on the road or practising. I've got a lot of pressure on me. I get really ratty and difficult to live with. No one understands what I have to go through. I would like someone there to look after me, but no one will have me. When I'm under pressure, I take it out on the ones I love.'

On the Richter scale of trouble, though, none of this registered in comparison with an incident which could have led to his disqualification from the championship.

The WPBSA, in one of its periodic surrenders to lunacy, had decreed that visitors to the pressroom must conform to a dress code. Since journos and photographers are not widely renowned for sartorial elegance in working hours, the concept of a dress code for visitors to pressrooms was not easily grasped, but Mike Ganley, son of Len, the redoubtable referee, was on duty as an assistant press officer and was there not to question the regulations but to uphold them.

A few weeks earlier, late one evening at the British Open at Plymouth, O'Sullivan took it into his head to urinate against an inside wall. Correctly, Ganley reported this. This may not have endeared him to Ronnie and may have helped to trigger the assault which followed when Ganley refused to allow his then guide, philosopher and friend, Del Hill, to remain in the pressroom because he was wearing jeans.

This activated O'Sullivan's highly protective instincts towards family and friends. He flew like a madman at Ganley, punching him in the testicles and biting through his lip. It was an assault which fell within the definition of actual bodily harm. Perhaps calculating that he could not count on continuing to work in snooker if he pressed criminal charges, and also acting on instructions from WPBSA worthies, Ganley locked himself away in his hotel room and remained tight-lipped about the incident – or at least as tight-lipped as he could until his lip healed and returned to its normal size.

No one challenged O'Sullivan's later mitigation that he had acted completely 'out of character' but he had nevertheless acted. The immediate question was: would he be allowed to continue in the tournament? The disciplinary committee met on the evening before he was due to play his quarter-final against John Higgins, who was in the unenviable position of not knowing whether he needed to gear himself up for an immense effort for the most important match of his life or whether he would receive a walkover. Neither Higgins, the assembled press or anyone else knew the disciplinary committee's decision until a few minutes before midnight.

The disciplinary committee considered not only whether O'Sullivan was guilty as charged but also factors like the desirability of aborting a quarter-final which was a prime television attraction or of unbalancing the event by having a walkover into the semi-finals. There was not much doubt which way BBC TV or Embassy, the sponsors, would bring to bear any influence they could.

This debate would have been unnecessary if the matter had simply been deferred until after the championship, a far more preferable option. What the WPBSA chose to do encompassed the worst of all worlds: hasty action, a decision flawed by considerations extraneous to the offence, loss of credibility to the game's administration and unfairness to Higgins. It was announced that O'Sullivan had been fined £20,000 plus a 'voluntary' contribution to two charities, a punishment which still enabled him to make a handsome profit on the event from his prize money of £60,000.

'A monumental abdication of responsibility' was the magisterial verdict of one of Britain's most eminent sportswriters, Hugh McIlvanney. Less than 11 hours after the verdict was announced, Higgins started a quarter-final which he had been uncertain he would have to play at all. He had been appalled by what O'Sullivan had done – as were most snooker people – and had been honest enough not to subscribe to any romantic nonsense about not wishing to accept a walkover. Higgins led 12–10, but O'Sullivan won the remaining three frames to go through to the semi-finals.

O'Sullivan fully acknowledged that he had been in the wrong and there was an exchange of handshakes with Ganley. 'I wasn't happy within myself,' he said. His contrition was genuine and he also took his 16–14 semi-final defeat by Peter Ebdon with good grace: 'Work and attitude reflect on you in the end. Maybe Peter deserved it more than me because he's more focused. Sometimes I've abused the game and haven't prepared for competitions like I should have or Peter does.'

Even for Ebdon's famed reservoir of mental stamina, the final that year was a match too far. Drained from beating Jimmy White 13–12, Steve Davis 13–10 and O'Sullivan, he woke on the morning of the final 'jaded and fatigued' and never seriously threatened as Hendry beat him 18–12 for his sixth title.

The world final brings the season to an end on a high emotional climax. The ensuing months return the players to the mundanity of ordinary life and the problems which go with it. Sinking into gloom and bad habits after the championship, O'Sullivan was eventually turned out of the house by his mother and told to fend for himself.

'I was too obese, too arrogant, too embarrassing,' he said. 'Just a waste of space and too time consuming for her really and for everybody around me. I just slobbed out. I wouldn't go out of the house.'

He responded by getting himself fit. 'I had to prove myself to her.' He always seemed to be needing to prove himself to either his father or his mother. A few months later, he reflected: 'Being fat and overweight was just no good, I'm fit now. When I put a suit and shirt on, I know I look good. When I go out there, I feel like I've got that aura again. My mum was upset with the way I was going. I was in a hotel for a month eating cheese sandwiches. I had to come back with my tail between my legs. My mum had to do that to me.'

There was also a new problem he had to face on top of the many he had already in that Sally Magnus gave birth to their daughter in January 1997. His first response was not only a doomed attempt to evade financial responsibility but also a denial of the implications of parenthood. DNA tests, made after the Child Support Agency had three times threatened to obtain a court order under which they could have sequestrated one-third of his assets, confirmed paternity. As is the way of these things, Sally and her mother, understandably resentful of his attitude, co-operated in an aggressive 'love rat' story for the *News of the World*.

Underneath O'Sullivan's brazen front, he is more sensitive than he would perhaps like to be and knows in his heart when he has behaved badly. He knew it was not right to inflict on his child any feelings of rejection which might arise from disclaiming all recognition and responsibility for her. While entitled to resist unreasonable attempts to take him to the cleaners financially, it was in his own interests to face up to the consequences of his actions. Eventually, he agreed a substantial settlement and support and belatedly attempted to establish some kind of parental relationship, but this did not last. The bitterness between Ronnie and Sally had gone too deep. The message he absorbed was that he was not wanted. He drifted away and tried to cope, as he was trying to cope with his father's imprisonment, with a sense of what might have been.

Like many players, O'Sullivan seemed to believe that if his game would come right, everything else would come right too but, more often, the reverse is true. Life is more than a succession of tournaments, although it does sometimes happen that the adrenalin that competition stimulates can for a time anaesthetise players from anything which is not happening on the eternal 12 x 6.

O'Sullivan's 1996–97 season embraced two world ranking titles, two other major finals, an abject first round capitulation, two more first round defeats to players not in his class . . . and the quickest 147 on record. His first round maximum at the Crucible took him only five minutes, twenty seconds and earned him £165,000. This was breathtaking virtuosity by any standards but, as the phrase goes with snooker's insiders, it won him only one frame. All season, he had played in fits and starts and he went out in the second round 13–12 to Darren Morgan.

O'Sullivan also had his moments in the 1997–98 season and came to the Crucible in reasonable psychological shape for a title challenge. A few days into the championship, though, he was notified that he had tested positive for marijuana during the Irish Masters, which he had won three weeks earlier in commanding style. Knowing that a storm would break about him when this information came into the public domain, there was a depressed air about his performance in losing 17–9 to John Higgins in the semi-finals.

'Some defeats hurt, but not this,' he said. 'I was never involved in this match. I'm looking forward to getting home.'

Why had he smoked marijuana, which is not conceivably performance enhancing for a snooker player but which is nevertheless on the banned list? 'Because I was bored.' The truth was that repose made him uneasy.

Hendry had been home a long time before O'Sullivan. Although he had won only one world ranking event that season, the Thailand Masters, no one had expected him to lose 10–4 to Jimmy White in the first round. They had played fourteen matches in the previous four years and Hendry had won them all but White, focused like a laser, produced one of the best performances of his life and also demolished Morgan 13–3. Unfortunately, by the time he played O'Sullivan in the quarter-finals, his game had reverted to its familiar mixture of promise and error. He had reached the stage where he could dare to hope that, at long last, he could make up for all his previous Crucible disappointments. Inevitably, this rubbed open the mental scars of the past and impeded his attempts to perform in the present.

During the Regal Scottish Masters, the first tournament of the 1998–99 season, I had breakfast on a few occasions with Del Hill, who confided that O'Sullivan was climbing the walls with depression. He was worried about him. So was Ian Doyle, who had taken over his management from Hearn. At my suggestion, Doyle obtained a series of consultations for him with Mike Brearley, the former England cricket captain, who was now practising as a psychoanalyst. Months later, O'Sullivan told me that the consultations had been useful but that he had discontinued them. My guess was that he was unwilling to probe too deeply into his relationship with his father. Instead, he resorted to a hypnotist, Paul McKenna, although, at best, hypnosis offers only short-term help. He turned to Prozac. He turned to the Samaritans. He turned to cocaine.

It was easy to warm to O'Sullivan as a player and impossible not to sympathise with someone who was so obviously inwardly tortured. When he later proved disloyal to people who were trying to help him, particularly Doyle, these feelings were modified by irritation. Under pressure, he sought role models from the world in which he grew up. That week, not for the last time, he won the tournament in the midst of deep depression. His dark mood was not to be alleviated either by the fear of losing or the satisfaction of winning. As far as he could, he played automatically, fatalistically. At the same time, he had zero tolerance for what he felt to be his own mediocrity.

His depression would not lift. A few weeks later, he was at the end of his tether and withdrew from his defence of the UK title, suffering from 'physical and nervous exhaustion'.

When he returned to the circuit after Christmas, he struggled to engage his higher gears, although he did hold Hendry to 12–12 in their 1999 semi-final at the Crucible before Hendry drew away to win 17–13 and, subsequently, the title. Their third session, which O'Sullivan won 5–3, was one of the highest quality ever produced there. It included five centuries in eight frames and, from 10–10, four in four, as Hendry made breaks of 101 and 108 and O'Sullivan of 134 (only pink and black short of a maximum) and 110.

There was no title for O'Sullivan until the China Open in December 1999, a drought of 15 months.

At the Crucible in 2000, Hendry succumbed uncharacteristically to negativity as he lost 10–7 on the opening day to a qualifier, Stuart Bingham, but O'Sullivan, who had demolished Williams 9–1 to win the Scottish Open a few days earlier, lost 10–9 to an inspired David Gray despite making five centuries, including three in three frames.

O'Sullivan could easily have won the championship in that form but that defeat was the first time he had ever produced his best and still lost. This shook him. The combination of disappointment and end-of-season emptiness precipitated a relapse into bad old habits and he fell apart so badly that summer that he eventually checked himself into The Priory clinic, Roehampton, for treatment for drug addiction.

That summer, a bizarre 18-month saga started on 4 June when he pulled up at traffic lights in Stratford, East London, alongside a sports car in which two young women were travelling. For reasons which were unclear, one was wearing only a bathrobe. As the lights changed, the two cars sped off. PC Paul Parkinson gave evidence that they were doing between 40 mph and 50 mph. 'When we stopped him, Mr O'Sullivan's eyes were bloodshot and glazed. He seemed agitated and his breath smelled strong,' he testified.

Three times, allegedly, O'Sullivan failed to provide a breath test through a breathalyser and at Plaistow police station told police that he could not give a blood test because of an aversion to needles or, despite drinking six cups of water, a urine sample. During his time at the station, he said that he had trained himself to go for long periods without using the toilet because of the demands of his sport. Since players are free to leave the arena between frames – and exceptionally during – it is difficult to understand why he did this – if he did. He was charged with refusing to give a breath, blood and urine sample but was acquitted 18 months later.

First, his defence applied for the case to be dismissed because the magistrate had tampered with vital evidence. He had been seen blowing into the mouthpiece of the relevant breathalyser. The prosecution agreed that there should be a re-trial, but the magistrate, William Rolstone, insisted that the case continue under his jurisdiction.

The next hearing was aborted because O'Sullivan overlooked the date and when the case was eventually resumed, the magistrate was observed winking at a reporter. O'Sullivan's lawyer, Nick Freeman, who had already built a high profile by representing various celebrity clients, argued that this was highly prejudicial to O'Sullivan, but the magistrate responded: 'Why would I wink at anybody? Do you think I'm gay or something?' Nevertheless, the pressure on him from both defence and prosecution sides was such that he was forced to withdraw from the case, which then came under District Judge Angus Hamilton, who ordered a re-trial, which he himself conducted.

The star witness at this was Dr Stephen Robinson, a police surgeon and sex counsellor, who told the court that O'Sullivan's inability to produce a urine sample could be attributed to his psychiatric state: 'I am aware of his psychiatric history and know that he was suffering from an anxiety depressive disorder. I also know that he had an obsessive personality. At times, he showed verbal agitation. This psychiatric condition could easily be linked to his inability to pass urine. It could happen to anybody. It is more likely to happen to someone with a psychiatric disorder. We are talking about a stress reaction. Any stressful situations, like being in a police station.'

Dr Robinson explained that when a person felt under pressure, the bladder could either be put into a relaxed state, making the brain think it did not need to go, even though it was full. Or it could lead to the tightening of the bladder muscle, which would then act like a stopper on a tap. After this evidence, Judge Hamilton halted the trial to find O'Sullivan not guilty.

In all, including adjournments without any progress being made, the case had come before the court 18 times before British justice delivered its verdict.

'I'm very relieved,' said O'Sullivan, unconscious of irony, paying tribute, as well he may have done, to his defence counsel, whose previous successes had included acquittals for David Beckham for driving his Ferrari at 76 mph and for Sir Alex Ferguson for driving along a motorway hard shoulder. He was able to persuade courts that Beckham had exceeded the speed limit in order to elude photographers and that Ferguson had driven along the hard shoulder in his desperation to find a toilet because of a stomach upset.

With his two most notable contemporaries, Higgins and Williams, having already won world titles, O'Sullivan was growing more anxious and frustrated in his inability to fulfil his prodigious talent. He was starting to feel that his prime years were slipping away. In the summer, with no tournaments going on, there was nothing much he could do about it because there was nothing on which to focus. It was very difficult, as it is for many sportsmen and entertainers, to have experiences of extreme emotional intensity in the full glare of the public gaze and readjust quietly to what most people would recognise as ordinary life. The buzz, the high, creates a need which has to be satisfied in one way or another. The calendar of the snooker circuit imposes a discipline, a pattern of a sort, but life away from it can seem shapeless.

There were highs to be had from drugs, drink, women, gambling, fast driving and various other pleasures, but there were prices to be paid as well and the problems of real life could not be evaded forever. As a player, O'Sullivan's chief problem was his impatience with any standard of performance inferior to his best, although there had been sporadic signs of preparedness to battle through these spells rather than indulge in the kind of careless shot selection and execution which is tantamount to self-destruction. Snooker had come easily to him and because of his father he had never been short of money. It did not come naturally to him to fight to the last when there was nothing in him.

His four week sojourn in The Priory changed his outlook and his view of himself. It cleaned out his mind and body and gave him 'time to reflect on a few things. I'm just trying to get myself right mentally and get to handle some of the situations which come through being a professional sportsman. I've been through a lot of stuff in the last few months, but I've got my life in order and the public will see a different side of me.' He recognised that for the preceding two years he had been 'a nightmare to live with' and that his pot smoking, far from relieving his depression, was making it worse. On his own admission, he attended more than 500 Narcotics Anonymous meetings.

Only shortly before the 2000–01 season did he feel like playing again. His preparation for the Champions Cup, a new event, consisted of a mere ten days' practice, five of them on his own, but when his mind is clear, his sublime hand–eye co-ordination takes over. His concentration, so often wayward, came easily to him throughout a week in which he made only a handful of unforced errors. He was prepared to be patient and shrewd in his shot selection without compromising his attacking instincts.

Even after he had beaten Hendry and Williams in the last two rounds for the £100,000 first prize, he was clear that happiness was not simply about winning: 'I've won tournaments and been in bits afterwards.' 'Feeling happy inside' was his desired state and he had come to recognise that talk of retirement, though deeply enough felt at times of frustration, had been a way of trying to evade his responsibility to his own talent.

'If I did pack it in, I know I'd regret it several years down the line. I really do love the game and I appreciate the support I get from the public and my family, but if I'm not happy inside, it's not the real Ronnie O'Sullivan I'm giving them. It's a bit of an act. I'm starting life again at 24. I'm very emotional. I haven't been able to reflect on what I've achieved before because in the past I've always been on a treadmill of turmoil.'

His next three tournaments yielded one second prize, a retention of the Regal Scottish Masters title and a quarter-final before his sense of well-being burnt out. Despite this, he retained the China Open in second gear but then went into a slump until he was again at full throttle in winning the Irish Masters in March. His father's re-classification, nine years into his life sentence, from category A to category B, usually a staging post towards category C, which permits home leave and other privileges, had lifted the spirits of the entire family.

At the Crucible, he at last claimed his destiny by winning the title or, to put it another way, he was able to dismiss the dreaded possibility that he might become the greatest player never to win it. This dread may have contributed to the intense depression he felt on the eve of the championship. In desperation, he turned to Prozac which, he admitted, alleviated his anxiety and promoted an ideal state of mind.

It may seem odd that he had once had to forfeit first prize in the Irish Masters for testing positive for marijuana, which is not performance enhancing, but could with impunity take Prozac which, at the very least, was performance enabling. Why, for that matter, were beta blockers on the banned list and Prozac not? There was, of course, no drug which could make him a better player, but Prozac certainly assisted him to produce his best.

'Ronnie is the Mozart of snooker. He's a genius. He was unstoppable,' said Peter Ebdon after an 8–0 middle-session drubbing had plunged him to a 13–6 quarter-final defeat.

'When Ronnie's on song, everybody else looks a carthorse in comparison,' said Steve Davis.

After beating John Higgins 18–14 in the final, O'Sullivan's first thought was for his father, alone in his cell on the final night, waiting for news of each frame. 'My dad might not show it, but this will mean so much to him. I owe him everything. I can't wait to go and visit him with the trophy. That will be special.'

When the euphoria subsided, though, reality reaffirmed that Ronnie senior would still be behind bars for several more years. Ronnie junior still had his own emotional volatility to cope with. Overall, life did not get any easier. Mentally, he continued to be delicately balanced, fascinating to observe from the outside but not much fun to experience from the inside. Possibly this was why his form tended to be cyclical. With maximum outside stimulus and maximum incentive, he could sometimes construct the cocoon of absorption in his game which led to peak performance but always, after the consummation these titles afforded, came the return to ordinary life and the same old problems, some of them intractable. His best was better than anyone else's but any number of factors, allied to the performances of his opponents, could prevent him from producing it.

Ebdon was always able to identify what he most wanted and pursue it. With his clutch of O levels, he was potentially university material but chose to give all this up and base himself at Kings Cross Snooker Centre to pursue a highly uncertain career in the racier world of snooker. His father, a prison officer, was understandably appalled, but their ensuing breach was fully healed by success.

On his 1992 Crucible debut, he beat Steve Davis 10–4 in reaching the quarter-finals. Most Crucible debutants are so nervous that they need all their concentration to avoid falling down the stairs into the arena. Ebdon, with his deep inner conviction that he was a star in the making, greeted the Crucible crowd with a friendly wave from the top of the steps.

Ebdon and Hendry never took to each other, even though each readily acknowledged the other's on-table qualities. Drawn to meet in the 1993 Dubai Classic, Ebdon was quoted as saying that the then world champion would be well advised to take his golf clubs as he would not be playing much snooker. Ebdon claimed that this quote had been put in his mouth by a journalist.

Much, much worse was the triumphalism Ebdon showed in beating Hendry in the quarter-finals of the 1994 Benson and Hedges Masters, Hendry's first defeat in that event after winning the title five years in succession. In potting the brown in the decisive frame, Ebdon left himself on the unmissably straight short range blue which guaranteed victory. Between potting the brown and the blue, he went into the kind of victory celebration seldom seen outside a documentary on African tribal dancing. Hendry was among those who thought this behaviour unacceptable.

Ebdon's mental intensity made him the hardest of competitors and assisted him to undertake and maintain long periods of highly disciplined preparation, not only in practising, not only in diet, but also in swimming half a mile a day to promote the physical conditioning which enabled him to concentrate and focus his mind for long periods. As a personal bible, he adopted *Think and Grow Rich*, a 1930 book by an American self-help guru, Napoleon Hill. He claimed also to be 'inspired by inspirational people' like Churchill. He always seemed to be sustained by a sense of his own destiny and was prepared to work to his utmost to achieve it.

An obsessive, a loner, his chief leisure interest lay in the bloodlines of racehorses, some million or so he claimed to have assembled on his computer. Knowing all about the breeding factors which point to success on the turf, he was asked if this methodology could be applied to humans. He volunteered that 'Prince Charles is actually line bred four by four to a full brother and sister. If he'd been a racehorse, he'd probably have been a champion two year old.' The heir to the throne's loyal subjects were no doubt reassured by this analysis.

Ebdon came to the Crucible in the spring of 2002 hardly mentioned as a potential champion. It had been a year since he had won a title, the Regal Scottish Open, but he was to depart with the £250,000 first prize by virtue of beating Hendry 18–17 in an epic final whose peak viewing figure, 7.4 million, was more than that for the FA Cup final. Together with the average of 5.4 million which was maintained throughout the four-hour transmission of the final session, these figures were timely reminders of snooker's capacity to produce drama not only of the utmost intensity at its climax but also of a high quality sustained over several hours.

Ebdon had been within a ball of going out in the semi-finals to Matthew Stevens. Trailing 16–14, he was required to clear the table from the last red to stay in the match but could not afford anything less than a pink from it to win the frame. The pink was a tricky cut which was effectively do or die. If he had missed, he would have required two snookers.

These days, as snooker careers at the top tend to grow shorter, a player can seriously challenge for the world title only a few times. The intrinsic difficulty of that pink would have been multiplied if Ebdon had been faced with it at a similar stage of any tournament but at the Crucible the multiplication factor was significantly higher. It was therefore one of the greatest single shots ever played there.

Overcoming some lesser but nevertheless substantial difficulties, he stole that frame on the black, fashioned a 138 total clearance to level and secured victory with a run of 55. He was to claim that when he left the arena at two down with three to play to compose himself, he had a vision: 'I actually saw myself shaking hands with Matthew, having just beaten him. I saw it and then it happened the way I saw it.'

The other semi-final, in which Hendry beat O'Sullivan 17–13, was even more highly charged emotionally because of an unprovoked verbal assault by O'Sullivan in which he remarked that he had 'no respect' for Hendry because in their semi-final at the Crucible three years earlier, he had been awarded a 'miss' which O'Sullivan felt he should not have accepted.

It seemed extraordinary that O'Sullivan could harbour a grudge for that long without previously saying anything about it when the worst accusation which could have been levelled against Hendry was that he was playing to the referee's decision, which all sportsmen are trained to accept. No one at the Crucible could even recall the shot to which O'Sullivan was referring. Even after the match, O'Sullivan was unrepentant, claiming that he had 'enjoyed' making those comments and that 'it made it a great atmosphere and you should buzz it up a bit. What could be better than a grudge match?'

'What happens off the table doesn't matter,' said Hendry in his victory press conference but puzzlement remained over O'Sullivan's real reasons for raising the emotional temperature. We at *Snooker Scene* noticed that he had been spending so much time with 'Prince' Naseem Hamed and his brother that he had adopted some of the Sheffield pugilist's habitual pre-fight big talk. O'Sullivan admitted as much a few months later after winning the Regal Scottish Masters in Glasgow, which was promoted by Doyle: 'I spent two hours with Naz at his gym and all the boxing talk got in my head. What I said about Ian and Stephen wasn't me. It was like somebody else talking. The worst thing now is that Stephen won't talk to me.'

This showed the all too easily suggestible O'Sullivan at his most naive. Did he believe that a retraction in front of 200 people could compensate for a personal attack splashed all over the media? Hendry continued to blank him and it was not long before O'Sullivan was accusing him of overreaction. O'Sullivan did eventually offer an olive branch of sorts, but by then Hendry did not care one way or the other. Eventually, though, time proved a healer.

The Ebdon v. Hendry final came to an almost incredible conclusion after Ebdon had led 11–6 and trailed 14–12. Back in the lead at 17–16 with the winning post of 18 tantalisingly near, Ebdon stood on the intersection of his life's desire and its fulfilment. It unnerved him. Just two pots short of victory, he missed a simple short range black, far easier than the final black Steve Davis had famously missed with his last shot of the 1985 final. Such a failure proved that the steeliest competitors can bend under abnormal pressure. 'I really thought I'd blown it,' Ebdon was to say.

Hendry forced a deciding frame, but he too was to display an uncharacteristic frailty of nerve, not in one ghastly error like Ebdon's but in his failure to capitalise sufficiently on three decent chances. Ebdon regained his composure to make the cool 59 which left Hendry too much to do.

Interviewed in the arena, both made all the right noises, but there is a distinction to be made between their opinions of each other as players and as people. Once political hostilities were resumed, Ebdon was defending the WPBSA board with all the passion of the most vehement Eurosceptic defending the pound and reserving, so it seemed to Will Buckley of *The Observer*, 'a particular venom for Hendry' who, said Ebdon, 'took the association to court and cost them £1.2 million but was never disciplined for bringing the game into disrepute'.

Ebdon could not seem to grasp how difficult it would have been for the losers of the substantive part of the High Court action to discipline the winners – Hendry, Mark Williams and 110sport – for having the temerity to expose WPBSA wrongdoing in the form of breaches of the 1998 Competition Act. This also raised the question of whether Ebdon was similarly critical of Jim McKenzie, on whom he had lavished praise and tried to restore for a third term as chief executive after his first two had provided him with successful actions for wrongful dismissal costing the membership first £68,000 and second £100,000. In his tunnel vision, Ebdon was not in the habit of lending his considerable intelligence to the cause of objectivity.

After the board had survived the November 2002 vote of confidence, Ebdon issued a statement saying that it had done so 'despite a block vote by one particular management company', though he coyly did not name 110sport. 'Snooker has shown the world that we want to be taking decisions for the right business reasons, not political ones. Now it's up to the players to set aside their personal differences and unite behind the current board.' He did not seem to realise that support for the board was just as much a political position as opposition to it.

Ebdon's year as champion brought him only two semi-finals during a season in which my stubborn optimism that all would somehow come right with snooker melted away. Against all reason, Altium's guarantee of sufficient investment to secure a world ranking circuit of at least nine world ranking events for five years had been rejected in favour of carrying on much as before with only cosmetic changes and no new investment.

Doyle acknowledged the absurd situation whereby any attempt to unseat the board that was backed, let alone instigated, by him was doomed to failure. With WPBSA very low in the water financially, some analysts believed that it would run out of money and go into liquidation, whereupon a new start could be made, but somehow it survived.

26

THE END OF AN ERA

IN SEVERAL WAYS, THE 2002–03 SEASON FELT LIKE THE END OF AN era. The British government's anti-tobacco legislation came into play, thus making it the last season in which Regal could sponsor the Welsh and Scottish Opens. Embassy were allowed to continue sponsoring the world championship until 2005 because the government wished to dispel suspicions of one-off special treatment for Bernie Ecclestone, whose £1 million donation to the Labour Party, later returned, was generally assumed to have been connected to Formula One's exemption from the ban.

The government's axe, though, did fall on Benson and Hedges, who had originated the Masters in 1975. It was, as Cliff Thorburn put it during the period in the '80s in which he won it three times in four years, 'the big daddy after the world championship'. Entry was confined to the top 16 in the rankings plus, in later years, two wild cards, so it could not be a world ranking event, which, by definition, had to be open to all players on the tour, but in terms of presentation, profile and public recognition, it had an exceptionally strong identity.

Its success was partly due to B&H keeping WPBSA out of it. B&H provided the entire prize fund, £750,000 in their last year, paid all the staging costs, including the hire of Wembley, and allowed WPBSA to keep the £1 million television fee. B&H threw an emotional farewell dinner on the eve of their 29th and last tournament, of which the star was Barry Jenner, managing director of Gallaher, the parent company.

'It wouldn't be right on an occasion like this not to mention the WPBSA,' he said at the end of his lengthy list of thank yous. 'There it is. I've mentioned them. I'm not too sure about their new logo: a man in a canoe without a paddle.' Pointedly, no one from WPBSA was invited.

Retrospection was natural in the circumstances and as the memories piled up it struck me that all the characters from what could be seen as the continuous saga of the world championship had been involved in another which had woven its own parallel narrative thread.

The first Masters was staged in the ballroom of the West Centre Hotel, Fulham. Television lighting not having reached its present sophistication, the players had to contend with considerable overhead heat which in turn dried out the cloth so drastically that the table was running between seven and eight lengths, as opposed to the ideal five and a half. Control was difficult and, for some shots, impossible. In the final, John Spencer and Ray Reardon went the full distance with the deciding 17th frame ending in a tie before Spencer potted the tiebreak black to win the £2,000 first prize.

An inspired decision took the tournament the following year to the New London Theatre, Drury Lane, snooker's first staging in a theatre-in-the-round, pre-dating the Crucible by a year. There was a new sense of prestige and occasion to which the public responded. Reardon, Doug Mountjoy and Alex Higgins respectively won the three tournaments held there before the first Masters to be held at Wembley Conference Centre was marked by a feat which will never be repeated: Perrie Mans won the tournament without making a 50 break.

Terry Griffiths, world champion at his first attempt the previous spring, also won the Masters at his first time of asking by beating Higgins 9–5, a result Higgins reversed the following year with a 9–6 victory after two extraordinary semi-finals. Griffiths beat Spencer 6–5 from 5–2 down and needed two snookers in the eighth to tie; Higgins, ashen-faced from being violently ill throughout the morning, for which he blamed 'some West Country mustard' he had eaten with a steak the previous evening, beat Thorburn 6–5 after trailing 5–1.

Steve Davis won the first of his three well spaced-out Masters titles in 1982; Thorburn then won his three out of four, his sequence broken by Jimmy White winning his only Masters in 1984 when the highlight was the climax to his 6–4 semi-final win over Kirk Stevens.

White was leading 5–3 when Stevens compiled only the fourth 147 break to be made in tournament play. It was to survive as the only maximum of B&H's 29 years in the sport. Stevens was 'just enthralled in it, lost in it' and, to add to his surreal feeling, he found, in the sea of faces which immediately surrounded him in congratulation, that he was looking straight at Donald Sutherland, the Canadian actor, who had arrived a little belatedly as a guest of B&H. This was the first frame of snooker he had ever seen. White was generous in his own congratulations but kept his concentration to make a break of 119 in the next frame to win 6–4.

An even more famous actor, Paul Newman, familiar with pool via his role in *The Hustler* but not with snooker, was nevertheless so fascinated by the 1987 Dennis Taylor/Alex Higgins final that he watched it until the very end as it ran live on BBC until 1.09 a.m. At 8–5, Higgins attempted the black from distance, which would have given him the £51,000 first prize, but it was Taylor who prevailed 9–8.

The 1988 final could hardly have been a greater contrast, a 9–0 whitewash for Steve Davis at the expense of Mike Hallett, who nevertheless provided an abiding memory by winning the deciding frame of his semi-final against John Parrott after trailing by 43 with only the combined value of the colours, 27, remaining.

Stephen Hendry, starting with his debut year, then won five consecutive Masters, a sequence which included his 1991 9–8 victory over Hallett in the most extraordinary reversal ever seen in a major final. Leading 7–0 at the end of the afternoon, Hallett would surely have won if he had potted the frame-ball pink in the first frame of the evening. Even as it was, the odds were overwhelmingly in his favour when he took the next to go seven up with eight to play. The first chink of light for Hendry came at 2–8, when Hallett missed a rest shot on the pink which, with black in addition, would have made him a 9–2 winner. Hendry began to play with renewed hope and purpose while Hallett, knowing that he should have already won, began to feel the agonising pressure of having a much longed for, and apparently certain, title snatched away. For all the chances he had in most of the remaining frames, he could not capitalise on any of them and lost on the final pink. To complete what he described as 'the worst day of my life', burglars ransacked his house during the final and stole property worth £4,500.

Masters titles went to Alan McManus in 1994, beating Hendry 9–8 in the final, then Ronnie O'Sullivan, before Hendry won for the sixth time in 1996, his 6–0 quarter-final victory over White including three centuries and a then record sequence of 487 unanswered points. He had never played better.

Yet it was not primarily excellence but, as ever, drama which stimulated the highest viewing figures. It did so in 1997 when Davis, 25 months without a title of any sort, came from 8–4 down in the final to beat O'Sullivan 10–8 in as fascinating a clash of styles, personalities and generations as snooker could ever produce. Add to it the archetypal appeal of an apparently fading champion sustaining a remarkable comeback and it is little wonder that the television audience averaged 5.2 million throughout its four hour evening session, peaking at 9.5 million.

O'Sullivan had begun irresistibly with breaks of 116 and 113 to lead 2–0 before Davis had potted a ball, but his spell of magical virtuosity was broken by snooker's first female streaker, who wriggled out of her clothes in an aisle seat 35 rows up before making her dash for glory – or at least a modelling engagement for a tabloid – as the *Daily Star* put it, 'to show off her frame'.

'She definitely broke Ronnie's concentration,' said Davis, who was able to split the afternoon session 4–4 before another unstoppable surge gave O'Sullivan the first four frames of the evening in only 49 minutes.

'At 8–4, I thought it was in the bag,' O'Sullivan admitted. 'Maybe I lost my head. I missed too many chances, but Steve stuck in there and put me under pressure. For the last two frames, I was a cabbage really.'

For Davis, few victories had tasted as sweet because he had begun to doubt whether he would ever win another major title.

The 1998 final was also a classic, an important career stepping stone for Mark Williams and the first indication of unreliability in Hendry's capacity to clinch winning positions. Three up with four to play, Hendry failed to nail down a couple of chances to secure the seventh B&H title which was still eluding him ten years later and also, at 9–9, had to watch Williams pot the last four colours to tie the deciding frame.

With the seventh shot of the exchange on the tiebreak black, Williams left it pottable to a middle pocket. It looked easier than it was, particularly with so much at stake. With the cue ball tight on a side cushion and the pot dead straight, all Hendry could do was roll it at dead weight. The black caught the far jaw, rebounded into the middle of the table and left Williams a straightforward pot to clinch the £145,000 first prize, even if it was a few days before he was able to bank it. The WPBSA, in charge of distributing the cheques, sent this one to his namesake, Mark Williams, the world no. 282 from Tottenham, who amused himself by flashing it round Camden Snooker Centre before returning it.

John Higgins emulated Steve Davis and Stephen Hendry by completing the last leg of their World/UK/Masters triple at Wembley in 1999, leaving Ken Doherty a 10–8 loser in the final as he was to be to Matthew Stevens in 2000, from which the most vivid memory was to be Doherty missing a regulation black from its spot for a 147 and the keys to a £80,000 Honda sports car.

'I potted all the hard balls,' Doherty reflected. 'When it came to the black, it was all a bit of a blur. I thought I couldn't miss, but I was shaking like a leaf. I should have taken a little more time and steadied myself. I took everything too quickly.' Even in the immediate aftermath he was adamant that 'missing the maximum doesn't hit as hard as losing the tournament. The title stands for a lot more than money. It's bigger than the UK. It has a lot more history.'

For Stevens, it looked like the first of many major titles, but the death of his father, Morrell, from a heart attack at the age of 48 during the 2001 tournament knocked most of the stuffing out of him and it was not until he won the 2003 UK title that he proved to have regained his commitment to the game.

Paul Hunter, who won the next two Masters, at least admitted that habitual boozing was incompatible with consistently producing top class snooker. A semi-finalist in the Regal Welsh Open at 17 in his first professional season, also enlivened by falling foul of the WPBSA disciplinary committee through a late night streak along Blackpool promenade during a qualifying competition, he won the Welsh Open at 19 but did not realise how much continuing application was required to consolidate this advance.

A positive test for marijuana cost him prize money and ranking points from one tournament but, more insidiously, it was alcohol which undermined his performances for the next two seasons before he realised that he needed to change: 'I used to get stuck into the vodka big time. I'd go boozing the night before a match and yet I couldn't understand why I was losing.'

There was never a danger that he would become teetotal and his lifestyle and boyband blond good looks still made him a hero for clubbers, carousers and ravers who readily recognised him as one of their own, even if he was bright enough to cut down on his own raving in the interests of fulfilling his potential. As anyone who has played on any sporting circuit can confirm, off-table good times are scant compensation for regularly losing in public when you know you could be winning.

As it happened, Hunter's 2001 Masters title gave journos a story that could be appreciated by anyone who did not know one end of a cue from the other. Trailing Fergal O'Brien, a metronomically efficient Dubliner at his best, 6–2 at the interval, Hunter returned in the evening to make four centuries in six frames in prevailing 10–9.

Entirely without embarrassment, he informed his victory press conference that he and his future wife had made good use of his hotel room in the two-and-a-half-hour break between sessions: 'Let's just say I was a lot more relaxed for the evening session.' Obviously, if this sort of preparation worked every time, everybody would do it. Hunter played up his image by hinting that he had again utilised it in the 2002 final in recovering from 5–0 down to beat Mark Williams 10–9 for the £190,000 first prize.

Sentimentally, it was hoped that B&H's valedictory Masters in 2003 would provide a classic final but, unsentimentally, Williams beat Hendry 10–4. The total attendance for the tournament was 24,329, the highest since 1988, so there was no diminution in public interest, even if we all left Wembley with an end of an era feeling. Television figures, as usual, were eminently satisfactory and the question asked on many sides was how, with such obvious evidence of support, snooker had commercially sunk so low in the water.

Snooker's appeal simply as a sport was emphasised at the Crucible three months later with one of the most remarkable championships ever staged there. Its development was almost like a novel, albeit less a whodunnit that a whowunnit. O'Sullivan's 147 break in the first round proved a red herring as he lost 10–6 to Marco Fu, easily the best player Hong Kong had ever produced and, as it turned out, a quarter-finalist.

Hunter, making his first significant showing at the Crucible, seemed certain to reach the final when he led Doherty 15–9 after three of their four sessions. When I entered the commentary box that Saturday afternoon, I did not expect to be detained much more than half an hour. Four and a quarter hours later, Doherty walked out of the arena the winner, 17–16, having won eight of the last nine frames. BBC1's *Final Score*, the cornerstone of *Grandstand* on the last but one Premiership weekend of the season, was delayed and a two hour overrun was accommodated on BBC2.

For students of the psychology of matchplay, this was prime source material. Hunter, in his heart, assumed victory. Mathematically, he knew it was possible to lose but did not believe that any player could beat him from such a position. He had never suffered from Clincher's Disease but when, in the second frame of the afternoon, he missed a straight yellow which would have put him six up with seven to play, tension spread insidiously through his body.

Adopting a truism as a truth, Doherty simply played it one frame at a time, each shot on its merits, not daring to hope at first but, as he progressively closed the gap, struggling to contain his excitement as hope was renewed. Married to a psychiatrist, Dr Sara Prasad, taking advice from a sports psychologist, Liam Morgan, and supported by his best mate, Mick ('you can do it') McLean, Doherty stayed within a cocoon of concentration as Hunter was forced to start thinking the unthinkable.

The traditional wisdom is that just as a runner's legs can take only so many races one after another, so a snooker player tends to flag in the later stages of Sheffield's marathon of the mind after a series of long drawn out close matches. This theory seemed eminently sound when Williams, having expended minimal mental energy reaching the final, led Doherty 10–2. Even from the overnight 11–5, an early finish was on the cards, but Williams felt uneasily that he should have been even further in front.

Next day, in the third session, Williams went from bad to worse as Doherty, again appearing fresh as a daisy, won seven of its eight frames to equalise at 12–12. Prior to the final session, Williams went back to his hotel with his lifelong friend and practice partner, Ian Sargent. Both have a tendency to be hyperactive and boisterous. The view of 'Sarge' was that Mark was 'bottling it'. Mark needed to discharge his frustrations in a way that could not be verbalised. 'I hit him a few times. He hit me back. He's only small, but he hits quite hard. I've got the bruises to prove it. When we came out again [for the final session], it was a different story, though I think that if Ken had got in front he might have run away from me.'

Nevertheless, when the evening intermission was taken at 14–14, Doherty was looking significantly more composed and Williams admitted his sense of panic to Terry Griffiths, his coach, whose deep understanding of the psychology of matchplay made a crucial difference to the outcome.

'Terry just said that if you're under pressure, the main thing is to realise it and not kid yourself. We had ten minutes in the practice room and it just gave me a bit of confidence before I went out. I think it was just instinct that got me over the line.' Suddenly, he was able to embody the Steve Davis ideal: 'To play as if it means nothing when it means everything.'

'At 16–16, I was singing songs in my head,' said Williams. 'I was singing Tom Jones's "Delilah".' Griffiths had done similarly in 1979, his championship year, with endless internal renditions of the Welsh song 'Myfanwy'. 'I just tried to take my mind off the arena, the crowd, everything.'

He was able to shut Doherty out of the next two frames to win 18–16. His mettle had been tested in the fiercest heat the Crucible could offer.

Devastatingly disappointed by his semi-final defeat, Hunter bore up with dignity and grace in his press conference and the following season won his third Masters in four years, coming from 7–2 down to beat O'Sullivan 10–9 in the 2004 final. That spring, though, O'Sullivan, at his most imperious, won his second world title and in 2005 was going strongly for his third until he lost his quarter-final 13–11 to Peter Ebdon from 8–2 up, reduced to 10–6 going into their controversial final session.

After two sessions, Ebdon was averaging 31 seconds per shot, on the slow side but within the bounds of acceptability. This average rose by the end of the final session to 37, which meant that his average for this session alone must have been well in excess of 40. Some shots do require lengthy consideration, but Ebdon's pace of play was so funereal that informed opinion was strongly against him: 'That was bordering on the ridiculous,' said Doherty; 'I've never seen anyone play that slow,' said John Parrott; 'He said he wasn't doing it on purpose and I believe him – though it's possible no one would admit it anyway,' said Cliff Thorburn.

The rules empower the referee to intervene in the event of 'a player taking an abnormal amount of time over a stroke or the selection of a stroke', but the late Colin Brinded did not do so. It did not take long for discussions to break out in the pressroom over the undesirability of a situation whereby a referee who depends for his livelihood on a contract with WPBSA has to make a controversial decision against a player who sits on its board, as by that time Ebdon did.

In *The Times*, Matthew Syed described Ebdon's tactics as 'shameless' and commented that while there was 'no suggestion that Brinded was fearful of Ebdon's position [on the board] there is a potential conflict of interest which needs to be reviewed'. When Ebdon sued for libel, *The Times* backed Syed to the hilt and successfully argued at a binding arbitration that he was expressing legitimate opinions on the basis of known facts while not asserting as a fact that Ebdon had cheated.

Meanwhile, back at the Crucible, Ebdon lost 17–12 in the semi-finals to Shaun Murphy, who became champion at the age of 22, beating Matthew Stevens 18–16 in a final which gave Embassy a worthy send-off after sponsoring the championship to the tune of £23 million in prize money alone in 29 years.

My last three words of BBC commentary on the final were 'amazing, astonishing, astounding' as Murphy, hitherto a promising but unfulfilled talent, completed his journey from the qualifying competition as a 150–1 outsider to the £250,000 first prize in front of a peak audience of 7.8 million, only slightly below that for the Liverpool v. Chelsea Champions League semi-final. It could not have been clearer that snooker the game still had a lot going for it, but WPBSA's running of it as a commercial activity was to be further undermined by tobacco money no longer being available.

27

THE CAST LEAVES THE STAGE

IN 20 YEARS, THE GAME'S SITUATION HAD DEGENERATED FROM ONE OF glittering promise to a bleak battle for survival. In some Orwellian fashion, the forces of honesty and progress had been demonised by the inept, the inert and the incompetent. The battle for power had been won by those who had no idea how to use it to the game's benefit.

It looked as if the game could go forward only with the collapse of the WPBSA and a new start, but somehow WPBSA tottered on, cutting everything not directly related to the survival of the circuit, seeking cheaper venues and requiring the players to compete for reduced prize money. Those who had voted to keep the board in place at the November 2002 EGM registered no complaint, knowing in their hearts that they had obstructed the course of progress and prosperity simply because they disliked Ian Doyle or had been duped by advisors who disliked him. It was difficult to keep a sense of futility at bay. I had loved snooker all my life and had devoted almost my entire career to it. Everyone in snooker could have been doing well out of it, but it was gurgling towards the plughole.

The cast which had made the '80s such a decade of liveliness and hope was dispersing – or had already done so – or was adapting to new roles as the demands of real life intruded.

Steve Davis, who had taken snooker to a new level in the '80s and struggled unremittingly against the forces of time and the Stephen Hendry generation in the '90s, had always cannily played up to the image created by the satirical puppet show, *Spitting Image*, of Steve 'Interesting' Davis. The satirical thrust of this was that he was an automaton, but the joke to those of us who knew him pretty well was that he really was interesting, wry, self-deprecating and shrewd. Steve invariably acquitted himself well in interviews, sports forums, telly commercials or light-hearted quiz shows like *They Think It's All Over* or *A Question of Sport*. Articulate, analytical, he was invariably fascinated by games and their systems. As a boy, he was the second best chess player in his school and continued to play, on and off, often postal games, against better opposition: 'I'd think for three weeks about my next move and back would come the reply by return of post with a move I just hadn't thought of.'

He became president of the British Chess Federation and often played, when he could find an opponent, in snooker pressrooms, in which he tended to spend much of his off-table time at tournaments: 'I like being in an atmosphere where there's a sense of purpose, some sort of work going on.' Fascinated by Scrabble, he once achieved a spectacular 100 point score, featuring an x and a y in a triple word count, and rose to his feet to accept our plaudits with a modest bow as if he had just made a century in the arena.

Since he was invariably forthcoming and quotable in his press conferences, no one badgered him when he was off duty. In Antwerp once, Hendry had tip trouble and flew his cue doctor over from Scotland to fix a new one, a task which most players learn to perform themselves. Next day, Steve walked into his press conference and declared solemnly: 'I've got a hole in my sock. I'm flying my mother over to darn it.'

Even when his heart was aching, he managed to front up. A minute after failing to pot the black which would have made him the 1985 world champion, he was asked by David Vine, 'Can you believe it?'

'It's all there in black and white,' was not a bad quip just before he was to collapse in anguish in his dressing-room.

After losing to Hendry once in Shanghai, having missed a blue to win which he could have potted with his eyes shut, he kept his press conference waiting for a few minutes. 'Sorry to keep you,' he said on arrival. 'I've just been to my room to try to kill myself.'

Perhaps because he knew how to deal with the press and understood what they wanted, he adapted naturally to his new role as a presenter of BBC snooker coverage in the 2001–02 season. When he and John Parrott, who also had considerable television experience as a resident team captain on *A Question of Sport* for almost ten years, were offered these positions, they were sliding down the rankings, but when Steve stopped trying to chase his past on the table, he started to play a lot better, holding down a top 16 ranking and reaching the 2005 UK final.

He appeared to be enjoying his family life with Judy and their two boys – until a separation was announced in February 2005 – a wide variety of television and public appearances and the challenge of adapting his skills to 9-ball pool, in which his manager and best friend, Barry Hearn, had worked himself into pole position by promoting the world championship and other top events. He liked his golf, his collection of jazz funk records (funding a niche magazine for that arcane form of music) and became fascinated by the Internet. When Barry promoted a pro-celebrity poker tournament for Sky, Steve got himself up to speed with innumerable low stakes games online and performed respectably in the tournament, albeit not as well as Jimmy White who, in dashing if unorthodox fashion, beat all the pros to secure the £100,000 pot, thereby doubling his prize money for the season.

Hendry had scaled his own peaks and was not so far on the way down as Davis but the symptoms of decline were there, even as he remained in contention for, and sometimes won, major titles. One of the first signals is not so much in missing more difficult shots, because top players automatically address these with more deliberation, but easy ones because concentration is no longer as automatic or so deep.

Ambitious young players cannot wait to practise because they see themselves as journeying to the fulfilment of a dream but when success is achieved, particularly on Hendry's scale, motivation tends to become weaker and intermittent. In his case, practice became a chore at times. He had his marriage and young sons to enjoy and there were many attractions in living like a human being instead of like a potting machine searching for perfection. He loved his golf, and life was to be enjoyed in all sorts of ways, although he still knew that, without putting the time in on the practice table, there was no chance of significant further success. He had the money to retire but no amount of it could replace the range of feelings and satisfactions he was accustomed to experiencing through competition. If he was going to compete, there was no point unless he gave himself his best chance of winning.

Hendry acquired new impetus through taking on Terry Griffiths as his coach. Technically, he may not have been telling him anything very different from what Frank Callan, the retired Fleetwood fishmonger who had become the father of modern coaching, had been telling him, but perhaps there was a different way of telling it and a more productive personal connection because it had not been so very long since they had been fellow competitors. Perhaps also Terry had more to offer than Frank in terms of psychological support and advice, for Frank, knowledgeable as he was, was essentially a technical purist. Unquestionably, Terry helped Hendry stay near the top and he was consistent enough – a description he hated – to regain top spot in the 2006 world rankings even as his last ranking title, the February 2005 Malta Cup, was receding into the distance. Creditably, he intensified his commitment, practising five to six hours a day on his own when he was not on the road.

Griffiths himself never recaptured the spontaneity and inspiration which carried him to the world title in 1979, the Masters in 1980 and the UK in 1982, which stood as his last major success until his retirement in 1999 after 18 years in the top 16. His interest in technique at times bordered on the obsessional but could not have provided a better grounding for his subsequent career as a coach. He was doing a fine job as WPBSA's director of coaching until he declined to continue working in the poisonous atmosphere of the Rex Williams regime. There was no one in the game who was better or more widely liked, but even this popularity, politically, was outweighed by the forces of reaction, self-interest and stupidity and he did not have the talent for backstage intrigue that was required for success in this murky area.

The other three leading Welsh players of the '70s were Ray Reardon, who let himself down badly in retirement through his connivance as vice-chairman in some of the dirty tricks and petty aggrandisement of the Rex Williams regime; Doug Mountjoy, who was ruined by one gross misjudgement and losing a lung; and Cliff Wilson, who died in 1994, who could have been a superstar if he had been born later.

Mountjoy's mistake in 1992 was to put his affairs in the hands of his son-in-law, a step which was to lead to bitter family disharmony, bankruptcy and in 1994 the loss of his £200,000 house, an unlikely fate for a player of moderate habits whose professional career had brought him £775,851 in prize money alone. During the 1992–93 season, he suffered in turn from gallstones, pneumonia, pleurisy . . . and cancer. He won a match at the Crucible with a tumour in a lung which was removed two months later.

Never a headline seeker, content to concentrate his mind and efforts simply on playing to the best of his ability, he was the epitome of the solid dependable pro. Masters champion in 1977, UK champion in 1978, he was runner-up to Davis at the Crucible in 1981 and remained a member of the top 16 for ten years. It did start to irritate him that he stopped improving, although he attributed 'missing easy balls and not knowing why' to his temperament rather than his technique. After one particularly depressing loss in January 1988, he pessimistically thought that he was on the verge of being finished as a leading player, but Frank Callan simply took him to a practice table, analysed his technique and told him how to change it. He understood straightaway what had to be done and stuck to this task throughout a series of defeats that culminated in a 13–1 trouncing from Neal Foulds at the Crucible. After a summer's hard practice, it was clear early the following season that he was playing much better, although results did not fully bear this out until he reached the UK final in December. 'I was playing really well. I had never played like this in my life.'

The 19-year-old Hendry had become the red-hot favourite after taking out Davis in the semi-finals, but Mountjoy made a hat-trick of centuries in beating him 16–12 in the final to regain the title after a ten year gap.

'Without that guy, I'm nothing,' was his generous tribute to Callan, who not only worked with Davis, Hendry, Griffiths, John Parrott and countless others at various times but found disciples like Griffiths and Mountjoy to disseminate his ideas and methods when they became coaches. Mountjoy, with age and illness eroding his skills, went to Dubai for three years as national coach to the United Arab Emirates. He could have stayed there but came home to where his heart was only to find that anticipated coaching work did not materialise and that he lacked the stamina to resume his career.

Wilson, a swashbuckling, Falstaffian figure whose snooker career was split in two, was in his youth a phenomenal potter: quick, instinctive, fearless. Had snooker not been in the doldrums, he had the personality and the game to have been a superstar. Like Reardon, he was born in Tredegar, South Wales. Reardon's base, amongst his father, uncles and the mining community, was the Miners Institute, Wilson's among a racier element in the Lucania billiard hall. From time to time, they played money matches which split the town in two, and they clashed each year in the Welsh Amateur Championship and the Welsh qualifying competition for the English Championship – which offered the then rare prospect of a rail fare paid trip to London. Reardon, who won six Welsh amateur titles, always beat Wilson in that competition; Wilson always beat Reardon in the English and reached the final in 1954.

Wilson's trips to London were eagerly awaited by the subculture in which snooker was then confined, as the newspapers ignored the game almost totally. The plush, intimate amphitheatre of Burroughes and Watts in Soho Square, then the home of the amateur game, had only 180 seats, more than enough for most attractions, but when Wilson played, there were frequently dozens locked out. This was at a time when snooker as a public entertainment was going nowhere. The professional game had taken no steps to recruit, let alone encourage players like Wilson who might have given it a shot in the arm, and the main amateur championships and local leagues proceeded year by year with little to sustain them but force of habit.

The Reardon family moved in search of a better future from Tredegar to Stoke, thus paving the way for Wilson at last to win the Welsh amateur title in 1957, but the absence of his old rival – and the death of his father, who had been so much part of his good times in snooker – led to him losing interest. After playing the odd few matches for a couple of seasons, he retired for more than 15 years, working long, hard hours for British Steel at Llanwern, where he became a shop steward. In his latter years, he was apt to reflect that many of his workmates, particularly those who had worked in the notorious Tin Shop, had failed by some considerable margin to reach their three score years and ten.

He returned to snooker only because he was asked to organise a works team to compete in division five of the Newport League. The boom years had not yet arrived, but the snooker scene had become much livelier and his interest began to revive. The snag was that his eyesight had seriously deteriorated. His left eye was virtually useless and his right was much weaker than it had been. Long sight in one and short sight in the other compounded the problems.

In his youth, his cue had run in the classically even-sighted way underneath the point of his chin. Returning to the game in middle age, he found his cue coming naturally under his right eye. As his blurred left-eye vision was nothing but a distraction, he tried playing Long John Silver style with a patch over it. 'This was lovely, like looking down a rifle,' he was to recall. The trouble was that after three or four frames, this eye also became tired and so blurred that he could not effectively see at all.

He took to spectacles and regained enough form to win his second Welsh amateur title in 1978, 21 years after his first. This qualified him for the World Amateur Championship in Malta, which he won later that year by beating a future world professional champion, Joe Johnson, in the final. By far his most remarkable win, though, was against one of the Maltese hopes, Joe Grech, in the quarter-finals which, at the insistence of an angry mob in the national stadium at Ta'Qali, had been re-drawn after Grech had initially been paired with the other remaining Maltese, Paul Mifsud.

The trouble was not with the Maltese snooker fraternity but with those who could see no further than their own national prejudices, as was the case when Wilson, 4–0 up against Grech, began to be systematically distracted with meticulously timed coughs, bangs, clatters and the lighting of cigarettes. With a crowd of 4,000, the largest I have ever seen gathered round a snooker table, in an ugly and intimidating mood, Grech levelled at 4–4 and led by 37 in the decider. With his robust personality and humour, Wilson was exceptionally adept at handling crowds, but there was no handling this one. Even so, he closed the gap and, amidst chaotic scenes, with virtually the whole crowd on its feet baying to distract him, managed to scramble in a flurry of colours for victory.

As we waited in the pressroom, guarded by police, until the mob had dispersed, Wilson was soon philosophical: 'The game's made of memories. If I'd won 5–0, I'd have forgotten it this time next week, but I'll always remember this.' He did not turn professional immediately, as perhaps he should have done, because he could then have taken up an invitation to play in the 1979 Benson and Hedges Masters. Later that year, though, he did.

Reardon thought it 'amazing the adaptations he was able to make from his original style', although he was never the player that he was in his youth. He still potted exceptionally well at times but leant much more heavily, in a manner he would have considered beneath him in his youth, on a shrewd tactical game. When he turned professional at the age of 45, he was already too old to establish himself as a contender for major titles, but this was not something over which he lost much sleep. He had his pride of performance and he wanted to do well enough to earn money for good times. Blessed with one of the happiest and most enduring marriages the circuit has ever seen, he was quite happy to skip the glory as long as he had the money to take Val on holiday.

In his rollicking, gregarious way, Wilson was extremely popular on the exhibition circuit and his advertising slogan – 'You've never seen anything like it' – was no infringement of the Trade Descriptions Act. He was a man's man, a man for a drink, a smoke, a bet and, famously, a curry. Once, in Dubai, he said that he liked curries the hotter the better. The staff was Indian and made him one so hot that they could not believe he was eating it. The sweat was pouring down his face. The staff from the kitchens watched through a small window. Cliff said, 'The bastards are watching me, aren't they? I'll eat this if it kills me.'

If, as a professional, he had played only when he was fit, he would never have played at all. His eyesight problems exercised the ingenuity of many opticians but even with darkened lenses he found it very difficult to adapt to television lighting. He had ongoing problems with knee, hip and back; he had to take tablets for his heart; and his better eye developed a cataract. Even so, he beat many good players, and reached 16th in the world rankings. If he could do this at the age of 55 with all these problems, what could he have done if he had been in his prime?

Canada had three players ranked in the top eight in the '80s but, with snooker yielding increasingly to 9-ball pool in the preferences of the cue bearing public, had no one in the top 50 by the turn of the century and no one in the top 100 a year after that.

Cliff Thorburn developed a sighting problem and by the time he had adjusted to it found himself in the qualifying maelstrom at the Norbreck Castle Hotel, Blackpool, not knowing, as he put it, whether to shake hands with some of his opponents or pat them on the head. Having been accustomed to playing in front of sizeable crowds and television cameras, he was unhinged by playing in tight three-walled grey cells with a crowd of ten at most and sometimes none at all. He last qualified for the Crucible in 1994, losing 10–9 to Nigel Bond after leading 9–2. It was as if the 'so near yet so far' inability to clinch winning positions when he first became a world class player had returned with a vengeance and he left the circuit as Kirk Stevens had without regret in 1991 after losing in the last 16 of the UK Championship to John Parrott: 'I won the first three frames, lost the next nine and that was it. I just wanted to come home.' So utterly had he fallen out of love with snooker that he did not watch it on television for two years and did not play for three, spending most of his time with his then wife and two very young children, working in landscape gardening, lumberjacking – only to discover he was scared of heights – and selling cars.

'The problem was, I couldn't really screw people into the ground. I was too nice,' he said of his inglorious career as a car salesman. 'I sold five cars in six months. I couldn't even sell one to my sister. She went down the street and spent twice as much on a car from another dealership. The only reason I was kept on was because I helped organise a pool competition at the dealership every Friday night. While the people were there, we tried to sell them a car.'

This former world no. 4 found his way back to snooker, albeit at a less exalted level, and won three of the five Canadian national championships between 1997 and 2002, but a couple of abortive attempts to make it back on the UK circuit, a divorce and three visits to rehab for his recurring drug problem also featured.

'Have you ever been addicted to anything?' he asked rhetorically. 'If you have, then you'll know how hard it is to give it up.'

I asked him once about his various near misses for major titles – two semi-finals at the Crucible, one at Wembley. 'It's never fate, it's always you,' was his response. He accepted responsibility for his ruined career, but it was easy to see how the classic factors of divorced parents, expulsion from school and early drug abuse set him up for adult problems.

At least Kirk reached his 40s with his looks and his health more or less intact. This was never likely to be true of Bill Werbeniuk, who died in 2003 at the age of fifty-six after spending his last three months in a Vancouver hospital suffering from heart problems.

This fate seemed implicit in the prodigious consumption of lager which made him a cult hero and allowed it to be too easily forgotten what a very good player he was, four times a quarter-finalist at the Crucible with a career high ranking of eighth. His girth, his moustache, his rolling gait were all reminiscent of Oliver Hardy of Laurel and Hardy fame and his apparently limitless tolerance of alcohol was legendary. In an all-day pint for pint drinking contest, he rendered a Scottish professional, Eddie Sinclair, himself a world class toper, horizontal after he had consumed 41 with Bill ready for more on 42.

Like Thorburn, Werbeniuk went on the road playing for money long before he even knew there was a legit circuit. Sometimes, they travelled together. Once, they fetched up in Billings, Montana, in the heart of cowboy territory. On the grapevine, they had heard that the Montana 9-ball champion also liked to play snooker, a rarity in that part of the world. They parked their car, whose Canadian number plates would have given away that they were likely to be snooker players, well away from the pool hall and Cliff quickly won a pile of money at 9 ball. The Montana man was so keen to win it back at snooker that he offered to give Cliff 9 points start for $200 a frame.

'He couldn't play snooker at all and I took nearly all his money,' Cliff was to recall. 'So now this guy is desperate. He challenges Bill, thinking Bill was just my back-up, not knowing that Bill was a better 9-ball player than I was. Bill took what little money he had left.'

On the tournament circuit, Werbeniuk beat just about everybody at one time or another, but the good times ended when he was banned for using Inderal and found that he could not play without it. He went home, lived with his mother, played cards for a living for a while, but eventually just stayed at home, watching sport on television and living on disability benefits. He became bitter about his fate, denouncing the modern players en bloc as 'boring'.

Here was a man of great heart and skill, whose very largeness made it more difficult for his heart to support life, reduced to railing against the game which made him a star like the last man propping up a deserted bar.

There were other deaths.

Eddie Charlton, the epitome of implacable competitiveness, left the circuit in 1995 but continued with a heavy schedule of exhibition engagements that left few towns in Australia and New Zealand unvisited. Both his marriages ended in divorce and the latter part of his life, when he was not on the road, he spent by himself in an apartment on the outskirts of Sydney, practising alone in a nearby club and usually eating alone in a nearby bistro. He developed a tumour in his bile duct but touring was his life and if he had to die, as he did in Palmerston North, New Zealand, at the age of 75, it was akin – as would have been his wish – to an old soldier dying with his boots on.

Fred Davis died at the age of 84, his memory shattered. Widowed, he lived his latter years on an isolated farm near Denbigh, North Wales, with his two daughters. Long after he should have done, this great champion kept playing in qualifiers simply to get out of the house for a change. Troubled by a hip condition, he had to alter his stance and could not beat anybody in his last couple of years.

John Spencer, the Crucible's first world champion in 1977, died in 2006 at the age of 70. The deterioration of his eye muscles, the form of myasthenia gravis which shortened his career, and a combination of the side effects of necessary drugs, a bowel condition and ultimately inoperable stomach cancer made the last 20 years of his life almost unremittingly miserable. His decision in 2005 to have no further radical treatment cleared his mind so he did, at least, derive some enjoyment from his final months. Rather a year in which he could feel relatively normal than another ten simply kept alive was his brave attitude.

John Pulman, who had preceded Spencer as world champion, fell down stairs shortly before Christmas 1998. With his girlfriend away for the night, he lay there unable to move for almost 24 hours and died in hospital on Christmas Day at the age of 75. He had presence and a nice line in quips but believed, as a former world champion, that the world owed him a living and that it was more blessed to receive than to give. Divorced after 25 years of marriage and almost a quarter of a century of womanising, he was twice bankrupt, first in the late '70s to my own disadvantage.

With the explosion of public interest in the game, there had been a sudden demand for instructional snooker books. I secured contracts and wrote them for John Spencer, Ray Reardon, Rex Williams, Fred Davis and even Ted Lowe. I also persuaded Stanley Paul, the publishers, that their Pulman book, *Tackle Snooker This Way*, could benefit from a re-write and new pictures. My arrangement with Pulman was two-thirds for him, one-third for me, but I made the cardinal error (never repeated) of allowing the contract to be drawn in his name so that all the money went initially to him. When I was fed up with asking for my share, and even more fed up with his refusal to provide any explanation or apology for non-payment, I put the matter in the hands of my solicitor. I did not want to be personally involved any more, so I said simply, 'Do what you have to do.'

John never replied to letters, so the matter trundled on and on, step by legal step, until one day he was arrested by the Tipstaff and bundled into the cells at Bow Street for the night. When he appeared, unshaven and dishevelled, before the beak the following morning, he was unstinting in his criticism of me for putting him in this predicament whereas, if he had only acknowledged the situation and/or admitted that he was short of money, I would have done my best to be accommodating. What riled me was his apparent determination not to face the issue at all. Actually, he succeeded in this. Within a few days of the magistrate releasing him, he was declared bankrupt. No more than a week after that we were both at the Crucible. His match finished before mine and he was told to join me in the box. I cannot say that he seemed pleased to see me but such was our mutual appreciation of the action that there was nothing in our commentary to suggest any animosity.

When ITV offered him more money, he left the BBC and had the voice, the authority and of course the knowledge to do the job well, even if he tended to regard such work as his right rather than a craft to be worked on. Twice he was ordered out of the box in a state of inebriation judged unacceptable by the producer. One gem did pass his lips during the Yamaha Organs tournament, in which one of the sponsor's products was offered as the highest break prize. As someone was clearing up the last few colours, his co-commentator, Dennis Taylor, remarked that it was possible for him to equal the highest break.

'That may be so, Dennis,' replied Pulman. 'But what can you do with half an organ?'

Dennis I was to find very enjoyable to work with. He loved competing and was reluctant to give it up but there comes a point where a player of his calibre cannot any longer stomach a diet of persistent defeat in the obscurity of the qualifying competitions. With his outgoing personality and reliable repertoire of jokes, he continued to be in demand for exhibitions, after-dinner speaking and a range of corporate work, much of it on the golf course, and even *Strictly Come Dancing*. With the proviso that nothing beats playing, he was happy with his post-competitive life and if ever he was not, he had only to unroll in his mind the videotape of the deciding frame of the 1985 final.

Other former top level players – John Virgo, Willie Thorne, Neal Foulds, Terry Griffiths and Mike Hallett amongst them – also gravitated to the commentary box. John, with second billing to Jim Davidson on BBC's highly successful game show, *The Big Break*, also trod the boards in pantomime, specialising in the role of Baron Hardup. During a performance of *Dick Whittington* at Northampton one night, the mechanical ship which featured in the first act closer collapsed, taking much of the scenery with it. John, amongst others, was carted off to hospital. 'That was the night we sailed to Morocco and never came back,' was how he described it. Willie, bankrupted by gambling, worked up a sideline in Big Willie underpants; Mike, also bankrupted, commentated for Eurosport and Sky and played exhibitions on the holiday camp circuit.

Bankruptcy was only one of the problems which came calling on Silvino Francisco who, surrounded by clouds of suspicion but no proof that he had been guilty of match fixing, was undone by his addiction to gambling. Under pressure to pay off his debts, he agreed to smuggle 47 kilos of cannabis worth £155,000 into Britain and was sentenced at Canterbury Crown Court to three years' imprisonment.

By then, he was 51 years of age and his ranking had sunk from his career high 10th to 166th. His eyesight demanded spectacles; his marriage broke up; unable to meet an Inland Revenue demand for £100,000 in back tax, he was declared bankrupt in September 1996. Living in a tiny council flat, he enrolled to study anatomy and nutrition at Chesterfield College of Further Education and was also hoping to move into coaching, a possibility which vanished with his drug smuggling conviction. There was also the possibility of using his knowledge of table construction from his younger days with Union Billiards in South Africa when he could not only erect a table but make a century break on it. The reality was that in the immediate need to keep body and soul together he had to work late-night shifts in a Chesterfield fish and chip shop.

Francisco wanted to stay in snooker . . . but he had to have money. Eleven customs officers were waiting for him at 3.45 a.m. when he drove off the cross-Channel ferry at Dover. Stashed in the spare tyre compartment behind the driver's seat of the classic convertible Fiat X19 sports car – not his own – that he was driving was about eight stone of cannabis resin. Offering what was regarded as the standard defence in such circumstances, he said that he did not know what he was carrying but it seems inconceivable that he could have brought in such a quantity of stuff without prearrangement of how to dispose of it.

'I've done a stupid thing,' he told me. 'I was set up.' He declined to go into details but gave me the impression that he was frightened to name names in case his four children should be the objects of retaliation.

Snooker's supporting cast, unable to earn enough prize money to make a living, went their various ways. Danny Fowler, who reached a couple of world ranking semi-finals, became a delivery driver for a maggot supplier; Les Dodd qualified three times for the Crucible, once when Eddie Charlton was tantalisingly suspended in mid-air en route from Norfolk, Virginia, to their tryst at Preston for the final qualifying round, and achieved further fame as the 1988 slimmer of the year, fining down from 19 stone to 12 stone 10. Back up his weight went, though, like a rubber ball to 25 stone 4 before he embarked on another battle with the scales. When Channel 4 paid him a call, Dodd was working in his club in Southport, preparing a chip butty for one of his members. 'You don't see Stephen Hendry doing this,' he commented wryly.

Some coached or worked in snooker clubs; some loafed about, apparently supported by betting; some either obtained a place on the WPBSA board (and the £1-a-mile travel allowance which went with it) or cultivated a favourable relationship with it; others had no visible means of support.

In a category all his own was Alex Higgins, who in the 2002–03 season entered the qualifying competitions for the Benson and Hedges Masters and the Embassy World Championship – only to withdraw from both, citing urgent appointments for extensive dental work, a by-product of the treatment for cancers of the palate and the throat which had not just blackened but almost cinderised his teeth. Some thought he had entered in the first place only as a means of recapturing some limelight, others that he was so deluded that he really believed he could still compete with the best at the age of 53. Not even contemporaries in good physical shape like Taylor, Griffiths and Thorburn could do that, so how could he?

It was easy to sympathise with his wish to play, and no one begrudged him that, but there was far less sympathy for his boastful ravings. Journos who knew nothing about snooker were eager to talk up a comeback because this was easy to write about; his namesake, John Higgins, put it in perspective: 'I've been reading all this stuff about how great his contribution was for the game, but I think it's terrible for the game if he's going to be coming back in the state that he's in.'

As 'wars of words' and animosity between players are the staple fare for papers like the *News of the World*, Alex's reaction was immediately invited: 'Tell him I'm ready to have a little match.' The sort of fans who seemed to believe that a player stays at the same standard forever fed excitably on visions of him playing again at Wembley or the Crucible. Jimmy White, trying to give his old mate a leg-up, actually suggested he should be given a wild card for the Masters.

'He'd be given some reception,' it was suggested to me in a television interview.

'Yes, then there'd be a match to play and he wouldn't be up to it,' was my reply, all too accurate as it was to prove when he eventually did return to competition three months later in an unofficial Irish Championship. In front of 49 spectators at the Millennium Forum, Derry, he made a top break of 23 in losing 5–1 to Darren Dornan, a 16-year-old Northern Ireland junior international so little known even locally that he appeared as Darren Dorrian on the draw sheet and thus in some newspapers.

At *Snooker Scene*, we received a letter from a Higgins fan of long-standing (who did not wish to be named) who had travelled a considerable distance for this eagerly awaited comeback only to find him 'not even a patch on the player who retired at Plymouth six years ago, never mind anything else. I was looking forward to seeing him play again but I'm sad to say that watching him is no longer pleasurable. It is just a torture as you sit there wondering who he's going to start bullying next. As a player, there's nothing left. All in all, a very sad and somewhat gruesome reminder of the realities of getting old. Killing some time in the shopping centre while waiting for my bus home, I happened to catch another glimpse of Higgins, now almost unrecognisable, in a long black coat and a fisherman's hat, beside the Millennium Forum. A kid whose voice hadn't broken yet invited him round the corner for a drink. Higgins followed.'

Unchastened by defeat, or anything else, and perhaps incentivised by payment and/or a free plug for one of his upcoming benefit evenings, Higgins alleged in the *News of the World* current widespread match fixing without naming names or providing a scintilla of evidence. 'People in snooker stopped taking Alex Higgins exclusives seriously several years ago,' said Steve Davis, forbearing to add that Brian Radford's byline on the piece was itself likely to provoke scepticism.

It seemed that he had only his unappeasable anger and his increasingly threadbare cloak of celebrity to keep out cold reality. Born with an extraordinary talent, obsessively honed, and an acute non-verbal intelligence which could read quicker than anyone the implications of how the balls were dispersed, there was always, it seemed to me, something damaged about him, some sense that nothing could ever compensate him for some monstrous injustice. In his lifelong attempt to recapture the unconditional love he had received from his doting mother, he had compulsively pushed his demands from any relationship he ever had to breaking point. Interested neither in analysing the past nor planning for the future, he lived off the cuff, instinctively gauging how much he could extract from any given relationship, deploying a variety of ruses with which to cajole or bully his way to a free bet, free drink or interest-free loan.

Everyone acknowledged that his emergence and the advent of colour television were the chief elements in snooker's sudden explosion and expansion, and Higgins played this role for all it was worth and more. The truth is that he did not wake up on a certain Thursday and ask himself: 'What can I do for snooker?' but, in trying to get snooker to do what it could for him, he gave it constant drama and bankable notoriety as his authentic genius came to be fatally undermined by outlandish and at times obnoxious behaviour.

The one-man play, *Hurricane*, written and mesmerisingly acted by Richard Dormer in an uncannily accurate and evocative impersonation of the protagonist, ends with him standing, fag in one hand, glass in the other, trademark fedora on his head, amidst the detritus of his life – money, beer cans, fag packets, betting slips – declaring defiantly: 'Don't pity me. I've stood on top of the world.'

Such moments, a glorious satisfaction at the time, can often be a consolation in a player's declining years, but Paul Hunter, winner of his third Masters title in four years in February 2004, was to be dead at the age of 27 in October 2006.

Cheerful, unassuming, carrying lightly the knowledge of just how talented he was, his golden hair braided or ponytailed according to fashion, he was a golden boy with a golden future which he was to be cruelly denied.

Diagnosed with multiple neuro-endocrine tumours in March 2005, he endured the hellish side effects of chemotherapy and the disease itself as they eroded his stamina and the feeling in his hands and feet. Gamely and uncomplainingly, he strove to keep his snooker career going, his opponents torn between human sympathy and their own necessity for results. After his last match, a first round defeat at the Crucible in 2006, he admitted, 'The pain in my side is 24/7 now,' and spoke movingly of his baby daughter. When a player makes his exit at the Crucible, his press conference usually ends with a phrase like 'see you next season' but those of us who could see, close up, how ill he was, could not restrain the thought, all too accurate as it was to prove, that for him there would be no next season. All that was left for him was to bear his unspeakable ordeal steadfastly right through to his final black.

28

THE WAY WE ARE NOW

THE REJECTION OF THE ALTIUM PROPOSAL IN 2002 WAS TO PROVE the tipping point in the circuit's prosperity. If it had been accepted, the players, from the world ranking circuit alone, would have been the better part of £10 million better off five years into the Altium contract.

Blaming WSE Ltd, whom it never should have appointed, the WPBSA board sacked them only nine months into their ten year contract. This was after Jim McMahon, the board's *primus inter pares*, as the game's Latin scholars would have described him, had hailed WSE as 'a different breed' and 'the best solution for the future of the sport and our players'.

On 11 December 2003, WSE obtained summary judgment in the High Court for its claim of £412,602.29 for breach of contract and was awarded £30,000 in costs. Sky demonstrated its disenchantment with WPBSA around this time by declining to renew its £800,000 a year contract to cover two world ranking tournaments.

The WPBSA balance sheet as at 30 June 2003 had showed its reserves down to £417,348, including £356,975 in fixed assets such as scoreboards and desks, even after a £1.2 million reduction in prize money and dropping ranking events in Thailand and China. Deloitte & Touche had charged £171,000 for advice in identifying a commercial partner, although what that advice was worth, WSE rather than Altium having been identified, was open to debate.

Sir Rodney Walker, who had recently served as chairman of UK Sport and Sport England, was cast in the role of saviour and empowered to hand-pick his own board. In essence, this proved to be a re-run of the coup Ebdon had proposed in January 2002. Walker's involvement was conditional on WPBSA directors being paid instead of having to make do with the infamous £1-a-mile travel allowance. Out of desperation, the Walker option was supported by 110sport, whose chairman, Ian Doyle said, 'Sir Rodney's plan offers a possible escape from the tried and failed methods of running the game.'

Doyle welcomed the news that the existing board were all prepared to offer their resignations: 'Given their recent history in losing television contracts, failing to attract sponsors and a rapidly diminishing prize fund, the time would seem right for them to move on. Indeed, we would have serious misgivings if Sir Rodney were to invite any members of that board to remain for any appreciable length of time in any significant role within the association.'

Doyle's misgivings were amply justified: Walker chose to retain Jim McMahon and Tony Murphy, the two most dominant members of the board that had plunged WPBSA so deep into difficulty. Ebdon was also invited to join the board as 'the eyes and ears of the membership'. In McMahon, Murphy and Ebdon, Walker could not have invited three more anti-110/Altium figures if he had tried, thus perpetuating snooker's internecine strife.

Walker's choices as non-executive directors from outside the sport were David Richards, chairman of Football's Premier League, Sir Robin Miller, chairman of HMV, and Adrian Metcalfe, formerly head of Channel 4 Sport. All, including McMahon, Murphy and Ebdon of course, were to be paid £15,000 a year and Walker £30,000 as chairman.

Even then, those implacably imposed to Doyle/110, or even *Snooker Scene*, who had supported the Altium proposal and Doyle's criticisms of how the game was being run, were not satisfied. At the 2004 AGM eight months later, Metcalfe was ousted in a coup achieved by some heavy-handed gathering of proxies.

Paul Sweeny, a bright, well-educated, low-ranked professional, just the sort of new blood that was needed, stood for the board but was told that his election address would have to be approved by the board – one of whom he was trying to displace – and was subjected to a great deal of unpleasantness by supporters of the 'old guard'. Proxies were aggressively gathered on the basis that the only way to ensure a new BBC contract was by retaining the board en bloc to demonstrate 'stability'. Armed by such open proxies, supporters of the old guard not only defeated Sweeny's candidature but ousted Metcalfe, not least because he was suspected of being too friendly with me. So much for 'stability'.

'Of all the people I have brought in, Adrian has been the one doing the most work,' said a bewildered and annoyed Walker, describing Metcalfe's ousting as 'beyond my comprehension'. It looked even more extraordinary when Tony Knowles was elected in his stead, again by means of assiduous gathering of open proxies.

When *Snooker Scene* reported this episode, quoting with approval Walker's remark, 'The whole voting system is a disgrace and a shambles caused by members abdicating ownership of their own votes,' the old guard on the board moved to get even with me and prevailed upon Walker to assist.

First, Walker circulated to the membership an extraordinary letter in which he called upon me 'to give your support to the board and allow it to work without constant undermining of its position'. This was tantamount to a plea not to subject the board and its allies to legitimate journalistic scrutiny. I published Walker's letter, together with my reply, in which I did not hold back on my disappointment that he had chosen to 'shoot the messenger'.

My enemies then resorted to the WPBSA's disciplinary rules in an attempt to put *Snooker Scene* out of business through involving me in legal expense and trying to discredit me. Initially, WPBSA blustered about inaccuracy, an allegation with which they did not persist. I was attacked through WPBSA's draconian disciplinary rules which in essence forbid any member making critical remarks about any other, a rule honoured more in the breach than the observance, and enforced highly selectively.

My Achilles heel turned out to be my love of billiards. Some 30 years past my best, I had retained my billiards-only membership in order to play in their one remaining annual tournament. But for this I would not have been a member and would therefore have been beyond their disciplinary reach.

In more issues of *Snooker Scene* than not in the previous 30 years, I had criticised some aspect of WPBSA's governance, but now, for the first time and without warning, I learned that the rules would be enforced against me literally. It was, WPBSA said, immaterial that I was a journalist. I was a player and would be treated simply as such.

I was not disposed to allow without demur the WPBSA to walk all over me. Fourteen months into the legal toing and froing, WPBSA's lawyers admitted that the 'truth or falsity' of what I had written 'is nowhere put in issue by WPBSA in these proceedings'. Earlier in the case, I believed that truth and/or fair comment would be a defence, but it was now clear that it would not.

It took more than a year for WPBSA to disclose the letters of complaint, which to my lack of surprise turned out to be from three past or present board members – Peter Ebdon, Tony Murphy and Mike Dunn – who did not like what I had written. These letters, all dated 8 or 9 February 2005, bore the hallmarks, as did the board minutes when they were disclosed, of a concerted attempt by the board to shut me up.

This chimed in with the board's exploitation of an anomaly in WPBSA's rules to expel, without charge, explanation or trial, Mark Wildman, WPBSA's chairman at the time the Altium bid was being discussed. Having earned an honorary membership through his service to the game, he did not have the right of appeal that an ordinary member would have had. In reality, the unfair expulsion of Wildman was an unprincipled act of revenge instituted by an opposing internal political faction and supported by new members of the board who were unaware of relevant history. Wildman wanted to appeal to the Sports Disputes Resolution Panel (SDRP), but this body is not empowered to consider complaints unless both parties agree. The WPBSA did not.

In my own case, lawyer-to-lawyer correspondence churned on until a hearing at the SDRP on 16 March 2006. My solicitor, Rhory Robertson, pointed out that while I was being charged under the tournament rules, I had committed no offence at a tournament. All the matters complained of arose from articles on snooker politics that the board did not like.

WPBSA's barrister, Paul Harris, engaged for a fee of £20,000 for a preliminary hearing which lasted less than three hours, argued successfully to the adjudicating barrister, Bruce Brodie, that the tournament rules did not apply exclusively to tournaments. Brodie did agree with us that WPBSA had not properly particularised its case. When it did so on 14 April, making not a single allegation of inaccuracy in a document that spanned 35 pages, containing 107 paragraphs, I resigned my membership.

This was no admission of guilt. It was simply that what I was defending – the right to play in one billiards tournament a year and attend AGMs – was insignificant in terms of the expenditure of time and money I would have had to commit to a full-blooded defence.

WPBSA claimed £76,288.84 in costs. I said they were not entitled to anything. Brodie arbitrarily cut them by half to £38,000, his idea of compromise, I suppose, although this did nothing to shake my view that establishments tend to stick together. My view of Brodie was not dissimilar to the BBC's of Lord Hutton.

WPBSA's pious line was that they owed it to the membership to recover these costs, but if they had behaved properly and fairly there would have been no costs.

They issued through a bankruptcy court a Statutory Demand, which if successful could have cost me my house, for all they knew. This dragged on for months through various postponements until, one day before this book had to be passed for press, my application to have this set aside was successful, leaving WPBSA to pay my costs of £13,419.26 and its own of £19,389.55. This meant that, in total, WPBSA had committed over the 30 months of this saga no less than £109,097.65 of the membership's money, chiefly in legal expenses, in trying to put *Snooker Scene* out of business. While it was the members, not the directors, who footed the bill, it was the directors, not the members, who had issues with me.

If the board believed that I would be frightened into failure to criticise when criticism was merited, they were wrong. Prompted by the case of Chris Small, winner of the 2002 LG Cup and a top 32 player for a decade, who had been refused a grant despite being forced into retirement by a degenerative spinal condition, I instituted a *Snooker Scene* investigation of the WPBSA Benevolent Fund.

Based on our articles, the Charity Commission identified certain areas of concern, including 'potential conflicts of interest which are not being managed' and that the WPBSA itself owed the benevolent fund £33,182 as at 30 June 2003. Furthermore, it was difficult to imagine that the five players who had received grants from the fund in 2005–06 could have been more deserving than Small.

Snooker Scene also highlighted commissions paid to a company controlled by Sir Rodney Walker of £75,237, plus another £20,000 due to him but waived in favour of a high profile donation of this amount to the NSPCC. When *Snooker Scene* asked Walker on what contracts these commissions were based, WPBSA company secretary, Elaine Eyers, replied: 'This figure is an accumulation of commissions paid to Myerscough Developments under the terms of a consultancy agreement and is commissions payable in relation to several agreements that Sir Rodney was instrumental in closing.' While it was interesting that the commissions were for 'closing' rather than 'introducing' such contracts, this took us no nearer to defining what they related to. Nor had any consultancy or commission arrangement ever been previously mentioned to the membership.

Walker had played a role in negotiating the renewal of the BBC TV contract until 2010, albeit at a figure understood to be in the order of £1 million a year lower, but all tournament sponsorships – 888.com for the world championship, Royal London Watches for the Grand Prix, Maplin Electronics for the UK Championship and Saga Insurance for the Masters – were negotiated by IMG/TWI, WPBSA's sponsorship agents. In the absence of any explanation, the possibility remains that some commission may have originated from the decision to award the championship to Sheffield until 2010, despite it being, as Walker said, 'not the highest cash offer'. IMG/TWI also substantially increased income from overseas television sales. But for their efforts and the BBC contract, the WPBSA could scarcely have continued to exist.

These sponsorships helped prize money rise year on year, though by nothing like the margins which would have rivalled the Altium deal in 2002. Neither were players happy that WPBSA signed away to event sponsors, for no additional payment, one of the two waistcoat logos they were permitted to wear. With leading players able to command anything between £20–70,000 per logo, their earnings from this source were roughly cut in half. There were grumbles aplenty but, as the WPBSA was the only game in town, no concerted protest action.

Within tournament arenas the game continued to proceed serenely enough for the public at large to be oblivious of commercial and political issues. Ronnie O'Sullivan continued to be snooker's greatest box office attraction and the chief stimulant to the column inches it received. Nevertheless, buffeted by mood swings, acutely self-critical of his performances, he reached the end of the 2006–07 season without having won a world ranking title for 26 months.

His lowest point was his 8–0 third session drubbing as Graeme Dott defeated him 17–11 in their 2006 Crucible semi-final, clinching proof that on any given day O'Sullivan's mind and game could unravel. In this championship, his irrational insecurities were externalised in a search for the holy grail of the perfect tip, of which he tried about 20. Even more eccentrically, as he left the arena in defeat, he presented the cue with which he had won two world titles to a boy in the audience he had never met. There was, he admitted, 'nothing wrong with this one' but that he 'felt like a new start', a yearning related to far more than a new cue.

In his restlessness, nothing could shift for long his underlying unhappiness. Emotionally volatile, easily bored not so much by snooker as what goes with it, in terms of hanging about between matches, he played the first match and the last at the 2005 Grand Prix at Preston. By semi-finals day, he was climbing the walls and it was as if he was on autopilot when he prevailed 6–5 over Barry Hawkins with a break of 117 in the decider.

'I'd rather be at home in the garden, planting a few shrubs,' he declared, evincing a hitherto undisclosed interest in horticulture.

Uninspired and flat for the early frames of the final, he was trounced 9–2 by John Higgins, whose superlative performance included two world records: centuries in four consecutive frames and 494 unanswered points. It was Higgins, too, who was to deny O'Sullivan the 2006 Masters title with perhaps the finest substantial clearance ever seen in the deciding frame of a major tournament, 64 from 0–60 to prevail 10–9 on the final black.

However, with Higgins losing in the first round at the Crucible and O'Sullivan imploding, it was Dott who, to the surprise of those of us who did not believe he possessed the extra gear a world champion requires, lifted the trophy. Nor did he demonstrate this extra gear in beating Peter Ebdon 18–14 in a final that lasted 13 hours, 39 minutes in all, with the last ball potted at 12.52 a.m.

Ebdon's sting had been drawn in the semi-finals, in which, from the commanding position of 15–9, he only managed to nail Marco Fu 17–16, and with Dott struggling for fluency there was a preponderance of long, grinding frames. Dott was leading 15–7 when the penultimate session had to be curtailed two frames early. There was therefore a possible 13 to be played in the evening, of which Ebdon won the first six, one boasting the championship record duration of 74 minutes, to trail 15–13. At 16–14, Ebdon was 60 in front and hot favourite to reduce his arrears to a single frame when Dott somehow managed to overcome his doubts and fears to produce a 68 clearance, his highest of the final, to go three up with four to play.

Dott's title was a trier's triumph, an example of what grit and perseverance can achieve. It also imbued him with a new depth of confidence for the 2006–07 season, in which he came to the Crucible as provisional world no. 1 only to lose in the opening round to Ian McCulloch. O'Sullivan could hardly have been drawn less favourably at the Crucible, but his 10–2 trouncing of Ding Junhui, virtually reproducing the 10–3 dismissal he had inflicted on the 20-year-old Chinese to win the Masters three months earlier, confirmed that he was the man to beat – if he could sustain such form.

Bereft as his mantelpiece had been of world ranking trophies for two years, he had won not only the Masters but also two Premier League titles, even if these successes, on reflection, owed something to their circumstances. Only four matches are required to win the Masters, an event to which he can commute from home; the Premier League consists of a series of one-night stands in front of capacity crowds, again ideal, as is the 25 seconds per shot time limit, for O'Sullivan's restless nature. Self-critical as he was, O'Sullivan also played pretty well in beating the fast-improving Australian left-hander Neil Robertson 13–10 but, increasingly struggling for form, was outplayed 13–9 by Higgins in the quarters.

There was an extraordinary quarter-final recovery from Shaun Murphy to beat Matthew Stevens from six down with seven to play, and two dramatic semi-finals in which Mark Selby, a rank outsider, won the last three frames to beat Murphy 17–16 and Higgins, from 14–10 down going into the final session, beat his fellow Scot Stephen Maguire, who was at last regaining the form which carried him to the 2004 European and UK titles, 17–15.

It was a championship which raised serious questions about the futures of Stephen Hendry, 38, comprehensively beaten 13–6 by Allister Carter, and another former champion, Mark Williams, 32, whose first round exit meant that his dreadful season had produced only two match wins. O'Sullivan's quarter-final exit also hinted that, in his inconsistency, he was a declining force, although it was another player from his generation, Higgins, who became champion by beating Selby 18–13, a success he attributed in part to giving up alcohol a year earlier.

For Hendry, and even for O'Sullivan, Williams and Higgins, time was starting to run short in terms of improving their career defining statistics. The championship, and the season as a whole, emphasised the rise of a new generation embodied by Robertson (winner of two ranking titles), Murphy and Ding (one each), Jamie Cope (who reached two finals), Mark Allen, an outstanding prospect from Northern Ireland, Maguire, Selby, a late developer, and possibly Judd Trump, at 17 the third youngest player ever to qualify for the televised phase of the championship.

Not since the Crucible had become the home of the championship in 1977 had I missed a session there. The middle Saturday of the 2007 staging was my 500th day, an occasion nicely marked by a BBC featurette which included some words from Steve Davis of which I was particularly appreciative: 'On behalf of all snooker fans around the world and certainly in this country, certainly from my own perspective anyway, over the years you've been a very important part of snooker, through *Snooker Scene* and as a commentator. Thanks very much for all the memories and thanks very much for being such a snooker fan. You've given a lot of people a lot of pleasure by continuing with the magazine and all of your enthusiasm. Thank you.'

Never mind that I slipped on the highly polished floor of my hotel bathroom and spent the second day of the final in a recumbent posture in Sheffield General prior to becoming the proud possessor of a titanium hip replacement, this kind of appreciation from players and enthusiastic followers of the game far outweighs the petty enmity of those in authority demonstrating far less interest in the good of the game than in defending their own positions. For snooker to have survived as a public and television entertainment, considering all the mismanagement, incompetence and worse to which it has been subjected, underlines what a great game it is.

INDEX